Late to Class

The Urbana Free Library

To renew materials call
217-367-4057

SUNY series, Power, Social Identity, and Education

Lois Weiss, editor

Late to Class

*Social Class and Schooling
in the New Economy*

Edited by
Jane A. Van Galen
and
George W. Noblit

Foreword by
Michael W. Apple

State University of New York Press

3-09
34-

Published by
State University of New York Press, Albany

For information, contact State University of New York Press, Albany, NY
www.sunypress.edu

Production by Diane Ganeles
Marketing by Anne M. Valentine

Library of Congress Cataloging-in Publication Data

Late to class : social class and schooling in the new economy / edited
  by Jane A. Van Galen, George W. Noblit ; foreword by Michael W. Apple.
     p. cm. — (Suny series, power, social identity, and education)
  Includes bibliographical references and index.
  ISBN-13: 978-0-7914-7093-0 (hardcover : alk. paper)
  ISBN-13: 978-0-7914-7094-7 (pbk. : alk. paper)
   1. Educational sociology.   2. Social classes.   I. Van Galen, Jane.   II. Noblit,
George W.

LC191.L293   2007
306.43'2—dc22

2006020754

10 9 8 7 6 5 4 3 2 1

CONTENTS

FOREWORD

As I began writing this foreword, the images of the tragedies unfolding in New Orleans were everywhere. The deaths and destruction, the human drama of trying to survive in conditions that were almost beyond comprehension, all of this and more, were ever-present, and rightly so. There were jarring words that kept emanating from the media, with sentences such as, "This was the worst natural disaster ever to be experienced by the United States." Yet these words sat side by side with more explanations. "It could have been avoided." This latter sentence seems much more compelling to me.

Why? The horrors of New Orleans are not explainable by phrases such as "natural disaster." This situation had its genesis not in a hurricane, but rather in a slow-moving political and ideological storm that eroded our collective sensitivities, which consciously refused to fund public institutions, which saw public as being by definition "bad" and private as being by definition "good," which engaged in one of the most massive programs of (upward) income redistribution in the history of our nation, and in a willful refusal to take seriously the possible effects of all of this on "our" economy, on the public infrastructure, on our educational institutions, on our social ethics, and on the structures of inequality of the larger society. In short, this was about *class* and its interconnections with race (see also Apple, 2000, 2006).

Yet, an understanding that class counts and counts in absolutely crucial ways has largely withered in the United States. This is constantly brought home to me when I am outside our borders. When I am in Brazil, or England, or Korea—or nearly anywhere else—the comparative absence of class discourses and understandings in the United States is so striking that one realizes that it has taken more than a century of creative ideological work by dominant groups to create a situation in which class talk seems either strange or somehow almost illegitimate in this nation.

Yet, I and many others have argued that class—and its complex intersections with race and gender—must be taken much more seriously than it has been in most of the ways in which we think about this society and especially about educational policy and practice. It is interesting that some of the best work on how we might best understand class has actually been done in the United States (see, e.g., Weis, 2004; Wright, 1978, 1985, 1989, 1997). And even the popular best-seller list will occasionally feature a book on the realities of, say, the upwardly mobile fractions of affluent classes (Brooks, 2000) or on the lives of the poor (Ehrenreich, 2001; Shipler, 2004). Given all of this, however, it still feels as if we need to constantly swim upstream to take class relations as seriously as they deserve in education. The book you are about to read helps rectify this situation.

There are important questions that need to be asked about class. What are the processes by which class inequalities are reproduced over generations and thereby over decades and even over centuries? How do the affluent and the middle classes retain their privileges and power in nations like the United States as well as other parts of the world? How have the affluent and the middle classes proved successful in resisting legislative attempts, such as increased educational opportunities for disadvantaged groups, to create more equality? Does this mean that such efforts have basically been a failure? Should governments do more or less to deal with such inequalities (Devine, 2004, p. 172)?

To these questions a number of others need to be asked. What roles do our educational institutions play in reproducing or interrupting class dynamics? What are the interconnections among different dynamics of dominance and subordination inside and outside schooling? How is class *experienced*? Do these lived experiences provide the space for counterhegemonic possibilities? What can education and educators do to expand these spaces? An emerging body of literature has sought to deal with a number of these issues (see, e.g., Anyon, 2005; Apple, 2006; Apple and Buras, 2006). The book you are about to read continues this path in important ways.

In order to answer these and other questions, we need to remember that what class means is more than simply one's place in an economic structure. In essence, class needs to be seen not only as a noun but as a verb. This is made clear in the following quote: "Class has both objective and subjective components. That is, it is not simply a position, but a complex lived cultural and bodily reality. It is a process, not merely a 'thing.' Thus, it should always be seen not as a static entity, but as a set of processes that are both creative and destructive and in constant motion. Furthermore, it is a relational concept in that it is defined in opposition to other classes. Finally, it is historically contingent" (McNall, Levine, and Fantasia 1991, p. 4).

The realization of such nuances may make class analysis more complicated, but who ever said that understanding the social realities and inequalities—and the struggles to change such realities and inequalities inside and outside of schools—was easy? But even given the conceptual and historical complexity of the ways in which class functions as a structure and as a process, as both economic and cultural, it is still more than a little visible in our daily lives inside and outside of educational institutions. Let me give a concrete example of how this works in real life.

I have taught at the University of Wisconsin in Madison for over three decades. Certain conditions have now had predictable effects, such things as budget cuts, the ever-rising cost of going to college, the fact that employment security for many working-class and middle-class people is now nearly nonexistent, and the high rates of under- and unemployment; the list could go on and on—all of these conditions have changed the character of my university and of so many others. Thus, the average family income of the entering class at Wisconsin is reported to be over twenty thousand dollars higher than before (and rising), this at a time when family incomes among many groups have either stagnated or fallen. This is one of the best indicators of who gets to study at "world-class" universities and who does not. It stands as a mute witness to the ways in which income is linked to social advantage in complicated ways.

To say that there are connections between income and advantage is to repeat a truism. However, is this condition totally explained by economic resources? We might say, along with Fiona Devine (2004), that income is usually a necessary condition, but it is not sufficient. Cultural and social resources are crucial as well. Particular dispositions, propensities, and appreciations—and an "ease" in displaying them—as well as who you know, play important roles here. Readers familiar with Pierre Bourdieu will recognize that this equates with his taxonomy of various kinds of capital: economic, cultural, and social. Bourdieu has argued that in terms of class advantage, symbolic struggles count and they count in important ways. At the same time, however, they are also struggles over economic and political power, as well as cultural power. There are complicated conversion strategies at play here, in which the accumulation of one form of capital—say, cultural capital—is used to "trade" for social and economic capital (Bourdieu, 1984). The ways in which such class conversion strategies privilege particular class actors in education, and de-power others, is striking and an analysis of these strategies is crucial if we are to more fully comprehend the ways in which the struggle over what counts as "legitimate" culture versus "popular" culture are so important in this society (Apple, 2006).

The authors included here, recognize the importance of these struggles and of the ways in which differently positioned actors engage in them. The authors are unusually reflective about their own structural location and about the dangers of imposing their "solutions" on others. All too much of the socially and culturally critical literature in education is written in such a way that it is either largely rhetorical or so overly theorized that its style itself serves to latently act as a new rule of exclusion. The authors are aware of the need for conceptual and empirical substance.

But this is not all. In the process of demonstrating the realities of class and of why we need to focus on class analysis, they are also fully aware of the ways in which class experiences are formed out of the intersections of race and gender as well. The word "experiences" is important here. The book illuminates not simply structural positions, but *lived* experiences. In this way, it is able to show us class as a process that includes moments of meaning making, struggle and resistance as well as domination (see also, Dance, 2002; Fine and Weis, 1998).

Finally, and in my mind one of the most important characteristics of the book, is its attempt to answer the question of "What is to be done?" By taking seriously the issue of "emancipatory" pedagog*ies* (the plural is crucial here), they are not satisfied with bearing witness to negativity—although this is a crucial act for researchers to engage in. They also want to open the spaces for possible interruption and intervention. As I have argued at length elsewhere, this is one of the more significant roles that critical scholars can play in a time of conservative attacks on everything we hold dear (Apple, 1996, 2006, Apple et al., 2003). For all of these reasons and more, this is a book that deserves our attention.

Michael W. Apple

References

Anyon, J. 2005. *Radical possibilities: Public policy, urban education, and a new social movement*. New York: Routledge.

Apple, M. W. 1996. *Cultural politics and education*. New York: Teachers College Press.

———. 2006. *Educating the "right" way: Markets, standards, God, and inequality*, 2nd ed. New York: Routledge.

Apple, M. W. et al. 2003. *The state and the politics of knowledge*. New York: RoutledgeFalmer.

Apple, M. W. and Buras, K. (Eds.) 2006. *The subaltern speak: Curriculum, power, and educational struggles*. New York: Routledge.

Bourdieu, P. 1984. *Distinction*. Cambridge: Harvard University Press.

Brooks, D. 2000. *Bobos in paradise: The new upper class and how they got there*. New York: Simon & Schuster.

Dance, L. J. 2002. *Tough Fronts: The impact of street culture on schooling*. New York: RoutledgeFalmer.

Devine, F. 2004. *Class practices: How parents help their children get good jobs*. New York: Cambridge University Press.

Ehrenreich, B. 2001. *Nickel and dimed: On (not) getting by in America*. New York: Metropolitan Books.

Fine, M. and Weis, L. 1998. *The unknown city: Lives of poor and working class young adults*. Boston: Beacon Press.

McNall, S., Levine R., and Fantasia, R. 1991. Introduction. In S. McNall, R. Levine, R. Fantasia (Eds.) *Bringing class back in* (pp. 1–13). Boulder: Westview Press.

Shipler, D. 2004. *The working poor: Invisible in America*. New York: Knopf.

Weis, L. 2004. *Class reunion: The remaking of the white working class*. New York: Routledge.

Wright, E. O. 1978. *Class, crisis, and the state*. New York: New Left Books.

———. 1985. *Classes*. New York: Verso.

———. 1989. *The debate on classes*. New York: Verso.

———. 1997. *Class counts: Comparative studies in class analysis*. New York: Cambridge University Press.

INTRODUCTION

Jane A. Van Galen

Nowhere is there a more intense silence about the realities of class differences than in educational settings.

—bell hooks

What does it mean to speak of social class in the United States at the beginning of the twenty-first century? In times when the social terrain between the "haves" and "have-nots" has grown ever wider, how can renewed consideration of social class deepen our analyses of educational reform—reform that has been invoked in the name of global economic competitiveness and opportunity? Why, even as we've come far in our understanding of race, ethnicity, and gender in schooling, do we seem to be late to class?

The authors in this volume, who found such questions particularly compelling, present theoretical, empirical, and pedagogical perspectives on social class and schooling in the United States. In compiling this collection, we hope to provoke a critique of the assumptions of "classlessness" (Reay, 1998) within which educational reform and education research has too often been constructed, toward the eventual goal of generating dialogue about the new meanings of "class" in U.S. schools in a rapidly shifting economy.

We believe that we have been late in coming to these conversations. As Sherry L. Linkon (1999, pp. 2–3) has observed, "the principles of inclusion and recognition that have been so important in creating spaces for gender studies, black studies, queer studies, and ethnic studies [in educational settings] have generally not been extended to class." Within the litany of "race class and gender" among critical scholars, class analyses

1

are by far the least developed. Apart from a long tradition of study of the schooling of poor urban children of color, educational researchers have paid relatively limited attention to the complexities of social class in shaping educational experiences in the "new economy" of knowledge and service work (Brantlinger, 1993, 2003; Brown, 1998; Chafel, 1996; Faulkner, 1995; Grant and Sleeter, 1996; O'Dair, 1993; Van Galen, 2000, 2004; Weis, 1990; Zandy, 1990).

While the academy is relatively silent about class, public discourse about the purposes of schooling actively denies its existence. As state and federal policy resonates with promises of opportunity if only individuals learn more, neither students nor their teachers have access to alternative interpretive lenses for explaining and navigating the constraints of their shared institutional lives. As Julie Bettie (2003, p. 195) observes, "class is largely missing as a category of identity offered by popular culture and political discourse in the early twenty-first century United States. Class is not a central category of thought, making it difficult to have a cultural or political class identity."

How, then, do we revive conversations about class? Marxist analyses and functionalist justifications no longer seem to work, but scholars have been less clear about how to conceive of class within newer theoretical perspectives. As Susan L. Robertson (2000, p. 19) observes, scholarship on class is confounded by

> . . . profound economic, political, and intellectual changes marking our time. The numerical decline of the old manual or "working class", the emergence of new forms of "post-Fordist" production, the shift in employment and investment from production to consumption, together with the new intellectual currents centred around feminist/identity politics and the individualism of neoliberalism, have all worked to challenge the sovereignty of class and dislodge it as a fundamental analytical tool in social theory. . . . It has become unfashionable in academic circles to talk about class, as if class suddenly no longer mattered and the historic concerns of class theorists—such as inequality—have disappeared.

The authors in this volume have worked to illuminate what few in their research settings could even have named: the shifting landscape of social class in the lives of young people and their families, and in the work of their schools.

This book was crafted against a backdrop of unprecedented policy work that presupposes that schools can equalize opportunity for all (Aronowitz, 2003, p. 25). State and federal educational policy reverberates with confidence in the inherent fairness of life outside of school; standards-based reform policies promise that after a long history of sorting and stratification, schools, will, at long last, bring poor and working-class children into opportunity limited only by their own ambitions.

Yet the promise of personal and global prosperity toward which young people are encouraged to aspire is contradicted by basic labor market data: the most rapid job growth is not among high-tech, high-wage sectors of the economy, but rather among low-wage service-sector jobs, few of which require high levels of education or skill (Bureau of Labor Statistics, 2000). Recent volatility in technology sectors and in the stock market, outsourcing, and the rise of contract work have left even highly educated workers experiencing an unprecedented sense of economic vulnerability (Berhnhardt et al., 2001; Ehrenreich, 1989; Perucci and Wysong, 1999). Even as academic and political interest in social class may have waned, movement through and within the rules of a new economic landscape has become turbulent for many families.

As recent social theorists have noted, the lived experience of class runs more deeply than economics. As M. Zweig (2000, p. 11) succinctly notes, "Class is about the power some people have over the lives of others, and the powerlessness most people experience as a result." If power does matter in the shifting landscapes of economic stratification, the challenge of closing achievement gaps (and ultimately, economic gaps) between poor and working-class children and their more privileged peers would not be a matter of simply enabling the lower-achieving students to "catch up" in competitiveness for a diminishing number of middle-class jobs. Instead, in times of volatile wealth and eroding job security across class lines, those with the power to do so are likely to position their own children at the winning ends of ever-more uneven playing fields (Brantlinger, 2003; Lareau, 1989, 2003; Lareau and Shumar, 1996; Reay, 1998). Quite simply, if children who currently are not doing well in school begin to do well, those for whom schooling *now* works would find ways do even better. While business leaders and policy makers may have envisioned a generally stronger and smarter workforce for a global economy coming from school reform, middle-class parents sensing their own economic vulnerability are likely to infer that in a rapidly changing and very competitive labor market, their *own* children had very well better become stronger and smarter than everyone else.

As Pierre Bourdieu (1984, p. 133) notes:

> When class factions who previously made little use of the school system enter the race for academic qualifications, the effect is to force the groups whose reproduction was mainly or exclusively achieved through education to step up their investments so as to maintain the relative

scarcity of their qualifications and, consequently, their positions in the class structure. Academic qualifications and the school system which awards them thus become one of the key stakes in an interclass competition which generates a general and continuous growth in the demand for education and an inflation of academic qualifications.

In this volume, then, scholars will examine the educational experiences of poor, working-class and middle-class students against the backdrop of complicated class stratification generated by a shifting global economy. Together, the chapters will explore the salience of class in understanding the social, economic, and cultural landscapes within which young people in the United States come to understand the meaning of their formal education in times of shifting opportunity.

The Chapters

As readers consider these individual chapters and the collection as a whole, we hope to generate dialogue in several areas.

Coming of Age in the Shifting Landscape of Class

First, the collection offers intriguing glimpses into the meaning that young people make of schooling as they come to terms with their relative power and status, even as they are likely to have little fomal understanding of the myriad ways in which their lives are shaped by class stratification. In the new economy, class has been rendered nearly invisible. As Valerie Walkerdine (2003, p. 241) has observed, "We no longer have a large manufacturing base which provides the pivot for an understanding of class stratification based on class divisions. What used to be the working class is now dispersed into service industries based on individual contracts, piecework, home work and work in call centres, with jobs for life having disappeared."

Unlike the lads of Paul Willis's (1977) classic study of working-class youths in an industrial community, young people today cannot frame their sense of the meaning of school within alternate, oppositional identities. Today, young people growing up at the margins of the economy do not face the more stark tensions between identities as workers and aspirations toward "more"; instead, the children and grandchildren of factory workers are more likely to embark upon career paths such as those that culminate, after years of shuffling documents, in their appointment as assistant manager of the night shift of the copy center. Meanwhile, those who in previous generations may have assumed that the professional positions were theirs for the taking are now more likely to contract themselves (and in the process, reinvent themselves) through a series of shifting corporate alliances and career changes.

How then, do young people coming of age in today's economy come to understand who they might become? As Ellen A. Brantlinger notes in her chapter, whether consciously or not, identity *is* shaped around social class markers, and in the shifting landscape of the new economy, even middle-class students experience commodification, alienation, and exploitation in the processes through which social distinctions are generated and sustained.

A number of chapters in this volume, then, consider the ways in which poor, working-, and middle-class students form identities of possibility, even while explicit identities of class may elude them. Deborah Hicks and Stephanie Jones draw us into the lives of young girls on the far social fringes of their communities, weighing the invitation to venture further into the alien but communal terrain of literacy. In the work of Luis Urrieta Jr. and of Jill Kayoma and Stephanie Jones, we encounter ambitious, talented, and academically driven working-class students of color whose sense of self is crafted within daily interactions with more privileged peers, many of whom assume that they have already earned the right to disdainfully exclude the lower-status students by virtue of their superior academic and social accomplishments (Bullock, 1995, p. 125). In the chapter by Richard Beach, Daryl Parks, Amanda Thein, and Timothy Lensmire, we observe working-class youths who have earned a place in a program for students with academic aspirations, struggling with acknowledging the privileges of their whiteness while at the same time grappling with their class oppression.

In each of these chapters, we see poor and working-class students tallying the relative costs of loyal identification with their economically vulnerable families, against the untested hope that schooling can, and will, serve the interests of people like them. Meanwhile, in Brantlinger's recasting of her previous work on class, we see the "winners" also coming to slowly understand that while they may be on top, they have precious little idea of how to navigate the rules of a game that are no longer stable nor clear, even though they had thought that success in school would have assured them of their capacity to succeed "as a constantly changing successful entrepreneur of oneself" (Walkerdine, 2003, p. 241).

We see these young people living out the central questions of class, always at the intersections of gender and ethnicity and geography, yet rarely able to name the myriad ways in which their lives are shaped by cultural and economic influences that operate well beyond the reaches of own agency.

Writing of girls at the center of these social confluences, Julie Bettie (2003, p. 190) observes: "Girls sorted through all of this and began drawing conclusions about what is or is not 'for the likes of me and my kind' as friendships were increasingly organized by race/ethnicity and class as girls began to formulate identities based on the possible futures they imagined for themselves."

While academic attainment is certainly a part of the construction of a possible future, the complex social fabric of school and community offers much more powerful messages of what one is entitled to imagine for oneself. For children coming of age in decaying industrial towns, in isolated rural communities, in schools in which "the haves" display clear and exclusionary advantage, much more than rising test scores would be needed to invigorate the imagination.

Because identify is formed within particular social spaces, these chapters suggest that we can learn much more about the formation of class identities by also considering more carefully the geographic and cultural contexts of schooling, Most of the studies in this volume were conducted in diverse urban settings, in which relative privilege is always visible to young people. Whether to suggest things that might be possible for themselves, or to underscore the seemingly insurmountable social distances between themselves and others, young people in metropolitan areas have regular encounters with individuals from broad class backgrounds. One can imagine the "coalition building" advocated in Noblit's chapter taking place in vibrant metropolitan areas, in which young people will have daily encounters with those living very different lives. Yet as Van Dempsey reminds us, most poor and working-class students live in small towns and rural areas, and the social cohesion and relative homogeneity of these communities may simultaneously mask the their relative disadvantage while also narrowing the range of possible futures to which they might aspire. What might we better understand about stratification and opportunity by becoming more mindful of the cultural geographies within which identities are formed?

And finally, how might we imagine ways in which repressive educational structures might be circumvented? Might we imagine new possibilities for pedagogies of the poor and working class through which young people might come to imagine new possibilities for themselves and for their communities? The authors of these chapters offer a foretaste of possible new frameworks for exploring class, in part by reconsidering what it might mean to envision schooling as a genuine instrument of possibility.

Social Mobility: Probing the Fractures in the System

While clearly documenting the numerous ways in which poor and working-class students come to understand the limits of what is "for the likes of me and my kind," the chapters also offer intriguing glimpses of fractures within the system, as we encounter those for whom schooling seems to be working as an avenue of social mobility. We are long overdue for scrutiny of the experiences of the "ones who got away" (Reay, 1997, p. 20) in spite of the obvious constraints of schooling and the economy. While we have amassed considerable data about achievement gaps between more privileged students and their less-privileged peers, we know relatively little about the experiences of those for whom education has opened doors. While each of the authors in this volume would concede that social mobility through schooling is very much the exception rather than the norm, each would also likely concede that we can understand more about oppressive social structures when we better understand the limits of their reach.

We venture cautiously into this discussion, for as Brantlinger wisely cautions, we must distinguish between social mobility that genuinely does mark fractures in the system and other forms of mobility that merely foster mythical ideologies of opportunity for those who work hard. For too long, Brantlinger observes, success stories have been used to merely "bolster and mystify" divisive relationships between more privileged and subordinate students, as the successes of a few are then turned against their many peers.

Yet these chapters complicate each of these positions, and closer scrutiny of the schooling of the young people in these chapters suggest rich terrain for further study.

Across these chapters, for example, we see much more than the individual ambitions of particular students. We see, instead, students being supported by quietly subversive teachers, by educational programs built to counterbalance formal school structures, by the advocacy of parents (their own and others), and by community activists offering young people alternative narratives for understanding the work of their schools. We simply do not see students making it through the complicated social structures of school on their own merit alone.

As we meet these young people who are poised to circumvent the limits of their lives and their schooling, we most often do so in places other than the traditional classroom. Beach and his colleagues write of a rare and rigorous college prep program created for students in a working-class high school. Urrieta powerfully documents the processes by which some poor and working-class Chicana/o students are actively recruited into educational structures that will provide material and symbolic capital for their educational success. In his work, the synchronized advocacy of community activists, teachers, and parents enabled students to imagine new possibilities for themselves. Kayoma and Gibson write of support systems created explicitly to enable students to construct identities other than those ascribed to them by higher-status students and by teachers and that enable them to envision success in school on their own terms. Hicks and Jones, in their after school literacy program, invite young girls to more

closely read their communities and their formal schooling and to imagine
other possibilities for themselves.

Other chapters suggest more possibilities. Both Fields-Smith and
Kroeger portray families exercising agency that includes action for the
collective good, and their work enriches a literature that too often represents parent involvement in single dimensions. These chapters suggest
(as Noblit notes in his chapter) that teachers and parents might well move
beyond adversarial relationships to explore potential alliances in the
interest of creating better schools for all children.

Yet there is more beneath the telling of these stories than mere inspi-
rational accounts of attaining the American Dream. Instead, these stories
collectively reveal how complicated the work of upward mobility is. For
example, it's clear that the resources available to the successful students
in these chapters are simply not available to all who might benefit from
their supports. In defining recipients of these resources as distinctively talented, school structures that sort on the basis of race, class, and gender
remain unchallenged. In Urrieta's chapter, for example, access to the advocacy of teachers was often dependent upon allowing oneself to be defined as smarter and otherwise "different" from one's peers, complicating
the development of a healthy ethnic identity. Often too, the strategies
used to facilitate the success of students are merely borrowed from the
strategies long invoked by middle-class white students and by their parents, strategies that obviously intensify the competition for limited resources but do nothing to broaden the discourse about why resources are
so limited in the first place. One might ask the parents in the Fields-Smith
chapter, for example, if rather than stepping into the traditionally supportive and subservient roles of parent involvement, African-American
(and other) parents might also negotiate new roles for themselves—roles
that Kroeger suggests will be essential if schools are to serve diverse populations well.

Clearly, then, in some schools, poor and working-class students are
being invited to the game, and in others, the very rules of the game are
being subject to greater scrutiny by students who enjoy the advocacy of
mentors and advocates. Yet it's clear that this is not enough. The "game"
itself continues as privilege defends itself. The rules still favor more privileged students, and the costs of the game are still extraordinarily high for
poor and working-class students.

For all of the obvious limitations of the avenues to mobility represented here, these chapters also suggest that there is much more going
on "beneath the radar" that warrants our collective curiosity. We see
here the potential of extra-institutional structures, of student support
groups that enable the formation of alternative identities, of the alternative renditions of parent involvement, and of community cultural

brokers who name the obstacles that they have faced in pursuing possibilities that schooling itself did not open to them. We need to understand these possibilities.

In these chapters there also are glimpses of how the very structure of school itself might be otherwise.

Poor and Working-Class Pedagogy

While we have come to envision varieties of feminist pedagogy or of critical multicultural education, we are harder pressed to imagine schooling in which poor and working-class students recognize themselves in the curriculum and discover their voices within the pedagogy. In these times in which the purposes of formal education have been narrowed to preparation for work in an increasingly competitive labor market, it has become difficult to imagine how school might serve deeper purposes of justice and equity. What alternatives can we imagine? What would the ends of such a new pedagogy be? As the authors of this volume attest, we cannot simply settle for enabling more students to attain individual mobility; nor can we settle simply for more working-class students acquiring the analytic and intellectual capital of middle-class peers. These questions point us toward questions of a pedagogy of class.

Critical scholars have long embraced a political project of critical pedagogy for public schooling. Lynch and O'Neill (1994, p. 313), however, question the very assumption that government-sponsored schools that now serve the interests of the powerful will ever become sites of emancipatory curriculum and pedagogy. Apart from isolated pockets of critical practice, there is little evidence that years of academic writing of the possibilities of a Friere-ian model of learning have led to significant changes in the schools of poor and working-class children, and while we might continue our advocacy for more politicized forms of schooling, we might also expand the conversation to consider additional possibilities.

In pursuing these projects, we must first acknowledge that focusing on the schools of lower-status children can never be enough, for as Noblit writes in this volume, "From race we have learned that what must be changed is whiteness, from gender we have learned that what must be changed is patriarchy, and from class I will argue we learn that what must be changed is hierarchy." Maike Ingrid Philipsen and Brantlinger each write in their chapters that we must imagine a pedagogy of privilege in which "the haves" come to realize how they benefit from the hierarchies that suppress the accomplishments of poor and working-class children.

How, then, to begin? The chapters in this volume suggest that we might explore two interconnected avenues: The first is to pursue what we have begun here: to examine extraschool structures and supports that are

working to open new ways of creating meaning out of the formal structures of school, and the second is to explore what a pedagogy of class itself might entail.

LOOKING MORE CLOSELY AT WHAT IS THERE. As academics have examined
schools for evidence that classrooms are invoking particularly politicized
forms of curriculum and pedagogy, we are perhaps missing more subtle
ways in which teachers work on behalf of poor and working class children. Michael Apple (1995, p. 146) suggests that in early efforts within
critical research traditions to cast teachers as powerless agents of capitalist forces, scholars have missed the potential in teacher's "resistance"
to formal and informal mechanisms of stratification. He notes: "Just as
blue- and white-collar workers have constantly found ways to retain their
humanity and continually struggle to integrate conception and execution
in their work . . . so too will teachers and students find ways, in the
cracks, so to speak, to do the same things. The real question is not
whether such resistances exist . . . but whether they are contradictory
themselves, whether they lead anywhere beyond the reproduction of the
ideological hegemony of the most power classes in our society, whether
they can be employed for political education and intervention. . . . Our
task is first to find them."

  Resistance is evident in many of the chapters in this book. Noblit
suggests that we look more carefully at the ways in which teachers invoke
caring and relation to shelter students from the harshest manifestations of
school reforms. Urrieta writes of teachers who actively resisted stereotypes of Chicano/a students to formally designate some as "smart" and
worthy of extra school recourses. Facing prescriptive literacy curriculum
in the schools in the neighborhood in which they were working, Hicks
and Jones created alternative literacies in their after school program. In
few of these examples did teachers invoke explicitly political motivations;
in none did the curriculum formally politicize the work of the school. Yet
perhaps, while some may find these efforts incomplete, there are lessons
in many schools about ways in which quiet resistance is working on
behalf of children.

RETHINKING A PEDAGOGY OF CLASS. Yet quiet resistance cannot ultimately
be enough, and we must continue to press our understanding of what a
pedagogy of class might involve. Beach and his colleagues reference the
work of scholars such as Renny Christopher (1999) or Sherry L. Linkon
(1999) who have begun to write to broader audiences about working-
class pedagogy. Ironically, this work is being done mainly in the college
classroom, where relatively few poor and working-class students will
ever be found.

This work is complicated in part by our confused discourse about class. Unlike race, ethnicity, and gender, Lawrence MacKenzie (1998) posits, class identity is often not considered to contribute to cultural pluralism. "Why? Because non-middle class identity is *supposed* to be invisible; it is viewed not as a cross-cultural asset but a condition to be repaired" (p. 103, italics in original).

He elaborates: "From what I've seen, life for many poor and working class students is erosively perplexed by the clinging, deep-rooted suggestion that their class identity is a badge of cognitive failure, an identity that an individual of sufficient merit can and should leave behind—and that one's parents, if clever and enterprising enough, and unless they're first-generation immigrants, should have already left behind. The message is this: Working class students must remediate their identities, and most of them will receive little or no respect until they do" (p. 100).

Arguing instead for a "pegagogy of respect," MacKenzie admonishes educators to move beyond conventional approaches to multicultural curriculum, to move beyond required reading on race, class, and gender to think about "what might be learned from the groundskeepers at work outside the . . . window, the electrician remodeling the library's lighting, the heating engineers. . . ." (MacKenzie, 1998) and the relationships between all of these and the professional staff of schools. In the very halls of educational institutions, he argues, are the seeds of powerful lessons on class hierarchies.

Challenges to imagining a more deliberate pedagogy of class clearly remain, and resolving them is beyond the scope of this volume. Yet the lives of the young people in these chapters illuminate many of these challenges. Students who might once might have grown up understanding the inherently contradictory interests of bosses and workers from the artifacts of their parents' union involvement, now have little or no access to discourse about worker interests. Public deliberation about the need for higher academic standards is disconnected from labor market data that predicts that most students will face low-wage work involving only minimum cognitive skills. The tensions inherent in making success in school contingent upon assuming an identity that distances oneself from family and community, make it clear that broader conceptualizations of academic achievement are necessary.

We imagine a pedagogy of class that will be created not by middle-class academics, but with members of the community who can name the "in between-ness" of the upwardly mobile. We envision work by community advocates who can envision alternative routes to mobility that sometimes challenge the structures of school, and sometimes sidestep school altogether. Cultural brokers with one foot firmly in the community and the other working with and beside the school may someday make the rules of success more clear and more subject to critical scrutiny.

Someday, middle-class students may understand that becoming educated obligates one to examine one's own privilege.

And, we believe, a pedagogy of class may well also contain the lessons of thousands of committed and caring teachers who have long served students well.

Carrying the Project Forward

As we've compiled this volume, we found ourselves asking ever more questions about the scholarly work that remains to be done at the inter- sections of social class and schooling. As we considered the next steps, we were reminded of Bettie's accounts of high school girls imagining only limited futures for ourselves, as we realized that the imagination of even middle-class scholars can be limited by the contexts of work and of our lives. We will work in these final pages to stretch our imaginations, in part to imagine decentering our status as middle-class intellectuals as we wonder about ways to move forward.

First, we want to imagine multiple ways of capturing the life trajec- tories of young people from all economic backgrounds. While we've learned much from reading and rereading these works, we fully realize the limitations of point-in-time studies such as these for understanding class dynamics. Given what we know about the complex intertwining of K–12 schooling, higher education, labor markets, idiosyncratic circum- stances, and structural obstacles to mobility, we find ourselves wanting to look far beyond the end of the book to see how things turned out for the young people whose lives are represented here. We want to know where their lives have taken them, and we want especially to know what they will come to understand about the many possible permutations of "turn- ing out well." But such is not the nature of educational research, that we can place ourselves in the position of chronicling life trajectories. We be- lieve that if we are to understand social class, we need research that fol- lows young people through the milestones of their lives. Examples such as Michael Apteds's series of "7 and Up" films, or Lois Weis's (2004) pro- ject revisiting students in young adulthood that she first interviewed when they were in high school, suggest the richness that we're missing in our more limited conceptualizations of educational research.

Second, we continue to try to imagine schooling in which class strati- fication is named but not reproduced. How do we imagine the possibilities of poor and working-class pedagogy, in which class is finally named and analyzed? How do we conceive of education in which poor, working- class, and more privileged students all come to better understand how so- cial class has been at very core of their imaginations of who they might be and become? We believe that these questions can only be addressed by scholarly work done in collaboration with public schoolteachers, and with parents and community activists who serve as advocates for young people. We need to better understand what schools are now doing "beneath the radar," whether as quiet resistance or as explicit practice, which disrupts the day-to-day work of schooling. We encourage our colleagues to imagine ways in which such scholarly partnerships might be realized.

Finally, we want to imagine how our work might become part of a project in which class is named in broader social settings. What would studies look like that foregrounded class, and from there, went on to considerations of gender, sexuality, and ethnicity? Or, as Noblit so cogently argues, might we "start" with either race or gender (or disability or sexuality) and then eventually come to the place where the oppressions of class can be seen and named? Drawing from critical race theory, what might we learn about educating young people for the political work of coalition building and local activism? What if our work went beyond analyses of the schools to projects of social change?

We trust that this volume is *a* beginning.

References

Allison, D. 2001. A question of class. In R. Coles, R. Testa, and M. Coles (Eds.) *Growing up poor: A literary anthology* (pp. 77–78). New York: New Press.

Apple, M. 1995. Ideology and power, 2nd ed. New York: Routledge.

Apted, Michaels. "7 and up" film series: *Seven Up/7 Plus Seven* (1964); *21 up* (1971); *28 up* (1985); *35 up* (1991); *42 up* (1990); *49 up* (2006).

Aronowitz, S. 2003. *How class works: Power and social movement*. Cambridge: Harvard University Press.

Bernhardt, A., Morris, M., Handcock, M. S., and Scott, M. A. 2001. *Divergent paths: Economic mobility in the new American labor market*. New York: Russell Sage Foundation.

Bettie, J. 2003. Women without class: Girls, race and identity. Berkeley: University of California Press.

Bourdieu, P. 1984. *Distinction*. London: Routledge and Kegan Paul.

———. 1986. The forms of capital. In J. G. Richardson (Ed.) *Handbook of theory and research in the sociology of education*. New York: Greenwood Press.

———. 1990. *In other words: Essays towards reflexive sociology*. Stanford: Stanford University Press.

Bullock, H. 1995. Class acts: Middle-class responses to the poor. In B. Lott and D. Maluso (Eds.) *The social psychology of interpersonal discrimination*. (pp.118–59). New York: Guildford Press.

Bureau of Labor Statistics. 2000. Employment Projections. Table 4: Employment and total job openings, 1998-2008, by education and training category. [on-line]. Available at http://stats.bls.gov/news.release/ecopro.t04.htm.

Brantlinger, E. A. 1985. Low-income parents' opinions about the social class composition of schools. *American Journal of Education*, 93 (3), 389–408.

————. 1993. *The politics of social class in secondary school: Views of affluent and impoverish youth*. New York: Teachers College Press.

————. 2003. *Dividing classes: How the middle class negotiates and rationalizes school advantage*. New York: RoutledgeFalmer.

Brown, L. M. 1998. *Raising their voices: The politics of girls' anger*. Cambridge: Harvard University Press.

Chafel, J. A. 1997. Societal images of poverty: Child and adult beliefs. *Youth and society*, 28, 432–63.

Christopher, R. 1999. Teaching working-class literature to mixed audiences. In S. Linkon (Ed.) *Teaching working class*, (pp. 203–22). Amherst: University of Massachusetts Press.

Ehrenreich, B. 1989. *Fear of falling: The inner life of the middle class*. New York: Harper.

Faulkner, C. 1995. My beautiful mother. In J. Zandy (Ed.) *Liberating memory: Our work and our working class consciousness* (p. 203). New Brunswick, NJ: Rutgers University Press.

Fine, M., and Weis, L. 1999. *Unknown city*. Boston: Beacon.

Grant, C. A. and Sleeter, C. H. 1996. *After the school bell rings*, 2nd ed. New York: Falmer Press.

House of Representatives. H.R. 1. The No Child Left Behind Act of 2001. Text available at http://edworkforce.howe.gove/issues/107th/education/nclb/nclb.htm.

hooks, b. 2000. *Where we stand: Class matters*. New York: Routledge.

Katz, M. 1975. *Class, bureaucracy, and schools: The illusion of educational change in America*. New York: Praeger.

Lareau, A. 1989. *Home advantage: Social class and parental intervention*. New York: Falmer Press.

————. 2003. *Unequal childhoods: Class, race, and family life*. Berkeley: University of California Press.

Lareau, A. and Shumar, W. 1996. The problem of individualism in family-school policies. *Sociology of Education* (extra issue), 24–39.

Linkon, S. L. 1999. Introduction: Teaching working class. In S. L. Linkon (Ed.) *Teaching working class* (pp. 1–11). Amherst: University of Massachusetts Press.

Lynch, K. and O'Neill, C. 1994. The colonisation of class in education. *British Journal of Sociology of Education*, 15, 307–24.

MacKenzie, L. 1998. A pedagogy of respect: Teaching as an ally of working-class college students. In A. Shepard, J. McMillan, and G. Tate (Eds.) *Coming to class: Pedagogy and the social class of teachers* (pp. 94–116). Portsmouth, NH: Boynton/Cook Publishers.

National Center for Educational Statistics. 1999. NAEP 1998: Reading report card for the nation. NCES Report 1999-459. United States Department of Education: NCES.

Nunez, A., Cuccaro-Alamin, S., and Carroll, C. D. 1998. First generation student undergraduates whose parents never enrolled in postsecondary education. U.S. Department of Education: National Center for Education Statistics. NCES 98-082.

O'Dair, S. 1993. Vestments and vested interests: Academia, the working class, and affirmative action. In M. M. Tokarczyk and E. A. Fay (Eds.) *Working-class women in the academy: Laborers in the knowledge factory* (pp. 239–50). Amherst: University of Massachusetts Press.

Perrucci, R. and Wysong, E. 1999. *The new class society.* Boulder: Rowman and Littlefield Publishers.

Reay, D. 1997. The double-bind of the "working class" feminist academic: The success of failure or the failure of success. In P. Mahony and C. Zmroczek (Eds.) *Class matters: "Working class" women's perspectives on social class* (pp. 18–29). Bristol, PA: Taylor and Francis.

———. 1998. *Class work: Mothers' involvement in their children's primary schooling.* London: University College London Press.

Riley, R. 1999. New challenges, new resolve: Moving American education into the 21st Century. The Sixth annual State of American Education Speech. Long Beach, CA. February 16, 1999.

Robertson, S. L. 2000. *A class act.* New York: Falmer Press.

Van Galen, J. 2000. Education and Class. *Multicultural Education,* 7(3), 2–11.

———. 2004. Seeing classes: Toward a broader research agenda for critical qualitative researchers. *International Journal of Qualitative Studies in Education,* 17, 663–84.

Walkerdine, V. 2003. Reclassifying upward mobility: femininity and the neoliberal project. *Gender and Education,* 15, 237–48.

Weis, L. 1990. *Working class without work: High school students in a deindustrializing economy.* New York: Routledge.

Weis, L. 2004. *Class reunion: The remaking of the American White working class.* New York: Routledge.

Willis, P. 1977. *Learning to labor.* New York: Columbia University Press.

Wexler, P. 1996. *Critical social psychology.* New York: Peter Lang.

Zandy, J. 1990. Introduction. In J. Zandy (Ed.) *Calling home: Working class women's writing.* New Brunswick, NJ: Rutgers University Press.

Zweig, M. 2000. *The working class majority: America's best kept secret.* Ithaca: ILR Press.

PART 1

GETTING TO CLASS

We came up with the title *Late to Class* on a walk through downtown Seattle with Bill Johnston. We liked it because of its double entrendre. We are both late in coming to a different understanding of social class and late in rethinking education in terms of social class. We also liked the title because it signaled a small transgression (in school and in social thought). We will likely be "disciplined" by the adherents of various theoretical schools of thought. Much like the student coming to class late—we expect some public reprimand and sanctioning as well. Nevertheless, the volume achieves more than we could have hoped on that long walk in Seattle. We are late to class and potentially in a liminal space where the authors in this volume reveal our assumptions and try to think much more clearly about social class and education.

The interconnections between the chapters are multiple, complex, and contested. This volume opens up our contestations about class even as it provides a rich base for future thought and action around social class and education. We decided to organize the text so that the reader was first faced with the juxtaposition of how we understand class.

On the one hand, class is lived experience and on the other hand, a history of ideas that people and states use to understand themselves. This opening section "gets us to class" in these two different ways. It also gets us to class in two of the competing views about social class: as warranted social theory and as narrative. Beth Hatt grounds class in a narrative of her life. For her, narrative is both a powerful way to unpack the dynamics of social class and education and a pedagogy she is employing for "educated" people. William Johnston was one of the trio that designed this volume. His ideas about class have informed ours in many ways. In his chapter, Bill gets us to class by examining the history of ideas about class that now exists as both implicit and explicit theories about the nature of social class, stratification, and identity. Together these chapters give us a basis to rethink how class works.

1

GROWING UP AS POOR, WHITE TRASH

STORIES OF WHERE I COME FROM

Beth Hatt

The idea of "poor, white trash" conjures many different images in people's minds. For some, they think of raggedy clothes, bad teeth, and dirty hair. People also picture trailers and roaches crawling across kitchen counters. A final assumption would probably be that they have "no education." For me, I think of my family, of people I care deeply about. I think about where I come from.

I would like to think that the following narrative about my own life is part of an education of "educated" people. Literature concerning the working class has taught us a lot about working-class culture, gender, and race construction within the working class, and about schooling within working class life. However, I am hesitant to think that it has personalized the working-class beyond the stereotype. It has not typically made the issue of growing up poor a personal one or as something urgently needing to be eradicated. Furthermore, the focus of critique has often stayed upon the working class rather than highlighting the destruction caused by hegemonic middle-class culture joined with capitalist ideals.

In this chapter I will provide a personal narrative of rural, white working-class life and the people who live it. It will be grounded in Dorothy Smith's (1990) perspective of the "feminist sociology of knowledge." She claims that within academia we, as women, are forced to work under the dominance of the "father tongue," which was constructed through years of the disciplines being dominated by men. The father tongue is characterized by impersonal and objectified relations with the right to speak for others, whom Smith specifically identifies as women.

This is particularly applicable to dominant notions of what is appropriate academic writing and rhetoric, which often distances itself from the emotional and relational aspects of the writer's life as well as those with whom we conduct research.

Smith's work could be expanded to include notions of whiteness and elitism as being part of the father tongue. Intellectual, political, and cultural worlds are not only structured through patriarchy but also through notions of white racial superiority and economic elitism. These worlds are dominated by men but are also very white and wealthy spaces and ways of being. We need to work against, and move beyond, the father tongue in order to allow greater, more diverse participation in various spaces such as the intellectual and political. For these reasons, I purposefully aim for my writing to be personal and reflective in opposition to a very formal or overly academic style.

Before beginning my narrative, I must first make some concessions. This is "my" story rather than "our" story. To clarify, I fully realize that I cannot speak for all of the rural, working class. Additionally, I cannot say our story because I left. I no longer live in the same small town nor live the same life. Instead, I see myself as being somewhere in between Karl Marx's categories of the bourgeoisie and the proletariat. I have wined and dined too much to be considered a proletariat, yet my working-class roots and identification keep me from being completely accepted and comfortable with/by the bourgeoisie. It makes my identity a bit schizophrenic. Also, I am torn between romanticizing the white working-class way of life while also being aware of the bigotry that is often included.

Finally, I do not want my narrative to be read as a success story nor as a story of hardship. I do not define it as a success story because success to me is about much more than schooling. I do not see it as a story of hardship because mixed in with the story is my privilege in being white. Additionally, I am well aware of the fact that I did not grow up as poor as many other people. I know that many children have struggled much more than I ever have or will. What I hope my story does, is shift how we think about class, people who are poor or working class, and the lived experience of class.

(De)Valued Knowledge

My environment growing up included blue-collar parents, a single-parent household, limited adult supervision, and a low-level family income. I believe my family background provided me with a unique perspective from that of many people in academia. Also, it enabled me to be aware of some of the ways in which financial and educational power can be used to oppress the working class.

Growing up, our food came from either the garden or from my father's hunting trips. We never ate beef. Instead we had deer, squirrel, and rabbit that my father hunted himself, not to mention, rocky mountain oysters (i.e., pig testicles) fresh from my grandpa's hog farm. My dad taught me a lot about nature. When accompanying him on hunting trips, I learned how to look at deer tracks in the sand and know whether it was made by a doe or a buck. I also learned how to recognize deer paths, skin a squirrel, and look for mussels in the river.

Some other lessons I learned included the importance of the value of family. Rarely do people in my community move outside of the county. Even those who move away to attend college often choose to stay and work in a factory rather than move away to begin a career in their field of study. In fact at one point in time, a large portion of my family all lived on the same road. I have also observed my aunts and father take care of my grandmother by cooking, cleaning, and driving her to her appointments. My decision to move away to attend graduate school was difficult for my family to understand I since had been taught to value "home" and "community."

Learning to Labor

My mother has worked in a glass factory for the past fifteen years, while my father has worked for the past twenty-eight years in a millwright factory. I began working in the eighth grade busing tables at a local cafeteria and continued to work in food service until I entered college. Being from a small town, I was often serving food and cleaning up after my fellow, wealthier classmates and their families. A few years ago, I ran into an old classmate of mine whose father was the town doctor. He told me that while in college he had to work fifteen to twenty hours a week.

He then proceeded to tell me that he would think of me. His family were regulars at the cafeteria where I bussed tables from the time I was thirteen to fifteen years old. To keep going, he would say to himself, "If Beth could manage working in middle school and high school, then surely I can do this [too]." His romanticization of my "hard work" denies the different material realities that he and I operated under as classmates. It denies the inequities inherent within our different material realities and makes them appear "normal." This romanticization toward the working-class way of life glosses over the real-life struggles of making enough money to have food to eat, worrying about a lack of medical coverage, being forced to work under dangerous conditions, and lacking job security.

My family has experienced literal pain for their labors. Two years ago, my mother mangled her hand in a piece of machinery and will never regain full use of it. Her employer forced her to return to work two days later to avoid increasing their accidental rate of injury. My father broke his leg while working and has a hole in his foot, while my older brother is missing a thumb as a result of an accident in a furniture factory. Just in this past year, my sister broke her kneecap and femur while working at a puppy day care and will never regain full mobility in her knee. If "murder" was redefined as deaths due to poor working conditions, the number would be significantly more than the amount of traditional murders. In 1990, 2.4 times more people were killed in the workplace due to purposeful violations of the law than were murdered at home or in the street (Lynch, Michalowski, and Groves, 2000).

Gender also plays a large role in being working class, particularly when most of the available high-paying jobs involve physical labor. Time and time again I have witnessed the women in my family "stuck" in miserable marriages due to financial dependence and husbands who abused this economical power they had over their wives. My parents divorced when I was ten years old and my mother was devastated emotionally and economically. Good paying work was hard to find, food was scarce, and I remember searching harvested cornfields for leftover corn to sell for cash, which was then used to buy groceries.

I also remember my mother going through trash dumpsters to see what treasures others had thrown away. In fact, my most favorite childhood stuffed animal, a sheep dog I named "Snuffy," came from a Dumpster. Those times gave me strength and determination that I don't think I would have had otherwise. I swore I would never be financially dependent upon a man and I perceived education as my way out. Acquiring an education became an act of independence and would ensure my future children that they would never want for their basic needs.

(Mis)education

It wasn't until I entered school that I remember being treated differently due to my social class and being ashamed for the first time. One of my best friends through grade school was Nicole. Nicole entered kindergarten knowing how to read. Everyday she was taken to the "special" room to receive advanced instruction in reading. In an effort for us to stay side-by-side, Nicole told the teacher that I could also read. The teacher believed her and the next day I went to the special room with Nicole. Of course, I could not read. Despite Nicole's efforts at whispering the words in my ear, the specialist was not fooled and I never went back to the special room with Nicole again.

Then there were the spelling bees. I really wanted to win! But every year, kindergarten through the fifth grade, it always came down to Nicole and me and she always came out ahead. She cried along with me when I lost. Her mother forced her to study for the spelling bees while my efforts were more self-motivated. I envied Nicole for her mother's attention, but Nicole resented it.

Her mother was a kindergarten teacher and her father worked at the local power plant—for a white, working-class town, they were the upper class. Nicole had the hippest clothes, always received compliments from teachers, and had a swimming pool, which was *the* sign of wealth in my community.

I have a distinct memory of standing in line beside Nicole during grade school as a teacher complimented her on a new outfit. I looked at Nicole's new, neatly pressed clothes and compared them to my worn-out shoes and hand-me-down blue jeans while feeling ashamed. It was one of the first times I realized that my family was not necessarily poor (depending on your point of view) but that I was "without." A large part of my memories connected to schooling are about feeling shame—embarrassment of being without, of being ugly. At one point in time, I even got lice and to this day still vividly remember the names I was called. I had been marked with the true stamp of being poor, white trash—I had gotten lice.

Throughout my schooling, success was typically narrowly defined to mean educational achievement. At times, I have struggled with the question, "If education equals success, then are my parents and brother failures because they do not have a formal education?" Also, throughout college I encountered numerous downcast faces and eyes accompanied by silence when I answered the question, "What do your parents do for a living?" When I receive this reaction, I think about when I worked with my mother in her factory. I saw her pass out due to working in extreme heat without any breaks and forced to work at the fastest pace possible. I also think about how she worked a swing shift (i.e., a weekly shift from days to evenings to midnights) for many years and I have seen the toll it has taken on her. My mother works much harder than I ever have in undergraduate or graduate school. I want to look at the people asking those questions and tell them these this. But this is a voice that has been silenced by "educated" people because of the higher esteem placed on educational credentials than working-class experience or knowledge. I continue to struggle with understanding how much value should be given to educational credentials because I have chosen to be a part of the institution of education.

Finally, my working-class roots taught me that no matter how many degrees a person has after their name, they do not automatically deserve your respect. In my community, posturing resulted in isolation rather than admiration. I was taught that you earn respect by being humble rather than by reminding people how great you are. That's your family's job. The rules in academia are quite different. We are often implicitly and explicitly taught that acquiring "an education" entitles respect from others, or rather from those without "an education." This still confuses me—especially since being humble can be so much harder than acquiring an education.

Race and Class

A part of white, working-class, rural culture is a careful construction of an "us versus them" dichotomy. The category of "them" can include people who are not white, academics, people who live outside the county, and people from the city. The most deeply embedded construction is that of people of color. Growing up, my community was 99 percent white except for the only doctor in the county and his family, who were Filipino-Canadian. I used to argue with my grandmother for saying negative things about African-Americans and with my mother's racist comments always framed by a fear of African-Americans. Through my own reasoning, I had concluded that skin color was not enough of a reason to judge a person, but that was the limit to the depth of my understanding. At that point in time, my ideology was that everyone should be "color-blind" when it came to race.

While a freshman in college, I decided to take African-American Literature. Little did I know how it would change my life. Within the classes, for the first time I was a racial minority. We read works by W. E. B. Dubois, Maya Angelou, Alice Walker, Zora Neale Hurston, Richard Wright, and Malcolm X. I heard a discourse that contradicted my life. I learned the history of racial bigotry in the United States that had been omitted from my previous education. My K–12 schooling had not even included the common surface level attempt at celebrating diversity through the Martin Luther King Jr. holiday.

Not until years later was I confronted with the reality of a middle class that was not 100 percent white. How was I to fit this into my schema of seeing all people of color as having suffered more than myself? How was I to make sense of the notion that all white people had more privileges than people of color when meeting a person of color who grew up with parents that were physicians? Due to growing up in a white, working-class family, I believed that all someone needed in order to have an easy life was money. It was then that I began to understand white privilege. I had previously connected my privilege with economic capital—not with the actual color of my skin. Through this realization, I began to understand that I was privileged just by simply being white.

My first academic job was in my home state of Indiana. Going home, however, was a very different experience. I had married a Mexican man and had a beautiful baby girl. So going home meant experiencing lessons in white oppression. Suddenly, a world that once seemed so familiar had become strange by "seeing" things that the presence of my husband and daughter brought into view. I especially became aware of the assumptions embedded in white privilege. For example, despite my husband's impeccable English laced with a Southern drawl, many people from my community assumed that he still needed to learn English. My biracial marriage allowed me to be aware of the practice of racial oppression where previously it had been blind to my "white" (blue) eyes. While standing beside my husband, I saw us being ignored by sales clerks in stores, and felt the constant gaze upon us as we walked through the mall.[1]

I may have grown up working class, but I also grew up with privileges in speaking English, largely experiencing cultural continuity between home and school, and always having authority (teachers, bosses, professors, etc.) figures who looked similar to me. I had lived most of my life without having to think about my race and how it influenced the ways in which people perceived me and the numerous spaces it allowed me to occupy.

Turning Points

At times I've wondered how I managed to get to college and then through graduate school. Consequently, I decided to write about the turning points, which had a strong influence on my education. As I think about these turning points, I want to be clear that it was never about hard work. It was about being provided with opportunities and being connected with people who had cultural and financial capital. When you're poor, you can work as hard as you want, but if someone doesn't provide a bridge so that you can cross the gulf of poverty, then it doesn't matter.

Figuring out how to get to college was difficult for me because I didn't have anyone who could guide me. The bottom line was money. I didn't have the money for application fees and knew that if I didn't get financial aid, that I couldn't go at all. I only applied to two schools because that was what I could afford. I remember that I really wanted to go to Cornell University but the application fee was fifty dollars and there was no way I could come up with the money. It wasn't until years later that that I learned I could have had those fees waived.

The summer before my junior year of high school, I participated in an eight-week summer science program at Indiana University for "economically disadvantaged" youths. Through this program, I was able to get a glimpse of college life and began to believe that I was capable of doing college level work. I also became connected with a faculty member who had a huge impact on my life. I ended up attending Indiana University. That faculty member got me into the honors program, and talked to me about applying to graduate school. Without her intervention in my life, I most definitely would not be writing this chapter. The summer science program ended two years after I had participated due to federal funding cuts.

To pay for college, I was fortunate enough to receive a Pell Grant, a grant from the state of Indiana, Perkins loans, Stafford loans, and a scholarship. Without these forms of financial aid, I simply would not have been able to go to college. I personally feel a sense of desperation when I hear about decisions made by President Bush to cut or reduce funding for programs such as the Perkins Loan Program, the Perkins Vocational and Technical Education Program, LEAP, Upward Bound, Talent Search, and Gear Up, which are all programs targeting low-income and/or disadvantaged youths (Selingo and Brush, 2005). Simultaneously, the state has been cutting funding to state universities (Digest of Education Statistics, 2002). To maintain financial stability, many universities have responded by raising tuition (Choy, 1999). Consequently, costs for attending college are steadily increasing while opportunities for financial assistance are quickly declining. There are becoming fewer and fewer bridges to help low-income students attend college. As bell hooks (2000) states, "Our nation is fast becoming a class segregated society where the plight of the poor is forgotten and the greed of the rich is morally tolerated and condoned" (p. vii). We have to pay attention to what is happening and focus on building up rather than tearing down those bridges.

Graduate school was also a whole new world for me. I was amazed at how often others assumed that I had money to pay for tuition when the financial aid office was late (as always) in paying. For example, I have a distinct memory of talking with someone in the university cashier's office about my financial aid being late. The person could not seem to understand why I could not just pay $5,000 and then get reimbursed later when I would receive financial aid. In fact, I was going to be forced to withdraw if I did not pay that $5,000. My mother cashed in part of her retirement so that I would not have to drop out.

I was also amazed at how often I heard other graduate students talk about being "poor" or not having any money. At first, it made me feel as if I wasn't the only one. But then through conversations with many of those students, I discovered that being poor for them meant having less than $500 in their checking accounts or if they did run out of money, they had family that could back them up. It was clear that many of the students had no clue what it meant to be poor.

Thankfully, I had a graduate adviser who understood my dilemma. He came from a working-class background himself and never forgot where he came from. Even though it wasn't required, he went out of his way to help us get by. A large part of his energy went to securing funding for graduate students. Additionally, he was not stingy with the funding like some other faculty. He not only paid us well, but also ensured that we had funding to travel to conferences. If he would not have been sensitive to those issues and would not have been willing to work with me during times of financial desperation, I would not have finished graduate school. Finally, he helped me and many others to understand how to maintain who we are against the pressure to conform to the "rules" of the academy.

Conclusion

I still struggle with meshing my working-class values of humility, family, and home with my lifestyle as a professor. When I visit my family, a part of me still longs to return. Although my income potential has been greatly enhanced, I wonder if it is worth it. I feel as if I am taking for granted what really matters in life: our relationships with others—my sense of community and family. By society's definition, I am successful, but in my heart I wonder if by investing myself in social mobility through schooling, if I have lost more than I have gained.

I now find myself more comfortable in "academic" spaces than in my home community. I sense that I have become an outsider through my class mobility and by seeing issues of race and gender differently than most people in my community now. How can I claim a working-class identity when I drive an SUV and don't have to punch a time clock? My work is rarely seen as work by my family due to the fact that I don't have someone controlling my time and that my job does not involve physical labor. My family doesn't know how to ask about my work or how to make sense of it, particularly since it is grounded in working toward racial, class, and gender equity. My mother regularly chastises me for not having a clean house—the sign of a "good" woman in her eyes. To me, however, my priorities have changed and I interpret her ideas of "good" women and housework quite differently now. Don't get me wrong, my family is proud of me. There is just more of a disconnect now from simply moving away to also rethinking much of my previous socialization. Additionally, I can listen but can no longer really share in their stories of struggle.

Whenever I get discouraged about my job, I remember my family. I remind myself of the struggles many of them have overcome and many that they still face. I remind myself of what I am taking for granted. I then remember that one of my main purposes in getting a Ph.D. was to give back to my family. I never want to lose sight of the fact that getting my doctorate was about becoming a bridge for my family. When a family member cannot pay their medical bills due to a lack of insurance, I want to be able to help them out. When my niece is ready to go to college, I want to ensure that she is able to go. I also want to be a bridge for the many first-generation college students I come across as well. It is what provides the meaning for my work.

I would like to end with a quote by bell hooks that I present as a challenge to those of us in academia. She states: "To see the poor as ourselves we must want for the poor what we want for ourselves. By living simply, we all express our solidarity with the poor and our recognition that gluttonous consumption must end. . . . Solidarity with the poor is the only path that can lead our nation back to a vision of community that can effectively challenge and eliminate violence and exploitation. It invites us to embrace an ethics of compassion and sharing. . . ." (2000, pp. 48–49).

The idea of solidarity with the poor is a complicated issue. We need to think through how the aim to own more and become wealthier reproduces class stratification and justifies the assault on the poor in our society. How do we justify to ourselves having more than our neighbors? Through wanting more for ourselves, how are we keeping others back? We must make this struggle our own by asking these questions. To achieve solidarity with the poor, we must make sacrifices ourselves and truly embrace an "ethics of compassion and sharing."

Note

1. I am referring here to instances such as looking for apartments or complaining of poor treatment in businesses.

References

Chow, S. 1999. College access and affordability. *Education Statistics Quarterly*, 1(2). Retrieved May 2, 2005, from http://www.nces.ed.gov/programs/quarterly.

hooks, b. 2000. *Where we stand: Class matters*. New York: Routledge.

Lynch, M., Michalowki, R., and Groves, W. B. 2000. *The new primer in radical criminology: Critical perspectives on crime, power, and identity*, 3rd ed. Monsey, NY: Criminal Justice Press.

National Center for Education Statistics, *Digest of Education Statistics 2002*, Table 330. Retrieved May 2, 2005, from http://nces.ed.gov/surveys/AnnualReports/reports.asp?type=digest.

Selingo, J. and Brush, S. 2005. Bush takes aim at student aid and research. *Chronicle of Higher Education*, 51(24), p. A1.

Smith, D. 1987. *The everyday world as problematic: A feminist sociology*. Boston: Northeastern University Press.

2

CLASS/CULTURE/ACTION

REPRESENTATION, IDENTITY, AND AGENCY IN EDUCATIONAL ANALYSIS

Bill J. Johnston

Introduction

This chapter attempts to explore whether and in what manner the construct class remains a useful category for social and educational analysis. At one time class was unabashedly identified as one of, if not the central, category of sociological analysis. This is not to suggest, however, that the class construct has ever been unproblematically embraced. Karl Marx is probably identified as the first great class theorist, but never unambiguously defined class (Crompton, 1998). Max Weber spent much of his professional career engaged in a debate with Marx's ghost over matters of class and social theory. A variety of theorists throughout the twentieth century have attempted to clarify, elaborate, or modify the original conceptions of class offered by Marx and Weber. Likewise, over the years there have been repeated declarations of the demise of class and/or class theory, just as others have lamented the imprecision, impurity, or simple neglect of class analysis (Eder, 1993; Pahl, 1993; Pakulski and Waters, 1996).

More recently, economic restructuring associated with processes of postindustrial and post-Fordist forms of production, transformation of the occupational structure, the triumph of global capitalism, and the dissolution of the former Soviet Union, has led to renewed questioning of the continued utility of class theory, and by implication, the utility of class analysis.

There are two primary reasons why we should examine the effects of class on education: one empirical and the other theoretical. First, as Steven E. Tozer, Paul Violas, and Guy Senese (2000) points out in his brief discussion of class, family background is closely associated with educational attainment. He notes, for example, that "compared to White non-Hispanics, Asian Americans drop out of school somewhat less, African Americans drop out slightly more, and Hispanic students drop out twice as often as the White comparison group. Girls drop out slightly less than boys. Taking all ethnic groups and genders, low-SES students drop out *six times as often* as high SES students and almost three times as often as middle-SES students" (p. 154, italics in original). Other studies of educational attainment obtain similar findings. To report attainment differences by race/ethnicity and gender, but not by SES, is at best to misrepresent the nature of the educational challenge. Moreover, given the history of class antagonism, to employ the language of class, or its cousin SES, is to invoke a social memory of working-class repression carried out by, or with the nodding approval of, the state. And to implicate the state in such a manner is to both threaten the legitimacy of the state and to highlight relationships of interdependency between the economic and political order. From the statist perspective, far better to invoke the legacy of Parsonian structural-functionalism, with its assumptions of meritocracy, order, and stability, to attribute school failure to the inadequacy of family or student, and to dismiss conflict as an event of individual deviance rather than as a structural problem. From a critical perspective, on the other hand, to ignore class and/or SES in analysis serves little purpose other than to mystify hegemonic relations and to protect the privilege of the privileged.

Second, Raymond E. Callahan in *Education and the Cult of Efficiency* (1962) traced the general adoption of business interests and values in education since 1900; a tendency reinforced during the past two decades beginning with the publication of *A Nation at Risk* (1983). The contribution of education to the labor force and to general economic development is now so taken for granted that it has become the primary focus of policy discussion, often to the exclusion of other interests. The tendency to exclude class from an analysis of education, however, deflects attention from the economic correlates of achievement, and more importantly relationships of domination and subordination relative to production and consumption. In a decidedly peculiar twist of logic we are left to engage in an analysis of an institution being defined and judged in terms of its contribution to economic production without recourse to a core construct by which to characterize economic relationships and potential conflicts.

Thus, we undertake a review of the construct of class, with the intention of exploring whether and how educators might more productively conceptualize social class. We conclude that while the class construct need not be abandoned, it may require reconceptualization. Consequently, we explore more culturally derived and emergent notions of class. As a component of identity formation, components of class such as economic status, conditions, and relationships remains important, but how to productively and analytically join class with analysis of other factors (primarily race and gender, but also sexuality, religion, disability, etc.) remains problematic, especially if one's interest is to engage in the analysis of collective action and policy formation for school improvement and individual achievement. Moreover, while class theory and class analysis may continue to have significant implications for general social theory development and institutional analysis, it may be that at the level of the school and classroom in which educators, who themselves occupy class positions, attempt to counter the potentially negative effects of class among their students, that different emphasis and understanding of class may be warranted.

Conceptualizing Class:
The Founding Fathers: Marx and Engels

For good reason Marx and Weber are considered to be the founding fathers of class analysis; the discussion of class throughout the twentieth century has primarily revolved around the competing formulations of class first advanced by Marx and then by Weber.

Karl Marx (1818–1883)

Marx and Engels, coauthors of *The Manifesto of the Communist Party* (1848), were clearly heirs to an established tradition in which the concept of class and the analytic division of society into class and status groups was already established, and in which there was precedent, albeit in a rudimentary form, of attempts to understand and influence the development of civil society. They were not alone in recognizing that in nineteenth-century France and England, the rise of industry was creating a new binary opposition between workers and propertied interests. Marx was the first, however to make class a central component of social theory.

> The history of all hitherto existing society is the history of class struggle. . . . The modern bourgeois society that has sprouted from the ruins of feudal society has not done away with class antagonisms. It has but established new classes, new conditions of oppression, new forms of struggle in place of the old ones.

Our epoch, the epoch of the bourgeoisie possesses, however, this distinctive feature: it has simplified the class antagonisms. Society as a whole is more and more splitting up into two great hostile camps, into two great classes directly facing each other: bourgeoisie and proletariat. (Marx and Engels, 1848/1976, p. 485)

In this formulation we find the seeds of reconceptualization of class from a hierarchy of status positions to a binary opposition. We have the basis of class theory as the essential dynamic explanation of social structure and change. And we have the privileging of economic relationships, relative to the social and political, as determinant (at least in the last instance). The basis of the great antagonism is identified as possession of the means of production that allows the bourgeoisie to exercise domination over the laboring class. While ownership was the ultimate basis of economic authority, social relations of domination and subordination was the defining characteristic. And in this we find a clear attempt to associate class with analytic positions (rather than as attributes of persons); positions that are knowable, and that can exist, only in relationship to other positions.

For Marx, relationships of *production* are of primary significance. Within a capitalist form of production, ownership of productive forces are critical and give rise to the necessity of exploitation of *labor power* as opposed to the mere exploitation of labor. Labor may be thought of as a commodity, which has a use value and price that will be determined through market forces and exchange. A worker may exchange labor for a wage, the value of which will be determined by more or less unencumbered market mechanisms. There is little inherent exploitation in such a market exchange; indeed workers may receive full and fair market value for their labor. The capitalist, however, obtains not just labor, but also labor power; the productive force that maintains and multiples capital itself, and without which capitalist forms of production could not be sustained. The application of labor power leads to the creation of *surplus labor* that may be appropriated to generate *surplus value*. The essence of the class relationship, and the nature of capitalist exploitation, is not found in the market exchange of labor for wages (which is ultimately a relationship between persons), but in the abstract, yet real, structural coupling of capital with labor power during the process of production. What happens to surplus value once it is transformed by exchange into money is of considerable social interest but remains distinct from the theoretical issue of capitalist forms of exploitation. From a Marxist perspective then, class position, associated with ownership of the means of production, or lack thereof, becomes a primary *analytic construct* and the central dynamic of history.

The structure of economic relationships is thought to be assessable and objectively determined through analysis. Thus, one may presume that material conditions potentially may determine consciousness and ultimately social movements, but the logic of class theory is not dependent upon the existence of class consciousness and action as a class for itself. It appears then that the potential for disconnection between the analysis of class relationships and the application of class theory, on the one hand, from the development of class consciousness and social action, on the other hand, has created an enduring tension. One is not entirely remiss to ask, however, what good is a theory of historical change and development if it does not lead to observable conscious social action. On the other hand, to the degree that class relationships are a fundamental component of capitalist structures and forms of production, then class theory and analysis serves the important function of making visible, and perhaps demystifying, forces that are often mediated and obscured by market relationships. Such knowledge as may be gained from class analysis may not set one free, but its absence is certainly no contribution to emancipation.

The analysis of class (treated as an analytic construct) within capitalist forms of production is thought to allow the determination of objective class interests that may be independent of the subjective perception or consciousness of class; in part, this relates to Marx's distinction between a class in itself and a class for itself. Now if one is concerned only with class positions, then it probably doesn't matter a great deal whether the relationship is one of exploitation or not. But the fact of the matter is that both class and occupational positions are filled by people, thus identification of structural forms of exploitation and the inevitable inequalities of income and opportunity associated with relationships of production, have significant social consequence. This point is made forcefully by Maurice Zeitlin (1980, pp. 2–3) who notes that no adequate social theory (as may have happened with some variants of structuralist Marxism) can focus only on structures, and that social actors are never merely effects of determinate structural factors. In a dialectical fashion, "Men and women make the social relations and material conditions of life that make them" (p. 3). Class relationships thus always contain a "latent historical content," grounded in the material conditions of production and conditioned by forces of contradiction and exploitation. Whether persons occupying particular class positions become conscious of the nature of exploitative relations and act in ways consistent with self-interest is a question of historically contingency. For example, Marx's expectation that the proletariat would eventually rise in opposition to their exploitation, appears to have been merely wishful thinking.

Max Weber (1864–1920)

In contrast to Marx's assertion that the relations of production are the real foundation of society, Weber considered economic power to be only one available form. Weber notes that one may identify class situation as an analytic construct; status groups, which tend to be actual social groups; and parties that are affiliations of individuals for the purpose of acquiring social power.

Weber associated class with life chances and with the acquisition of goods and income, governed by principles of market exchange. It is the exchange relationship rather than the production relationship that is the primary defining characteristic. Persons who share a common market situation may also be considered as belonging in the same class situation. Clusters of (economic-based) classes within which mobility is relatively easy, may be described as social classes. In this formulation, class remains a potentially relational construct, but is revealed much more personally and hierarchically. Because Weber was not bound to a binary understanding of exploiting and exploited classes, he was able to allow the possibility that a variety of class positions might be identified. As Anthony Giddens (1971, p. 164) points out, however, Weber, following Marx, privileges ownership/nonownership as the primary basis of historically significant social class division within competitive markets. Weber identifies four primary social classes: dominant entrepreneurial and propertied groups; propertyless white-collar workers, technicians and intelligentsia; petty bourgeoisie; and the working class internally differentiated by skill level (p. 165).

Having positioned class as one among other sources of influence, Weber also is free to identify multiple dynamics governing social action and historically contingent change. During periods of economic or technological transformation, for example, class may be determinate, whereas during periods of relative social stability status may predominate (Crompton and Gubbay, 1977, p. 7). Moreover, associating class with consumption and exchange, then class identification becomes a task of differentiating various life chances, incomes, and goods acquisition along a continuum. Class identification requires empirical description rather than theoretical explication; in practical terms class identification becomes reduced to a process of occupational grouping associated with status hierarchies.

Neither Marx nor Weber engaged in a thorough and explicit discussion of class as such. Rosemary Crompton and Jon Gubbay (1977, p. 5) note, for example, that Weber develops the concept of class in only two brief passages, whereas Marx is described as never having provided a precise definition (Crompton, 1998, p. 26). Consequently, much subsequent theoretical work has been an attempt to more adequately conceptualize and describe class. What is clear, however, is that both Marx and Weber are positioning class within the context of developing a broader theory of society and that they privilege different social forces and dynamics.

The Competing Logic of Industrial Society and the "New" Middle Class

In the United States of 1900, Marx's account of the labor process in factory-based production and the general critique of capitalism was the most advanced theoretical statement available. Nevertheless, while Marxism may have offered a potent explanation of emerging social dynamics, it did not achieve widespread acceptance. There are a variety of reasons for this. First there were a number of competing general social theories. Because Marx's theory was clearly inhospitable to those interested in furthering capitalist development, one should not be surprised that it did not achieve widespread acceptance among the early industrialists and their political supporters. Alternatively the work of such thinkers as Spencer, Veblen, and Pareto, while containing critical analytic elements, could more easily be incorporated into emerging liberal evolutionary, structural functionalist theories more hospitable to capitalism and its supporters. (e.g., Parsonian functionalism).

Second, while some within the nascent labor movement were clearly influenced by Marx, they were cautious in adopting too revolutionary a position in relation to the bourgeoisie and the state. Throughout the nineteenth century, worker resistance in Europe and in the United States was typically met by bloody repression (Beaud, 1993) either at the hands of factory owners acting independently or by the aid of the state. While labor may have been predisposed to adopt Marxist theory, there was little authentic opportunity to express such sentiments.

Finally, emerging developments within the structure of capitalist forms of production were to create internal tensions within Marxist theory. Indeed, much of twentieth-century Marxist thought has been an attempt to rescue Marx from contemporary developments. Most notable during the first half of the twentieth century was the rise of corporate forms of industrial organization and a concomitant increase in the number of white-collar workers. These two developments were to influence subsequent general social theory development and to stimulate reconceptualization of class structure.

Adolf A. Berle and Gardiner C. Means, in *The Modern Corporation and Private Property* (1933), Burnham in *The Managerial Revolution* (1941), and Berle in *The 20th Century Capitalist Revolution* (1954) proposed that control of the "modern" corporation had slowly shifted from the hands of owners (either family or collectively through stock) into the hands of managers. Quoting from Charles Francis Adams writing as early as 1869, "The system of corporate life is a new power, for which our language contains no name; . . . We have no name to express government by monied corporations" (Trachtenberg, 1982, p. 3). *Corporatism* and *industrialism* were being positioned to compete with *capitalism* as the essential force of modern society, and the hired managers and waves of clerical workers were portrayed as constituting a new class of workers, neither owner nor laborer in the traditional sense. This "new middle class" of workers posed something of a problem for traditional class theory by substituting a three- (or more) class stratum for the binary opposition of bourgeoisie and proletariat. Now it is the case that Marx himself had responded to the problem of class strata in identifying the petty bourgeois and underclass of the disenfranchised proletariat. But this modification never threatened the underlying binary logic of class theory. The rise of a new middle class, however, was something of a challenge. The mass of clerical workers, who were typically women, was more easily handled. In terms of the nature and relationships of work, there is little functional difference between the assembly line and the typing pool. Clerical workers were firmly associated with subordinated labor. But managers, especially top managers, were an entirely different case. These positions were associated with varying levels of authority and control, and as the argument was advanced, mere ownership without control is of questionable value in terms of explaining social structure, function, and dynamics. The shift in the basis of domination and subordination from economic relationships to organizational authority has been a continuing theme by those attempting to account for the rise of the middle class and for the effects of continued economic restructuring associated with intensified concentration and centralization of power into fewer and larger corporate units.

Drawing on the work of Durkheim and Spencer in social theory, and Malinowski and Radcliffe-Brown in anthropology, an evolutionary form of social theory emerged that attempted to explain extant structures, including stratification, through an analysis of functions served. Talcott Parsons, drawing upon the work of these theorists as well as others (e.g., Weber and Pareto), produced *The Structure of Social Action* (1937) and *The Social System* (1951) provided perhaps the most influential statements of the functionalist perspective. A primary objective of this approach is to explain the creation and maintenance of the social order. As outlined by Percy S. Cohen (1968) social order theories tended to be grounded in reference to three primary factors: coercion, common interest, and/or value-consensus. As a general theory of society, Parsonian functionalism emphasized value consensus and institutional structures and process, attempting to identify the functional prerequisites and boundary maintenance processes that enabled an institution to persist. Within this perspective one might interpret class structure, or more likely following the Weberian influence and Warner's conflation of class with status, the stratification of SES positions, in terms of their contribution to maintaining the status quo. While such an analysis might be useful, a host of critics have also pointed out that by emphasizing the "consensual" aspects of system maintenance and social order, structural-functional explanations ignore the ever-present conflicts and tensions inherent in society.

Ralf Dahrendorf

Dahrendorf (1958), was primarily responding to the overly consensualist assumptions of Parsonian structural-functionalism in proposing a dialectical-conflict perspective grounded in the exercise of power relationships (Turner, 1974, pp. 92–96). In Dahrendorf's (1959) view, institutions are constituted by various organizations; what he describes as Imperatively Coordinated associations (ICAs). These ICAs are themselves characterized by a complex of roles/positions. Positions in ICAs tend to be differentiated by the distribution of power, which through normative processes, leads to the emergence of a new basis of legitimate entrepreneurial authority. In advancing the notion of ICAs, Dahrendorf is explicitly rejecting traditional Marxist theory while advancing a theory of industrial society. As outlined by Dahrendorf (1959, pp. 43–44) "[T]he separation of ownership and control involved changes in the structure of social positions and a change in the recruitment of personnel to these positions." Social positions are now to be differentiated on the basis of exercise of control rather than ownership. The functions and roles previously reserved to owner/managers have been redistributed to stockholders, executives, and investors and finance capitalists.

In Dahrendorf's (1959, p. 55) view, the new middle class is not one class but two: executives who occupy command positions and are more closely associated with the interests of capital, and the mass of "clerical" workers who are associated with the working class. Dahrendorf asserts that there are still classes, but the basis of class formation and structure are no longer grounded in production or markets, but rather in the unequal distribution of authority among groups and quasi groups within imperatively coordinated associations. This division within the middle class is significant for the examination of social order and conflict, since one can observe the relative similarity of interests between owners and executives, on the one hand, and the mass of white-collar and working classes on the other hand. The legitimation of power is the basis for the creation and maintenance of a particular social order. Nevertheless, power is also the resource and grounds over which role occupants compete. While power may be hierarchically distributed among roles/positions, roles also tend to cluster along the binary dimension of authority over others versus the relative absence of such authority, with the result that social conflict tends to become polarized as conflict between the rulers and the ruled.

While there are many similarities between Dahrendorf's and Marx's formulation, a significant difference is that the former locates the source of conflict within institutionalized authority relationships. As a consequence of the convergence of interest in the effects of corporatism and industrialism, a theory of industrial society gradually emerged as an alternative to traditional Marxist class theory. The essential characteristics of the theory of industrial society that gradually developed have been summarized by Anthony Giddens (1987, pp. 26–29) and includes the following:

1. The most significant set of changes to be found in the contemporary world . . . [has] to do with the transition from "traditional" societies, based primarily upon agriculture, on the one hand, to "industrial societies", based upon mechanical production and exchange of goods, on the other.
2. The transition from traditional to industrial society represents a progressive social movement. [Conflicts tend to be counterbalanced by the] beneficial features of the industrial order, which both generates material affluence and is associated with the dissolution of traditional constraints.
3. In the early origins of the newly emerging industrial society, class divisions were acute, and class relations were the focus of major tensions. But these tensions have been largely displaced as accepted modes of industrial bargaining became established, in conjunction with the extension of political citizenship rights. . . .
4. The rise of the liberal-democratic state is an essential element accompanying the transition from tradition to modernity.
5. [T]here is an essential unity to the industrial order wherever it emerges. [Following Weber some proponents of industrial society theory argue that] *large-scale organization* is a necessary feature of contemporary societies and that this has certain universal features (italics in original).
6. The conception of industrial society has often been closely associated with so-called modernization theory. The key idea in modernization theory is that the 'underdeveloped' societies remain trapped within traditional institutions, from which they have to break free if they are to approach the economic prosperity achieved in the West.

For purposes of our discussion, the essential features of this approach is to enable discussions of the declining significance of class theory and class analysis, legitimation for examination of occupational status rather than traditional class relative to identify formation and social action, and legitimation of assumptions of meritocracy and processes of credentialism within an examination of structures of social mobility. Within general social theory, the industrial society thesis became a primary theoretical alternative to Marxism.

Structural Marxist Developments:
Althusser and Bourdieu

Although Althusser shares with Dahrendorf and the industrial society theorists a recognition that the class structure is evolving, he retains an interest in the primacy of production relations as determinant, at least in the last instance. In essence, Althusser in political-economic theory and Bourdieu in development of the notion of habitus, are developing a perspective that retains much of the thrust of Marx's original work, while purporting to better represent extant political, social, and economic conditions (Resch, 1992).

Louis Althusser

Althusser rejects whatever historicist and teleological elements that may have plagued Marxist theory, advancing instead a nonlinear, modernist, and materialist "science of history." Whereas Marx proposed that the capitalist mode of production determined rather directly the political and legal superstructure on the one hand and ideology on the other hand, Althusser proposes that the mode of production remains determinant in the last instance, although the last instance may never come. This recognition allows examination of the relative autonomy of various institutional sectors of the social formation, be they political, economic, or ideological. The state, for example, may be more or less directly representative of the accumulative interests of capitalists, but more likely to represent the general interests of capital while also attempting to balance a variety of other competing interests (including its own) in attempting to maintain social perceptions of legitimacy. The various institutions that comprise the social formation are considered to retain a distinctive character and influence, yet together constitute a structured whole. Social actors must effectively navigate these various institutional orders, each with its own axis of power. The consequence of this line of argument is to introduce an element of confusion. Historically manifest class structures and relationships, allowing recognition of a variety of competing fractions and strata, within a social formation characterized by the presence of competing modes and forms of production, introduces the idea of a hierarchical structure of positions and roles (Resch, 1992, p. 28) without clear determination of when and how hierarchical positions influence social processes.

In "Ideology and Ideological State Apparatus," Althusser (1971) positions ideology as of particular significance. Beginning from the question of the "reproduction of the conditions of production" of a social formation, Althusser makes a distinction between *state power* that may be considered in a traditional sense of a monopoly of the means of repression, and *state apparatus* considered as the organizational manifestation of the political, and also the object of contestation by parties in order to wield power. Since the raw exercise of power may generate opposition and resentment, it is preferable to disguise the exercise of power through other means. One means is to develop ideological state apparatus such as the schools. There, children may be taught not only the knowledge and skills (the know-how) necessary to meet the technical needs of production, but also may be socialized and enculturated to accept the habits of mind, forms of analysis, and dispositions to view the extant social formation as natural and rational, or at least as inevitable. In this regard, ideology is considered an imaginary symbolic system, representing prevailing visions of the society. That ideology constitutes an imaginary system that may not reflect the "objective" interests of its carriers or even of "objective" conditions of the social formation is of little matter. The evaluation of ideology is not to be found in determinations of truth, but rather in the degree to which it provides *cohesion* (Poulantzas, 1973), and beyond that, to the manner in which it shapes the practical interests and practices of individual agents formed as subjects. Paralleling the analysis of imperialism considered not so much the projection of capitalism upon a subordinated people, but rather the imposition of a worldview, the objective of an ideological state apparatus is to engage in a process of domestic imperialism.

Pierre Bourdieu

One of the difficulties with Althusser's description of ideology and subject formation is that individual agents are portrayed as little more than autonomic and passive recipients of the determinant dominant ideology. Bourdieu (1977a, 1977b), while not a Marxist, arrives at a somewhat similar position to that of the structuralist Marxists. For Bourdieu, the location of oneself or others in social space becomes a two-dimensional (class and culture) rather than a one-dimensional (class) enterprise (Rupp, 1997). While the political and economic power exhibited by dominant groups allows considerable class-based influence over ideological agencies such as schools, such influence is not absolute. Robert Paul Resch (1992, p. 216) notes that for Bourdieu, individual subjects "are not imprinted with a fixed set of [ideological] rules and procedures as much as they are endowed with a social sense of cultivated disposition." Bourdieu (1977b, p. 487) is careful to focus analysis at the structural rather than at the individual level. And it is in this light that one should consider his development of the concept "habitus, [the] system of dispositions . . . [which] acts as a mediation between structures and practice"; dispositions that are differentially distributed across class positions, but act to reproduce extant structures. Habitus is posited as representing various class-stratified, taken-for-granted, and structured symbolic systems. Habitus inhabits the collective unconscious establishing generative guidelines and boundaries upon individual and collective action. Among the most important functions of habitus is to identify the relative status and symbolic relationships differentiating various class and social positions. To be identified, and to identify with a particular class one must have acquired, through socialization in families, schools, and elsewhere, the symbolic and cultural capital associated with that class. The result is that the analysis of class structure and identity requires assessment of one's access to, and exchange value of, economic, cultural, social and symbolic capital (assets). In some regards, habitus may be considered the functional equivalent of dominant ideology, but in a softer yet more pervasive form.

For Bourdieu, both the economic and cultural constitute analytically identifiable and separate fields. While Giddens tends to emphasize the individual's ability to navigate between various fields (e.g., economic, cultural, and political) in the process of socially situating themselves, Bourdieu retains a more determinant role for class and habitus. In essence, Bourdieu retains a materialist grounding of class, but mediated by the habitus, and continually evolving during processes of intergenerational reproduction of economic and cultural assets.

In summary, the structural Marxists are attempting to respond to a number of difficulties emerging from traditional class theory. One is that the anticipated progression from class structure to class consciousness to class action has not typically been observed. The response was a combination of attempts to separate an analysis of determinant structures from social consciousness and action, to reconceptualize the basis of class structure and the manner in which class-based influences were manifest (often in combination or mediated with other social factors), and to shift emphasis to concrete patterns of general ideological reproduction at the institutional level and strategies of class-based inheritance of power and privilege across generations. In making these moves, however, the field was set to elevate the analytic status of strategies and mechanisms of social reproduction (through symbolic systems and patterns of discourse) relative to traditional economic structural determinants. This in turn facilitated a theoretical shift from assuming the primacy of class and class struggle toward exploration of alternative theoretical positions attempting to explain emerging patterns of social differentiation, exclusion, and mobility under conditions of disorganized capitalism and postindustrial society.

From Structure to the Search for Identify:
Lenin and Lukacs

Marxist theory is grounded in the belief that the mode of production determines the class structure; class structure provides the basis of class
struggle and ultimately of historical class action. Unfortunately, the general failure of the proletariat to manifest their historic revolutionary role,
the failure of the working class to exhibit a consistent collective consciousness and action, and the rise of the new middle classes that generated questioning of whether they, rather than the working class might
occupy the revolutionary position, all served to generate a crisis for
Marxism. Likewise, alternative theoretical explanations, associated, for
example, with the industrial society thesis, predicting the withering of
class, class identification and class action also have been disappointing. In
essence, throughout the twentieth century, to paraphrase Marx, class has
remained an important factor of social theory and analysis, but not just
as theorists and analysts would have it. In the following, we will explore
the contributions of Lenin and Lukacs, Gramski and Giddens.

Lenin and Lukacs

One line of argument attempted to retain the emphasis upon class by
highlighting the cultural dynamics of class formation, action, and reproduction. The Marxism of Lenin and Lukacs, for example, addressed class
consciousness but in a very peripheral way. For Lenin it was proper that
the leaders lead the party, and that the party lead the mass of workers.
Acquisition of power and the imposition of a new social order was the
objective. In obtaining this objective, the revolutionary class consciousness of the workers was potentially useful but not the necessary means of
power acquisition. On the other hand, mastery of the means of ideological production/ legitimation by the party was considered a necessary step
in the acquisition and institutionalization of revolutionary authority. In
recognizing the importance of ideology in the development of Praxis,
Lenin is moving away from traditional economistic accounts and legiti-
mating a more prominent place for an analysis of ideology. Lukacs followed the Leninist argument, but placed a different emphasis upon class
consciousness. Since class structure was determined independent of actual
persons, one should not attempt to infer the structure of capitalist society
from the consciousness of citizens; likewise one should not infer the
"true" consciousness of the working class from the perceptions of actual
workers. It is class not persons that is the historical subject. The Communist Party, however, was thought to serve as the concrete historical
representative of the interests of the workers. To identify the historical

manifestation of the class consciousness of the historical subject of history (i.e., working-class consciousness) one must turn not to members of the working class, but rather to the party.

Antonio Gramsci

Gramsci (1971; also see Kolakowski, 1978), broke with the Leninist tradition by advancing the idea that the development of a revolutionary consciousness, that is, working-class consciousness, was a prerequisite to historical action. Classes, not persons, may constitute the historical subject, but members of the working class could not be authentic participants in class struggle unless they understood their own interests in opposition to the bourgeoisie, the structure of capitalist forms of production and exploitation, and their role in history. For Gramsci, the objective of revolution is not simply to capture the reins of state power, that is, to monopolize the forces of coercion, but rather to interpolate a democratic and egalitarian worldview. Gramsci observed that the ruling class inevitably employed systems of ideological and cultural hegemony to advance their interests, and to counter this tendency called for the emergence of organic intellectuals to champion the working class. In advancing these beliefs, Gramsci also modified Marx's conception of base/superstructure. For Marx, economic relationships constitute the structural bases of civil society; law, polity, and ideology constitute the superstructure. For Gramsci, civil society must be conceptually divided into two parts. Relations of production still constitute the base of civil society, but the superstructure of the social relations of civil society are identified as cultural, ideological, and intellectual. It is these superstructural elements that constitute the collective "common sense." The dominant class becomes a hegemonic class by creating or controlling the institutions and from there are allowed to dominate the principles of judgment of law and the state. Within this framework, the rule of the dominant class is found to be grounded upon ideological manipulation (hegemony, reification, etc.). This constitutes a break with the prevailing notion that one could engage in "objective" analysis independent of the actual conditions of history. While Gramsci opened Marxist theoretical discussion to the central role of consciousness, and to the forms of development of class consciousness, the problem remained, as Gramsci well understood, that no historically oppressed group had ever succeeded in imposing its worldview as a means to the ascent to power. In a similar vein, Andrew Gorz (1982, p. 67) exploring the possibilities of socialism, notes that "In the immense majority of cases, whether in the factory or the office, work is now a passive, preprogrammed activity which has been totally subordinated to the working of big machinery, leaving no room for personal initiative. Loss of the ability to identify with one's work is tantamount to the disappearance of any sense of belonging to a class."

At present, it appears that several different research tendencies are being exhibited. One is to treat class as an empirical construct, which may be variously defined. One then searches for relationships between class and some dependent variable of interest, possibly followed by an attempt to generate a model of effect. At best this may lead to deductive approaches to theory building or may languish as another example of what C. Wright Mills (1959) described as "abstracted empiricism." A second tendency is to concede that the identification of determinant relationships between class structure and consciousness may be so tenuous that further work in this direction is unwarranted. A third approach is to attempt a reconceptualization of the structure—agency relationship. Giddens's theory of structuration is perhaps the most well-known example of this approach, but interesting work is being done within this broad tradition by Margaret E. Archer (1996) and in the focus on the symbolic and exchange value of various "assets" (Robertson, 2000).

Anthony Giddens

Giddens's thinking about class has evolved over the years. Following a flirtation with evolutionary liberalism in the 1960s and the examination of class (1971, 1973), Giddens (1984) developed a new theory of society that he called "structuration." Society and social structures are not to be considered things that determine the actions of individuals. Rather, the interaction of various actors, involving the mutual interpretation of meaning through a process of reflexive monitoring, over time gives rise to *interaction regularities,* that is, social systems (Rossides, 1997, p. 68). Such systems of habit and routine enable the efficient collective engagement for access and control of economic and other resources and constrain the range of social action that is deemed appropriate. In this, Giddens is advancing an interpretive sociology, but his theoretical project of structuration is much broader than this. Indeed, it is to develop a form of social theory that integrates the structural and interpretive.

Structure as the abstract set of constitutive rules, does not exist in time and space. Rather, it is the instantiations of structure through situated human action that is space/time bound. Structuration refers to the "conditions governing the continuity or transmutation of structures, and therefore the reproduction of social systems" (Giddens, 1984, p. 25). The duality of structure is found in the fact that "the constitution of agents and structures are not two independently given sets of phenomena, a dualism, but represent a duality. According [to] the notion of the duality of structure, the structural properties of the social systems are both medium and outcome of the practices they recursively organize" (p. 25).

The manner in which this discussion connects with our interest in class, is that class represents one structuring field (economic) among a variety of others (e.g., status, race, and gender), that may be employed by agents in the manifestation of social action. Derived from a Weberian notion of class, Giddens attempts to integrate structure and agency in a manner that retains recognition of the class structuration processes within a capitalist economic system, but in a form that does not privilege class analysis in the analysis of social systems.

Empirical Studies of Class, Consciousness, and Action

While there is considerable debate on the proper way to conceptualize class, the available empirical evidence is actually much more consistent. Empirical work can be grouped within several traditions. One is the status attainment and social mobility approach that was dominant during the 1960s and 1970s. Here one may locate the well-known studies by Peter M. Blau and Otis Dudley Duncan (1967), Duncan, David L. featherman, and Duncan (1972), William H. Sewell, Robert M. Hauser and Featherman (1976), Hauser and Featherman (1977), Featherman and Hauser (1976), and Christopher Jencks (1979). Following primarily from within the Weberian tradition, these studies link occupational status hierarchies with a variety of outcome variables (e.g., educational attainment, occupation mobility and attainment, income, lifestyle, and life-chances). Whether one chooses to employ the construct of class or socioeconomic status to interpret these findings, it is clear that economic conditions have a direct and important influence on individual and collective social outcomes.

A variety of studies have indicated that the majority of citizens in the United States and Europe have a relatively consistent idea of the class structure of their society. Typically within this line of research, class is considered as a subjective status-group ranking of related occupational positions, rather than being considered relationally as derived from the structure of production or organizational authority. What appears clear from these studies is that people are engaged in a process of identifying (and distinguishing) self and other on the basis of a variety of socially available structures. Class is clearly one of the these structures (others may include race/ethnicity, gender, religion, region, and sexual orientation). Whether class is the primary dimension of social identification is not at all established. Nevertheless, that some image of class structure is a factor of social identification appears beyond dispute.

Another research tradition has been to explore the degree to which various forms of collective social action derive from class identification and identity, concluding that social identification and action is the result of a variety of intersecting fields. Only rarely does one find a pure situation in which one says, "Now I am going to act on the basis of class interests. Now I am going to act on the basis of gender." Nevertheless, there is a body of research to indicate that class action is an inherent component of class consciousness. G. William Domhoff (1967), Goran Therborn (1978), Zeitlin (1980), and T. B. Bottomore and Robert J. Brym (1989) have all engaged in an examination of the dominant class. They find that this class does tend to have a high degree of self-identification of themselves as a class, and participate in both formal and informal policy-making centers that allow them to express their class interests in a relatively unified and dominant manner. This finding, while of interest and importance from the perspective of both class analysis and theory, is consistent with Marx's belief that the ideas and interests of the ruling class would dominate the society.

A more interesting theoretical question is the manner in which the working and middle classes orient themselves toward social action. Mike Savage (2000, p. 101) argues, following Bourdieu, that class is relational in the sense that social groups differentiate themselves from others in various "fields," so that class culture is best conceived as a mode of differentiation rather than as a type of collectivity. Individual identity construction is the ongoing process of interpreting a variety of "assets," associated with class structure, class culture, gender, organizational position, and so forth. That is, social action is the consequence of a complex calculus of assets and opportunities derived from intersecting interpretive fields. To the degree that each of these fields are socially derived, then individual identity formation is structured (consistent with Giddens and others' notion of structuration); in this manner individual and relational (e.g., class) identity may be more closely connected than some theorists have proposed. In his empirical work, Savage finds a high level of consistency in the perception of class structure, the relative status ranking associated with various class positions, and the political and social implications that class position holds for the individual's life history. As noted by Savage, class serves as a benchmark by which to compare self with other and a field by which to locate self in social space. It is important to note that especially among the working and middle classes, class structure is oftentimes used less as means of invoking a sense of belonging than a dimension by which to differentiate themselves. In this regard, for the majority of respondents in Savage's study, identification with the middle class was perceived to mean that one was "ordinary, average, and in the middle"; one was neither exclusionary like the upper class nor part of the lower class. Independence, dignity, and responsibility are now coming to be associated with middle-class careers realized within an ever-changing work environment.

So What are Educators to Make of All This?

Marxist class theory, as do competing explanations such as the industrial society thesis, offer a creation story about social practices and social formation. Such stories are important and interesting, but to the extent that they are portrayed as the whole story or the foundational story, one must remain skeptical. One may question, for example, Marxist class theory but still retain an interest in class analysis. Within the class analysis project one is perhaps more inclined to turn to Weber rather than to Marx for inspiration. Class analysis need not consider class antagonism to be the engine of history, but rather considers class along with other dimensions (e.g., race gender, occupational and status groups, political power, and cultural capital) to be potentially determinate alone or to be in combination within any particular historical conjuncture. In this regard, the observations of two contemporary commentators on class are instructive. "Individuals are not *members* of a class; they *engage* in various class *actions*—individually and collectively, in everyday life and in relation to extraordinary events, and not just in relation to production and occupations. In these acts, individuals may have multiple, overlapping, sometimes contradictory, sometimes reinforcing interests based on their participation in multiple, heterogeneous markets" (Hall, 1997, p. 21, italics in original). And, from Savage (2000, p. 149), class analysis is a mode of cultural analysis. "The traditional strengths of class analysis lay precisely in interest in the cultural meaning of class."

Schooling is a complex enterprise, but at base, it represents an attempt to socialize, enculturate, train, and perhaps stratify the young and prepare them to take various positions in the society. In essence, schooling represents an agency of the state charged to reproduce (and occasionally transform) the extant social formation (Althusser, 1971; Bowles and Gintis, 1976; Carnoy and Levin, 1985). In order for educators to fulfill either a reproductive or transformational role, however, they must possess, (either implicitly or explicitly) an image of the social formation, that is, a set of beliefs which, following Therborn (1978), influence their perceptions about what is good, possible, and desirable at the general social level, and that they employ in determining the curriculum and practices to be used with the particular mix of students who happen to be in their charge. The primary question from a systemic perspective is the degree to which structures and practices are, or are intended, to serve primarily reproductive or transformative purposes. Nevertheless, it is also the case

that few educators tend to represent their work as reproductive or transformative. Rather, they most often express their intention as "making a
difference" in the lives of children; by which is meant to contribute to
children's personal and social development and to provide these children
with the social and intellectual skills that will allow them entry to higher
education or to the job market.

The question we pose here is, how might teachers employ the concept
of class in such a manner that they are better able to realize their own instructional interests to make a difference in the lives of children and simultaneously contribute to the social interest in contributing to the social
good by reducing forms of structured social inequality? We suggest that
since the primary social correlates with academic performance of children
are related to class, race, and gender, then one place to begin is for teachers to explicitly recognize these basis of influence. To propose a renewed
emphasis on the study of the social purposes and institutional structures
that influence schooling and educational outcomes, tells very little about
how this emphasis might be accomplished. Here we propose that one
promising way to proceed is to engage in an analysis of the economic, organizational, cultural, and social assets associated with various institutional fields (Savage, 2000). Such an analysis leads to identification of the
knowledge, competencies, symbols, and beliefs that any individual must
master prior to entry into various occupational and civic spaces. Moreover, the teacher is provided with a common metric from which to engage in an analysis of the particular asset sets that are privileged by state
departments of education, the district and school, and various local community groups and may engage in assessments of student mastery of valued assets. This is not a new form of analysis for teachers who have long
attempted to generate developmentally appropriate plans of study for
their students. It may, however, introduce a new focus of analyses; one
that more explicitly links classroom activities with broader social and institutional structures, functions, and processes. In one regard, the recent
emphasis on "policy alignment" that is driving the standards and accountability movement is precisely such a form of analysis. The prevailing policy alignment focus, however, is less oriented to attaining
outcomes of social equity and justice and more oriented toward reinforcing dominant forms of stratification based on possession of technical
knowledge and decontextualized skills, which serves to further privilege
property over person rights (Apple, 2001).

Having engaged in an analysis of various assets, the task then becomes a more familiar one of selecting instructional methods that allow
the students to begin to acquire additional relevant assets such as cultural, civic, and political-economic understandings. Since the assets approach imbeds knowledge, skills, and perspectives within the social

context, it would seem necessary to adopt instructional strategies that also are contextualized. One way to accomplish this is suggested by Margaret R. Somer's (1997) discussion of narrativity and Donald E. Polkinghorne's (1995) discussion of narrative analysis. Within this general approach the task is to examine examples of narratives in order to discover the underlying perspectives, frameworks, and interests that motivate the speaker. One typically finds that individuals employ various socially available interpretive frameworks during the process of determining what they may reasonably expect to accomplish, the manner in which they should act in various settings, and reciprocally to determine their own identity in social space. I am reminded here of a school principal talking about the low-income students in his school. I paraphrase only slightly. "These students understand the minimum wage job structure, but they can neither conceive nor have the language to talk about the high-wage job structure. Nothing in their experience prepares them to project a future different than what they have already experienced." We would propose that the instructional task in a democratic society is to explicitly convey to students the types of economic, organizational, cultural, and social assets required in various domains, and to develop among students the systemic and structural understanding to critically assess and project personal trajectories of access into these domains. Understanding class structure, class formation, and class action is not the only factor that must be considered, but it remains one important factor.

References

Archer, M. S. 1996. *Culture and agency: The place of culture in social theory*, 2nd ed. Cambridge: Cambridge University Press.

Althusser, L. 1971. *Lenin and philosophy and other essays*. Trans. B. Brewster. New York: Monthly Review Press.

Apple, M. W. 2001. *Educating the 'right' way: Markets, standards, God and inequality*. New York: RoutledgeFalmer.

Beaud, M. 1993. *Socialism in the crucible of history*. Trans. and intro. by T. Dickman. Atlantic Highlands, NJ: Humanities Press.

Berle, A. A. 1954. *The 20th century capitalist revolution*. New York: Harcourt.

Berle, A. A. and Means, G. C. 1933. *The modern corporation and private property*. New York: Macmillan.

Blau, P. M. and Duncan, O. D. 1967. *The American occupational* structure. New York: Wiley and Sons.

Bottomore, T. B. 1956. *Karl Marx: Selected writings in sociology and social philosophy*. New York: McGraw-Hill.

Bottomore, T. B. and Brym, R. J. 1989. *The capitalist class: An international study*. New York: New York University Press.

Bowles, S. and Gintis, H. 1976. *Schooling in capitalist America: Educational reforms and the contradictions of economic life*. New York: Basic.

Bourdieu, P. 1977a. *Outline of a theory of practice*. Cambridge: Cambridge University Press.

———. 1977b. Cultural reproduction and social reproduction. In J. Karabel and A. H. Halsey (Eds.) *Power and ideology in education*. New York: Oxford University Press, 487–511.

Burnham, J. 1972, 1941. *The managerial revolution: What is happening in the world*. Westport, CT: Greenwood Press.

Callahan, R. E. 1962. *Education and the cult of efficiency: A study of the social forces that have shaped the administration of the public schools*. Chicago: University of Chicago Press.

Carnoy, M. and Levin, H. M. 1985. *Schooling and work in the democratic state*. Stanford: Stanford University Press.

Cohen, P. S. 1968. *Modern social theory*. New York: Basic.

Crompton, R. 1998. *Class and stratification: An introduction to current debates*, 2nd ed. Malden, MA: Blackwell.

Crompton, R. and Gubbay, J. 1977. *Economy and class structure*. London: Macmillan Press.

Dahrendorf, R. September 1958. Out of utopia: Toward a reorientation of sociological analysis. *American Journal of Sociology*, 64, 127.

———. 1959. *Class and class conflict in industrial society*. Stanford: Stanford University Press.

Domhoff, G. W. 1967. *Who rules America?* Englewood Cliffs: Prentice-Hall.

Duncan, O. D., Featherman, D. L.; and Duncan, B. 1972. *Socioeconomic background and achievement*. New York: Seminar Press.

Eder, K. 1993. *The new politics of class: Social movements and cultural dynamics in advanced societies*. Thousand Oaks, CA: Sage.

Featherman, D. L., and Hauser, R. M. 1976. Prestige or socioeconomic scales in the study of occupational achievement. *Sociological Methods and Research* 4 (March): 403–23.

Giddens, A. 1971. *Capitalism and modern social theory; An analysis of the writings of Marx, Durkheim and Max Weber*. Cambridge, England: University Press.

———. 1973. *The class structure of the advanced societies*. London: Hutchinson.

———. 1984. *The constitution of society*. Berkeley: University of California Press.

———. 1987. *Sociology: A brief but critical introduction*, 2nd ed. San Diego: Harcourt.

Gorz, A. 1982. *Farewell to the working class: An essay on post-industrial socialism*. Trans. M. Sonenscher. London: Pluto Press.

Gramsci, A. 1971. *Selections from the prison notebooks*, Trans. Q. Hoare and G. N. Smith. New York: International Publishers.

Hall, J. R. 1997. Introduction: The reworking of class analysis. In J. R. Hall (Ed.) *Reworking class*. Ithaca: Cornell University Press.

Hauser, R. M. and Featherman, D. L. 1977. *The process of stratification: Trends and analyses*. New York: Academic Press.

Jacoby, H. 1973. *The bureaucratization of the world*. Trans. E. L. Kanes. Berkeley: University of California Press.

Jencks, C. 1979. *Who gets ahead?: The determinants of economic success in America*. New York: Basic.

Kolakowski, Leszek. 1978. *Main currents of Marxism: 3-the breakdown*. New York: Oxford University Press.

Lukacs, G. 1971. *History and class consciousness: Studies in Marxist dialectics*. Trans. R. Livingstone, London: Merlin.

Marx, K. and Engels, F. 1978, 1848. Manifesto of the communist party. In Robert C. Tucker (Ed.) *The Marx-Engels reader*. New York: W. W. Norton and Co., p. 473–74.

Mills, C. W. 1959. *The sociological imagination*. New York: Oxford University Press.

A Nation at Risk. 1983. A report to the nation and the secretary of education United States Department of Education by The National Commission on Excellence in Education. Washington, D.C: U.S. Government Printing Office.

Pahl, R. 1993. Does class analysis without class theory have a future? *Sociology*, 27, 253–58.

Pakulski, J. and Waters, M. 1996. *The death of class*. Thousand Oaks, CA: Sage.

Parsons, T. 1937. *The structure of social action: A study in social theory with special reference to a group of recent European writers*. New York: McGraw-Hill.

———. 1951. *The social system*. Glencoe, IL: Free Press.

Polkinghorne, D. E. 1995. Narrative configuration in qualitative analysis. *International Journal of Qualitative Studies in Education*, 8(1), 5–23.

Poulantzas, N. 1973. *Political power and social classes*. London: New Left Books.

Resch, R. P. 1992. *Althusser and the renewal of Marxist social theory*. Berkeley: University of California Press.

Robertson, S. L. 2000. *A class act: Changing teachers' work, the state, and globalization*. New York: Falmer Press.

Rossides, D. W. 1997. *Social stratification: The interplay of class, race and gender*, 2nd ed. Upper Saddle River, NJ: Prentice Hall.

Rupp, J. C. C. 1997. Rethinking cultural and economic capital. In John R. Hall (Ed.) *Reworking class*. Ithaca: Cornell University Press.

Savage, M. 2000. *Class analysis and social transformation*. Philadelphia: Open University Press.

Sewell, W. H., Hauser, R. M., and Featherman, D. L. 1976. *Schooling and achievement in American society*. New York: Academic Press.

Somers, M. R.. 1997. Deconstructing and reconstructing class formation theory: Narrativity, relational analysis and social theory. In J. R. Hall (Ed.) *Reworking class*. Ithaca: Cornell University Press.

Therborn, G. 1978. *What does the ruling class do when it rules?* London: New Left Books.

Thompson, E. P. 1978. *The peculiarities of the English*. In *The poverty of theory and other essays*. London: Merlin.

Tozer, S. E, Violas, P. C. and Senese, G. 2002), *School and society: Historical and contemporary perspectives*, 3rd ed. Boston: McGraw Hill.

Trachtenberg, A. 1982. *The incorporation of America: Culture and society in the Gilded Age.* NT: Hill and Wang.

Turner, J. H. 1974. *The structure of sociological theory.* Homewood, IL: Dorsey Press.

Weber, Max. 1930. *The Protestant ethic and the spirit of capitalism.* Trans. T. Parsons. London: Allen and Unwin.

————. 1946. *From Max Weber: Essays in sociology.* Trans. and intro. by H. H. Gerth and C. W. Mills. New York: Oxford University Press.

————. 1978. *Economy and Society.* In G. Roth and C. Wittich (Eds.) Berkeley: University of California Press.

Zeitlin, M. 1980. *Classes, class conflict, and the state.* Cambridge, MA: Winthrop Publishers.

PART 2

CLASS WORK

To participate in the social world, people must engage in class work—in everyday life. Class work is both the embodiment of a class position and work to maintain and change class position. Deborah Hicks and Stephanie Jones reveal how young girls live in an urban neighborhood and school. These girls struggle to find a safe place. Being "good" is linked to class mobility if only in the rhetoric of the school. Being "bad" reaffirms one's working-class origins. Jill Koyama and Margaret A. Gibson reveal the class work when race and class overlay. The middle-class students are white and the working-class students are of Mexican origin. The marginalization of the latter group is in some sense the work of the middle-class school. The Mexican-descent students resist the white construction of them as "other" even as they work to construct their own identities in such a way that allows the possibility of school success and possibly class mobility. Luis Urrietta Jr. pushes the examination of class work by Latinos in his study of Chicana/o social mobility and the role of education in such. The class work he analyzes reveals how subordination creates internal divisions within the Chicana/o community and a form of class stratification he terms a *third class system*. This system is marked by a plural hybridity, permeability, and improvisation.

Richard Beach, Daryl Parks, Amanda Thein, and Timothy Lensmire reveal that school culture works to perpetuate white privilege, and show how a dynamic young teacher uses critical literacy to try to penetrate this culture for working-class youths of many races. He challenged many discourses including that of individualism by having students examine how institutional forces shaped both discourse and social practices. Encouraging alternative and conflicting value stances while discussing literature became a means to challenge existing dominant discourses. Class work can lead to the realization of how discourses construct social class, race and gender, and to imagined alternatives.

Cheryl Fields-Smith interrogates class differences in African-American families negotiation with schools, and how some of these families came to mimic white patterns of parental involvement in order to get the school to work for their children. She notes that current conceptualizations of parent involvement do not capture the class work of working-class Black parents but that the middle-class Black parents had similar social capital to draw on as whites and thus better fit the largely white, middle-class model of parent involvement that schools use to define who is supporting them and not. Yet the middle-class African American parents did more than support the school on the school's terms. Rather, they extended the curriculum to include content about African Americans and engaged in a form of advocacy for their raced children.

The class work of the middle class in home-school relations is further examined by Janice Kroeger. She uses the idea of heteroglossia to interpret how middle-class parents both constitute their own advantage even while they open up venues that may allow another language to be spoken at times. She emphasizes the responsibility of the school and educators to question the activities of the middle class to reproduce their class advantage and to actively use the various languages in the school to get beyond class as a reproductive force.

3

LIVING CLASS AS A GIRL

Deborah Hicks and Stephanie Jones

Listen to the voice of a girl growing up in a small, working-poor community in a Midwestern city. Brandie, at the time in the fifth grade, has composed a poem modeled after George Ella Lyon's (1999) collection, *Where I'm From*. Brandie's poetic rendition captures some of the language, experiences, and feelings that are shaping her life as a young girl.

> I am from a ghetto neighborhood where people fight in the streets.
> I am from the other end of Garner where people are always arguing in the streets.
>
> I am from the past who died.
> I am from my Grandpa who died in World War Two.
> Underneath my bed is a box full of pictures falling out like old memories just coming back to me.
> It's like the past who died and they came back to say hi.
>
> I am from my Grandpa with gray hair, strong coffee and World War Two.
> He is kind, he has loving collections of knifes and he was never mean.
>
> I am from the park where I play in, to the slide I slide down.
> I am from the God who made me.
> I am from Jesus who died on the cross for me.
>
> I am from the eagles flying the sky.
> I am from the swings that go high into the sky.

I am from the deep blue sea where the whales swim.
I am from the pool where I swim.

I am from the red white and blue which are the colors of my country.
I am from the heroes who saved our country and sometimes even
  died.

I am from the pictures I take and the pictures I draw.

I am from the *Tears of a Tiger* because it is sad.
I am from the books I read because it is something to do.

I am from the know-it-all because my brother thinks he knows it all.
I am from the pass-it-on because my brother tells my secrets to his
  friends.
I am from the attitude because my sister always has an attitude.

I am from my Mom who had me.
I am from my Grandmother who took care of me.

Brandie's poem conveys in literary terms the ways in which the social, cultural, and religious aspects of life in her "ghetto neighborhood"
become refracted dimensions of voice and psychology. Lower Bond Hill,
the urban community in which Brandie is growing up, is a close-knit
neighborhood in which *family* is at the core of one's identity and values.
Brandie captures this through her frequent references to family members,
all of whom share the tight physical spaces of a run-down wood frame
house. Brandie is being raised by her grandmother, a matriarchal figure
who has struggled to hold things together for a family living in extreme
poverty. In hard times and in better times, a belief in God and Jesus, provides a source of strength and spiritual comfort. Books also make their
appearance in Brandie's poem. The novel *Tears of a Tiger*, like Brandie's
real life, takes place within a landscape of urban poverty. The distinctive
slice of working-poor America that Brandie depicts in her poem, however, is one that the critical educator bell hooks (2000) once called the
hidden face of poverty—poverty as lived by working-poor white folk.
Though diverse in the ways in which all urban neighborhoods are culturally, racially, and linguistically hybrid in contemporary times, Lower
Bond Hill has, since the postwar years, maintained a distinctive identity
as a historically Appalachian enclave within a Midwestern city.
    During the Johnson administration's War on Poverty, there emerged
attempts among educators and psychologists to understand the particular
landscapes of poverty shaping the lives of youths across America. The face

of white poverty, as seen in Appalachia, among sharecroppers and migrant workers, and in cities was captured in the work of writers such as Robert Coles (1967). This concern about the distinctive ways in which particular landscapes of poverty are formative of thought, feeling, imagination, and identity is our focus as well. We reach back to an era during which white poverty was a concern of policymakers, psychologists, and educators, and yet bring this focus into a contemporary context focused around the lives of working-poor girls. As researchers, we draw on ethnography as a tool for developing a deeper understanding of life and learning among girls growing up in poverty. As literacy educators with activist agendas—we want to help girls shape strong and viable futures for themselves in Lower Bond Hill and in the middle-class worlds around it—we draw on the writings of educators who have made similar commitments. We develop the argument that critical educational efforts have to be *answerable*, in the sense used by Mikhail M. Bakhtin (1990) to the ways in which voice and psychosocial history emerge in particular landscapes of poverty.

In her essay, "A Question of Class," the novelist Dorothy Allison (1994) writes about how she became aware of the fact that for middle-class people, she and her family were "they" or "those people." Growing up female, poor, and white became a complex web through which thought, feeling, and identity became refracted. "The central fact of my life, " Allison writes, "is that I was born in 1949 in Greenville, South Carolina, the bastard daughter of a white woman from a desperately poor family, a girl who had left the seventh grade the year before, worked as a waitress, and was just a month past fifteen when she had me. That fact, the inescapable impact of being born in a condition of poverty that this society finds shameful, contemptible, and somehow deserved, has had dominion over me to such an extent that I have spent my life trying to overcome or deny it" (p. 15).

In our efforts to understand the experiences of girls growing up in Lower Bond Hill, we wondered how young girls negotiated such tensions as those articulated by Allison. Our stories and analyses concentrate on the lives of four girls, two in the second grade and two in the fifth grade, whom we have known as teachers and ethnographers. Like scholars, fiction writers, and critical educators whose work has informed our own— hooks, Allison, Myles Horton, Paulo Freire, and Bakhtin—we have attempted to maintain a focus on the concreteness of a particular landscape and history, and on the speaking voices of girls growing up in that landscape. This kind of vision, informed as much by literature as social science, offers the best hope for pedagogical activism that is, indeed, *answerable* to the lives, hopes, and dreams of girls who are at risk of becoming "they."

Everyday Life and Work
in Lower Bond Hill

James Fallows (2000) has argued that poverty in contemporary America
has become increasingly invisible, as the middle-class workforce has
moved out of older industrial workplaces and into more secluded professional locales associated with the new work order. Though Michael Harrington (1962/1993) once wrote of a similar kind of invisibility in his
book *The Other America*, communities such as Lower Bond Hill have
unquestionably become more isolated as the economy has moved away
from an older manufacturing base. In the postwar economy, this was a
stable blue-collar community. Warehouses and factories offered employment for locals and an incentive for their rural kin to head north from
eastern Kentucky and Tennessee, or west from West Virginia and Virginia. Middle-class professionals from the city worked alongside local
community residents. These once thriving local businesses are now
largely deserted factories and warehouses—ghostly vestiges of times
when locals who were laid off could walk down the street and find another job within a day. In the changing social landscape of the new global
economy, middle-class professionals have little or no contact with this
isolated community. In a complementary way, many residents of Lower
Bond Hill spend their entire lives in the neighborhood, leaving mostly to
work first, second, or third shifts in the service industry and factory jobs
that are available beyond Lower Bond Hill's borders.

Its geography contributes to the isolation of Lower Bond Hill relative
to the city whose affluent business center lies just minutes away. Driving
into the community, one is struck by its resemblance to what those living
in rural Appalachian areas would call a *holler*. Behind the neighborhood's center, basically a crossroads in which the essentials of a bank,
health center, and popular coffee shop can be found, rises a steep hill that
adds to a sense of landscape familiar to original rural migrants. Its
boundaries are marked on one side by a busy road that shadows the trajectory of a local river, and on the other side by an industrial area that extends under a viaduct. The only road without such distinctive geographic
boundaries has also become emblematic of the changing demographics of
Lower Bond Hill. Sandwiched in between apartment buildings occupied
largely by white residents is a stretch of apartment dwellings and a small
grocery store where Latinos live and work. These new immigrants are
named by local residents as "Mexicans," though their small subcommu-
nity actually reflects a sometimes uneasy alliance of Mexicans and Gua-
temalans. Also strewn along Garner Street, depicted by Brandie in her
poem, are clusters of black families. As this road winds its way further
out of Lower Bond Hill, the predominate whiteness of the community

begins to shift toward the racial identities more frequently associated with urban poverty in the minds of many middle-class whites.

At the center of the neighborhood lie groupings of small brick apartment buildings, tightly clustered along side streets typically two or three city blocks in length. Out on the streets, locals congregate to share news; children play with friends, cousins, and siblings or half-siblings; folks stop in the local coffee shop for a bite to eat and a smoke; a young Latino couple waits at the bus stop without being acknowledged by community residents walking by.

Like working-poor communities across America, Lower Bond Hill has faced its share of challenges. Industrial pollution has, since the postwar years, been the Achilles' heel of a community in which factory work was for years the primary source of income for men. A toxic waste storage facility was once a source of air pollution that led to a government crackdown. The facility still operates, though it is now bound by stricter regulations about how toxic waste is stored only blocks from where children spend their growing years. Because the community sits in a valley, on humid days the air can become heavy with the sickly sweet smell of chemical pollutants stored in barrels or emitted into the air from the smokestacks of the few working factories. Combine this with the smells from the city's main sewage treatment plant, located only blocks from the neighborhood elementary school, and it becomes a challenge to be inside an apartment building or inside a classroom with no air-conditioning.

Over the past five years, the neighborhood has been riddled with a new kind of challenge—a pernicious street drug called OxyContin. Paul Tough (2001) has referred to OxyContin as the Trojan horse of street drugs. A prescription painkiller with an opiate base, OxyContin doesn't appear at first that different from other prescription drugs that have long been used to achieve a mild recreational high. OxyContin, however, packs a dangerously addictive punch. When crushed (thus changing the time-release chemistry of the painkillers) and either snorted or mixed with water and injected, it produces a warm, long-lasting high that can become addictive within weeks. As Tough writes, OxyContin "might look like a casual Saturday-night drug, but it it's a take-over-your-life drug" (p. 63). OxyContin made its way through rural America, starting in Appalachian communities and in rural Maine and moving into cities.

As this prescription drug's diversion became known in the medical community a crackdown on legal prescriptions ensued, driving street prices upward. Some residents who first developed an opiate addiction through OxyContin have since turned to heroin—a cheaper street drug, but also one connected with needle use. With the introduction of these new and challenging social realities have come other ones. This small community loses about one person each month to drug overdose. There has been an increase of HIV and hepatitis C infections in a community where street drug-related needle use was once relatively rare, and an increase in prostitution as one way that women (and some men) can support a drug habit that can cost up to—and beyond—a hundred dollars per day.

Schooling in Lower Bond Hill

Nestled amid residential side streets in the heart of Lower Bond Hill is a 1930s school building. Once an elementary (pre-K–6) school, Linden Elementary School has recently added junior high grades at the bequest of its urban school district. Parents and kin of children at the school can be seen outside the school doors morning and afternoon, dropping off children or waiting to pick them up. Otherwise, the school has been shaped by a class ideology that aims, to appropriate Beverly Skegg's (1997) phrasing, to help students "become respectable." Teachers drive in largely from suburbs, their SUVs and Toyotas parked safely close to the school building. Due to district-wide budget cuts, most instructional assistant positions, many of which were occupied by local community members, have been cut. As a result, the faces of adult community members present in the building are largely those of parents going into the school's main office for a special occasion or meeting, often an unpleasant one, and the community women employed as lunchroom servers. Children going to school in Lower Bond Hill walk into a different social order when they enter the building that has provided an education for their parents, aunts and uncles, and sometimes even grandparents. The in-your-face working-class language that goes with having an *attitude* is unwelcome. As one teacher at Linden School described things, "They [the students and families] don't share our values."

Lower Bond Hill has struggled with an exceptionally high dropout rate among its young people, rates that can reach 70 percent. For some, dropout has become a way of life, and generations have depended on the help of government assistance or through the unregulated economy. Coupled with these high rates of dropout are low rates of academic "achievement" as measured by proficiency tests that have become important for students in the second grade or higher. Linden School, as with schools across the nation, is now being held accountable for the test performances of its students. Accountability measures are always tied to the high-stakes tests given in early March of the school year. If Linden School fails to meet its mandated test score targets over the coming years, it faces the possibility of redesign, where faculty and professional staff clear the building and a new administration and faculty are put into place by the district.

The school's response to these challenges has been a tightening of the curriculum and a rigorous disciplinary order. Two security guards parade the hallways of the school, their walkie-talkies always ready for a needed communication with the school's administrative staff. Each year, there is a push to achieve test scores that meet the targets set for specific grade levels. In January and February of the previous school year, for instance, the school's leadership implemented a "proficiency boot camp." Teachers were urged to wear army gear (e.g., fatigues) and lunchroom servers were given bandannas with army fatigue patterns. Children in the second grade and beyond spent much of the two months rehearsing skills and strategies for the high-stakes tests. Military images were posted around the school building and military music was broadcast over the loudspeaker at the end of each school day.

Though teachers grumble about the proficiency tests and about the heightened meaning they have assumed in recent years, an outright challenge to this system has become virtually unthinkable. In the ways described by Michel Foucault (1978) the system of accountability and regimes of testing have become a *technology*—supported by discourses centered on academic standards (specific skills and strategies listed out by content area and grade level), the proficiency tests that avowedly measure children's progress toward reaching standards, and test score mandates. In the idiom of new literacy research (see Collins, 2000; New London Group, 1996), educators write about multiple literacies required for participation in a new work order, and about the value of hybrid language practices. In working-poor communities such as Lower Bond Hill, however, the language of schooling in the twenty-first century has moved in the opposite direction—toward what Bakhtin (1981) termed *authoritarian discourses*. A monologic discourse of achievement and standards has become the *only* means through which success can be measured.

As a result of these varied factors, everyday pedagogical practices at Linden School are not in a deep or defining way connected with students' lives in Lower Bond Hill. Teachers, who are under increasing surveillance (see Miller, 1996), feel squeezed by increasing expectations and declining resources. The creative energy among teachers that Shirley Brice Heath (1983) documented in the years of desegregation in the 1970s has given way, at least in this neighborhood, to a gritty determination to help students achieve higher test scores. Students, parents, and teachers alike seem to hold their breath until the test results are announced in late May. The hope of responsive or activist pedagogy, described at length in the writings of educators such as hooks, Myles Horton, and Paulo Freire, seems a forgotten dream— a barely audible whisper amid a militaristic call to arms, and instantiated in systems of control that effect teachers and students alike.

Ethnography and Activist Teaching

Flannery O'Connor (1961) once wrote that an identity lies beneath what is immediately visible, particularly what is visible to an outsider. "[An identity] is not made from the mean average or the typical," she wrote, "but from the hidden and often the most extreme" (p. 58). O'Connor argued for the strengths of the regional writer—one immersed in the concrete language and values of a particular social landscape. "The isolated imagination is easily corrupted by theory but the writer inside his community seldom has such a problem" (p. 54).

In the community in which we sought to become ethnographers and teachers, the very things that contribute to the strength and resiliency of children and adults—the close bonds of family and kin for instance—made the kind of depth described by O'Connor more precarious to achieve. Both of us grew up in working-class family and community settings, and one of us (Stephanie Jones) grew up in a neighborhood not unlike Lower Bond Hill. However, as we sought to develop research understandings about the lives and identities of young girls in the neighborhood and to construct an activist pedagogical agenda *with* girls and in response *to* them, our well-meaning intentions as educators and ethnographers bumped up against a core neighborhood value: What happens here ain't nobody's business. It has taken years to be able to hear the nuanced meanings in girls' language, and to develop sufficient trust among community members who have already been "researched" and often portrayed negatively. For one of us (Hicks), this effort has been a three-year history of educational research and activism with the same girls and their caretakers; for the other (Jones), the process has stretched out over a two-year history with younger girls and their caretakers.

The vision that has shaped our pedagogical efforts is one that would bring class into wider research and policy discussions about how educators might address the needs of culturally diverse youths. A growing body of educational research that examines "how people live culturally" (Lee et al., 2003) has shown that differences in language, race, and culture, formerly connected to discourses of deficit and disadvantage, are in fact powerful tools for teaching responsibly, critically, and effectively. Anne Haas Dyson (1993) has used the term *permeable* to describe pedagogies that make space for diverse identities and languages. As Kris Gutierrez (see Gutierrez, Baquedano-Lopez, and Tejeda, 1999) has argued, these create a "third space" where the languages and systems of knowledge of students and teachers can enter into teaching dialogues that are richer and more effective because of their hybridity. Seldom have these research literatures, however, considered the distinctive differences lived by poor and working-class white students (for a notable exception, see Heath, 1983). We wanted to address that void by creating and researching pedagogical practices that would allow working-poor girls to engage in more productive *kinds* of hybrid language and subjectivity. This kind of engagement, we reasoned, might allow girls something we knew to be missing in their lives: a deep attachment to school and academic practices. Our perspective on creating a critical literacy pedagogy with girls thus builds on a tradition of cultural research and on traditions of educational activism that are sometimes known as critical pedagogy. This vision has been shaped by these varied literatures, and by our own histories. Our voices and identities have been shaped in contradictory landscapes of class, and we have drawn on our experiences to help us understand the tensions and contradictions faced by young girls.

Our effort to create this kind of teaching and research agenda is feminist in its focus and its intent. The work draws on a tradition of feminist ethnography in which the focus is on the lives of girls and/or women, and in which there is an effort, in the words of Angela McRobbie (1991/2000, p. 135), to "make talk walk." Much like McRobbie and other feminist researchers studying gender, class, and pedagogical relations, we draw on multiple disciplines—education, psychology, cultural studies, anthropology, and literary studies—in an effort to understand identity. Our efforts draw on the work of British feminists such as Angela McRobbie, Diane Reay, Beverly Skeggs, Carolyn Steedman, and Valerie Walkerdine[2]—all of whom have grounded their inquiries in the materiality of how relations of class are *lived* by girls and women. Walkerdine's work in the field of critical psychology provides an important bridge to our project. In a recent book, Walkerdine, Lucey, and Melody (2001) depict the perspective on psychology that drives their efforts to understand what it means to "grow up as a girl" in contemporary Britain: "It is the situated and specifically local character of how people live and transform their lives that is important. The new cultural geography has attempted to get to grips with some of the local specificity of space and place. It is the deep embeddedness of the production of subjectivity in the social and cultural that we are exploring here. The social, cultural, and psychological are so strongly entwined with each other that a disciplinary teasing apart does violence to the actual mechanisms" (p. 15).

This statement about inquiry that is focused on the "production of subjectivity in the social and cultural" provides an important starting point for our own study of girlhood lives. However, we approach this kind of inquiry from a different angle—that of educators, and in particular literacy educators, interested in how girls growing up in working-poor America engage with the languages and ideologies of school. From this perspective, our lenses shift to a focus both on psychology—how thought, feeling, imagination, fear, and desire are shaped within this specific social and material landscape—and literacy—how girls read cultural texts (e.g., literature, film, photography, television, and classroom talk) and how we in turn (as teachers and researchers) read girls' language and respond to them. *Reading,* in this sense, is both a metaphor for how girls engage in language practices that are always filtered through class relations and identities, and a method for conducting ethnography that supports activist teaching.

This kind of responsive, activist pedagogy has become increasingly difficult to create in regular language arts classrooms. As the two of us confronted the demands faced by language arts teachers at Linden School to bolster students' achievements on certain kinds of language tasks, we decided to conduct our work within an after-school environment. The school's administration has generously supported our work, as the school has been anxious to provide meaningful after-school programs for students whose regular school day ends at 1:45 p.m. The two of us have created after-school reading programs for girls in two grade levels. Eight to ten fifth-grade girls met weekly with Hicks across their fourth- and fifth-grade years, and seven second-grade girls worked with Jones first in her capacity as a classroom language arts teacher (for eleven weeks) and then in a weekly after-school program. These teaching practices have been supported by ethnographies focused on girls' community lives. We have interviewed girls and their primary female caretakers, attended community meetings, interviewed community organizers, spent time in the community spaces that have been opened to us, and sometimes taken girls to other kinds of spaces—museums, theaters, libraries, and shopping malls in more affluent city landscapes.

You will meet four girls from Lower Bond Hill in the stories and analyses that follow: Cadence and Heather (second graders) and Alison and Mariah (fifth graders). Their struggles to negotiate the complexities and contradictions of class differences become visible, as does their tenacity in rising to those challenges. These are smart girls, loving girls, and sometimes badass girls. These are girls whose voices, identities, and futures are being shaped in the complicated social landscapes of Lower Bond Hill and Linden School.

Attitude Girls

At first glance, Cadence and Heather seem to be a study of contrasts. Heather, with light freckled skin, long blond hair, and bright blue eyes, comes to school well-groomed and often wears stylish studded jeans and an "Angel" T-shirt. Olive-complected, brunette, tangled-haired Cadence has deep green eyes and often wears clothing that is either too small or too large. Heather is the "good girl" in school—Cadence is the "bad girl." Heather is often praised in class for her good behavior; Cadence is punished several times a day with her name on the board, check marks by her name, lost recess, or even detention.

An after-school girls' group opened up an alternative pedagogical space where the multiple voices of girls growing up and living in material conditions afforded by poverty were not only welcomed, but utilized in specific ways so that the girls could begin to actively construct hybrid identities, attaching themselves to school in meaningful ways while holding tight to their community, class-specific identities.

The following transcript is from the second-grade after-school girls' group that Stephanie led. We were discussing the main character of the Junie B. Jones books (Park, 1992). The girls read some of the books in the series and had begun talking about what *kind of girl* Junie B.'s character is:

SUSANNE: She has an attitude.

CADENCE: A BIG attitude.

STEPHANIE: What does it mean to have an attitude?

CALLIE: You're not listening to your teacher and you ain't following the rules and you need more time to become better and go to college and get out and do whatever you want.

STEPHANIE: So has anyone in your life told you that you had an attitude?

CALLIE: Yeah, my mom did.

HEATHER: Yeah—Heather Ann Pike! You quit that now! (Heather yells in a tone of voice that sounds parent-like.)

STEPHANIE: I remember when I was a little girl when my stepdad would yell at me he would say, "Stephanie Renee, wipe that attitude right off your face!" and I would know I was being mean—sometimes I was mean to him.

HEATHER: When I cuss my mom sticks soap in my mouth.

STEPHANIE: Has that happened before?

HEATHER: Once.

STEPHANIE: So let's think about Junie B. Jones. What kind of girl is Junie B. Jones?

HEATHER: She's nice and mean.

ABBEY: She's only MEAN. She's an *attitude girl*!

STEPHANIE: Do you like Junie B.?

> (All of the girls shake their heads "no" except for
> Cadence—who says yes.)

STEPHANIE: Cadence, you said yes—what do you like about Junie B.?

CADENCE: I like the way she have an attitude because I have an attitude like that too.

STEPHANIE: Oh, so you can understand [her]?

HEATHER: It's a connection.

At this point a couple of the girls began to quietly voice some positive perceptions of Junie B. Callie, a quiet, often withdrawn girl in the group said, "I like her because *sometimes she says yes* in a nice way—like when she said yes to her mother about riding the bus—*but inside she said no*."

Every girl in the group identifies with having an "attitude" at one time or another. Some of the girls, however, have learned to voice, or perform, a different identity while they're within the walls of school or under a particular adult's supervision. When faced with the character of Junie B. as "an attitude girl" and asked whether or not they liked her, only one student said yes—Cadence. Junie B. is a girl with an "attitude," much like all the girls in the group—but she and Cadence have something in common that some of the others don't quite share. They are both just beginning to tinker with the idea of saying or acting in a way that differs from what they feel on the *inside*. Many of the other girls, Heather in particular, have already bought into the notion that they must be somebody else when they enter the school building. This somebody else is often characterized as a girl who listens quietly, follows directions without question, and follows the established (though sometimes unspoken) expectations of school, including presenting a sweet, docile, feminine identity. Though the other girls insisted that they didn't like the main character, it was clear that they enjoyed the stories, as they had each read book after book in the series. The identity of the "attitude girl" may be one that the girls believed I would not value as a teacher; therefore, even if they secretly admired Junie B. for being *herself* inside and outside school, the girls did not readily admit to liking the character.

This phenomenon of internalizing the expectations of a dominant "other" is described in the works of Freire (1970). Through this internalization, the girls have created an automated filtering of their community language. The filter, which serves as a "personal automated surveillance" technology was documented by Tammy Schwartz in her work with adolescent girls from Lower Bond Hill (2002, p. 105). The activist pedagogy engaged with here aimed at reducing the personal surveillance and using the home discourses as positive resources for young readers and writers.

Cadence, in her typical form of *not* silencing her community voice, spoke her mind and connected herself personally to the character with an attitude. People (like her stepfather) have told Cadence that she has an attitude, and she has begun to take on this identity as one of which she is proud. "I *like* the way she have an attitude, because I have an attitude like that too." This attitude is demonstrated in a myriad of ways throughout the school day and at home. Exaggerated sighs, rolling eyes, wobbling her head back and forth with her eyes looking to the ceiling, and turning her back to the authority figure are all ways in which Cadence exhibits her attitude, power, and agency.

Cadence also uses a tone of voice, body language, oral language, and social conversational style similar to many of the adults in Lower Bond Hill. These characteristics, however, are punished in school—even when the student is clever, intelligent, and academically motivated. Teachers and even the principal can be heard reprimanding Cadence in the hallway, in the auditorium, and in the cafeteria. They think she has a "bad attitude." This is the same attitude that students witness their parents using to gain power in school. Students love to tell stories of a parent "going off" on a teacher or the principal—stories that end with the child being told to "do whatever you want" by the parent. This power, of course, is temporary and often retaliated against in coercive ways within the school system, an aspect of power relations the students don't yet understand. What they do understand is "having an attitude"—and Cadence makes a critical connection with a book character who she perceives is a girl like herself.

Heather, on the other hand, seems to be in a continuous mode of suppressing her community voice and experiences as she negotiates school and classroom expectations. There were times during the after-school group, however, when Heather performed an identity that she would never let surface in school—or even around her parents or other community adults.

A girl in the group shared a story about being punished because she was *messin'* with her brothers who had been *messin'* with her first. The girl was prohibited from going outside to play, but her older brothers didn't receive any restrictions on their privileges. The topic turned to one of 'fairness' and how their friend had been cheated. Heather, however, had something else on her mind.

"Did you punch 'em in the face?" Heather asked as all the other girls giggled.

The girl in question responded, "I popped 'em and I kicked 'em and I. . . ."

"I know *where* she kicked 'em at!" Heather added with a squeal.

Later in the conversation I asked the girls, "Have you ever kicked a boy there?" Heather and Cadence responded almost in unison, "Yeah!" and as our talk continued, girls began to share the *words* they use for the private area of a boy.

Cadence offered, "The noodle thing," and everyone laughed.

Heather added, "The hotdog," and more laughter followed.

A third girl reported that her brother called it a "penis" and I explained to the hysterical group that the *real* word, the biological term used, is penis. I was quickly put in my place, however, as Cadence informed *me* of what the *real* word is.

"Un-uh! That's not the *real* word though," Cadence said.

"What's the *real* word?" I asked.

"It starts with a . . ."

D! finished Heather.

In case I didn't know what D meant, one of the girls spelled it out for me, "D-I-C-K." This led into an extensive conversation about the alleged boys who curse all the time in school and the boys who simply identified curse words using the first letter as a representation of the entire word or phrase. "You named a lot of the boys who were using these words. Are there girls who use these words?" I asked the group. "I do," volunteered Heather, "I do when I just lose my temper."

Heather continued to tell us that she uses the B word and she calls people "Fat F-ers." When asked how she learned these words Heather replied simply, "My parents." However, then she replayed a story she has almost certainly heard at home about God and Satan. "I think Satan made the bad words." She also made it clear to us her decision about when and where to cuss. "I don't cuss *around* my parents." Heather also doesn't cuss around teachers, administrators, or around any other adults in the neighborhood. She is quite successful at suppressing this part of her language experience that is closely connected to her home and community—any teacher who knows Heather would be shocked to read these comments. Slightly below the surface of Heather's "good girl" identity lies an identity that she works hard to silence in school—the one that kicks boys in the hotdog, fights, and uses strong language that reflects a working-poor discourse.

Cadence's Attitude as the Source of a Powerful Voice

Following several weeks of reading Vera B. Williams's collection of poems in *Amber Was Brave, Essie Was Smart* (2001), I asked the girls in our after-school group to think of a word that described themselves.

When it was Cadence's turn, my instincts as a protective teacher took over, and instead of *hearing* what Cadence told the group, I insisted that she think of something "*good*":

> "Cadence is. . . ." I said to the group and paused, waiting for Cadence to complete the sentence.
>
> ". . . A *brat*," Cadence responded.
>
> Heather joined, "Cadence is uh . . . bothering."
>
> I looked at Cadence and wanted her to think of a positive characteristic to describe herself so that I didn't even hear what she was trying to tell me about her identity, "Something good inside you Cadence."
>
> Heather offered, "Cadence is nice."
>
> Cadence yelled, "No, I don't *wanna* write!"
>
> Cadence *did* decide to write, however, and the writing in her writer's notebook from that day follows:

> > Cadence is a football that gets thrown in the air.
> >
> > Cadence is a sock hung up in the air on a wire saying, "Help me!"
> >
> > I do not do my work.

The following week I carefully approached the topic with Cadence after we conferenced around a piece she had written about her family gathering at Thanksgiving. "Cadence, I want to work on another piece with you. I thought you might want to work on a poem called 'Brat.' I thought it would be sort of like a Vera B. Williams poem." I knew Cadence made a connection with these writings. Cadence walked away. I continued, "I don't think you're a brat, but you said some people do."

Cadence turned and looked at me, "You write. I like how you write."

"You tell me what to write." I got my pen poised.

"BRAT. . . . People—say—I'm—a—brat. But—I—really—am—not. Am—not—a—brat," Cadence spoke slowly and carefully, pronouncing one word at a time as she watched my hand scoot across the page. Finally Cadence was satisfied with the poem. It is one that mediates her voice and agency as she "talks back" to the people who tell her she is a brat. Cadence's finished piece is a powerful statement about taking control over her identity.

Brat!
People say I'm a
        BRAT.
But I really am
        NOT
        A BRAT!
Okay?
So, De'Andrew,

> Pokey,
> Brandon,
>   Tommy,
> Leave me alone!
> I am a sweet,
>   Smart,
>   Very smart
> Girl.

The Girls and Their Mothers

In early spring I sat with Cadence's mother, Lori, at Cadence's grandfather's kitchen table. His compact two-bedroom apartment is now home to Cadence, her two sisters, and her mother. Their belongings are piled high in the living room floor in reused cardboard boxes and in black garbage bags, and I glance at them as Lori tells me about getting evicted from their apartment a couple blocks away. ". . . I kept telling them 'we're gonna get kicked out if you keep making all that noise'." I see the stress on Lori's face. She's not smiling the way she usually does and there is a definite tension under her eyes that I've never seen before. Our conversation moves to Cadence. "How would you describe Cadence?" I ask Lori. "She's a headache. Opinionated. Hardheaded. Hard to keep her focus. Hard time listening. Kinda like how *I* was growing up." "How *is* she like you?" I probe. "Her smartness," Lori tells me. "I'm a big reader."

Lori was offered a scholarship to attend college, but aware that she didn't have the resources to pay for housing, food, books, or transportation, Lori declined the scholarship. Now, as a single thirty-one-year-old mother of three girls, Lori has a burning desire to attend nursing school but tells me simply, "I just hate to jump in and have to stop because of the hardships." The hardships, for Cadence's mother, include getting the money to feed, house, and clothe her children during the forty-eight-week long training period that would be required if she wanted to study nursing. With the girls' father in jail on drug charges, Lori's father unemployed and suffering from depression and emphysema, a mother who is struggling to make ends meet on her own, and a sister who depends on a man to "take care of her," Lori has more to worry about than caring for three daughters. Taking a year off work and trying to get by using federal and state assistance could be devastating. "What do you hope for Cadence?" I ask Lori. "I hope that she's better than me. That things won't be so hard for her, and that she won't have to work at a job she hates." Lori pauses and looks hard at me. "I hope she has everything settled before she has kids."

When I ask her how the school can help to make these hopes come to fruition, Lori responds, "Patience. A teacher has to have patience.

I'm dealing with a very bright, gifted child, but you have to have the patience to see what she can do—it might be easy to overlook because she's hyperactive. . . ."

I hope Cadence's teachers will have patience, too and that Cadence's life isn't as hard as her mother's has been, but I can't imagine her being any "better" than her mother. Lori, like millions of other mothers in the United States, is smart, resourceful, insightful, articulate, loving, caring, and devoted to her family. But Lori, like millions of other mothers, has been stifled at the hand of poverty.

After I leave, Lori puts her hair in a bun, pulls on her white work pants and comfortable shoes, puts a book and lunch in her backpack, kisses her girls, and heads out the door to walk up the steep hill to work the third shift at a local nursing home. She tells me, "I work—that's what I do."

Cadence wants to work, too. In two separate entries in her writer's notebook, Cadence wrote: "I wish that I could be my mom because she gets jobs and I don't get a job. I wish that I could too, but my mom won't let me. . . ."

Like Cadence, Heather wishes to be her mother—or even better, a princess version of her mother, as she writes in this piece: "Once upon a time there was a lovely princess. She lived in a castle. She lived with a handsome prince. She had eight children. She was a great cook. Her toilet was running. She wanted to have more kids."

Heather is indeed (at least in desire) the princess she writes about. During choice time at school Heather spends an enormous amount of energy designing and creating elaborate crowns and wands for herself. She prances around the room twirling and whirling gracefully with her long blond hair flowing behind her. Heather begs for her picture to be taken as she stands straight, chin high, lips curled upward, and eyes beckoning the wonder above her.

With the recent addition of a baby brother, Heather seems almost obsessed with caring for others, thinking of having children, and being a mother—despite her mother's urgings to "wait to have kids." Heather adores her mother and writes about her often. She wants to *be* her mother, in fact, as she writes, "I wish I can be my mom because you get to love your kids." Heather plays the mother role as she cares for her baby brother in this story:

> I have a new baby brother. He is beautiful. He looks like me. His name is Jed. He was named after my dad. I can hold him and I can feed him. I can push him in the stroller. I can make him smile.
> When he grows up I am getting him a car. I like to sleep by him. When he cries I can stop him and sometimes he can sleep with me in my bed.

When I get home I am going to give him a bath and take him outside
with me. I am taking him to the park and having a picnic and then I am
going to show him off.
I love my brother.

Like most of the young girls in this community, Heather is already at-
tuned to many of the details of caring for babies. After spending time
with Heather's mother, it's not hard to understand why Heather wants to
be like her mother, to *be* her mother. The following piece of writing conveys some of these reasons:

I love my mom.
She makes me laugh.
She loves me and my little brother.
She always takes care of us.
She always makes sure I eat.
She likes to read with me.
She likes when I pick flowers for her.
She likes when I write.
She likes to bake.
I love my mom.

Dena loves Heather as openly and outwardly as Heather loves her
mother. In a home-school communication journal I kept with families,
Heather's mother responded to my positive comments about Heather: "I
must agree on your compliments on Heather. She is a great child. She listens very well at home as well. She always tries to help me with lots of
things. I enjoy spending my time with her myself."
Dena spends much time with Heather, outside her recently acquired
full-time job at a local bank. Dena tells me, "Anything she wants to do, we
do." If Heather is watching *Nickelodeon* at home and a website address is
advertised for activities connected to the show, Dena helps Heather connect
to the Internet. If Heather is looking through a magazine at home and sees
a recipe for a cake, they make one together. One time Heather was watching one of her favorite television shows, *Zoom*, and had a question. Dena
helped her e-mail someone on the show. "I'm teaching her to type . . . I want
her to be hip to the real world—like where I am."
Cadence is still struggling to find accepted ways to fit in a middle-class
institution like school. And though Heather has learned to seemingly successfully juggle various ways of acting, talking, and being in different class
contexts, a strong classed identity lies just below the surface. If Cadence
and Heather aren't strategically invited to *attach* themselves to school and
academic success in a way that values their community identities—
strongly connected to their mothers' identities—they may be getting a job

sooner rather than later. And "growing up" to have children doesn't necessarily mean being grown. A thirteen-year-old friend of Cadence's family has just announced her pregnancy. All of this scares Lori and Dena, but they know these are simply more pieces of a complicated reality, particularly in a working-poor community like Lower Bond Hill. To overcome these challenges and pressures, teachers and schools must do more than increase standards and implement challenging curricula—they must listen, watch, understand, empathize, and *then respond* directly to the social, emotional, and historical needs within this particular place at this particular time. Then, and only then, can we help Cadence and Heather to sort through and realize their own cross-class, complex hopes and dreams for themselves:

By Cadence:	By Heather:
I want to be a vegetarian.	I wanna be an artist.
I want to be a hooker.	I wanna be an actor.
I want to be a tom girl.	I wanna have a nighttime job.
I want to be myself.	I wanna work at a gas station.
I want to help the old people.	I wanna be a mathematician.
I want to be a doctor.	I wanna be a nurse.
I want to be a character.	I wanna be a baker lady.

The Power of Language

Alison and Mariah, in the local idiom of Lower Bond Hill, are cousins. In some middle-class settings, they might be considered distant stepcousins. The two girls are neighbors, only needing to cross the street to reach one another's apartment buildings. Through these ties, the two girls have developed close bonds across their fifth-grade school year. Though they occasionally fall into the "you're my friend—you're not my friend anymore" cycle of preteen friendships, their family histories and shared neighborhood experiences eclipse an occasional fracas, even a threat to fight. The two girls sit near one another in their language arts classroom, sharing secrets and notes in the interstices of the official reading and writing curriculum.

For girls with such tight bonds of family and friendship, however, the two could hardly be more different. In the classroom, Alison conveys a "good girl" identity that is frequently connected in the minds of teachers to her being a "good student." She rarely causes her teachers any trouble. She is usually on-task—doing what she is supposed to be doing, completing her homework in a regular and timely manner. A sweet, little-girl demeanor is part of Alison's charms. She is small and thin in frame, with long blond hair and blue eyes. She acts the part of a princess: sweet, soft-spoken, and yet powerful in the attention she receives.

Mariah asserts a different kind of power. She is often perceived in the classroom as a troublemaker with what teaching adults call a "foul mouth," or what those in the neighborhood might call "an attitude." Mariah strongly voices a working-class identity. She is nearly one year older than Alison as well as many other girls in her classroom. Part of her maturity is a more overtly sexualized way of performing her working-class femininity. "A little hottie," is one description voiced by a visiting student teacher; "too hot, too fast," are other words spoken about Mariah or to her. In the ways described by Bakhtin (1984) in his writings about carnivalesque relations, much of Mariah's power is achieved by subverting the *official* discourses of middle-class schooling. Her darker kind of attractiveness (she has brown hair and expressive brown eyes) and frequent outbursts of anger evoke the tougher edges of growing up in a sometimes unforgiving landscape. Mariah cusses; she fights. She can play the badass girl that classroom teachers dread having to discipline and educate.

The girls' distinctive voices in relation to neighborhood landscapes can be heard in stories of near misses with sexually threatening adult men. Many of the eight girls in the after-school program for fifth graders talk about rape and other forms of violence aimed at little girls. In one after-school meeting, these stories come out, ironically, as the girls respond to some questions about the meaning of *romance* in their lives. One girl, Nicole, has invented her own question about "What girls should be like." Her response to her own question brings up neighborhood words for female sexual identity: *sluts*, *hoes*, *bitches*, and *doing tricks*. The power of these neighborhood words opens a door to community stories in which the girls in the group had to find the right language, or the right response, to ward off the advances of a creep.

Alison's story calls up a narrative theme that reverberates through several of the girls' stories of being approached by a man seeking sex. A man driving a red pickup truck with silver detailing, has cropped up in more than one girl's narrative. Alison tells about a time when she, her younger brother, and her aunt were walking by the Kitchen (a popular local coffee shop) and the man in the red truck made an attempt to physically grab her and drag her into his vehicle.

> We 'as standin' right here [*demonstrates*]
> An' up by Kitchen there's this red truck, and it had like silver lines
>   on it
> Had this big rusted ol' {uh, ladder on top of it
>   girl?: {pervert
> An' uh, so he start ridin' real slow and starin' at me like this
>   [*demonstrates*]
> I start lookin' over like this.
> He went down on the under / other end of Garner like this

He, uh, looked down on the other / Garner like this
He start comin' up like this and he stopped right here at the light
He turned over and looked at me, he start reachin' over to his door
    like this
An' he went like this, he went like this [*demonstrates man's arm
    movement*]
An' was openin' up his door
An' I started screamin, I was like Cheri, Cheri, Cheri HELP ME!
An' the light turned Walk an' I took off dippin' 'cross the street
I 'as screamin' and cryin'
The guy slammed his door shut and start ridin' up there
I was holdin' on to Cheri like this cryin'
I ducked my head underneath her shoulder
An' the guy came ridin' by

This story about a near encounter with this man (named a "pervert" by one girl's inserted comment) was met with rapid acknowledgment from other girls. Brandie proclaimed in a high voice that the same man was following her. Elizabeth announced that she knew someone with a car like that.

Listen to a similar story told by Mariah during the same after-school meeting. She conveys in a raw, working-class language a related kind of incident in which a man seeking sex approached her on the street. Woven into Mariah's story is a thread common to neighborhood sexual narratives: Male outsiders often associated with sexual violence or perversion are Mexicans and blacks. Mexican men (many of whom are young) are in the minds of young girls such as Mariah, connected with a darker side of community life in Lower Bond Hill. Prostitution occurs for drugs and for money—or both. Mexicans are believed to be more commonly connected with such illicit sexual practices as, in the words of Brandie, "they're rich." Mexican men are believed to carry around bundles of cash in their pockets and to seek out girls and young women as sex partners. Mariah's story, probably a mixture of fact and hyperbole, recounts two incidents in which Mexican and black men made lurid sexual advances toward girls. In this narrative, however, adult women (Nicole's mother), Mariah's older brother, and Mariah herself, use in-your-face language to counter these sexual advances. Hers is a different kind of identity than the one conveyed in Alison's story of a young girl hiding her face in the crook of an adult's protective arms.

There's this girl, I think it was Nicole and Tiffany
I guess they're walkin' down the street
And this Mexican asked them to get in the car
Nicole dipped, she said "*fuck you, HELL NO!*"
She dipped in Paradise

She told her Mom, her Mom got out of the Kitchen
She was like, YOU FUCKIN PRICK, I'M GONNA KICK YOUR
    ASS!
The Mexican drove off real fast!
But then again that time, it was like around, around 7:00
It was me and Nicole, we were walkin' home
'Cause she was gonna stay all night with me
'Cause my Mom said she could
An' we were walkin' home, cause I lived on Burns
An' uhm, this Black dude he was followin' us all the way home
I got to the door, he was like, "You wanna go for a ride?"
I was like, "Where?"
He goes, "Down the alley"
I said, "Fuck you no"
My brother looked out the window, my brother was like, "What
    the fuck you just ask?"
"Like I told him *'fuck you no'*"
He's like, "Told who?"
"Like this guy who's tryin' to make me get in the car"
My brother ran down them steps
My brother('s) like, *"You better get the FUCK away from my sis-
    ter 'fore I chase you down all the way to Brown, you BLACK
    MOTHER FUCKER!*

The differences in how the two girls voice language that either reflects the in-your-face identity of a girl with an attitude or a more middle-
class femininity familiar to many teachers can also be seen in their
readings of a cinematic text. In the girls' pre-teen peer group cultures in
the classroom and in the neighborhood, perhaps no holiday comes as
charged with meaning as Valentine's Day. In honor of the encroaching
event (or perhaps as a form of pedagogical acquiescence to its impas-
sioned hold on girls' imaginations), the girls were shown the George Roy
Hill film, *A Little Romance* (1979). Lauren, the film's twelve-year-old
heroine, experiences first love with a French boy, Daniel. The class differences between the two (Lauren is the daughter of a wealthy American
couple living in Paris; Daniel is the resourceful son of a taxi driver who
jilts customers by tinkering with his cab meter) are elided by their shared
high IQs. The two concoct a scheme to run off to Venice and kiss in a
gondola under a bridge at sunset, marking their love as eternal. Their ad-
ventures prior to this more dramatic conclusion run the usual gamut of
sneaking out to the movies together and stealing kisses in the subway.
Lauren's close friend, Natalie, voices an underlying theme of the liminal
qualities of pre-teen sexuality. As she and Lauren, visiting the Louvre,
stare upward at the male genitals of a Greek statue, Natalie asks her
friend furtively, "Have you done it?" Lauren fakes a response ("Sure, all

the time"), though on another occasion she recoils when Daniel and his working-class buddy sneak Lauren in the back door of a theater to watch a porn film. Running away in tears from the film's portrayal of adult sexuality, Lauren voices a middle-class ideology of love: She yearns for a romantic soul mate.

When asked to rate *A Little Romance* (on a scale of 1–5 "stars"), its stronghold on the girls' imaginations was apparent. Alison gave the film a rating of 98 stars, Mariah the even more hyperbolic rating of 5 million stars. However, the girls' readings of this cinematic text also revealed distinctive ways in which coming of age in Lower Bond Hill became layered with the screen images of Lauren and Daniel. To appropriate Stuart Hall's (1989) terminology, the girls produced *negotiated readings* in which distinctive ways of living femininity and class were voiced in relation to the text.

Alison, who had proclaimed the scene in the porn film theater as her favorite, identified with Lauren. Alison was taken with Lauren's response to the porn film. In her summary of the scene, Alison recounted a girl's shocked reaction to seeing a screen couple (described as "a girl and boy" in Alison's portrayal) doing "blah blah blah."

> An' I don't know what was goin' on in the movie but the girl [Lauren] said, it was like, it was like a porno movie, about this girl and boy blah blah blah
> An' the girl [Lauren] took off runnin' outside and was cryin'
> An' Daniel took off runnin' outside with 'er
> An' he was talkin' to her
> An' he said somethin' to her like, it's just makeup or something like that
> He said "I'd never do that to you"

Mariah also identified with Lauren. What she offered as a plausible reason for this identification was an experience that she claimed to have had. Like Lauren, she drank alcohol with her boyfriend. In *A Little Romance*, Daniel sneaks some champagne up to Lauren's room on her thirteenth birthday, where his working-class buddy (a cigarette-smoking, cussing sidekick) plasters a poster from the porn film on the walls and dances suggestively with Natalie, Lauren's naive girlfriend. Mariah remembered a scene from "when I was little" that she claimed was similar: "On my birthday, we were playing around, and, . . . this boy I know, he got some beer." Her story ends with a coda that may have been truth or fiction, or perhaps a little of each: "My mom found his [the boy's] picture on the wall and she tore it." Prior to that, she suggests, the two went a little too far, a theme that contrasts with Alison's reading of Daniel's *romantic* assurances.

On the surface, it would seem as though Alison's stronger embrace of middle-class girlhood identities would set the stage for a more successful experience in school. Though true in part, just beneath the surface, discernible only with the passage of time and within an alternative pedagogical environment, lie the more complex truths of how both Mariah and Alison struggle in contradictory landscapes of class.

We are in an after-school meeting in early December, and the girls have made the decision to cuss. It started when a graduate research assistant driving one of the girls home cussed in her car when nearly hit by a police car on a high-speed chase. "Fucking ass" were the words that slipped out. The following week, she shared a personal narrative where she talked about her right to cuss. The girls followed suit with their own decision to cuss.

Mariah and Alison have, along with the other girls, been working on narrative and photographic compositions about "My Life as a Girl." With the addition of cuss words seem to come the undercurrents of life in Lower Bond Hill. Mariah writes simply in her journal, "It fucking sucks being a girl." Alison composes a lengthier story about how she cannot leave her house alone and about how angry this makes her feel. "My life as a girl stinks because my brothers get all the damn attention like going to the country with my papa and I don't because my papa said it's too cold down there, so I have to go to the damn country in the summer. And I am not allowed out of the fucking house unless I go with my aunt. I think it also stinks because I don't get to go to the skating rink with my aunt because Mama says that me and her talk to boys. So in my head I get mad and say that fucking stinks because I don't talk to boys and she don't either."

If one peels away the surface veneer of a middle-class schoolgirl identity most successfully enacted by Alison, suddenly the voices of both Alison and Mariah ring with the language of Lower Bond Hill. Cussing is one way of naming one's identity as a girl in this distinctive landscape, in contrast to the middle-class school setting where this is viewed as being foulmouthed. These girls' life stories also exude anger, which is more readily associated with Mariah. In the classroom, it is often she who loses it—ending up in detention, having missed school outings, and generally getting reprimanded by adults. And yet, both girls voice anger in their stories about girlhood. Why does life as a girl, to use their language, suck?

In the bitching session that ensues (as the girls like to use the word *bitch* to describe women and girls and their unique styles of complaining and arguing), the girls raise the issues that constrain and confine them in a neighborhood characterized by patriarchal relations. When adult siblings, neighbors, or relatives bring young children to visit, "you get laid off with the kid" (as Mariah explains it). Moreover, boys get not only more attention but also more material goods. In Mariah's words, over Christmas what she got was "jack shit," whereas boys more often get what they want.

Deeply connected with the *words*, however, were the lives that the girls lead outside of the walls of Linden School, lives that must be more psychologically influential than any official curriculum. As the language of the after-school program was opened up to working-class language, so too did neighborhood stories begin to reveal aspects of the girls' lives that had remained hidden. It was as though, as James Paul Gee (1996) has argued about language, the power of cussing carried with it an "identity toolkit"—a discourse deeply intertwined with the girls' neighborhood lives. As the girls spoke, using a language more heavily inflected with these forms, stories of pain and loss also emerged as shared threads of neighborhood consciousness.

Both girls, we were to learn, had lost or been separated from their birth-mothers due to the drug culture that has now reached into neighborhoods such as Lower Bond Hill. In December, Mariah, teary-eyed and exhausted in the classroom, barely holding it together during a language arts lesson, said she had learned that her birth-mother (who had lived in a rural Appalachian location) had died from a drug overdose. Later the same day, Mariah rocked back and forth on the floor in grief, her head in her hands, as the girls began to map out narratives about their lives as girls. In March, both Alison and Mariah sobbed after a graduate research assistant shared a story about the heroin-related death of a family member. Alison had much earlier in the year been taken away from her mother, who had herself become an addict. The two girls sat on the floor, their backs to the wall, crying. Alison sobbed, "I want my mom back." After a long discussion of how drugs had taken their mothers from them, Mariah gave Alison, still in tears, a kiss on her forehead.

What does it mean, then, to grow up as a young girl in Lower Bond Hill? For these two girls at least, it means living a life in school that is partly concealed—the life associated with loved ones, anger, and sometimes fragmentation as the darker edges of neighborhood life reach into their homes. It also means living a neighborhood life of resiliency, devotion to family, and spirituality that provides stability and strong support. The speaking voices and life experiences of these two girls run deep, as Flannery O'Connor might argue—a reading of them must seek meanings that are under the surface. One girl, Mariah, in the ways described by Bakhtin in his writings on the carnivalesque, uses subversive language and female sexuality to subvert the official discourses of an authoritarian school setting. Another girl, Alison, appears to have appropriated norms for being a good schoolgirl. However, just beneath the surface of that seeming success lies the fragmentation of identity that Valerie Walkerdine (1990) has described as *splitting*. In the classroom, unlike Mariah, she keeps her mouth shut.

It may be, however, that working-class forms of language and identity hold as much power for Alison as they seemingly do for

Mariah. Alison's cinematic reading of an ideology of romance and love in *A Little Romance*, for instance, may show the relevance for her life as a leading neighborhood narrative for teen women: partnering and having babies of one's own. She evinces both fascination and familiarity with the new babies coming into her household and into the homes of kin living in Kentucky. She holds an aunt's new baby, feeds him, and burps him. She carries around a picture of the newborn, showing it to teachers and peers.

How will these two girls fare as they enter their teen years? Alison and Mariah are both girls who are easily drawn into literature and writing. They are smart, creative, and articulate. The tension for both girls seems to lie with the meanings of the language, identity, and values of Lower Bond Hill in a school setting where some of these would not be valued. For Mariah, her strong attachment to neighborhood values and language could easily preclude a productive future in school. Mariah's difficulties are attributed to her (alone) rather than to her distinctive way of living class in a classroom setting. For Alison, her attachment to a culture of romance (to appropriate Angela McRobbie's apt phrasing) and familiarity with babies could drive a wedge between her primary desires and a deeper attachment to literature, writing, or other areas of learning. For now she seems content, though worried. Each school year in the spring she waits anxiously, in the hopes that she has passed her reading proficiency test.

Language is powerful in the classroom. It provides a means of naming one's identity and of having one's identity named by others. It provides a way of narrating one's place in existing *figured worlds,* in the sense used by Dorothy Holland, William Lachicotte Jr., Debra Skinner, and Carole Cain (1998), and of imagining new figured worlds. It provides a way to bitch, to articulate anger, to argue, and to love. Finally, and perhaps most hopefully, language can become a means for empowerment, a way of gaining new kinds of voices and consciousness.

Over the course of weeks and months, the two girls whose voices and lives have been chronicled here experienced a shift in consciousness that is deeply educational. This could be most readily observed with Mariah, the older of the two and, at least in the after-school setting, a girl seen by Alison and others as a leader. The "I'm angry and resistant" voice that has been her frequent demise in the classroom has, in the after-school program, shifted to an "I'm angry and empowered" voice. While moments of intense feeling have come with the words connected to the girls' neighborhood lives, these seem more like healing moments leading to understanding rather than to moments of outright resistance. As I have begun to hear the articulations of life in Lower Bond Hill in the girls' voices, they have opened hidden parts of their lives to me. It creates the possibility for a pedagogy that is *answerable* to the students' life language, experiences, imaginations, and hopes for their futures. As this after-school literacy project has evolved, so has the curriculum itself. The girls in this project have begun work on a magazine that will feature realistic and fictional writing about their lives as girls.

Answering the Voices of Girls Living in Poverty

The call to create more critical, radical, or activist pedagogies has become a familiar refrain in some circles of the educational research community. What some scholars have termed the *new literacy research*, is connected to the goal of helping teachers, researchers, and students unpack the forms of language and practice that replicate existing—and sometimes inequitable—social relations.

Our work is indebted to this emerging interdisciplinary field of new literacy studies. At the same time, our efforts look back to earlier exemplars of pedagogical activism in which there was a long-term commitment to shaping practice in response to a distinctive social, historical, and material landscape, and in dialogue with the speaking subjects in those landscapes. The Piedmont mill towns where Shirley Brice Heath (1983) connected ethnographies of communication with teaching innovations, and the hill country of eastern Tennessee where Myles Horton founded a school for labor organizers and civil rights activists—these were responses to particular social geographies and histories. In these and in other similar exemplars, the "critical" part of critical pedagogies evolved out of what Mikhail Bakhtin, in his early philosophical essays, referred to as *answerability*. These educational efforts entailed discursive *responses* to particular kinds of language and narratives of experience, and *responsibility* toward the subjects whose lives were impacted by educational practice.

The ethnography and activist teaching described in this chapter is focused on young students, not on the adult laborers or peasants associated with the work of critical educators such as Freire and Horton, nor the university students associated with educators such as bell hooks (1994). The goals of this work shift slightly when educating children who have not sought assistance to overcome oppressive hegemonic relations, but instead have been sought out by researchers and advocates such as the two of us. More limited in scope, the *aims* of our teaching have been to engage girls in meaningful pedagogy that will aid their emotional and psychological attachment to school and to academic practices *and* to create an exemplar of critical practice that could have wider implications for the education of girls living in poverty.

Girls growing up in neighborhoods such as Lower Bond Hill are coming of age amid exciting forms of hybridity and global change, and amid troubling social realities connected with a poverty that is concentrated and isolated. Part of our attempt to understand the psychological implications of growing up in this unique enclave of poverty has entailed a writing focus on the lived experiences and speaking voices of girls—Cadence, Heather, Alison, and Mariah. This analysis has drawn on literature and on the literary arts of writing, as well as on the feminist and materialist psychological theory developed by Walkerdine and her colleagues.

Stories and analyses of how class is lived by young girls have revealed layers of complexity that defy the reductive educational fixes now in vogue. The rhetoric of parental involvement doesn't match the experiences of Heather and Cadence whose mothers are clearly involved in the literacy development of the girls. The belief that becoming somebody different within school spaces will promote academic success also fails to explain the continuing vulnerabilities of Heather and Alison—the two "good girls" who work hard to be the successful student their teacher expects them to be—but who also have hopes and dreams for a future that don't coincide with images of academic success in the United States. Raising standards, teaching more "skills," regulating progress with numerous formal evaluations, and training parents to work with their children will not meet the more complex needs of girls living poverty if they are to successfully position themselves in the twenty-first-century workforce. If these girls are expected to bridge the social class divide and to break the cycle of poverty in their families, they must be actively engaged in constructing identities that are reflective of their community (and in the case of these four girls—their mothers), but they must also be attached to academic practices.

Understanding that one can construct such a hybrid identity begins with opening up school spaces where home identities (including language practices and various ways of being) are genuinely valued and perceived as valuable resources. Cadence and Mariah share an "attitude" that reflects an assertive in-your-face working-poor identity. In an alternative pedagogy, their attitudes were used as powerful tools to begin constructing new identities—hybrid identities that don't shed the discourses formed within intimate relations of home and family. Heather and Alison perform identities closely aligned with community practices within an alternative pedagogical space—identities that they felt needed to be left behind as they crossed the threshold to school. Hybrid identity work continues for Heather and Alison too, as these seemingly successful students tease apart their class-complicated future aspirations that include having babies and getting jobs.

In Wendy Luttrell's study of two groups (rural and urban) of women returning to school to obtain a high school diploma, "bad attitudes" were used by twelve of the fifteen urban women as an explanation of why they weren't "suited" for school (1997, p. 63). This attitude was perceived as a character trait that interfered with their academic success. The remaining women who described themselves as good students felt they had to silence their own voices in order to be successful in school. One woman stated: "I learned at a young age to button my lip. . . . My sister couldn't put up with it and she didn't do well; I guess you could say it was more my style to take it, so I did real well in school"(p. 63). "Doing well" in school, however, is relative and perceived through class-specific webs of understanding. This woman was in an adult basic education class with the goal of achieving a high school diploma. Her notion of having done well in school does not coincide with the concept of doing well in school for upper classes in the United States.

Are Alison and Heather more apt to "take it" from teachers? Are Cadence and Mariah not able to "put up with it"? Whatever route the girls take, traditional schooling practices would not be aimed at changing the realities of their class oppression. This fact illuminates the imagined dichotomy of "good girl" and "bad girl" and problematizes the privileging of one over the other within school settings. For both, their futures look bleak without serious change in pedagogical focus.

Contemporary discourses of achievement and accountability in U.S. schools do not address students as classed and gendered subjects. An alternative pedagogy that is answerable to the social, emotional, material, psychological, and linguistic specificities of high-poverty girls' lives must be in place if these girls are to construct a deep attachment to school and to academic practices. Such an attachment could lead to the completion of high school and to the pursuit of postsecondary options that hold the possibilities of changing the material futures of girls who live in poverty. Though small in scope, our case studies are powerful in suggesting that such pedagogical change is possible in the language arts classroom. The speaking voices of working-poor girls and women can help keep the concreteness of their experiences and desires at the center of similar pedagogical efforts. As Cadence's mother so eloquently put it: Let her teach you.

Notes

The research described in this chapter has been supported in part through an AERA/OERI research grant and through funds from The Sociological Initiatives Foundation and from the Martha Holden Jennings Foundation.

1. For examples of this work from the United Kingdom, see McRobbie (1991/2000); Reay (1997, 1998, 2000); Skeggs (1997); Steedman (1982, 1994); Walkerdine (1988, 1990); Walkerdine and Lucey (1989); and Walkerdine, Lucey, and Melody (2001).

References

Allison, D. 1994. A Question of Class. In *Skin: Talking about sex, class, and literature* (pp. 13–36). Ithaca: Firebrand Books.

Bakhtin, M. M. 1981. Discourse in the novel. *The dialogic imagination: Four essays by M.M. Bakhtin* (pp. 259–422). Ed. M. Holquist. Trans. C. Emerson and M. Holquist. Austin: University of Texas Press.

———. 1984. *Rabelais and his world*. Trans. H. Iswolsky. Bloomington: Indiana University Press.

———. 1990. *Art and answerability: Early philosophical essays by M.M. Bakhtin*. Eds. M. Holquist and V. Liapunov. Trans. V. Liapunov. Austin: University of Texas Press.

Coles, R. 1967. *Migrants, sharecroppers, and mountaineers*. Vol. 2, *Children of Crisis*. Boston: Little, Brown and Company.

Collins, J. 2000. Bernstein, Bourdieu and the new literacy studies. *Linguistics and Education*, 11(1), 65–78.

Draper, S. M. 1996. *Tears of a tiger*. New York: Aladdin Paperbacks.

Dyson, A. H. 1993. *Social worlds of children learning to write in an urban primary school*. New York: Teachers College Press.

Fallows, J. 2000. The invisible poor. *New York Times Magazine* (March 19).

Foucault, M. 1978. *The history of sexuality: An introduction*. Trans. R. Hurley. New York: Vintage Books.

Freire, P. 1970. *Pedagogy of the oppressed*. New York: Continuum Publishing Company.

Gee, J. P. 1996. *Social linguistics and literacies: Ideology in discourses*, 2nd ed. Bristol, PA: Falmer Press.

Gutierrez, K., Baquedano-Lopez, P., and Tejeda, C. 1999. Rethinking diversity: Hybridity and hybrid language practices in the third space. *Mind, Culture, and Activity*, 6(4), 286–303.

Hall, S. 1989. Encoding/decoding. In S. Hall, D. Hobson, A. Lowe, and P. Willis (Eds.) *Culture, media, language*. Birmingham: Centre for Contemporary Cultural Studies.

Harrington, M. 1962/1993. *The other America: Poverty in the United States*. New York: Simon & Schuster.

Heath, S. B. 1983. *Ways with words: Language, life and work in communities and classrooms*. New York: Cambridge University Press.

Hill, G. R. 1979, Director. *A little romance*. Orion Pictures.

Holland, D., Lachicotte, W. Jr., Skinner, D., and Cain, C. 1998. *Identity and agency in cultural worlds*. Cambridge: Harvard University Press.

hooks, b. 1994. *Teaching to transgress: Education as the practice of freedom*. New York: Routledge.

———. 2000. *Where we stand: Class matters*. New York: Routledge.

Horton, M. and Freire, P. 1990. *We make the road by walking*. Eds. B. Bell, J. Gaventa, and J. Peters. Philadelphia: Temple University Press.

Lee, C., Spencer, M. B., and Harpalani, V. 2003. "Every shut eye ain't sleep": Studying how people live culturally. *Educational Researcher*, 32(5), 6–13.

Luttrell, W. 1997. *School-smart and mother-wise: Working-class women's identity and schooling.* New York: Routledge.

Lyon, G. E. 1999. *Where I'm from, where poems come from.* Spring, TX: Absey & Company.

McRobbie, A. 1991/2000. The politics of feminist research: Between talk, text, and action. *Feminism and youth culture,* 2nd ed. New York: Routledge.

Miller, J. 1996. *School for women.* London: Virago.

New London Group 1996. A pedagogy of multiliteracies: Designing social futures. *Harvard Educational Review,* 66(1), 60–92.

O'Connor, F. 1961. The regional writer. In S. Fitzgerald and R. Fitzgerald (Eds.) *Mystery and manners: Occasional prose* (pp. 51–59). New York: Farrar.

Park, B. 1992. *Junie B. Jones and the stupid smelly bus.* New York: Scholastic.

Reay, D. 1997. Feminist theory, habitus, and social class: Disrupting notions of classlessness. *Women's Studies International Forum,* 20(2), 225–33.

———. 1998. *Class work: Mothers' involvement in their children's primary schooling.* London: UCL Press.

———. 2000. Children's urban landscapes: Configurations of class and place. In S. R. Munt (Ed.) *Cultural studies and the working class: Subject to change* (pp. 151–64). New York: Cassell.

Schwartz, T. 2002. "Write me: A participatory action research project with urban Appalachian girls." Unpublished dissertation: University of Cincinnati.

Skeggs, B. 1995. *Feminist cultural theory: Process and production.* Manchester: Manchester University Press.

———. 1997. *Formations of class and gender: Becoming respectable.* London: Sage.

———. 2001. Feminist ethnography. *Handbook of ethnography* (pp. 426–42). Eds. P. Atkinson, A. Coffey, S. Delamont, J. Lofland, and L. Lofland. Thousand Oaks, CA: Sage Publications.

Steedman, C. 1982. *The tidy house: Little girls writing.* London: Virago Press.

———. 1994. *Landscape for a good woman: A story of two lives.* New Brunswick, NJ: Rutgers University Press.

Tough, P. 2001. The alchemy of OxyContin. *New York Times Magazine* (July 29).

Walkerdine, V. 1988. *The mastery of reason: Cognitive development and the production of rationality.* New York: Routledge.

———. 1990. *Schoolgirl fictions.* London: Verso.

Walkerdine, V. and Lucey, H., 1989. *Democracy in the kitchen: Regulating mothers and socializing daughters.* London: Virago Press.

Walkerdine, V., Lucey, H. and Melody, J. 2001. *Growing up girl: Psychosocial explorations of gender and class.* New York: New York University Press.

Williams, V. B. 2001. *Amber was brave, Essie was smart.* New York: Scholastic.

4

MARGINALIZATION AND MEMBERSHIP

Jill Koyama and Margaret A. Gibson

In high schools across the United States adolescents enter into social relations with many others, some whose backgrounds are similar to their own and others who are racially, ethnically, economically, culturally, and linguistically different. There, they interact with one another, constructing seemingly coherent systems of knowledge and engaging in complex patterns of social activities across a wide range of possible memberships available to high school students. These interactions are especially complex because of their placement within the social, economic, racial/ethnic, and political characteristics of schools and also because students, as well as teachers, administrators, and staff, bring to school their own histories and life experiences. Students, increasing numbers of whom are economically marginalized and recent immigrants, and teachers, who have attained middle-class status and are mostly native-born Americans, are, together, "people who started out from very different places (literally or metaphorically or both) [and] wind up occupying the same space" (Ortner, 1996, p. 182). And across the space, adolescents in essence "make" and "remake" themselves over and over again, refusing a singular or essentialist label of identification and struggling against the processes of class determinism. They are formed as social and cultural subjects as a result of their backgrounds—their social class, their ethnicity, and their race—but also as a result of their shared daily environment and interactions (2003, p. 169). Through their encounters with one another in various school settings, they construct themselves and the "others" repeatedly.

In this chapter we present a multifaceted account in which migrant students of Mexican descent are categorically made, unmade, and remade by interacting with each other, with nonmigrant students of Mexican-descent, with European American students, and with their teachers in a California public high school that serves students from white middle-class and Mexican-origin working-class and migrant families in nearly equal number. We focus on migrant students as a subset of Mexican-descent students who often find themselves in a "state of being but not belonging" (Gilroy, 2000, p. 77) as they try to negotiate the fluid boundaries of sociocultural and ethnolinguistic identifications in schools. They are, in essence, betwixt and between, both novices and "others" who are on the edge of full participation in the games of learning and being American high school students. They are often singled out and labeled by white classmates as "loners who keep to themselves" and as *cholo/as* or "gang members" by some teachers as "uninterested in school" and "academically unfocused," and by more assimilated nonmigrant students of Mexican-descent as the school's "underclass." These perceptions of migrant students take various forms, and throughout the chapter we show how the migrant Mexican students are "constructed," in the sense of being made and the sense of being made-up (Ortner, 1999), and also how they simultaneously contribute to, and work against, the constructions. However, it is clear to us that in general the construction of the marginalized "otherness"—of the class, ethnic, and sociocultural "others"—is not intrinsic to class, ethnic, or cultural differences between the migrant students and their classmates, but rather one outcome of the ongoing cultural work of becoming and being a high school student. Specifically, the constructions of the migrants in this chapter, some seemingly congruent with reality and others less so, are not, we argue, merely attributable to the differences between the migrant and the white students, but rather are the results of the overarching structures of inequality within a particular high school, where white middle-class students and working-class Mexican-descent students have their first sustained interactions with each "other."

Framed by the particular social and cultural contexts and constraints of the high school, the migrant students both struggle with the cultural process of becoming an American high school student and also negotiate the unexpected side effects. Drawing on practice theory or perhaps more accurately on theories of practice, we interrogate the ways in which the migrant students are simultaneously constructed as economically, linguistically, and ethnically marginalized "others" through their relations with their school, most of their teachers, and with many of their classmates—and also how they (re)make their own particular and academic identifications tangential to the dominant through their participation with each other and staff in the school's Migrant Education Program. We explore how class identifications, always less visible, but intricately joined with race and ethnicity, operate in the cultural beliefs and assumptions of teachers and students; manifest in the ritualized practices of the school; and inform how individuals attend to, and behave in, particular situations and contexts.

Theoretical Perspectives:
Theories of Practice

For a variety of reasons, different groups of people—some with more power and resources than others—encounter, interact with, and confront each other. Practice theory is a perspective that does not attend separately to the dominant group's representations (and their power to constrain others) or to the agency (and possibly "resistance") of the subaltern subjects, the members of the "weaker" group(s) in the encounters. It insists on exploring the two in process, together, in tension. It focuses on the highly patterned and ritualized behaviors and activities that underlie, organize, and often conserve systems, but also focuses on the ongoing enactment of these routines by actors who are shaped by the organizing patterns and who struggle at some angle against them (Ortner, 1994, p. 398). Relations between people and social structures are generated and regenerated similarly and differently in practical action. And it is precisely the ongoing matrices of interactions between the two, in particular moments and over time, on which theories of practice focus to account for social reproduction and change.

Social structures are produced and reproduced, and ongoing day-to-day human practices are constrained by structures, reproduce structures, and struggle within structures (Ortner, 1994). There is thus a complex relationship between human beings and social structures, one in which structure is both a source and product of social practices (Giddens, 1979). According to Giddens, individuals and groups act as intentional, reflective agents who have the capacity to see some aspects of the larger social forces and workings of systems and also analyze their own actions and practices. Their agency is not a series of discrete individual acts but rather a "continuous flow of conduct," a sort of situated practice to which power is inextricably bound (pp. 55–56).[1] Thus, less advantaged subjects in light of practice theory are people who need not be either compliant with the determining structures of a system or oppositional to them. They can simultaneously engage in activities and in practices, without being social and cultural dupes or countercultural revolutionaries.

To frame the complex and social intentional actions and practices of subjects in a life that is culturally organized and constructed, Ortner (1996, 1999) develops the idea of "serious games." Serious games capture the situational complexities of life that are precisely social, consisting of webs of relationships and interactions between multiple, shiftingly interrelated subjects and contexts, as well as consisting of the agency of actors, who play multiple simultaneous games with intention, skill, knowledge, and intelligence. S. B. Ortner's serious game metaphor also addresses power and situations of inequality that permeate social life. In her most recent work, a study of social class within her own peer group, her high school graduating class, Ortner (2003) chooses to use "games" without the qualifying adjective "serious" to refer to what she considers "the slightly unreal world of school status games" (p. 111) and reserves "serious games" to distinguish the games of power and success in broader sociocultural and political contexts.

And these games and the actors who play them are not isolated, not abstracted from the continuum of time. Practice theory considers the historical patterns and moments, as well as the more recent past within which social practices are embedded. In this sense, it provides a method to examine the ways in which the meanings of relations are derived from changing social, economic, and cultural contexts across a continuum of time. Practices are seen as long term. In particular, Sahlins (1981) demonstrates that cultural construction of subjects and agents occurs in historical processes and that social practices are mutually constituting and reflective of historical patterns. At particular moments, when people's interactions redefine them and their practices as different from that culturally presupposed, then they have the ability to "work back on the conventional values" (p. 35) of the system. When traditional or customary social practices do not reproduce the usual or expected results or relations, there are possibilities of redefinition, of remaking, and of reconstructing both the disadvantaged and their practices. This failed reproduction, according to Sahlins (p. 35), is change.

Paradoxically change is difficult ongoing social and cultural work and yet "[it] is largely a by-product, an unintended consequence of action, however rational action may have been" (Ortner, 1994, p. 395). Human behavior is not obligated to conform to the class and cultural categories socially determined by their own cultural presuppositions (Sahlins, 1981, p. 67). The effect of putting culture into practice can result in something that is not always pre-given, not always expected or usual. There can be a reworking of sorts of new relationships through which practices come to "mean" something different as shown in the work of Sahlins (1992), but the process of change is messy and there are likely multiple slippages back into the usual (Ortner, 1999).

As Ortner makes clear both in her studies of gender making (1996), mountaineering Sherpas (1999), and her high school graduating class (2003), games are not discrete, isolated objects, but rather interpretations of objects that are themselves parts of larger societal and cultural games. In fact, there are multiple games being played simultaneously and particular actors may have various roles across a number of them at any one time. There are games within games and players playing across multiple social fields. There are also multitudes of rules, goals, and stakes for these games. In this chapter, we rely upon the metaphor of games and (sometimes serious games) as a theoretical category to explore the ways in which migrant students of Mexican descent are defined by the limiting structures of their situations and are also intentional participants in both creating and re-creating those situations. To attend accurately to the data, we move beyond a kind of class determinism to explore both the social constraints, such as ethnic stratification and class structures, and the efforts by students and teachers who struggle against them. We look specifically at the students' school experiences at the level of games—what they need to do (or not do) to be particular types of American high school students—and we also make reference to the larger games of schooling, that is, of the processes by which high schools "push" students into categorical social identifications by obscuring class in favor of ethnicity and personal qualities, such as studious and hardworking.

The Study: Methodology and Setting

Hillside High School (HHS), a comprehensive public high school located in the rolling hills above California's central coast, draws students from two distinct communities, Hillside and Appleton.[2] Hillside is a predominantly white, middle- to upper-middle-class professional town where the median family income is $73,515 (U.S. Census Bureau, 2002). Appleton is a mostly Mexican and Mexican American working-class agricultural town where the median family income for Mexican families living in and near Appleton is estimated to be about $33,000.

Both Hillside and Appleton are part of a large unified school district that serves over 19,000 students and is the fourth largest employer in the county (Valley Unified School District Homepage). Hillside High and Appleton High are the only two comprehensive high schools in the district. Appleton High, a school built for 1,500 students houses over 3,000, even though the district buses some 600 Appleton students per day to Hillside High. HHS is currently, with the additional students from Appleton, also overcrowded, serving 1,900 students in a school designed for 1,200. In the fall of 1998, when this study began, the ninth grade at Hillside High was nearly equally divided between non-Hispanic white students, who comprised 44% of the class of 2002, and students of Mexican descent (both parents of Mexican origin), who made up 42% of the freshman class. Another 6% of the ninth-grade class had one parent of Mexican origin, and the remaining 8% were Asian American, African-American, non-Mexican Latino, or of mixed ethnic descent.

Beyond differences in ethnicity and residential neighborhood, students from Appleton and Hillside vary dramatically in their socioeconomic backgrounds and realities. Eighty-one percent of the Mexican-descent students have two parents who emigrated from small towns in northern

Mexico with limited educational opportunities. As a result, more than half of the Mexican parents and 73% of the migrant parents attended eight years or less of school; only 6% of the migrant students had a parent who had any postsecondary education. Contrastingly, 62% of the white Hillside students had at least one parent who had completed a four-year college degree and another 26% had a parent who had attended some college. Furthermore, while many of the white students live in affluence, most of the Mexican-descent students live near or below the poverty level. Over half of the Mexican-descent students (including 61% of the migrant students) receive free/reduced-price lunches and, based on the free-reduced lunch rate of 80% at the elementary schools attended by most of these students, more were eligible.

Not surprisingly, issues related to socioeconomic class are, according to teachers and students, as salient as ethnic differences at HHS, but are often obscured, perhaps lost in the discourses of race and ethnicity. As noted by Ortner (2003), while class is often recognized in high schools where students from different neighborhoods are brought together in one setting, class boundaries become less visible than other sociocultural boundaries, such as ethnicity. One HHS teacher remarked that over the past twenty years he had witnessed increased class stratification at the school, and another teacher repeatedly voiced concerns that the administration had focused too much on racial and ethnic conflicts between Mexicans and non-Mexicans and not enough on classism.

Many of the interviewed students, both white and those of Mexican descent, addressed the emphasis on money and socioeconomic class, noting that what one wears becomes a status and class issue. And this was one way in which class was often talked about at Hillside High—as a comparison of goods, such as clothing and cars, or as an economic gradation of privileges tied to ethnicity. In a related way, class becomes a nearly hidden referent of ethnic categories used to describe differences (Ortner, 2003). For example, one teacher explained: "At Hillside High, if you don't have money, you don't have crap. You [a Mexican-descent student] enter the school grounds, passing the palm trees and the gate. You see all the nice cars in the parking lots and then you arrive on the big yellow limousine [school bus]."

This scenario pertains to the large majority of the Mexican-descent students, 93% of whom are bused to HHS each day from their homes in Appleton. In sharp contrast, only 26% of the white students ride the bus to school, most as a matter of convenience rather than economic necessity.

In this chapter we focus on the school experiences of a specific subset of Mexican-descent students at Hillside High—the 160 migrant students in the class of 2002, all of whom qualified for supplemental support through the federally funded Migrant Education Program (MEP). Many choose also to be members of the program's associated club, the Migrant Student Association (MSA). Like the large majority of their non-migrant Mexican-descent peers, these students face multiple obstacles to academic engagement, chief among them a sense of not belonging in the larger school culture (Gibson et al., 2004). But, in contrast to their non-migrant Mexican-descent classmates, many also from working-class backgrounds, the migrant students construct a space of belonging through MEP and MSA in which they make "successful" academic identifications and "resist" socioeconomic and cultural determinism by preparing themselves to graduate from high school and in many cases to attend college. While the large majority of these students' families do not follow the agricultural crops seasonally and instead live most of the year in Appleton, nearly half of the students leave the area in December, many of them returning to Mexico for a least a part of the time their parents are laid off during the winter months, due to the lack of agricultural jobs. Roughly 20% of these migrant students miss at least some days of school during January.

The findings we present here on migrant students of Mexican descent emerged from a larger, four-year longitudinal and comparative study of the entire class of 2002 at HHS conducted by a research team that included Jill Koyama and that was led by Margaret A. Gibson. Data for the study were compiled from many sources: interviews with students, teachers, school staff, district administrators, and students' parents; collections of federal, state, district, and school documents; students' class work and academic records; observations and participation at informal after-school gatherings, cocurricular events, teacher-training sessions, school board meetings, district-wide convocations and seminars, departmental meetings, pep rallies, athletic events, and graduation; and student surveys, including one completed by 248 students of Mexican descent and 256 white students in the ninth grade, a follow-up survey completed by 272 of these same students in the eleventh grade, a survey on club and sports participation completed by 170 students in grades 9–12, and a survey given to 64 migrant students, all MSA members.

Interactions at Hillside High School

To capture the schooling experiences of the migrant students, it is important to contextualize their situations within the practices, social structures, and overall stratification of the school and the communities it serves; the larger cultural, ethnic, and economic differences between the two towns; the historical ongoing tensions and conflicts between the white students and those of Mexican descent that focus on ethnicity, but also include class differences; and the position of the migrant students within the larger Mexican-descent student population. We do not present the story of the migrant students as mere encounter between two different ethnic or social class groups, but rather as one deeply situated within the multiplicities of the institutional practices and the ongoing social relations and interactions within the high school during a particular time in history, a time when there were active social movements aimed at diminishing either the presence or rights of Mexican immigrants in California. Exploring how historically created conditions made it possible for the migrant students to actively play or not play the game of becoming academically successful high school students contextualizes the agency exerted by individual students.

Mexican Students Arrive at Hillside High School

Prior to the early 1990s when the district began busing Appleton students to Hillside High in order to relieve severe overcrowding at Appleton High, the HHS student body was predominantly white and middle to upper middle class. Soon after the initial transfer of the Mexican-descent students to HHS, many of the white parents began expressing concerns that academic standards at the school, which is known for its excellent college preparatory and Advanced Placement (AP) courses, had suffered. During the early and mid-1990s, a vocal body of Hillside residents advocated secession from the Valley Unified School District and pushed the state to allow them to form their own separate school district, a district that would (again) largely exclude Mexican students and serve predominantly middle- and upper-middle-class white students (for a further description of this movement, see Hurd, 2003). Although the movement to secede has faded, in part due to district reorganization that gave the schools in and around Hillside more local control, Hillside parents continue to make up the overwhelming majorities in HHS's Parent Teachers Association (PTA), Site Council, and Boosters Club, thus exerting substantial influence, often in the form of middle- to upper-middle class cultural capital, over the school's programs and practices.

Constructing "Them": The Non-English Speakers

In California, a state that has traditionally experienced high immigration from Mexico, the consequences of learning and speaking (or not learning and not speaking) English have emerged as important rallying points not only in boundary maintenance, but also as a way of defining and indexing "us" (those who fluently speak English) in comparison to "them" (those who do not). Across the state, English monolingual ideology has been repeatedly invoked to construct an "American ethnicity" (Ricento, 1998). During the 1980s and 1990s, a series of propositions that promote the use of English and limit the rights of Mexican immigrants, many who speak Spanish as their native (often only) language, were passed. In 1986, California voters approved Proposition 63: English as the Official Language. In 1994, Proposition 187 (parts of which were later overturned) made undocumented immigrants ineligible for public social services, including education; in 1996, Proposition 209, for all practical purposes, repealed Affirmative Action policies in the state and public entities; and in June 1998, Californians approved Proposition 227, which essentially brought to an end bilingual education in public schools.

At Hillside High, as in schools throughout the state of California, the propositions, which changed the rules and increased the stakes in the game of learning English, have had a chilling effect on the education of the students whose home language is other than English, which at HHS means 91% of Mexican-descent students. The impact is even greater for English learners, and at HHS 63% of the migrant students and 26% of the nonmigrant Mexican-descent students in the Class of 2002 were designated as Limited English Proficient (LEP) on entering the ninth grade. These students are placed for much, sometimes most of their school day in English Language Development (ELD) and Sheltered or SDAIE (Specially Designed Academic Instruction in English) classes, creating in practice a pattern of segregation. This type of segregation, although troubling to the teachers who teach "English learners," is not readily changed. One faculty member explained: "There's not any easy answer because we still divide the kids by their language needs sometime during the day. . . . we put them in SDAIE classes. We put them in ELD classes. That's great, and it gives them what they need academically, but it segregates them from . . . the rest of the population."

At HHS, as in many other schools, being classified as LEP and placed into ELD and SDAIE classes restricts students' contact with native English-speaking students and, more importantly, creates both physical and linguistic isolation and constructs "non-English" speakers as relative outsiders. This resonates with the findings of Valdés (2001), who points out that even students who are being taught entirely in English "have very little access to English" (13) because of the segregation, in classes and across campus, from their English-speaking peers (see also Hurd, 2004; Mendoza-Denton, 1999).

In addition, there are restrictions and practices in certain classrooms that define when Spanish is and is not spoken—and that in effect devalue the speaking of Spanish. For instance, in one reading skills class the teacher

discouraged the use of Spanish by students "for their own good." He remarked: "[If I don't] do bell assignments, they engage in social behavior
that may not be appropriate. They revert to Spanish, and then I have to get
them back again [into English]." Many at HHS fail to recognize the value
of Spanish for the Mexican-descent students. For example, 60% of the
white students surveyed in the ninth grade said that Mexican students
would "fit in better if they didn't speak Spanish to each other"; only 19%
said they liked being at a school where "so many people speak Spanish."
Some teachers also commented that if the Mexican students would learn
English and refrain from speaking Spanish they could become "successful"
and "fit in better at Hillside," an apparent assumption being that speaking
Spanish precluded the learning of English.

In general, English learners felt neither "encouraged" nor "supported"
to speak English. Even students designated as Fluent English Proficient
(FEP) expressed hesitancy about speaking English in certain situations.
Ronaldo, a migrant student who is fluent in both Spanish and English, explained that he spoke little in his classes because of his embarrassment in
speaking English in front of white students; our observations of him in
classes confirmed his comments. Many others, including some of the migrant students who were taking the toughest AP classes and were "on
track" for college, reported a similar reluctance to speak out in class for fear
of mispronouncing some word in English and embarrassing themselves, or
possibly even subjecting themselves to some more overt form of ridicule by
classmates (Gibson, 2005). Those who were still learning English were even
more unwilling to speak out in class, but not necessarily in other settings.
For example, a handful of Mexican-descent males who spoke very little in
their ELD classes, felt free speaking English to one another outside of class.
One of the students explained that speaking English outside of class was
"less dangerous" than in class, where he would be judged by the teacher and
by better English speakers. Another English learner, who consistently insisted on using Spanish in his ELD classes—when he could have attempted
English—suggested that he did so to confuse ("mess up") the teachers. Actions such as these of resisting or "not-learning" English reinforced some
teachers' perceptions that Mexican students weren't particularly interested
in being educated. However, student reluctance to use English in class, or
outside, may have other very different meanings. It may reflect fear of embarrassment or ridicule, since the school has not created safe environments
for students to make mistakes, which of course is a necessary part of learning, or it may reflect actual resistance to learning English and assimilation
into American culture due to the students' wish to maintain a strong Mexican identity (Mendoza-Denton, 1999). English may be seen as replacing
Spanish and, thus, viewed by Mexican-descent students as a form of *sub-*

tractive acculturation (Gibson, 1998). It may also indicate their refusal to play in the game of conformity, a form of play set by, and mostly followed by, the middle-class white students.

Belonging in Schools

Fitting in and belonging for Mexican-descent students is difficult given that students who live in Hillside in essence "own" the high school. It belongs to them and they know it. They form the dominant groups on campus (Gibson et al., 2004). Teachers confirm this view. "At Hillside High," one teacher explained, "white students occupy the space. It is their space. They are comfortable. They fill it. They are confident. They are conversing. They are at ease." In contrast, the same teacher noted that for students of Mexican descent "there's a feeling of otherness, especially with the limited English speakers and migrant students who come and go and have to work much harder to belong, to fit in, to make their places of comfort at school, if they can." It is as though there are two schools, one attended by Mexican students and one by the white students. Thus, within Hillside, social contact between students from different ethnic and class backgrounds is clearly organized and limited. In the game of overcoming such organization, of belonging, Mexican students struggle to play, perhaps even struggle to become legitimate players.

The intraschool segregation is firmly established in the use of physical space on campus. White students occupy the center spaces of the HHS campus, especially the central courtyard referred to as the "Quad," while Mexican-descent students almost exclusively congregate in the periphery of the campus, in particular, in and around the building referred to by many white students as "Mexicoville" because it houses both the Migrant Education Program and the Spanish for Spanish Speakers classrooms. As one teacher observed, Mexican-descent students "hang out around corners," because, as this same teacher concluded, they find comfort and safety along the margins. It is, she explained, the only place "left for them" as no other settings have been purposefully created for them by the school.

Other teachers, as well as many of the white students, believe that Mexican students segregate themselves due to their inability or unwillingness to integrate and participate and their strong tendency to "hang out with their own people." This view of Mexican-descent students was the focus of an article in the student newspaper titled "Students Practice Voluntary Segregation" (November/December 1998). In it, Mexican students were said to prefer to be with one another and thus chose not to enter the Quad. The ideas expressed in this article, like those of many of the teachers and white students, constructed Mexican-descent youth as students who preferred to remain separate, to be with *their* own people—who, in reality, did not wish to mix with white students or to participate in the social life of the high school. Migrant students perhaps fared even less well, being seen as students who not only wanted to socialize with other Mexicans, but in particular, wanted to hang out with "poor wetties," a slang reference to the derogatory term of *wetbacks* used by some white students to signify Mexican immigrants, usually poor, who cross the Rio Grande into the United States.

In sharp contrast, the large majority of Mexican students explain that they feel uncomfortable "hanging out in the Quad," many noting great discomfort even in passing through this area of campus because, they told us, white students made them feel like they don't belong there. Some described specific and repeated incidences of being verbally assaulted; food was even hurled at them by white students. As one eleventh-grade migrant student put it: "Hanging out in the Quad is not okay if you're Mexican. It isn't like really a place for Mexicans. Bad, really bad things happen there. . . . They [the white students] make fun of the way you look, like the things you wear, and the food we eat, and speaking Spanish, and well, it isn't worth it to me, even if I am hungry and want to cross it to get some lunch fast. . . . Or even if I want to listen to bands [which often play during lunchtime activities staged there], I walk around, you know, the back way . . . I hang out in the back just to hear, but mostly I just don't go there much."

Others said much the same, noting that "The Quad is only [for] white people," that white students "stare at you as you walk by," and they "judge you a lot." It is clear that many of the students of Mexican descent don't feel that they "belong" in the Quad and certainly, from their accounts, they do not seem to be welcomed. It is unclear, however, to what extent the students have internalized what Bourdieu (1984) refers to as "the choice of the necessary," where one's experience of social status, class, and cultural distinction makes certain behaviors unthinkable. In this sense, the students may be eliminating the option of going to the Quad because it has already been refused to them.

White students recognize the segregation of spaces on campus and the social divisions it represents. They, too, commented on feeling discomfort walking through parts of campus where large numbers of Mexican students hang out. For the most part, though, their discomfort does little to limit their sense of belonging or their overall social and educational opportunities. It certainly does little, if anything, to challenge or jeopardize their class or social status. As one teacher noted, white students tend to project an attitude of privilege and ownership, with many questioning why Mexican students even attend HHS or, alternatively, indicating that their presence is unimportant to them. As one white student explained, if the Mexican students stay "along the backs of the buildings when we're having our activities going on in the Quad, most of us don't even pay attention to them."

Moreover, the two groups of students often attend different classes, white students heavily represented in the college preparatory and AP classes, while Mexican students are overrepresented in the basic skills, general education, and English language development classes. Mexican-descent students are also underrepresented in school-wide events, student government, and extracurricular school activities. As one migrant student put it, "if you're Mexican, the biggest challenge [at HHS] is getting involved." In the ninth grade, for example, only 11% of the Mexican-descent students were involved in a school-sponsored sport compared to 52% of their white classmates. For those who completed four years at HHS, sports participation rose to 30% for the Mexican-descent students and 72% for white students. Club membership follows a similar pattern. Only 6% of the Mexican-descent students joined a club their freshman year, compared to 22% of the white students. Club participation increases each year for both groups, but Mexican-descent students mainly join clubs such as MSA, where all or most of the members are Mexican and Spanish speaking. Those who joined other clubs were usually third-generation students whose families had middle-class jobs, who fit easily into mainstream school activities—and for whom, because of their class irregardless of their ethnicity, such activities were designed.

Migrant students in particular and Mexican-descent students in general report many reasons for their low participation in sports including cost, lack of transportation, after-school jobs, and family responsibilities, but added to these economic reasons is the fact that many Mexican-descent students believe they will not fit in. One boy, a migrant student, explained: "Sports are, well, made for the white students and white coaches and well, white parents, families. I mean how many Mexicans do you see surfing or playing tennis or whatever. I mean many of us play soccer and we are good at it, and we hoop [play basketball] at our houses, but not at school. No. And we don't really feel comfortable playing because we know that the sports and groups are not made for us. They [the coaches] don't even like try to get us to play. . . . They, well no one really sees us as athletes or surfers or what."

In short, the students of Mexican descent do not feel that they belong. They do not feel welcome on athletic teams and hence do not play, thus helping to solidify a perception of Mexicans as "non-jocks" or not interested in participation. In this sense, they disengage from participating in what they knew were literally (and metaphorically) the games played by mostly middle-class white students and by some middle-class, more assimilated Mexican students. The less assimilated Mexican and migrant students' disengagement constructs participation in extracurricular activities, especially athletics, as a particularly middle-class game.

Ethnic Tensions: Making the Foreign Other

Very few of the Mexican-descent students who attend HHS participate in gangs, although they are frequently referred to by white students, in jest and otherwise, as *cholo/as*, "gang members," or as "gang wanna-be's." Still, overall, students and teachers indicate that ethnic tensions, including gang violence and physical fights between Mexican and non-Mexicans, or among Mexican students, have diminished since the mid-1990s. When asked about gangs, one teacher suggested that while only a handful of the Mexican-descent students were active gang members, she understood why they might like to reify the mainstream belief that they were affiliated with gangs. She explained:

> [S]ome of the students who are non-academically oriented can enjoy the rub off of coolness of being seen as a gang member because you can make yourself look gangish if you're not. And, well, that gives you a bit of control and power in perception from the white students that you wouldn't, you know, normally get because you're a geek. But you're wearing some big ole pants and a big ole shirt and so suddenly they're a little scared of you. It gives you a sense of power that you don't usually walk around with when you know the white students are walking around feeling powerful. Well, not so much powerful, but feeling confident and comfortable that this is my space and I'm supposed to be here. . . .

Others, who seemed less insightful than this teacher, let their perceptions (and possibly fears) about students' gang affiliations guide their daily behaviors and routines on campus. A teacher recounted the following dialogue: "I heard a comment in one of the classes, . . . when I was in one of the Anglo classes, and students were saying, 'I'm not going to that bathroom. It's a gang bathroom,' and I thought you know there aren't that many bathrooms for students and it's like the only bathroom in the entire upper campus. It's not a gang bathroom, but there appears to be Spanish students hanging out and using it, so it must be a gang bathroom obviously. I thought how absurd."

Another teacher and a few white students, in contrast, confided to us that they never used that bathroom, not because they thought it was a "gang bathroom," which they agreed would be an absurd designation, but because they had seen "Mexican gang members" hanging out there in between classes.

Still, despite a paucity of actual gang members or gang violence, visible signs of covert racism and ethnic tensions persist, and conflicts over celebrating Mexican holidays or special occasions highlight the ethnic divisions. Only 16% of the white students surveyed in the eleventh grade indicated that Cinco de Mayo and Mexican Independence Day should be celebrated at HHS, and in 1999 members of the South Side Surfers, a white clique, were accused by the school administration of planning to disrupt the school's Cinco de Mayo celebration (HHS Newspaper, 1999). In 2000, over half of the student body skipped school on May 5 due to planned Cinco de Mayo events, either not wishing to participate, using this as an excuse to skip school, or claiming that their parents kept them home to avoid conflict, or in the case of many Mexican-descent students, choosing to spend the day instead at Appleton High to participate in its more genuine and conflict free celebration (Regional Newspaper, 2000).

The troubles that erupt on these days are not unidirectional. For example, during the Mexican Independence Day Assembly in 1998, a vocal handful of Mexican-descent students "booed" the American flag and the National Anthem (HHS Newspaper, 1998). Yet many Mexican-descent students view these occasions as the only time when the school creates a space and time for them to publicly celebrate their ties to Mexico and to Mexican culture. As one Mexican-descent female student commented following the 2001 Cinco de Mayo celebration at HHS: "They [the white students] were dying because we brought the Mexican flag over. . . .We are proud we're Mexican. . . ." It also bothers some white students that first- and second-generation students of Mexican descent typically self-identify as "Mexican" rather than as Mexican American or American. Combined, these incidences and the multiple published reports generated from them (or perceptions about them) give rise to the definition of the Mexican-descent students as "anti-American," the construction of the foreign others.

In addition to nasty incidents that predictably occur at school-sponsored (and generally poorly planned) celebrations of Mexican Independence Day and Cinco de Mayo,[3] there are constant small, visible, and enduring symbols of ethnic tensions on the Hillside High campus. Confederate flags, White Power notations, and racist remarks, including the juxtaposed statements, "Mexicans suck" and "Whites suck more," are engraved in the steel door of a student bathroom, and similar graffiti appears intermittently in common areas such as the library bulletin boards, and on personal items, including students' notebook covers.

It seems likely that the behavior of the students of Mexican descent are the result of individuals resisting the hegemonic system of the school, of refusing to play the games of assimilation, and of "acting white." Practice theory provides a way of recognizing the importance of these individuals who exert their agency and who create "a whole variety of counterforces" (Ortner, 2003, p. 79) that were underestimated both by Bourdieu (1978, 1984) and Karl Marx (1965 [1867]) in their theories of social stratification and class struggles. The individuals who struggle against assimilation may or may not change their own academic outcomes. Many do, but the outcomes for some who refuse to play the games of assimilation look similar to those who had no access to the games or who played faithfully by the rules, but who failed anyway. However, in the aggregate, the counterforces created by the struggles inform and construct multiple and varied alternative pathways to positive academic outcomes that may over time, impact the rules that secure hegemonic practices in schools.

Academic Performance

Recent scholarship positively links a student's sense of belonging and acceptance in school to increased academic engagement and performance (Gibson et al., 2004; Goodenow and Grady, 1993; Osterman, 2000). The converse is also true; students who feel marginalized in school perform don't perform as well, and the national pattern of low academic attainment among Mexican-origin youths is reflected at Hillside High. While almost all white students on entering the ninth grade take either algebra or geometry, and a third are placed in accelerated English, only half of the Mexican-descent ninth graders are placed in college preparatory classes. Many of the white students, who are well prepared academically, also exhibit confidence in the classroom. One teacher, who observed a ninth-grade English honors class, had this to say: "They [the students] were running the class . . . they just ran it. The teacher was in the room, but I didn't really see any needed interaction. They had control. They went from one to the other. They did (the) questioning of each other, support for one another. They fed food to them (their classmates) when one of the presentations had some food associated with it. They organized that and got it all out. They were just totally running it in a confident way where everybody was moving forward with the academics that way because it was a communal expectation of 'hey, this is what we're going to do' . . . it was the middle class thing to do and they knew it, knew it well."

This class was made up entirely of white students, all of whom possessed the cultural capital needed to succeed and provided to them by their middle-class upbringings. At HHS, students of Mexican descent do not "run" classes. In fact, the few who do enroll in AP or honors classes (with the notable exception of AP Spanish) remain nearly silent. One teacher observed this to be the case with her teacher's aide, a Mexican-descent student who did not participate in his chemistry class. The student explained that he felt uncomfortable talking in a class where he was the only Mexican. Numerous other Mexican students, even third-generation students who were fluent in English, echoed this sentiment (Gibson, 2005).

The pattern of low achievement and a sense of not belonging among the Mexican-descent students persist over time. At the completion of the ninth grade, the mean grade point average (GPA) for white students was 3.03 (on a 4.0 scale), yet for Mexican-descent students it was 2.09; 57% of the white students but just 19% of the Mexican students had a GPA of 3.0 or better. By the end of the twelfth grade the gap remained even though many of the Mexican-descent students who were struggling academically, had left HHS. A similar disparity emerges in terms of successfully completed college preparatory courses. Among the students who graduated from HHS in June 2002, 64% of the white students compared to just 21% of the Mexican-descent students had completed all the courses required for admission to the University of California at Los Angeles (UCLA) or California State University. Furthermore, only 59% of the Mexican-descent students who entered HHS in August 1998 graduated from Hillside High four years later. Notably, however, 69% of migrant students stayed at HHS and graduated from the twelfth grade, compared to just 26% of the nonmigrant first- and second-generation Mexican-descent students and 60% of the third generation Mexican-descent students. In addition, 9% of the migrant students finished elsewhere in the area, bringing the migrant student high school graduation rate to 77%. Perhaps even more remarkable, 47% of those migrant students with a ninth-grade GPA of 1.8 or lower graduated from Hillside High, compared to just 11% of the nonmigrant students of Mexican origin and 13% of the white students with similar GPAs.

Paradoxically, while the migrant students at Hillside were exceeding both Hillside graduation rates for Mexican-descent students and nationwide graduation rates for migrant students, teachers repeatedly determined migrant students to be unfocused, undisciplined, and lacking command of the curricula materials. In one English Language Development classroom, the teacher's interactions with migrant students usually began with a qualifying phase: "I know you haven't been here for most of the year" or "you won't know this because I don't think you were here," or "just do what you can, but you won't know this material because you weren't here." This particular teacher's perceptions was that the migrant students' trips to Mexico handicapped them in the game of being "serious" and "focused" high school students. Unfortunately, such constructions were not only being made by this particular teacher. For example, in one of the mathematics classes, a teacher accused a migrant student of being "uninterested in graduating" because the student "had traveled to

Mexico again over the winter break." Nonmigrant students of Mexican descent in the same class told us that they hesitated to work on assigned group projects with migrant students because "who knows what they learn there [in Mexico] and what they've missed here [at HHS]." In fact, the so-called uninterested migrant student was an officer in the Migrant Student Association (MSA), had a cumulative GPA of 3.4, received an A in the math course, and expected to attend UCLA. Thus, the perceptions of this working-class migrant student were constructed more by the necessities of his family's class standing than by his actual achievement.

The Migrant Student Association

With its 110 members (2001–2002 school year) the Migrant Student Association at HHS is one of the high school's two largest student clubs. Its mission is to "promote higher education, celebrate cultural differences, participate in school activities, and organize community service activities" (MEP Handbook). MSA is designed to attend to the social and academic interests and needs of migrant students, but like other student clubs at HHS, it is open to all students who wish to join, and a significant 28 percent of the members are nonmigrant, including three of the club's four officers (2001–2002 academic year). Although almost all MSA members are students of Mexican-descent, there is considerable diversity in the membership—freshman to seniors, recent immigrants and U.S. born, and students in the top quartile of their class to those with failing grades. A few have gang ties, but only a few. Three-fourths are female and two-thirds are seniors, drawn to the club in part because of its emphasis on helping students gain access to higher education. One third of the seniors had a GPA of B- or better and, based on college preparatory courses taken and completed, were also on track for admission into the California four-year college system.

Participating in MSA

We look at the interactions between the MSA students and the club's two advisers within a context that is consciously designed to be supportive and inclusive. We focus on how the MSA members mediate their overall marginalization at HHS through their participation in MSA, and how MSA is purposefully structured and maintained as a space where migrant students "belong"—where they are encouraged to integrate and solidify their connections to each other, to academics, and to their Mexican heritage. Members and advisers work together to coconstruct academically successful, belonging, and engaged students. Members create positive

Mexican and school identifications that seem improbable, if not impossible, in other settings at HHS, given the larger social and cultural context of the school and its patterns of segregation.

When asked why they participate in MSA and why the club is important to them, members offer a range of responses but they all revolve around the sense of belonging and support the club provides. As one senior explained: "there aren't a lot of places [at HHS] where Mexicans feel accepted, and MSA has a type of environment where they make students feel comfortable." Others said they participated "because I like how this club treats us equally." It's "a special club for Mexican American students; it makes us feel important." "It allows people that are Mexican or migrant to have somewhere to go."

Beyond the community created within the club, students also explained that through their participation in MSA they feel more connected to the larger school, and are able to have a voice and an impact. "We feel wanted and we feel part of the school by doing activities with MSA," one student commented. Others said, "it makes us stronger. . . ." "Having the MSA club is important because Latino students can learn how to become more involved and comfortable with the campus." The migrant students, most of whom refused to play in or felt marginalized by the more "mainstream" organizations on campus, participated actively and enthusiastically in the MSA. It functioned as a countergroup that shared many of the values of the other school-sponsored organizations and through MSA, migrant students became active members of the school community, albeit in lower-visibility activities.

The club also emphasizes leadership and giving back to one's community. The two often go hand-in-hand, as students develop leadership skills as they plan and carry out a wide variety of service activities. During they 2001–2002 year these included erasing graffiti in their neighborhoods, preparing food baskets for needy families at Thanksgiving, organizing a clothing drive, and engaging in a pen-pal project with a fourth-grade class to let them know that success in high school and college attendance were within their reach.

Literally and metaphorically, MSA provides a space, a playing field, for the migrant students' voices and actions. All MSA members are Spanish speakers, and they are free to use either Spanish or English or both when talking to each other or to the club's advisers about social and academic concerns and situations. One MSA member noted, ". . . you feel you belong because there are people that you know and that even speak the same language you do." The ability to express themselves in the full range of their languages, in a "safe space made just for them," encourages students to voice their opinions and to participate in ways that are denied them in other HHS settings among their white peers and teachers. Within MSA, these students are engaged in the serious game of being a high school student, rather than peripheral "players."

More than individual players, the migrant students and other MSA members, together with the MSA advisers, become a "team" of sorts. "MSA is a club that unites all of the migrant students of HHS," stated one member. Another added that the club "unites all Mexicans in order to make a difference in this school." Together, the migrant students and the advisers bond to create what various members describe as "family" and "close friendships."

The club advisers acknowledge their conscious efforts to create a close-knit, caring atmosphere. One explained: "I think just the fact that making students feel that they're part of something and sharing personal things with them and for them to see you as, 'This is my friend, this is somebody that really cares for me' and I mean, just respecting the students and demanding the same from them, I think that it is something that I bring with me. . . . [O]nce they see that we really care and we want to help, I think they feel part of it, and it just becomes like a family."

Members recognized the advisers' efforts and many said that they participate in MSA because they know the advisers genuinely care for them as students, as youths of Mexican-descent, as community members—and as people.

Students also emphasize the importance of being able to identify with the advisers, who they trust with personal as well as with academic concerns. MEP teachers, who also serve as the club's advisers, are trusted mentors and role models for the migrant youths (Gibson and Bejínez, 2002). Both advisers attended local public schools, are themselves the children of migrant farmworkers, live in the same neighborhoods as many of the students, and are active participants in the Mexican community in Appleton. They point to the importance of creating strong relationships with students that extend beyond HHS and often associate with the MSA members and their families outside of the school setting. One adviser plays soccer and basketball with his students on the weekends and attends the same Catholic Church that many of the students attend.

At school, MSA members go to the MEP office for academic support as well as for personal guidance. The two advisers assist the migrant students with school assignments and preparations for college, but more notably, students assist one another, sharing academic resources and knowledge. Seniors often work together on college, scholarship, and financial aid applications. Numerous members credit their participation in MSA and the support they received there as their main motivation to attend college. More broadly, MSA members express the value of studying and interacting with other students. One nonmigrant MSA member commented, "I participate [in MSA] because it gets me to work with people and it doesn't matter if it's with friends or not." Many friendship and peer networks are formed in MSA that act as resources, or as peer social capital (for more on peer capital among working-class students of Mexican descent see Stanton-Salazar, 2004).

Students' connections with one another are also reinforced through their participation in MSA weekly meetings and committees, and sponsored events. Some students attend nearly every meeting and hold offices in the club, while others attend meetings and join in MSA-sponsored activities less frequently. Yet, these migrant students, who are nearly absent in larger HHS activities and ceremonies, are welcomed, even encouraged, to participate in MSA meetings and events. Some organize and facilitate an end of the year MSA ceremony and graduation banquet, held in conjunction with Appleton High's migrant students. The ceremony includes an optional religious ceremony, a dinner accompanied with mariachis, speeches delivered by the students, and a dance. This resembles the graduation ceremonies from Mexico and is one of the many ways in which MSA creates close ties between home, school, and community. The ceremony celebrates not only the students' academic achievements but also honors their Mexican heritage. Students who have been nominated by their peers, give speeches where they formally thank their families and MEP for their support.

Conclusion

In this chapter we have looked at the school experiences of migrant students of Mexican descent in a California high school by focusing on the interactions and encounters between the migrant students, their peers, both white and of Mexican descent, and their teachers. It is clear to us that in certain situations, like the encounters in the Quad, the white students' and teachers' representations of Mexican-descent students, migrant students in particular, construct the migrants as marginalized "others." It is also true that the migrant students have struggled against and "resisted" such constructions while simultaneously making their own identifications.

In spite of the many obstacles in their path, the large majority of Hillside High's migrant students graduate from high school. With the support and guidance of MEP and MSA, these students construct a successful pro-academic Mexican student identity (Gibson, 2005), in essence by creating a new set of game rules. In MSA, unlike other settings across Hillside High, they are encouraged to participate fully; they are legitimate players. It is there, with their migrant peers and advisers that they escape, if only temporarily, from the institutionalized daily rituals of the school that construct them as not belonging. Against all of the constraints of HHS—including the inequitable practices of tracking and isolation, the racist discourses promoting English monolingualism, and the class stratification—the migrant students, with their MEP teachers, create and maintain a space of belonging in an otherwise isolating campus. There, interacting with each other, the migrant students transcend the dominant representation, in which they are seen as academic and social outsiders—as ethnic, social class, and linguistic "others." Situated within the highly patterned and structured practices of the school, which serve to conserve the academic "success" of the white students, the migrant students construct themselves as engaged and achieving high school students.

And perhaps these migrant students' experiences have a great deal to do with class and less with ethnicity. However, in the United States, to speak of ethnicity, is often in many ways to speak of class. Ortner (2003) suggests that to consider the class/race/ethnicity linkage one "consider the ways in which racial and ethnic groups represent to one another their own class desires and fears" (p. 52). For most of the working-class, migrant, and Mexican-descent students in our study, who inhabit marginalized positions in the larger Hillside campus, the predominantly middle-class white students, with their cultural capital, represent the referent by which they gauge their own academic "success," their own ability to play the game of being a "successful" high school student. Most of the white students know exactly how to get decent, if not good grades, and know how to make out college applications, which is more an unspoken expectation than a distant goal. Most of the migrant students do not inherently know these things and must struggle to "construct" themselves as academically successful. Through their participation in MSA, the students create alternative pathways by "playing" with, and by appropriating the rules of, the "success" game. They struggle against the constructions of their white and Mexican middle-class peers—and in essence "reconstruct" themselves.

Finally, returning to the metaphor of serious games, we conclude that the migrant students of Mexican descent play multiple games simultaneously—broadly belonging and participating in high school, learning English, constructing alternative paths of possible social mobility, and developing pro-academic and ethnic identities in MSA. They are indeed "made," through their encounters with their teachers, and with their white and nonmigrant Mexican peers as the linguistic, cultural, and socioeconomic "others." Yet, they also "construct" themselves as belonging, engaged, and achieving students. Through their participation in MSA, they (re)define their positions within HHS in ways that challenge their configurations as foreign "others" and provide for the possibilities of participating in the larger game of schooling at HHS. At this point, there is an ongoing working out of things social—the identities constructed for and by the migrant students, the boundaries of contexts or playing fields in which the migrant students participate, and the determinants and values of rules and goals in the "serious game" of being a migrant student of Mexican-descent in an American high school.

Notes

1. Power does not directly make or determine "others," but it does structure the fields of action, guiding the course of conduct and ordering the possible outcomes. Power is central to the totality of ongoing social processes, which are characterized by positioned interpretations, values, and ideas (Williams, 1977, pp. 108–9). It is ever present in interactions by which we force "others" into comprehensible (and usually ordered) categories. Power, then, is not a static system of domination, but rather processes that define the "norm" while constantly being resisted and challenged.

2. All names are pseudonyms.

3. Due to the history of tensions, the school administration no longer celebrates these days at HHS. Rather than making a concerted effort to plan activities more carefully and to embed them in the educational curriculum, the school has decided instead to replace them with a more politically neutral "World Week." This lack of recognition of Mexican holidays is a major disappointment to the Mexican-descent students, three-quarters of whom stated on the eleventh-grade survey that these days should "definitely" be celebrated at school.

Acknowledgments

The research discussed in this chapter was made possible in part through generous grants from the Spencer Foundation (199900129) and from the U.S. Department of Education/OERI (r305t990174), Margaret A. Gibson, Principal Investigator. We also wish to acknowledge our gratitude to all of the students and staff from Hillside High School who have contributed to this work.

References

Bourdieu, P. 1978. *Outline of a theory of practice.* Cambridge: Cambridge University Press.

———. 1984. *Distinction: A social critique of the judgment of taste.* Cambridge: Cambridge University Press.

Gibson, M. A. 1998. Promoting academic success among immigrant students: Is acculturation the issue? *Educational Policy,* 12, 615–33.

———. 2005. It's all about relationships: Growing a community of college-oriented migrant youth. In L. Pease-Alvarez and S. Schechter (Eds.) *Learning, teaching, and community: Contributions of situated and participatory approaches to educational innovation.* Hillsdale, NJ: Lawrence Erlbaum Associates.

Gibson, M. A. and Bejínez, L. F. 2002. Dropout prevention: How migrant education supports Mexican youth. *Journal of Latinos and Education*, 1, 155–75.

Gibson, M. A., Bejínez, L. F., Hidalgo, N., and Rolón, C. 2004. Belonging and school participation: Lessons from a migrant club. In M. A. Gibson, P. Gándara, and Koyama, J. P. (Eds.) *Peers, schools, and the achievement of U. S. Mexican youth* (pp. 129–49). New York: Teachers College Press.

Gilroy, P. 2000. *Against race: Imagining political culture beyond the color line.* Cambridge: Harvard University Press.

Giddens, A. 1979. *Central problems in social theory: Action, structure and contradiction in social analysis.* Berkeley: University of California Press.

Goodenow, C. and Grady, K. E. 1993. The relationship of school belonging and friends' values to academic motivation among urban adolescent students. *Journal of Experimental Education*, 62(1), 60–71.

Hurd, C. A. 2004. "Acting out and being a "schoolboy": Performance in an ELD classroom. In M. A. Gibson, P. Gándara, and Koyama, J. P. (Eds.) *Peers, schools, and the achievement of U. S. Mexican youth* (pp. 63–86). New York: Teachers College Press.

———. 2003. "Belonging in school: The politics of race, class, and citizenship in the Pajaro Valley Unified School District." Unpublished doctoral dissertation, University of California, Santa Cruz.

Marx, K. 1965(1867). *The Communist manifesto.* New York: Washington Square Press.

Mendoza-Denton, N. 1999. Fighting words: Latina girls, gangs, and language attitudes. In D. Galindo and M. Gonzales (Eds.) *Speaking Chicana: Voices, power, and identity* (pp. 39–56). Tucson: University of Arizona Press.

Ortner, S. B. 1994. Theory in anthropology since the sixties. In Dirks, N. B., Eley, G., and Ortner, S. B. (Eds). *Culture/power/history: A reader in contemporary social theory* (pp. 372–410). Princeton: Princeton University Press.

———. 1996. *Making gender: The politics and erotics of culture.* Boston: Beacon Press.

———. 1999. *Life and death on Mt. Everest: Sherpas and Himalayan mountaineering.* Princeton: Princeton University Press.

———. 2003. *New Jersey dreaming: Capital, culture, and the class of '58.* Durham: Duke University Press.

Osterman, K. F. 2000. Students' need for belonging in the school community. *Review of Educational Research*, 70, 323–67.

Ricento, T. 1998. National language policy in the United States. In T. Ricento and B. Burnaby (Eds.) *Language and politics in the United States and Canada* (pp. 85–115). Mahwah: Lawrence Erlbaum.

Sahlins, M. 1981. *Historical metaphors and mythical realities: Structures in the early history of the Sandwich Islands Kingdom.* Ann Arbor: University of Michigan Press.

———. 1992. *Anahulu: The anthropology of history in the kingdom of Hawaii.* Chicago: University of Chicago Press.

Stanton-Salazar, R. 2004. Social capital among working-class minority students. In M. A. Gibson, P. Gándara, and J. P. Koyama (Eds.) *Peers, schools, and the achievement of U. S. Mexican youth* (pp. 18–38). New York: Teachers College Press.

U.S. Census Bureau 2002. Demographic profile (Table DP-3). Profile of Selected Economic Characteristics, Aptos CDP, California: 2000, published May, 14 2002. Retrieved May 17, 2002 from http://censtats.census.gove/cgi~bin/pct/pctProfile.pl.

Valdes, G. 2001. *Learning and not learning: Latino students in American schools*. New York: Teachers College Press.

Williams, R. (1977). *Marxism and literature*. New York: Oxford University Press.

Introduction

Adalberto Aguirre Jr. aptly expresses some of the frustration facing Latina/o faculty members encountering stereotypes in their careers in academia. His expression, "the field is still a field" is appropriate, but should be contextualized, for as the Native American educational anthropologist Bryan M. J. Brayboy (2003) correctly points out, "doing fieldwork" in the academy is not the same as "doing fieldwork out in the fields." Despite the clarification, this citation reflects a complex set of issues involving racial, meritocratic, and consumerist implications when analyzing social class. In general, the stereotype is that most educationally mobile Latinas/os, especially those of Mexican heritage, are of farmworking or poor working-class origins. The truth is that many of us are and many of us are not. Even within the income brackets known as "working class," there is considerable variation and intergroup oppression, for now we know that modernist interpretations of labeled groups such as "working class" are not coherent, collective, essentialized, homogeneous wholes (Morrow and Torres, 1995).

Scholarship on class analyses have not been as prolific as studies of race, while educational mobility studies for minority students have received some attention (Gándara, 1995). Academic research tends to be compartmentalized into variables, when in reality race, gender, class, and other "variables" are so interwoven that they are not exclusive, but mutually dependent and informing (Hatt-Echeverría and Urrieta, 2003). Scholars of color in particular, in an effort to combat the pathological images of minorities as deviants, disadvantaged, or as the products of "cultures of poverty" (Galdwin, 1990) produced by whitestream scholarship, have focused on race without clearly associating race to class and to other related variables. Sandy Marie A. Grande (2000) refers to "whitestream" as the cultural capital of whites in almost every facet of U.S. society. "Whitestream scholarship" would thus be academic scholarship, not necessarily produced by whites, but that produced by any scholar to support white cultural capital (perspective and values). The term *whitestream* is used as opposed to mainstream in an effort to decenter whiteness as dominant.

This chapter explores the intricacy of how social class is attributed with explicit and implicit racial, meritocratic, and consumerist characteristics in Chicana/o educational experiences. The data presented in this chapter is from a larger qualitative study of twenty-four educationally successful Chicanas/os. The bulk of the data is drawn from the "retrospective interview" (Gándara, 1995) method employed. Theoretically, using the concepts of the habitus and of figured worlds in practice and social practice theory, this chapter explores how educational mobility is tied to class in the history-in-person (Holland and Lave, 2001) of Chicanas/os in a complex array of experience. While some Latina/o students from working-class backgrounds learn to "play the game" (Urrieta, 2004) of education, many do not. The complexity lies in the social, cultural, and economic landscape of the Latina/o contextual "geography" of the United States. This contextual geography will be further discussed, as will the practices that allow some working-class students to enter and play the educational mobility game, and others not.

Background

The data in this study builds on the Chicana/o scholarship focusing on attainment in higher education and on the "survival" practices of Chicanas/os as resiliency and more recently as persistence (Gándara, 1995; González, 2001; González et al., 2001; Hurtado, 1994; Padilla, 1999; Stanton-Salazar, 2001). Agency in this literature is seen as the will and the drive to achieve academic "success," especially through social networks and strong familial ties, despite the barriers that the system might produce. The most influential work as a foundation to this chapter is Patricia Gándara's (1995) seminal work on low-income Chicana/o educational success.

Gándara's study (1995) is fundamentally important because it is a study of the first documented cohort of low-income Mexican-Americans with low family educational backgrounds to complete doctoral level education. Gándara (1995, pp. 114–15) highlights the importance of the active implementation of affirmative action programs, financial assistance, and active college recruitment during the 1960s. "These subjects attended college during a period when opportunities were opening up for minorities. Major civil rights legislation had recently passed and colleges and universities were recruiting minority applicants and, in many cases, funding their educations. . . . The importance of the time cannot be overstated."

Gándara's subjects attended college during the 1960s and 1970s and completed Ph.D.'s, M.D.'s, or J.D.'s. Her study includes a second cohort of Chicanas/os to compare to the first in fundamental characteristics and experiences. The second cohort completed advanced degrees between the late 1980s and mid-1990s.

Gándara found that the subjects in her study shared some common characteristics in their educational development. These characteristics are highly important when analyzing consultant[1] heuristic identity development K–12 in the life histories documented in this chapter. These characteristics were as relevant during the time when Gándara conducted her fieldwork as they are now. In effect, what I found are the "ripple effects," as one consultant in this study put it, of these first cohorts of Chicana/o scholars referred by Gándara (1995, p. 11) as ". . . the 'advance team' for a new generation of Chicano scholars, born in the fields and the barrios, but educated in the nation's elite universities."

The characteristics identified by Gándara were parenting styles with an authoritarian figure, most often with the mother playing an active role in education, and families sharing values believed to be attributed to the middle class. This includes a "hard work" ethic where children are well aware of their parents' work and oftentimes work with them. Family folklore included a "culture of possibility" and sustained the view that education is a strategy for mobility.

Gándara attributed educational attainment to intense personal drives for achievement where her subjects often made "vows" to not live in the kind of poverty they were born into, thus depending on persistence, hard work, and to a lesser degree on ability for educational mobility. "Opportunity" played a key role in gaining access to college preparatory curriculum and to the information and resources that made attending college a reliable goal. Contact with white peer groups was important and often Chicana/o students attending schools in racially mixed schools had greater access to resources (in economic and whitestream cultural and social capital).

Gándara highlights the fact that low-income students possessed some of the characteristics attributed to the middle class (i.e., a hard work ethic, persistence, and cultures of possibility). This variation in characteristics and practices illustrates that the working class is not a homogenous collective, as often outdated modernist and generalized quantitative validity claims would have us believe. The contextual "geography" (and I use this term in quotes because I am referring to the social-historical landscape of the Latina/o community) is thus multiple, intricate, and varied in terms of identity (including race, gender, class, sexual preferences, religion, and generational and linguistic differences). The following section will attempt to explore a brief and general explanation of what that landscape might look like in terms of the Latina/o working class.

Contextual "Geography" of the Latina/o Class Systems in the United States

There is an infinite possibility of interpretations of what the social-historical class landscape might look like for the Latina/o community in the United States. In order to begin to explore that landscape, however, keep in mind that even though the Latina/o community has recently been given media attention due to the 2000 U.S. Census reports, this community is not new to the United States. In fact, what we now call "Latinas/os" or "Hispanics" were living in what is now the United States long before 1776. The continuous flow of Latin American migrants over the centuries, but especially after 1910, has consistently strengthened and diversified the characteristics of this community.

Although the possibilities are multiple, I will argue for three major systems in practice in this Latina/o class landscape. The first is the Latin American class system, keeping in mind that social class is not independent of race, ethnicity, gender, sexual preferences, religion, educational levels, and so forth. The second system is the U.S. whitestream system, and the third is a hybrid system, a local system that fuses and orchestrates aspects of both. Latinas/os in the United States orchestrate aspects of all three in different degrees, especially those living in communities with a high Latina/o presence.

The Latin American class system tends to be well-defined and rigid. I will use the example of Mexico for context specificity and also because the focus of this work is on Chicanas/os, but I also wish to clarify that this system is also multiple and complex. *My interpretation of this system is but a glimpse of what could be written about it.* In Mexico there is, and has been, a visible economically wealthy elite group that is small and highly exclusive, an almost nonexistent middle class, and a rather large number of poor, working-class people. Keep in mind that poverty in Mexico is very different than in the United States. Historically, race has, and continues to play, a strong role. The active rejection of indigenous people has often equated being uneducated, lacking reason, and being marginal and poor to being *indio* (Indian) (for further discussion see Urrieta, 2003b). Mobility in this system is difficult and resources are scarce, since the national elite and foreign investors have an almost complete monopoly over production. This is especially true after the implementation of the North American Free Trade Agreement (NAFTA) in 1994 that caused the large waves of undocumented immigration to the United States. Class is especially important in defining people's place in this system, often more so than other variables such as race, although race is always associated with class, but you can escape your "race," if you can move up in class. An abundance of terms to clearly demarcate class exist such as *chusma, Naco, chúntaros, indios,* and *mal educados* (uneducated). Keep in mind, as Sophia Villenas (1996) and Guadalupe Valdes (1996) have pointed out, that the concept of *educación* (education) in Latin America means something very different than education in the United States. *Educación* is a system of manners, like habitus dispositions, which also indicate class status.

The second system is the U.S. class system. This system is too, rigid, and well-defined, but the differences are not as obvious because of the consumerist, meritocratic illusion of being middle class. In Latin America the poor know they are poor; in the United States many poor think they are middle class. People in the United States are often blind to the reality of their socioeconomic conditions. In the U.S. system, race and class are also interdependent historically, but race takes a much more prominent role that diverts attention from class. The opposite is true in Mexico, where until recently there was no acknowledgment of racial problems until the Zapatista rebellions in 1994 (Holloway and Peláez, 1998). The U.S. system actively promotes itself as a meritocratic, democratic, and just system where hard work and personal drive are rewarded with the American Dream, regardless of race, gender, disability, or religion. This is a system where successful minority people are showcased as the proof that racism does not exist and yet there has not been a single nonwhite president, a women president, and much less an openly gay president, or Muslim president to show for it. This myth of meritocracy equates people living in deplorable conditions of rampant crime, drug use, run-down schools, and so forth, as the working class, of any race, not as the result of societal inequalities and racist structural outcomes but actively places the blame on individuals and communities as failures.

The third system is a hybrid Latina/o system that is constantly being remade. In this system, some elements of the Latin American class system reform in the U.S. context, complimenting the U.S. class system in some ways, and clashing in others. This hybrid system varies according to locality and can be as particular as to a family unit and as broad as the Latina/o U.S. imagined community (Oboler, 1995). In this system *la chusma* and *los Nacos* still exist, but so do, *welferas* (women on welfare), narcotraficantes (Drug Lords), *cholos/as* (gang members), "white trash," "hood rats," "lowlifes," "bumbs," "wetbacks," "*mojados*," "sellouts," "High-spanics," and so forth. In this system there is a great division. Differences exist according to who is U.S. born and who is an immigrant, who is legal or undocumented, who speaks English, who is bilingual, and who is a monolingual Spanish speaker. There is a difference in who calls herself Hispanic, Mexican-American, Latina/o, Chicana/o, Salvador-eña/o, Boricua, and so forth. There is also a difference in who is of European, mestizo (of mixed racial heritage), Indian (Native), or black heritage, and the sociohistoric pigmentocratic hierarchy of skin color in Latin America (with white having the highest privileges and prestige) helps to sustain white supremacy in the United States. For example, studies have shown that Latinas/os of a more white-looking phenotype tend to be more successful in U.S. society. As an example, take the personal histories of the mostly white-looking Cuban refugees given asylum and economic assistance in the 1960s. Generation differences, educational attainment levels, religion, and age are all also important distinctions in this hybrid system as well.

The orchestration of the three systems explored here is constant for people who maneuver themselves in all three systems, and in many more.

As an example, this might include an individual spending time in Latin America with her grandparents in a rural indigenous village, living in a predominantly working-class urban U.S. Latina/o neighborhood, and working in an all-white business environment. The constant improvisation and orchestration is crucial to be able to function in such different environments. The focus here is on three very general and broad examples, yet the possibilities for many more macro- and micro-examples of class systems exist. In any case, people learn to perform within the dispositions of their environments (habitus) at an almost unconscious level due to how society has socially and historically positioned groups of people. In order to participate in another environment, people need to relearn those dispositions so that they are able to perform in those secondary environments. Such is the orchestration that I will explore in this chapter as it relates to Chicana/o educational success, but in order to proceed, I wish to revisit the concepts of the habitus and of figured worlds.

Theoretical Frameworks

Habitus and Figured Worlds

Pierre Bourdieu (1977) defines the habitus as a "way of being," a set of "dispositions," a "tendency," and "inclination" toward certain practices learned at an unaware level due to the social positioning of groups of people produced historically. For example, when Adalberto Aguirre (1995) refers to himself as a "curiosity" for his white students and colleagues that he is therefore a "stranger" to Stanford, he is conveying the dispositions of his working-class, farm-working origins. According to the material and symbolic experiences of his history-in-person as a working-class Chicana/o, he expresses his subjective and internalized system of structures, schemes of perception, conception, and action of his upbringing (p. 86). Regardless of how much "success" he enjoys, he always will have those humble origins as his primary habitus that will forever keep him estranged from full participation (both in reality and in his own perception).

Habitus is thus a "matrix of perceptions, appreciations, and actions" (Bourdieu, 1977, p. 83), produced historically and reproduced individually and "naturalized" and experienced as a "taken-for-granted." Jon Webb, Tony Schirato, and Geoff Danaher (2002, p. 15) provide a useful definition of habitus: "Habitus can be understood as, on the one hand, the historical and cultural production of individual practices—since contexts, laws, rules, and ideologies all speak through individuals, who are never entirely aware that this is happening—and, on the other hand, the individual production of practices—since the individual always acts from self-interest."

Habitus is thus more of a macro-defintion of the cultural practices that inform the dispositions of the working class. I wish to use this concept cautiously, however, because I refrain from generalizing in the modernist tradition and thus to essentialize groups of people as collective wholes. In whitestream U.S. society however, it is safe to say that "those groups that have alternate systems of habitus may have little opportunity for public participation" (Blackledge, 2002, p. 70), unless they learn to practice the practices of the secondary whitestream habitus.

Identity is key in understanding how habitus and figured worlds function in relation to class and other interrelated variables. Dorothy Holland, William Lachicotte, Debra Skinner, and Carole Cain (1998) current understanding of identity is one of becoming, not of being. Identity is thus a site for the social "authoring" of the Self, or auto-*naming*, embedded in a collective past and created in practice through life experiences, or through history-in-person (Holland and Lave, 2001). Therefore, identities are always in process, mediated by cultural artifacts and discourses, but are also capable of improvisation. Improvisation at particular moments or in specific situations and contexts is a key factor because it can lead to the creation of an altered identity. Thus, a person from a primary working-class habitus, can enter a middle-class habitus with the intent of "changing" some of the alienating practices of the secondary habitus through improvisations. Holland and her colleagues (1998, pp. 17–18) elaborate, "Improvisations are the sort of impromptu actions that occur when our past, brought to the present as *habitus*, meets with a particular combination of circumstances and contradictions for which we have no set response. . . . In our view, improvisations, from a cultural base and in response to the subject positions offered *in situ*, are, when taken up as a symbol, potential beginnings of an altered subjectivity, an altered identity."

Holland and her colleagues' (1998) social practice theory also incorporates the Bhaktinian concept of dialogism, which implies that humans can entertain different internal dialogues simultaneously, and can thus orchestrate participating in multiple habitus and figured worlds at the same time. This enables people, in practice, to embody internal tensions and contradictions. For example, Chicana writer Gloria Anzaldúa (1987, p. 85) writes, "*A veces no soy nada ni nadie. Pero hasta cuando no lo soy, lo soy.*" (Sometimes I am nothing and no one. But, even when I am not, I am.) Thus Anzaldúa expresses the ability to exist in the contradiction of being everything and nothing simultaneously.

In the same vein, Chicana scholar Dolores Delgado Bernal (2001, p. 626) states that a mestiza consciousness is both "born out of oppression and is a conscious struggle against it." These seemingly contradictory stances are in line with the notion of dialogism and *hybridity* that imply that Chicanas/os have multiple essences, *ni de aquí ni de allá*, "not from here nor from there" (Mexico or the U.S.). Implied is also in-betweeness, not really Indian or Spanish, not Mexican nor "American," not really English or Spanish but Spanglish, not really the United States nor Mexico, but Aztlán. And thus emerges the hybrid third-class system of Latinas/os in the United States, incorporating Latin American elements with U.S. whitestream class system structures.

The following excerpt from a poem, submitted as a personal document by a Chicana in this study, helps illustrate a few of the contradictions:

> I am a mixture
> Mestiza, indigenous, African, and gachupina
> All bloods run through my veins
> And pump the blood in my heart
> Chicana, Mejicana, Americana
> Mexican in America
> American in Mexico
> A mixture of three
> That combine into one

It is precisely these historical contexts, as described in the poem, often linked to place (the U.S. and Mexico) that help inform the collective/group memory in struggles against structural oppression (i.e., the cultural politics of Chicana/o identity).

Drawing from Aleksei N. Leontiev (1978) on activity theory, Holland and her colleagues' theory (1998) conceptualizes figured worlds as socially produced, culturally constructed activities to which we are recruited, drawn into, or enter and develop at different degrees and that we are dependent on one's position through interactions and participation. Figured worlds become more like processes or traditions as well as historical phenomenon to be apprehended as we are gathered up and given form as our lives intersect with them. "'Figured world' then provides a means to conceptualize *historical* subjectivities, consciousness and agency, persons (and collective agents) forming in practice" (pp. 40–41).

Thus, it is through participation (practice) in figured worlds that people reconceptualize historically who they are as individuals or collectives and through this consciousness come to understand their agency.

Holland and her colleagues (1998) state that figured worlds are social encounters, organized and reproduced by dividing and relating participants to each other while depending on these interactions and intersubjectivities for perpetuation. The significance of figured worlds is held by re-creating them by working with others in localized and temporal spaces that give voice to particular landscapes and experiences. Understanding figured worlds is useful to help us heuristically develop an awareness of how access to higher education and educational mobility is currently being acquired by working-class Latinas/os. In a sense the meritocratic and competitive model of educational spaces, enables only a very select few students of color real access to the "aspirations" of the American Dream and to others of the same group a deceptive lie that places blame on individuals for lack of success. For some students, educational success at an early age is already an "unthinkable" reality.[2]

Figured worlds compliment habitus in this chapter because figured worlds function from micro-locality to an infinite possibility of larger meaning; habitus is more rigid and defined, like the structures of society while figured worlds allow for more individual agency. Applying an understanding that there is a class habitus is thus appropriate in a broad sense due to the material and symbolic conditions experienced by groups of people historically. But access to micro-, local figured worlds allows for entry into a secondary class habitus—the "middle class"—through educational mobility. Such figured worlds are, for example, "ability groups" that lead a working-class student to be recruited to a magnet school, which may eventually lead her to a college education, as was the case with Isadora, who is discussed later in this chapter. The following section uses data from an ongoing two-year study of educationally mobile Chicanas/os in California to explore how Mexican-American students of working-class and upper working-class backgrounds (K–12) were allowed access to higher education and to social class mobility. This access was through recruitment into the figured worlds of ability grouping and tracking in schools.

Methodology

The Study

The anthropological methods used in this study fall within the general premise of "participant observation" (Davies, 2001). The general methods included (1) fieldnotes; (2) interviews; (3) observations of consultants in practice; (4) participant observations; (5) document and artifact analyses, including electronic mail; and (6) ethnography. Four groups of self-identified Chicana/o "activists" participated in this study according to the following group criteria: (1) undergraduates in the social sciences planning to enter the field of education at any level; (2) professional educators currently working in the field of education (K–12) either as teachers, counselors, administrators, and so forth; (3) graduate students in education programs; and (4) Chicana/o professors in the field of education.

Each group consisted of 6 people, 3 men and 3 women. Twenty-four interviews were used for the general analysis of the larger study (for further details on the study see Urrieta, 2003a). Consultant ages ranged from 19 to 57. To participate, consultants had to self-identify as Chicana/o, fit one of these four groups, and have a strong "activist" ideological orientation. Pseudonyms are used for all of the people in this study.

Interviews

Interview narratives were carefully analyzed before, during, and after transcription since this is the primary source of data. Although the interview protocol was semi-structured, most of the interviews were more like conversations rather than question and answer sessions. Interviews ranged between a forty-minute session and up to two, three-hour sessions, or six hours of recorded interviews.

Interviews were, for the most part, conducted in English. Some consultants used Spanish and others did not, or could not because they were monolingual English speakers or did not feel comfortable talking about academic matters in Spanish. All of the interviews were conducted exclusively through dyadic interaction except for one in which a consultant's significant other was present.

Retrospective Interview

Each consultant was asked to remember her or his development of their academic and social/cultural identities. Questions such as the following were asked:

Tell me about your educational experiences.

- Elementary, Middle School, High School.
- Was language ever an issue?
- What did you learn about being Chicano/Latino in school (K–12)?
- Undergraduate, Graduate School.
- Who have been your educational mentors? (Describe them.) How were they your mentors?
- What were you taught about how to be successful in school?
- Was that different from being successful at home?
- How would you say your culture defines success?
- How was what you learned in school different from what you learned culturally?

As already mentioned, the interviews were semi-structured so often the protocol questions were used to initiate the conversation only. Consultants were freely encouraged to recall events in detail. One consultant recalls that "My kindergarten teacher said I was smart and that I would do great things. She'd always tell my mom that."

In this study, similarities in K–12 experiences corroborate with Gándara's (1995) findings on the educational mobility of low-income Chicanas/os; income was not a criteria used in this study; each consultant self-identified as being of working-class (including upper working-class) origins. As opposed to most of their peers, almost all of the consultants developed a positive academic identity early on. This identification and invitation into the figured world of "smartness" (for a full discussion on smartness see Hatt-Echeverría, 2003) was created and nurtured mostly by teachers in the educational institutions that these students attended, whether these were public, private, or alternative schools. Once constructed as "smart," most consultants were placed in honors or gifted tracks that made them aware of being considered "smart," even if this changed for some in later grades. In private or rural school settings where student populations are not large enough to officially track, students were segregated into "high" or "low" ability groups. In all cases, students became aware early in their academic trajectory, with a few exceptions, that they were "different" from the "other" kids, even if the other kids were of the same racial/ethnic background, and were expected to perform well academically.

The main case where this was not found was with Julián and with those who entered the educational system as monolingual Spanish speakers. These students suffered under the stereotype of low teacher expectations of Spanish-speaking students, especially those enrolled in bilingual education programs. Another exception of this early "smart" identification is the case of a much older consultant in his midfifties. This was due primarily to highly racialized expectations of Mexican-American students in the time and context of his youth. However, "being an athlete" and attending an integrated, primarily white middle-class school was the impetus for his recognition as "smart" and for his subsequent placement into a "college track."

In such cases, students had to fight, literally and/or figuratively, against the perception of not being expected to be smart. Julián, for example, recalls teachers being frustrated with him for not knowing what a bonnet was. Such items of whitestream culture, although they seemed like "little things" to his teacher, were completely foreign in Julián's cultural world where bonnets did not exist, but *rebozos* did. Despite Julián's "demoralizing" experiences in low-quality English as a Second Language (ESL) programs, he became an avid reader. He was identified as "college material" by the time he was in high school, even though he refused to change his academic track, which was not considered to be "college bound."

Another example is Jaime, an undergraduate and second-generation immigrant.[3] Growing up in southern California in the late 1980s, he entered the public schools as a monolingual Spanish speaker. He enrolled in bilingual education programs in primarily Latino and African-American elementary schools. Although several teachers tried to "test him out" and officially track him as "gifted," his official redesignation was delayed until the fifth grade.

> Starting with kindergarten, my teacher said I was very smart and would do great things . . . I was in bilingual education until . . . the fifth grade because every time a teacher wanted to test me into the gifted program, we would end up moving. So in third grade a white teacher again said I was smart and would do great things and he took . . . four of us out and gave us separate work to prepare us for this test. So I took the test and got labeled as gifted and talented, but then we moved again and I was again placed into a bilingual classroom. And it wasn't till . . . fifth grade that I won a Math competition that they [teachers] finally checked my record and saw that I had been labeled GT two years before. Then I was moved to the GATE classes.

Despite teachers' efforts, every time Jaime had to change schools, his label as "bilingual" automatically placed him back into a bilingual track that is often disassociated with being "gifted." The reality is that there are probably thousands more like Jaime who are bilingual and gifted and never identified or even sought out because of mainstream educators' perceptions of children in bilingual classes (González Baker, 1996).

Another exception to the early identification as "smart" is Juan, a second-generation Chicano who entered an almost entirely Latino Catholic school in greater Los Angeles as a monolingual Spanish speaker in the late 1970s. His case is atypical of being identified as smart at a young age, but is quite typical of not having a memory of early educational experiences, probably attributed to the "sink or swim" English language learning approach and to the language learning process. "I really don't remember those days [in Catholic school]. I remember playing in the playground, talking to my friends . . . messing around in class, but in terms of education, I don't remember anything. I believe it's because it was English only and my language being Spanish, I probably don't remember what the teachers were teaching me."

Johnny remembers being pulled out of class to attend "special" classes in reading and he was fully aware of the fact that "special" did not mean it was good. "I remember them sending me to these special reading classes, but they were all in English with no Spanish support, so I learned how to read, but I didn't really understand what I was saying. I guess I knew I was slower and that made me feel bad."

In middle school, when he moved to another part of the city and transferred to public schools, he was automatically placed in bilingual and remedial classes based on his grades and standardized test scores. Johnny admits that he felt "more comfortable" because "other kids would speak Spanish," but did not feel that his classes were "challenging." It was not until high school that he insisted that his academic counselor transfer him to honor's classes because his older brother was in this track and he wanted to do the same. "Finally, after several times, I would say after the seventh time, he [counselor] got mad at me and told me if you don't make it don't say I didn't warn you and come back crying to me! And he finally authorized the permission for me to transfer to the honor's classes."

Johnny got A's, did exceptionally well in his honor's courses, and later attended a major public university and is now a bilingual public elementary schoolteacher in his home community.

Other than these three cases, all of the twenty-four consultants developed a positive academic identity early on. Most were tracked in the early elementary school years either in separate "high" groups, gifted and talented classes, or schools, such as magnet schools. In cases where consultants later deviated from this positive academic identity, this early identification served as a motivation for them to be able to again be perceived as academically oriented. In the cases where this early identification did not occur, as in those just mentioned, a later recognition of academic promise, even if with reluctance, was recognized. These students were eventually tracked into programs and classes that enabled them to have access to the officially labeled college-bound curriculum and later to colleges and universities. Of all the consultants, Julián and Johnny were identified the latest as "college material" by the tenth grade in high school, and in Johnny's case, this was mainly after several attempts and with great reluctance and communicated predictions of failure.

Alicia, now a continuation high school teacher, was the only female exception to continuous tracking, although she was identified as "smart" early on. Because of barrio social and economic conditions, Alicia deviated from her designation as smart, and became involved in high-risk activities that eventually led to her multiple pregnancies, and attending continuation school. It was not until much later that she met a Chicano teacher, and was able to regain her academic identity. She subsequently completed her Associate of Arts degree at a local community college, and later her bachelor's degree and teaching credentials from a prominent public university.

The sorting practices and subsequent labeling of the students in this study as smart created physical and social distancing between them and other Chicana/o, Latina/o students. Isadora, for example, thought of the "regular" students as "dumb." Through her new consciousness as a Chicana, she recognizes them as being in her own ethnic/cultural group by using the term *Raza*. ". . . like there were *Raza* at my school, but they were in regular . . . everyone always talked bad about like the regular kids and stuff . . . it's kind of bad, but I did feel like oh I'm not a regular kid. I felt kind of extra special or something. . . . I don't think I ever outwardly made fun of them, but I know that I would look at them and think, you're dumb!"

Eva, a second-generation Chicana now completing undergraduate studies at a state university also recalls, "Like B track was all the ESL people and we'd say, 'oh you know all the wetters [version of wetback] are all on B track,' and things like that."

In Juanita's case, the distinction between herself as a Catholic school student and those in public schools, even though she grew up in a predominantly Latino/a neighborhood, has a clear class connotation when she referred to them as *chusma* (low class) because they did not attend Catholic schools.

Even in cases where the distinctions made were not in such antagonistic terms, the identification as smart and subsequent tracking created distancing, especially for students like Phillip who attended schools that were physically, socially, and economically removed from the physical boundaries of the barrio. Because of his upper working-class status, Phillip had access to wealthier, more diverse, schools and access to whitestream society through his student peers. His mother's employment as a paraprofessional at a less wealthy school made him aware of the distinctions.

> . . . she (his mother) was a teacher's aid and worked with monolingual Spanish-speaking students. So I was totally exposed to that and exposed to people that just spoke Spanish and didn't speak much English and also who didn't have a whole lot of money, didn't have [a] whole lot of resources cause where she was working [it] was a very poor school. . . . I'd always go with her to events and things like that. She'd put on the assemblies for those schools and I'd be there watching those kids. So I knew at that time that there were kids that were different than me that were also *Mexicano* that spoke mostly Spanish and . . . lived in those kinds of environments.

Even though Phillip remembers having an active identification as Mexicano, his English language, and economic and upper working-class status, created distance from "those schools" and from "those kids" who lived in "those environments." For other students the separation occurred within the school. Tracking within schools was also identified by some to be culturally isolating because of the distancing from members of the same ethnic group. Therese recalls, ". . . it [school] was kind of isolating because my best friends didn't think they were smart. Like my little Chicanita friends, one of my friends I remember . . . she was in the slower class and she was like, 'You know I'm not smart like you.' She would always say things like that . . . but [in] K–6 a lot of my friends were white . . . high school was a little different; all my friends were Asian. It just transformed because they were in the honor's classes. . . ."

This isolation occurred in Therese's experience even though her school community was "about 80 percent Mexican." Phillip's case illustrates the physical removal from the community, while for Therese, it was the physical removal within the community and the "schools within schools" effect of tracking, even in schools with high minority populations.

Chicanos in U.S. society are also divided with internal strife that in many predominantly Chicana/o, Latina/o neighborhoods is manifested through differences between the generations, language use, and in gangs, as already mentioned. Henry, for example, described being "very critical" of his "own people" and using "derogatory terms" like *wetbacks* toward members of the immigrant generation. Making distinctions within the community was also evident in Eva's case where she recalls referring to ESL students as "wetters," or in Isadora's case as *chúntaros*, or to certain lower working-class neighborhoods as "chuntyville," or in the case of Santa Ana, California, as "Chuntana." In Therese's experience for example, her father was adamant about her not comparing herself, even physically, to Mexicans from Mexico. Yet her father was a "fighter" for rights and proud to be Chicano, a pride he instilled in his children at a young age.

Alexandra had a similar experience where a *mojado* (wetback), in her family's lore, was not a suitable marriage partner. "I do remember family members and people saying *mojado* all the time and using it in a negative way. Sometimes it was used just as an identifier to distinguish between second, third generation, and immigrant, but a lot of times, especially when it came to marriage, it was seen as a negative thing. Like if you're a Mexican-American and you marry a Mexican, they're using you to get their citizenship. I remember [my] family saying that."

Thus, differences illustrating internal community division and internalized oppression with implicit class distinctions abound, reflecting the effects of subordination and if not physical, then psycho-emotional self-destruction. Divide and conquer is in place.

Most consultants recall these differences becoming more pronounced during and after middle school, especially with regards to race, class, gender, and sexuality. In primarily Chicano/Latino communities there is a constant differentiation made between those "American" born and those born elsewhere, primarily Mexico. Those distinctions become quite pronounced and even lead to violence and aggression among students and community members. On the other end *pochos*, "wannabe gringos," or

"High-spanics" were common retorts by members of the first generation. The terms *norteño* (northerner for U.S. born) and *sureño* (southerner for Mexico born) also became identifiers for groups and gangs. Alicia, the continuation high school teacher, recalls such divisions. "I didn't see too many differences between them [gangs]. Besides of course, you know the *Norteños* were all Chicanos and the *Sureños* were all from México ok. By the way, my kids' dad actually was a *Sureño*; he was a *Norteño* at first until he found out he was from México. And when he found out he was born in México, then he was hanging out with all the *Sureños*. . . ."

This example is not only indicative of distinctions made among Latino students, but also of the hybrid forms that emerge from a Mexican-origin identity. This example shows the plurality in the hybridity of the third class system explored earlier, but also in this case illustrates the permeability and constant improvisation of that hybridity.

For some of the consultants these feelings of difference translated into feelings of "embarrassment" or even "resentment" of the home culture and language, or dialect (i.e., Spanglish or other hybrid forms of language). Some consultants recalled feeling uncomfortable speaking "pure" Spanish or being around relatives speaking only Spanish in whitestream settings. Alexandra, for example, did not like having her third-generation fully bilingual mother speaking Spanish to her teachers.

> I didn't even think about that [the language issue] until maybe junior high or high school, the fact that my mom spoke Spanish. Like I didn't even think about that, like the only reason I knew is because when she would go to school and speak Spanish sometimes I would feel uncomfortable because I knew she knew English. . . . I didn't realize it but at that time I was privileging English because I was thinking well if she speaks English then they'll [teachers] realize that she can speak English to them.

Early on Alexandra was made aware of the fact that if her mother spoke in English she would somehow get better treatment and more attention from the teachers and administrators at the school.

Class plays an important implicit role as consultants in their K–12 experiences often equated lower working class with being more "Mexican," or having more "Mexican" cultural traits, somewhat like the classical Mexican context in which poverty is associated with being "more Indian" (Urrieta, 2003b). In Juanita's case she equated shopping at the swap meet (flea market), for example, as somehow being more "Mexican," "TJ" (for Tijuana), or *chusma* as opposed to shopping at name brand and expensive department stores like Robinson's May. Her father's old station wagon was also an issue because she was always comparing what she had to what she saw white people had on television.

All of the consultants felt that they had developed a positive academic identity at the expense of their ethnic identity to varying degrees and a good academic identity often equated being able to be of, or moving toward, a higher economic social class. Even when family and community provided supportive ethnic/cultural environments, the school devalued nonwhite culture and contradictions emerged. Phillip, Therese, and Anabel, for example, all said they had always had positive ethnic identities, yet Phillip and Therese, for example, both are primarily monolingual English speakers and Anabel's Spanish is limited. Spanish is not the first language for any of the three and none are of the first generation. Anabel had successful Chicana/o role models in her community, while Phillip and Therese had exposure to higher education through their parents' temporary, yet significant community college experience. Furthermore, Phillip's mother worked in the field of education as a paraprofessional.

Of those who had very negative, conflicted, and uncritical ethnic identity perceptions, most are fully bilingual, second generation, and spoke Spanish as their first language. Such is the case with Juanita and Miguel, and others such as Alicia and Alexandra who after coming to initiate the process of Chicana/o consciousness (learning about one's history) made a concerted effort to regain full literacy in the Spanish language. Most consultants, though, said they had developed from negative to ambivalent to positive feelings about themselves and their native home identities and culture because of their schooling and societal experiences.

There were some consultants for whom self-realization, self-identification, and self-recognition as Chicanos or Mexican-Americans or Mexicanos was always known, but not necessarily appreciated. For some, especially the younger consultants, it was both known and appreciated, but not critically. By critical, I mean that there was no revisionist analysis of the history behind the terms. For older consultants, a lack of self-appreciation was more defined and pronounced especially compared to younger consultants, who had already benefited from having socially conscious Chicana/o educators or community activists in their K–12 experiences. The implicit institutional message portrays nonwhite cultures as less valuable, even in communities where the majority is non-white.

Tracking Mechanisms and the Figured Worlds of K–12 Schooling

The following diagram can help to visually organize the academic and ethnic identity development arrived at through the life experiences, or history-in-person accounts in the larger study. It will also serve to facilitate the discussion of the findings in this section because it focuses on the narratives of academic and ethnic/cultural identity development that will be explored. The box represents the rigidity of schooling institutions.

K–12 Education

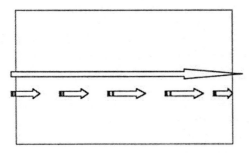

elementary/middle/high school

In this diagram, the interaction between community and institution is most prevalent in the K–12 phase, especially in the elementary school years, but it is not encouraged in significant ways.

Studies claim that Chicano/Latino parents in general have low levels of school involvement and participation. But, too much parent involvement is not welcomed especially of monolingual non-English-speaking parents. Language and cultural barriers in the formal structures of schools impede their participation, except when teachers with an activist consciousness, such as Juanita, intervene. Parents intending to advocate for their children's best interests and who are thus critical of certain educational institutional practices, are also not welcomed. As we progress to high school, participation diminishes and is also less encouraged and welcomed although there is plenty of rhetoric to the contrary. All of the consultants in this study reported that in most cases, both of their parents, or at least one, was very supportive of education. In the case of the *mujeres* it was often the mothers who were most vocal and encouraging.

The thicker arrow in the center of the box represents the tracking mechanisms used to segregate "smart" students in the K–12 system. It is within this arrow that the "successful" academic identity development of Chicana/o students is traced. The tracking of these students is manifested through segregated ability workgroups, classes, official tracks, or schools (i.e., figured worlds of "smartness"). This arrow is thin, rigid, and segregated compared with the overall student population, which would fill the entire box, because only a small number of students are allowed in gifted tracks that in later grades are called "college bound," "college prep," "honors," or "AP." This arrow becomes even narrower because the number of these academically successful students as identified officially in schools, gets smaller as students progress through the system so that by high school only a select group of students remain and are "eligible" for college admission.

Of those then who enter and graduate from colleges and universities in California, the number is even smaller. For example, in 1990, only 4.0% of Hispanics 18 and over in the state had completed a B.A. degree, 1.1% a master's, and 0.8% a doctorate or professional degree.[4] Laws such as SP-1 and SP-2 at the University of California that eliminated race or ethnicity as a consideration for admissions as did Proposition 209, which eliminated Affirmative Action in admissions decisions statewide in both the University of California and the California State University systems, worsened this situation.

A similar report (Gándara, 2000, p. 3) shows that the numbers of Chicanos/Latinos entering higher education in the state significantly declined post-209, especially in the University of California system. "In 1997, while affirmative action was still in effect, 13.2% of the entering freshman at the University of California were Chicano/Latino (of this 11.9% were Mexican-American). This percentage dropped to only 11.8 (and 8.8 for Mexican-Americans) in 1998—the first year in which the provisions of Proposition 209 were imposed." This report also concludes that those numbers are more significant at the University of California at Los Angeles (UCLA) and at Berkeley in the University of California system and at CSU San Diego and Cal Poly Pomona in the California State University system. The numbers of Chicanas/os, like those in this study, is minuscule compared to the larger K–12 Hispanic student population in the state that in the academic year 2000–2001 accounted for 43.2% of the total student population (California Department of Education, 2002). The university continues to be an isolating experience, especially for students coming from highly segregated Chicana/o, Latina/o neighborhoods, as did some of the consultants in this study.

Despite the large demographic presence, the arrow parallel to the academic identity development track arrow representing the ethnic/cultural identity development is broken. It is broken because there is no constant flow of support for the healthy and complete ethnic/cultural development of Chicana/o students in schools, except through community and family support networks usually not complimented in school structures and in the official curriculum. In the experiences of younger consultants this ethnic/cultural identity line is sporadically nurtured by the presence of a socially conscious Chicana/o, Latina/o teacher in the K–12 system, especially in high school. But that complimentary support is sporadic because the overall presence of Hispanic teachers in California was only 13.5% of the entire teaching force in 2000–2001 (California Department of Education, 2002, p. 213), and not all Hispanic teachers have a critical identity consciousness.

This number of educationally mobile Chicana/o students is thus quite small, not only in the state of California, but nationally. Census data

Table 1
Educational Attainment, Overall Hispanic- and Mexican-Descent
Population in the United States

Total	Overall Hispanic	Mexican
Less than 9th Grade	7.0%	32.3%
9th–12th Grade		
(no diploma)	8.9%	16.8%
High School	33.1%	26.4%
Some College or AA	25.4%	17.7%
BA	17%	5.1%
Adv. Degree	8.6%	1.8%
BA +	25.6%	6.9%

(2000) summarized in table 1 reveals the following national educational attainment percentages for Mexican and Mexican-descent populations in the United States as compared to the overall Hispanic population; keep in mind that Cuban-American educational attainment levels exceed those of non-Hispanic whites. The number of Mexican-American students who are educationally successful is indeed a small percentage. That issue itself should raise questions of access and equity for socially conscious educators, policy makers, education researchers, and activists.

This is especially alarming given that the total Hispanic population in the state of California was 32.4%, with Mexican residents and U.S. citizens of Mexican-descent accounting for 25% of the total California population in 2000. The Hispanic population also accounted for over 50% of the K–12 dropouts in 2000–2001 and only 32.48% of the high school graduates.[5] All of the consultants interviewed are part of this tiny group of people of working-class origins who have been educationally mobile by participating in the figured worlds of educational success; thus, having access to learn the practices of the middle-class habitus. The Chicana/o group is even smaller than the mainstream "Hispanic" category because not all people of Mexican descent self-identify as Chicana/o, and even less develop a critical identity consciousness.

Overall Findings

The findings of this data focusing on life histories and on the development of a positive academic identity through the figured worlds of academic success, are for the most part consistent with those found in Gándara's (1995, p. 114) study on the educational mobility of low-income Chicanos. Her study is historically significant because it documented Chicana/o educational mobility "during a period when opportunities were opening up for minorities." Gándara found the following to be important characteristics for low-income Chicanos/as who want to access higher education: (1) the importance of parental support, (2) a hard work ethic and the view of hard work as a mobility strategy, (3) family myths or folklore that creates a culture of possibility where mobility is possible, (4) and an intense personal drive and persistence. All of these characteristics coupled with the opportunity to have access to college-bound curriculum and to information and resources on the possibility of college attendance were of most importance in achieving higher education. Similar findings were found in this study.

All of the consultants had parental support; in cases where both parents did not support educational attainment at least one was very supportive. Because of language barriers, lack of formal schooling, or other factors, many parents did not know how to support education, but were always supportive of their children. All, but especially those children who more directly identified with working-class culture in this study, had a hard work ethic and often worked with their parents early on. This carried through to college where people like Therese worked three jobs through college and was currently working part time and running her own consulting business while finishing her Ph.D.

Several consultants expressed a folklore of wealth in their family's past. Anabel, for example, described her mother as "a working-class snob." Andrew's collective family memory recalled being landowners and losing that land in the 1800s after the U.S. invasion of New Mexico. This collective and family history might have been part of the motivation for his educational mobility, but also for his identification with Reies Lopez Tijerina and the Chicano movement. Nearly all of the consultants recall and still feel they have a strong personal drive. Phillip, for example, recalled this as always striving to be "the best." "I wanted to be the best at anything I did, so I wanted to be the best in school, the best soccer player, the best at football. . . . So college to me came as part of that motivation to be the best."

All of the consultants were persistent and goal oriented because they knew that educational mobility was a possibility. Such is the case of Johnny, for whom the possibility of being in the honor's track was a reality because his older brother was already in one.

In terms of access to the college-bound curriculum, with the few exceptions discussed, all of the consultants were identified as "smart" early on. This identification was really an exclusive invitation and recruitment into the figured worlds of tracking through ability groups, classes, programs, or schools that eventually got them into college-bound tracks in high school. Alicia is the only exception. Positive reinforcement in terms of academic achievement was influential in most of the cases since they were responsible for the students' drive and persistence. For those tracked early, this contributed to a very positive, but often judgmental academic identity that viewed students in lower tracks as "dumb," or "lazy." Tracking, along with peers, older siblings, partners, and minority recruitment programs provided the main means to access resources and information (social capital) about college and financial aid through the figured worlds of educational success.

The main differences with Gándara's work are that more established Chicano/a teachers and student organizations now have an effect on community life and on Chicana/o students in the K–12 system by impacting the lives of students and by advocating for them and their parents (for further discussion on the impact of community activists see Urrieta, 2003a). By providing opportunities for self-recognition and by motivating them, students like Julián are presented with a possibility usually not considered—attending a university. Higher education is usually not considered a possibility because of the working-class habitus that has historically positioned Latinas/os as not being college bound. Access to the knowledge and practices of the secondary habitus (the middle class) create the aspirations for educational mobility in those selected students. And the aspirations are created by participation in the figured worlds of smartness that make educational attainment an accessible possibility and that create a positive academic identity. Recall that identities are in effect also the outcomes of figured world participation. Jaime, for instance, was recruited to the university he now attends because of his academic identity even though he had already decided to attend a technical institute.

This study differs from Gándara's by tracing along with academic identity development the ethnic/cultural identity development of Chicanas/os prior to attending the college campus. The findings indicate that there is no consistent support system for the healthy ethnic/cultural identity development of Chicana/o students, even when strong family and community support networks exist. The U.S. educational system and society at large do not support the positive ethnic/cultural identity development of non-whitestream cultures. Thus, students developed either negative, ambivalent, or positive, yet uncritical views of themselves, their home cultures, communities, and society in general.

Orchestrating Habitus and Figured Worlds

The goal of this chapter is to speculate how a few select Latinas/os who have a working-class primary habitus (upbringing) are able to develop a secondary habitus that allows them to "play" the (middle-class) game, while most others are not. According to Bourdieu, the secondary habitus, if it is acquired at all, is acquired through social institutions like schools or through other forms of secondary habitus formations. Habitus is thus a broader macro-structural, sociohistorical outcome that creates the dispositions of being "working class." Important to remember, however, is that to use the concept of the habitus to essentialize to entire groups is also problematic and for that reason I recognize that not all working-class people share exactly the same dispositions.

Figured worlds in this chapter are more local and temporal, and function like habitus but at a more micro-level (although they can function at the macro-level as well). Figured worlds, like habitus, distribute power and teach its participants how power works, both in society at large (the habitus) in relation to the figured world and its participants, and within the figured world. From figured worlds people can emerge with altered identities.

In this study, all of the participants claimed to be of a working-class upbringing, yet because they possessed some of what are believed to be middle-class and whitestream dispositions, they highlight that the group labeled as Latina/o "working class" is not a collective whole. For some of the consultants in this study, those dispositions included being able to read in kindergarten, being articulate, knowing the story of the *Mayflower*, recognizing a bonnet, or simply being able to speak English. Furthermore, those middle-class and whitestream dispositions were recognized by teachers (the representatives of whitestream culture and its institutional agents) and are thus recruited, or invited into the figured worlds of smartness (i.e., educational success).

The figured worlds of smartness (e.g., ability groups) position its participants in relation to society as whole, in relation to their "average" and "slower" peers, and in relation to each other. In these figured worlds people are ordered and ranked (i.e., the smartest and the valedictorian) and power is distributed to the group in relation to its place in society and to its members in relation to each other. All the members of the honors' track, for example, have a positive academic identity and are considered to be smart. But, not everyone within this figured world has an equal claim to smartness, and some members are considered to be smarter than others.

These figured worlds, however, are the entry point that grant access to the material and symbolic resources and whitestream cultural capital that leads to higher education. Higher education, in a symbolic and not just material way, is the entry point into the middle-class habitus. Keep in mind that someone can win the lottery, for example, and become materially wealthy, but still not have the dispositions of the middle-class habitus, nor the credentials (symbolic capital) to grant her entry into that world.

All of the consultants in this study were recruited into the figured worlds of smartness early on, even though they were of a primarily work-

ing-class upbringing. Through the symbolic power distributed in these figured worlds, consultants emerged with a positive academic identity and access to higher education, even if at their ethnic/cultural identity's expense.
Recall Aguirre's statement cited earlier, "I have lost some of myself in that
(academic) journey." I must concur that so have I. The consultants in this
study, however, are actively engaged in regaining that ethnic/cultural identity through Chicanismo/a,[6] while a vast majority of successful Hispanics
and Latinos/as are not. People like Richard Rodríguez and Linda Chávez,
for example, have completely lost themselves in the process and uncon-
sciously bought into middle-class, whitestream culture and values.

Conclusion

Developing a positive academic identity is essential in gaining access to
educational and social class mobility. Tracking mechanisms like ability
grouping, magnet programs, and honor's tracks are the figured worlds
that select a few Latina/o working-class students who are recruited into
them and from which they emerge with the aspirations and whitestream
cultural capital to have access to higher education. The outcome is that a
handful have access to social class mobility and most do not. Education
thus functions as an enabling and disabling system.

To conclude, I wish to state clearly that I do not advocate that tracking is a means for working-class students to have access to higher education, even though it is for a select few. If anything, this system of seriated,
hierarchical power distribution serves to maintain the inequalities of U.S.
society and a racialized, consumerized, meritocratic system of deceptive
myths and promises of empty dreams to most working-class people.
Moreover, social class mobility should not be at the expense of one's eth-
nic/cultural identity. And when the symbolic violence of internal community division, internalized oppression, and self-hate within the Latina/o
community are also outcomes, the hegemony of whitestream culture and
white supremacy are in place.

Notes

The author wishes to express his gratitude to the Spencer Foundation and the
Gates Millennium Scholars Program for funding this research and to the editors
of this book for reading and commenting on previous drafts of this chapter. An
earlier version of this manuscript was presented at the annual meeting of the
America Educational Research Association, San Diego, 2004.

1. The reference to "consultants" in this chapter is another critical attempt
and choice of wording referring to "informants" or even previously known "subjects." This reference hopes to problematize the "relationships," or lack of, which

develop or do not develop while conducting research and the power dynamics involved that often exploit, misrepresent, or simply dismiss consultant knowledge as secondary to researcher knowledge. The notion of consultants shifts the roles and treats them as "experts" in community knowledge, actively involved throughout the research process; thus the reference to them as consultants rather than informants, participants, or subjects (Baugh, 1983; Hinson, 2000; Lassiter, 1998).

2. As a former eighth-grade teacher working with bilingual students, it became very apparent to me that some students already knew that they were not going to be academically successful. They were aware of the fact that they were not considered "smart" and that they were enrolled in classes where students like them were lucky if they graduated from high school. On many occasions students communicated to me that trying to convince them that they could be anything they wanted to be career wise was indeed a deceptive lie on my part.

3. In this chapter, first generation refers to the immigrant generation not born in the United States, second generation refers to the those born in the United States from immigrant parents, third generation refers to those born of second generation parents, and so forth.

4. According to the 1990 Census data in a California Postsecondary Education Commission Report, April 2001.

5. California Department of Education.

6. Chicanismo/a are the male-oriented and female-oriented ideological foundations behind the politics of the Chicana/o identity, namely, self-determination, an end to material and symbolic colonization, and to community empowerment.

References

Aguirre, A. 1995. A Chicano farmworker in academe. In R. Padilla and R. Chávez (Eds.) *The leaning ivory tower: Latino professors in American universities.* Albany: State University of New York Press.

Anzaldúa, G. 1987. *Borderlands/La Frontera: The New Mestiza.* San Francisco: Aunt Lute Books.

Baugh, J. 1983. *Black street speech: Its history, structure, and survival.* Austin: University of Texas Press.

Blackledge, A. 2002. The discursive construction on national identity in multilingual Britain. *Journal of Language, Identity, and Education,* 1(1), 67–87.

Bourdieu, P. 1977. *Outline of a theory of practice.* Trans. Richard Nice. Cambridge: Cambridge University Press.

Brayboy, B. M. J. 2003. The history of anthropology and future research: Conducting "fieldwork." In G. Noblit and B. Hatt-Echeverría (Eds.) *The future of educational studies.* New York: Peter Lang.

Davies, C. A. 2001. *Reflexive ethnography, A guide to researching selves and others.* London: Routledge.

Delgado B. D. 2001. Learning and living pedagogies of the home: The mestiza consciousness of Chicana students. *Qualitative Studies in Education,* 14(5), 623–39.

Galdwin, T. 1990. Poverty is being poor. In J. Spradley and D. McCurdy (Eds.) *Conformity and conflict: Readings in cultural anthropology.* Glenview, IL: Foresman and Company.

Gándara, P. 1995. *Over the ivy walls: The educational mobility of low-income chicanos.* Albany: State University of New York Press.

Gándara, P. 2000. Latinos and higher education: A California imperative. Chicano/Latino public policy seminar and legislative day proceedings. Sacramento, CA.

González, K. P. 2001. Inquiry as a process of learning about the other and the self. *Qualitative Studies in Education,* 14(4), 543–62.

González, K. P, Marín, P., Pérez, L. X., Figueroa, M., Moreno, J. F., and Navia, C. N. 2001. Understanding the nature and context of Latina/o doctoral student experiences. *Journal of College Student Development,* 42, 563–80.

González Baker, S. 1996. Demographic trends in the Chicana/o population: Policy implications for the twenty-first century. In D. R. Maciel and I. D. Ortiz (Eds.) *Chicanas/Chicanos at the crossroads: Social, economic, and political change.* Tucson: University of Arizona Press.

Grande, S. M. A. 2000. American Indian geographies of identity and power: At the crossroads of indígena and mestizaje. *Harvard Educational Review,* 70(4), 467–98.

Hatt-Echeverría, B. A. 2004. "Make Good Choices": Social Positioning, Control, and Silencing through the Cultural Production of being "Smart." Ph.D. diss. University of North Carolina at Chapel Hill.

Hatt-Echeverría, B. A. and Urrieta, L. 2003. "Racializing" Class. *Educational Foundations,* 17(3), 37–54.

Hinson, Glenn. 2000. *Fire in my bones.* Philadelphia: University of Pennsylvania Press.

Holland, D. and Lave, J. (Eds.). 2001. *History in person: Enduring struggles, contentious practice, intimate identities.* Santa Fe: School of American Research Press.

Holland, D, Lachicotte, W. Jr., Skinner, D., and Cain, C. 1998. *Identity and agency in cultural worlds.* Cambridge: Harvard University Press.

Holloway, J. and Peláez, E. 1998. *Zapatista! Reinventing revolution in Mexico.* London: Pluto Press.

Hurtado, S. 1994. Graduate school racial climates and academic self-concept among minority graduate students in the 1970s. *American Journal of Education,* 102, May 1994.

Lassiter, L. E. 1998. *The power of Kiowa song.* Tucson: University of Arizona Press.

Leontiev, A. N. 1978. *Activity, consciousness, and personality.* Hillsdale: Prentice Hall.

Morrow, R. A. and Torres, C. A. 1995. *Social theory and education, A critique of theories of social and cultural reproduction.* Albany: State University of New York Press.

Oboler, S. 1995. *Ethnic labels, Latino lives, identity and the politics of (re)presentation in the United States.* Minneapolis: University of Minnesota Press.

Padilla, R. 1999. College student retention: Focus on success. *Journal of Student Retention, Research, Theory & Practice,* 1(2), 131–45.

Stanton-Salazar, R. 2001. *Manufacturing hope and depair: The school and kin support networks of US-Mexican youth.* New York: Teachers College Press.

Urrieta, L. 2003a. "Orchestrating the Selves: Chicana and Chicano negotiations of identity, ideology, and activism in Education." Ph.D. diss. University of North Carolina at Chapel Hill.

Urrieta, L. 2003b. *Las Identidades También Lloran*/Identities also cry: Exploring the human side of indigenous Latina/o identities. *Educational Studies Journal, 34,* 147–68.

Urrieta, L. 2004. "Playing the game" versus "selling out": Chicanas and Chicanos relationship to whitestream schools. In B. K. Alexander, G. Anderson, and B. Gallegos (Eds.) *Performance theories in education: Power, pedagogy, and the politics of identity.* Mahwah, NJ: Lawrence Erlbaum and Associates.

Valdés, G. 1996. *Con respeto, bridging the distances between culturally diverse families and schools: An ethnographic portrait.* New York: Teacher's College Press.

Villenas, S. 1996. "Una buena educación: Women performing life histories of moral education in Latino communities." Ph.D. diss. University of North Carolina at Chapel Hill.

Webb, J., Schirato, T., and Danaher, G. 2002. *Understanding Bourdieu.* Thousand Oaks: Sage Publications.

6

HIGH SCHOOL STUDENTS' EXPLORATION OF CLASS DIFFERENCES IN A MULTICULTURAL LITERATURE CLASS

Richard Beach, Daryl Parks,
Amanda Thein, and Timothy Lensmire

One of the interesting political developments since the 1980s is the degree to which white working-class people, particularly males, are voting and registering as Republicans. White working-class males continue to identify with the Republican Party despite the fact that conservative Republican economic policies have resulted in no mean wage increase since the 1970s; large-scale reductions in well-paying manufacturing jobs; downturns in union memberships; and increased concentration of wealth, resulting in a disparity in income gaps between rich and poor, lack of affordable health care, cuts in benefits/retirements, and increasing tuition for higher education necessary for many jobs (Frank, 2004).

These political attitudes represent a shift away from the1930s and 1940s in which many white working-class males participated in Socialist and working-class organizations that articulated populist issues of class and government support for working-class people (Frank, 2004). In our own state of Minnesota, up until the 1970s, there was a strong, progressive, pro-labor/union tradition that successfully fought for and passed pro-labor legislation and relatively high taxes for social services and schools. Since that time, union membership has declined and the Republican Party has now gained control of most of the state's government, resulting in pro-business, anti-labor legislation, large tax cuts for the wealthy, and cuts in job training, education, health care, and social services designed to help working-class people.

In his review of economic history, Richard Ohmann (2003) notes that a major shift in economic policy occurred beginning in the 1970s with the rise of conservative and neoliberal agendas. Prior to the 1970s, the American economy was organized around highly stable companies, what David Harvey (1989) describes as "Fordism." In the 1970s, the breakup of these companies and the rise of "fast-track" economic theories resulted in the instability of "flexible accumulation" through "new sections of production, new ways of providing financial services, new markets, and, above all, greatly intensified rations of commercial, technological, and organizational innovation" (Harvey, 1989, p. 147). Ohmann notes that the "instability and excesses of this casino capitalism" (p. 33) has resulted in a shift from stable, well-paying, long-term, full-time jobs with benefits (Ford believed in paying workers so that they could afford his cars and decent housing) to "flex-time, part-time, and temporary labor; subcontracting and out-sourcing; job sharing, home work, and piece work; workfare and prison labor" (p. 34). This shift since the 1970s has resulted in a parallel shift away from the New Deal politics of strong government support programs and government regulation to a diminution of government support and deregulation, resulting in funding cuts for education, job training, health care, social security, child-care, and housing, particularly for low-income people.

These shifts have placed working-class people in a double bind. On the one hand, the transformation from manufacturing to "knowledge-economy" jobs requires increased higher education beyond high school. On the other hand, cuts in state and federal spending have resulted in large increases in tuition at state colleges and universities (tuition at the University of Minnesota increased by 38% from 2001 to 2004), pricing many working-class students out of higher education. A study by The Century Foundation (2004) found that at four-year institutions, two out of every three students from the wealthiest quartile enroll within two years of high school graduation, compared with one student in five from the bottom socioeconomic quartile. Seventy-four percent of students at the nation's top 146 colleges come from the richest socioeconomic quartile, and just 3% come from the poorest quartile. The fact that a wealthy student is twenty-five times more likely to be attending these colleges than a poor student is partially due to reductions in Pell Grant funding, most of which was designed to support low-income families. In the 1980s, Pell Grant funding covered nearly 60% of total costs of attending four-year colleges; now it covers only about 40% (The Century Foundation, 2004).

Americans dream of rising expectations for each new generation (Apple, 2003). All of this leads to the question, why do working-class white males support a conservative political agenda that has benefited upper-income people and hurt working-class people? One explanation of the appeal of a conservative agenda has to do with cultural values that take precedence over economic realities. Thomas Frank (2004) argues that working-class white males respond positively to a political appeal to "cultural authenticity" associated with "basking in the easy solidarity of patriotism, hard work, and the universal ability to identify soybeans in a field" (p. 40). This prototype is set against what is perceived to be the effete, intellectual, snobbish, morally questionable, white-collar worker aligned with the "knowledge-economy" that has excluded white working-class males, particularly those without advanced education. Frank quotes a Missouri farmer who described the kind of work he does as "measured in bushels, pounds, shingles nailed, and bricks laid, rather than in the fussy judgments that make up office employee reviews" (p. 39). Politicians such as President Bush seek these voters' identification by emphasizing down-home, conservative values, including an appeal to evangelical voters through references to "faith-based initiatives." This appeal to working-class people masks the economic realities of small-family farmers and business owners who have been put out of business by agribusiness conglomerates and corporations who funnel millions of dollars to fund conservatives' political campaign. As Frank notes: "Deregulated capitalism is what has allowed the Wal-Marts to crush local businesses across the Midwest and, even more importantly, what has driven agriculture, the region's raison d'être, to a state of near-collapse" (p. 46).

Society Economic Policies

To avoid focusing the blame on corporate owners, Frank documents that ways in which conservative politicians direct the blame on "liberal," secular intellectuals associated with New Deal/Great Society economic policies. He also shows how these politicians legitimize their claim to making economic arguments through cultural appeals based on anti-abortion, gay marriage, and anti-gun control issues as well as evangelical Christian values.

Working-class adolescents are very much aware of the problematic status of their low-income family world and the unfairness of the overall education and community-support system that provides little opportunity for future success (Beach, Lundell, and Jung, 2002; Eckert, 1989; Phelan, Davidson, and Yu, 1998). As one social worker noted (Sadowski, 2003, p. 25): "They really feel that they cannot make it. This is not just reflective of the family of origin from which they come, but from looking at society as a whole. These kids are not stupid; they are just aware of what is going on socioeconomically."

This sense of resignation suggests the need for educators to challenge conservative's appeal to adolescents by interrogating the values inherent in these appeals. If adolescents begin to perceive the problematic nature of these appeals, they may be less likely to support such policies and look more favorably at the kinds of alterative progressive agendas of the 1930s and 1940s.

Working-class students also face a diminution of support for public education due to cuts in school funding, education that might provide them with cultural capital. James P. Gee (2002) argues that a primary difference between the Fordist "Old Capitalism," which created an expansive middle class based on consumption practices, and the "New Capitalism," is that the New Capitalism is marked by the capacity to not only build one's portfolio, but to also manage and use it to define oneself as being the "right" sort of person. "If you have no Portfolio or don't view yourself in Portfolio terms, then you are surely in the 'lower class'"(p. 63).

This redefinition of class points to the importance of cultural capital available to middle- and upper-middle-class adolescents through family and institutional resources, particularly in terms of expensive after-school activities/technology tools, resources often not available for working-class adolescents. Even if affirmative action programs are available for working-class students, these students may therefore have difficulty accumulating certain credentials necessary for admissions to elite schools. And, while working-class students do succeed in academia, their struggles are rarely made explicit, particularly in terms of acquiring the cultural capital associated with being the "right" sort of person. This was evident in a longitudinal study tracking the development of Crystal, a rural working-class female, over a five-year period from her senior year through four years of college (Payne-Bourcy and Chandler-Olcott, 2003). In high school, she posed as middle class by appropriating middle-class literacy practices, but continually struggled during college because she had difficulty linking these practices to the dominant discourses operating in her college courses. She also lacked the resources, support systems, and access to faculty afforded to middle-class students. Her high school and college coursework rarely addressed issues of class difference shaping her experience, creating a sense of alienation from academic work. While her English course dealt with issues of language and power related to students' identity, "No real dialectic was established that allowed for learners to move back and forth in their consideration of personal, community, and societal issues. Such a dialectic would have allowed the exploration of social class but also would have allowed inquiry into the ways that social class intersects and interacts with such factors as gender, race, and the sense of geographic place that was so important to Crystal and many of her rural peers" (p. 582).

Laura Payne-Bourcy and Kelly Chandler-Olcott recommend that secondary literature classes directly address portrayals of class difference in texts as a means of helping students such as Crystal examine the often implicit relationship between class and power underlying her struggles.

Loss of Working-Class Workplace Community

The shift to New Capitalism also resulted in the loss of traditional socialization trajectories into a workplace community associated with defining one's masculinity, in which young workers followed in the footsteps of parents, relatives, and peers as mentors who help them move seamlessly from secondary school to a strong workplace community supported by labor unions. Lacking that traditional socialization trajectory into masculinity, adolescents then turn to alternative forms of male-bonding communities as substitutes for the lost workplace bonding. One study of adolescent white males in northeast Britain found that, faced with few employment opportunities, these males turned to active participation in soccer fan clubs involving physical, ritual display of team support (Nayak, 2003). These males also closely identified with their local community site or family, rejecting work that required them to move to another community, a reflection of their need for symbolic stability to counteract the instability of a shifting, global economy. While it is easy to dismiss these practices as doing little to alter the economic or political systems that undermine their self-worth, these findings point to the larger human need for a community that preserves a lost sense of dignity.

Other research finds that participation in sports, particularly football, is equated with masculinity, an identity construction mediated by discourses and narratives of violence and toughness (Burgess, Edwards, and Skinner, 2003). Other research indicates that white college athletes who strongly identified with athletics as constituting their identities were more likely to subscribe to the importance of their racial identity, while black athletes were less likely to subscribe to the importance of their racial identity, suggesting that active participation in sports may only enhance white athletes' sense of white privilege (Brown et al., 2003).

White Working-Class Males' Identities
and Attitudes toward Affirmative Action

Conservatives also build a cultural appeal to white working-class males around the notion of white privilege under attack. Politicians since the 1800s have employed a "race-card" strategy of pitting low-income whites against low-income people of color by arguing that people of color are "taking away your jobs." In his documentation of the evolution of white privilege, David R. Roediger (2002) noted that in the 1800s, wealthy whites provided poor whites with small tokens of economic privilege and social status that served to create an economic hierarchy that set low-income whites against blacks, and positioned blacks as inferior "others." To construct their sense of white privilege, whites distance themselves from what they perceive to be low-level "slave-labor" work done by blacks and Latinos and attempt to achieve what they perceive as middle-class status in terms of not being or living near blacks or Latinos.

At the same time, in a post-civil rights era, whites seldom adopt blatant expressions of bigotry. Instead, they adopt a discourse of what Eduardo Bonilla-Silva (2001) describes as "color-blind racism," as evident in statements of denial such as "Everyone is equal, but . . ."; or "I am not prejudiced, but . . ."; in arguments such as, "I didn't own slaves, so I'm not a racist," or in denials of the structural nature of discrimination as reflected in critiques of affirmative action programs (Blum, 2002; Reisigl and Wodak, 2001; Wiegman, 1999). They adopt this stance of "color-blind racism" because they are participating in an institutionalized economic system that privileges whites at the expense of people of color. While they may claim that race "does not matter," they still support systems that perpetuate economic inequality.

This discourse of "color-blind racism" is reflected in conservatives' attacks on affirmative action policies related to college admissions and to job-hiring practices. Conservatives frame the issue of affirmative action in terms of personal or individual benefits or losses—the fact that affirmative action limits whites from achieving, as some argue, their rights to a college education or employment (hooks, 2000).

This "race-card" appeal has been effective in setting working-class whites and people of color against each other, shifting the blame for job losses and flat wages away from fast-track capitalism and corporate downsizing. In one study, white working-class males perceived affirmative action as an "unfair quota system" that gives blacks and Hispanics jobs they believed should be theirs (Fine and Weis, 1998). They also perceived blacks and Hispanics as abusing government programs, while whites use these programs only on a temporary basis as a necessary means of supporting their families. These males therefore defined themselves as distinct from the "other"—as not engaging in the "unfair" practices associated with blacks and Hispanics. Attributions of laziness were evident in a survey in which only 16 percent of whites ranked blacks on the "hardworking" end of a scale; just under half ranked blacks on the "lazy" end of the scale (Feagin, 2000, p. 211).

Conservatives also attack affirmative action as one more governmental imposition on themselves as "free" agents who should not be constricted by institutional or governmental forces (Center for Individual Rights, 2004).

The issue of loss of job opportunities and competitive college admissions is framed in terms of race rather than class in order to appeal to a working-class white audience racial resentment. The argument is made that lack of employment opportunities and college admissions/financial support are due to government programs favoring people of color and not whites (Guinier and Torres, 2003). This argument serves to pit whites against people of color as a scapegoat for their problems, as opposed to focusing on cutbacks in government support programs designed for all low-income people.

These critiques of affirmation are also framed in terms of individual rights as opposed to rectifying institutional practices. In an analysis of college classroom discussions, Frances Maher and Mary Kay Tetreault (1997) noted repeated instances in which white students perceived themselves as individuals, while describing people of color as groups. They perceived issues of affirmative action as a threat to their "individual mobility rather than a response to a group history of discrimination" (p. 327). As a result, the white students "could not see that White people, too, were not simply individuals with common personal experiences, but differentially placed members of an unequal social order" (p. 336).

Framing affirmative action around individual rights and personal attributes fails to recognize its larger purpose of transforming what have been exclusive institutional practices. As Robert K. Fullinwider (1998, p. 14) argues: "The purpose of affirmative action is *not* to distribute benefits and burdens according to personal desert—or merit or need; *it is to change institutions*. It is to make white institutions multi-racial. Now, if that is our purpose, and if that purpose is sufficiently compelling, then the personal deservingness of the beneficiaries and victims of affirmative action is beside the point."

These attitudes toward affirmative action are also expressed by middle- and upper-middle-class whites. White lawyers expressed negative attitudes toward a mandated affirmative action program at their law firm (Pierce, 2003). They described persons of color hired at their firm as "unqualified" and not "fitting in." They consistently adopted a stance of innocence related to their racist treatment of these persons of color, a stance that reflected a discourse of individualism:

As Jennifer Pierce (2003, p. 213) noted, "By defining social life as the sum total of conscious and deliberate individual activities, these white lawyers are able to ignore the very systematic practices they themselves deploy, practices that exclude and marginalize African-American lawyers.

Attitudes toward affirmative action also differ according to gender. Bonilla-Silva (2003) finds that white working-class males were less likely than working-class females to espouse progressive perspectives given their traditional gender role in the economy:

> It has been the white *male* workers who have historically supported the racial order. Why? Because whether in periods of economic security or insecurity, white masculinity has provided white men with economic and noneconomic benefits. During good times, working-class men have been the "kings of the castle" (the home) and, during bad times (when "their" women have had to work in the paid labor force), they have been able to maintain a sense of control by demanding a traditional patriarchal organization of the home and by "patrolling neighborhoods" and the family from racial "pollution." (p. 145, italics in original)

Bonilla-Silva (2003) also finds that working-class females were often most likely to espouse more progressive perspectives on issues of affirmative action because they were more likely to have close personal relationships with blacks, resulting in a sense of solidarity with working-class blacks, not shared with white working-class males.

At the same time, white working-class males do not blame lack of access to higher education or jobs on conservative policies that redistribute wealth to upper-middle-class whites. As Michelle Fine and Lois Weis (1998) note: "None challenged economic restructuring or the historic privileging of white maleness in the economy. Left totally unexamined, and even unrecognized, by working-class white men, many of whom are highly marginal in this economy, is the role of white elites who self-consciously closed industries or enabled legislation which moved capital across state and international borders, thus interrupting far more white male jobs than affirmative action ever was intended to or ever could" (pp. 27–28).

Framing issues of affirmative action around individual benefits and burdens as opposed to transforming institutional forces reflects a larger historical shift from collective social and labor movements to a conservative/neoliberal discourse of individualism that challenges notions of community action and collectivity (Aronowitz, 2003). In that discourse, the individual is assumed to be responsible for their own status or success, as opposed to collective efforts of groups to organize and define value as a community.

High School Students' Perceptions of Identity in Terms of Race and Class

All of this shapes the ways in which high school students construct their identities in school contexts in terms of racial as opposed to class differences. Based on her ethnographic analysis of twelfth-grade working-and middle-class females in a Central Valley California high school, Julie Bettie (2003) found that these female students perceived differences between each other primarily in terms of race as opposed to class. Mexican-American working-class females, for example, wore darker lipstick or nail polish to connote the fact that they were not be perceived as white. Similarly, white working-class females defined themselves as not being affiliated with practices associated with Mexican-American students.

At the same time, despite their marginalization in the school by the school staff, both Mexican-American and white working-class females had difficulty critiquing the school's institutional bias against working-class students and their favoritism toward middle-class students. Given the middle-class culture of high schools, even teachers from working-class backgrounds adopted a middle-class discourse that constructs their own and students' identities around physical control/order, constraints on emotional expression, neatness, and so forth, as a way of marginalizing what is perceived to be undesirable aspects of working-class culture, often framed in terms of race. As a result, the teachers did not make explicit allegiances to their working class backgrounds.

The school staff as well as middle-class students frequently explained problems in working-class students' academic performance by adopting a deficit model in which working-class family practices were perceived as lacking in comparison to middle-class families, which was perceived as supportive, educated, warm, drug-free, articulate, confident, and hard-working. As a result, the working-class white students adopted a subordinate habitus that took the form of resisting or not participating in activities celebrating preppy status such as school dances or pep rallies. While they believed that the middle-class students were often caught up in an insincere obsession with achievement markers and status, the Mexican-American working-class females associated this more with "acting white" than with class differences. Bettie posits that they were framing differences in terms of race rather than class mainly because they lacked a discourse for discussing class difference: "Without a critical discourse on class, they were unable to locate themselves more clearly in relation to their various peers or to locate themselves historically in class terms in relationship to parents and grandparents" (2003, p. 81).

Bettie argues that the students' lack of a larger discourse for discussing class differences reflects the larger society's propensity to use race to trump class differences. She cites the example of California's Proposition 209 that eliminated state affirmative-action programs based on the argument that income rather than race is a more important admissions criterion. Working-class whites who supported the repeal of affirmative action programs perceive race as "brown," and assumed that they were being discriminated against by such programs as victims of "reverse discrimination." In reality, she found that when the white working-class students reached their senior year in the vocational education track, they lacked the coursework necessary to go to college:

> Although white working-class students experienced a feeling of unfairness in relation to preps regarding educational achievement and college, they lacked a discourse of class that could explain their own and their parents' "failure" and that would allow them to articulate the class antagonism they felt toward middle-class students. In its absence, a discourse of individualism and meritocracy helped render institutionalized class inequality invisible and consequently left white working-class students feeling like individually flawed "losers." . . . Ironically, because it offered class instead of race, not in addition to race, the discourse surrounding Proposition 209 encouraged students to understand inequality solely in racial terms and in the end worked as a racial project creating an alliance among whites across class and among Mexican Americans across class. Because any clear understanding of institutionalized class inequality is missing from U.S. popular and political discourse, "class" was read as racial code and used to rearticulate white privilege. (pp. 174–75, 176)

Bettie argues that by thinking of class as a performance allows for the potential of challenging deterministic notions that class origins limit potential for changing or developing new identities, as well as the ways in which class differences are institutionally or politically perpetuated and challenged.

All of this suggests a pedagogical agenda to help adolescents interrogate their discourses of individualism for framing issues of race and class difference. It also suggests the need to help them move beyond simply defining difference in terms of race to help them recognize how class shapes their perceptions of difference.

Entertaining Hybrid Discourses

One approach for helping students interrogate discourses of individualism is by responding to multicultural literature that portrays alternative discourses of race, class, and gender. Engaging with alternative, hybrid discourses serves to challenge students' status quo discourses, leading them to interrogate the limitations of these discourses of individualism constituting their attitudes toward affirmative action.

In responding to and discussing multicultural literature, students are exploring dialogic tensions associated with hybrid discourses, leading to what Cynthia Lewis (2004) describes as a re-articulation of their existing, often fixed, stable discourses. In research on white teachers' book club discussions on teaching muliticultural literature in a rural Iowa town, Lewis and her colleagues find that teachers begin to interrogate a discourse of "liberal humanism" and individualism that frames racism as a matter of individual prejudice and choice by adopting a counterdiscourse of "critical multiculturalism" (Lewis, Ketter, and Fabos, 2001). Some teachers in the group resisted the group's prevailing white privilege by taking up a discourse of "critical multiculturalism" that focuses on institutional racism portrayed in the literary texts they were teaching. Through their discussions and exploration of hybrid discourses, the teachers were exploring alternative stances and positions that served to redefine their own identities and teaching practices.

Adolescents' Responses to Multicultural Literature

To illustrate the ways in which white working-class males may entertain these hybrid discourses, we cite some of their responses to multicultural literature taken from a study on high school students' responses to multicultural literature that was conducted at Thompson High School (a pseudonym), a diverse, urban high school of 1,550 students in a "working class" section of a large, Midwestern city (Beach et al., 2003). This school was chosen for its diversity (the student body is 42% white and 58% students of color: 30% Asian, 17% African, 10% Hispanic, and 1% Native American) and because the recent demographic shifts in the school and the community created a unique site for studying racial and social class tensions. Students in this study were enrolled in a multicultural literature class for eleventh- and twelfth-grade students who receive college credit for taking this course while still in high school. The 14 participant students in the class consisted of 8 females and 6 males: 8 white, 3 Asian-American, 1 Hispanic, and 1 student of African descent. Most of these students can be identified as working class given their parents' occupations; of the 14 students, 2 students could be considered as middle class.

Each of the four authors participated in different ways in this study. Richard Beach, a professor and literacy researcher at the University of Minnesota with background experience in studying responses to multicultural literature (1997), was the primary investigator. Daryl Parks, a doctoral student in literacy education, was the teacher of the class. Parks, a popular English teacher in the school who has won several teaching awards, was explicit to the students about his working-class background experiences and how those experiences shaped his own responses to literature. Amanda H. Thein, also a literacy researcher, observed classroom discussions, interviewed the students, and conducted an ethnographic analysis of the school. And Timothy Lensmire, also a professor of literacy at the University of Minnesota, has applied critical literacy and Bakhtian perspectives on classroom interactions in writing workshop classrooms (2000), and is currently examining the development of white male masculinity practices.

In the course, Parks encouraged the application of various critical theories (Appleman, 2001), including Marxist, feminist, structuralist, New Historical, and Critical Race Theory. Participants engaged in taped large and small group discussions for each of the texts read in the course—*The House on Mango Street* (Cisneros, 1994), *Bless Me, Ultima* (Anaya, 1978), *Kindred* (Butler, 1979), *Their Eyes Were Watching God* (Thurston, 1986), *Woman Warrior* (Kingston, 1989), *Obasan* (Kogawa, 1993), *Love Medicine* (Erdrich, 1989), *Smoke Signals* (film), *Bastard Out of Carolina* (Allison, 1992), and *A Yellow Raft in Blue Water* (Dorris, 1987)—and wrote journal entries and essays for each of these texts. The researchers also conducted observational analyses of the school culture. Transcripts of selected group discussions, all interviews, and focus groups were coded using QSR NVIVO.

The School and Classroom Culture

A key factor shaping students' identities and their responses to literature was the school and classroom culture. The school culture reflected the largely working-class neighborhood community, which had become increasingly diverse, particularly with a large influx of immigrant Hmong people. The school culture reflected an attempt to perpetuate a past white hegemony in resistance to this increasing diversity through school events and traditions that harked back to a time in which the school was largely white. This attempt to perpetuate past white privilege was most evident in the emphasis on a discourse of competitive sports that equates school spirit with the identity of school athlete or jocks as successful football or hockey players on what are largely white, male teams. One student noted that the principal "likes sports players a lot cause she thinks they're like role models throughout the school."

Interviews with school athletes reflected their adherence to this discourse of competitive self-achievement that was associated with the strong athletic tradition at Thompson. Athletes evoked narratives of hard work and training consistent with a discourse of competition. Being involved with sports served as an extrinsic means for students to attain self-discipline. In order to participate in sports, students must maintain *control* of themselves both in school and outside of school. When one female study participant wrote an article for the school newspaper regarding athletes' use of alcohol, she was criticized by the school's athletic director for undermining the positive image of athletes in the school. Students, both male and female, who were involved in athletics at Thompson, were not only supported on the field, but also in positions of school leadership, as a form of symbolic display of the importance of physical self-control and self-discipline as central to the school that did not allow students to leave campus during the day for lunch and that did not provide them with any free periods.

This control extended to school events such as the annual "Winter-Fest" coronation ceremony in the school gym where white students were crowned. During this event, the gym doors were guarded by ROTC students dressed in full regalia and carrying swords. Many students at Thompson did not support such events that center around who they perceived as the mainstream "popular" white students; these potentially disruptive students were actually encouraged not to attend and were provided with movies in classrooms.

This physical control of students was also reflected in the control of classroom activities. Observations of classrooms indicated largely teacher-directed activities resulting in high levels of student passivity in which students seemed uncomfortable when given freedom to think critically and speak openly (Bettie, 2003; Yon, 2000).

The teacher of the multicultural literature class, Parks, attempted to create a classroom culture that deviated from the larger school culture of physical and intellectual control. He valued dialogic, intellectual exploration around issues of class and race that were rarely addressed in the larger school culture. He also modeled ways of interrogating texts and constructively challenging others, as well as providing support for expression of minority or alternative interpretations. His influence was increasingly evident in students using notions of "subtext," "voices," and "culture," as well as their practice of citing textual evidence for their hypotheses.

Because Parks explicitly described his own identity as constituted by his white, male, working-class background, he gained identification with some of the students in the class. He frequently used stories and personal narratives to situate himself within these competing discourses. Parks mediated different class worlds of his students and these academic worlds by describing how he had learned to negotiate differences between his working-class background experience and other worlds. He shared childhood narratives of financial destitution, family members' run-ins with the law, and the prevalent drug culture of his factory-employed neighborhood. He also shared anecdotal experiences of white privilege operating in the larger high school culture and community, modeling self-critique for the male athletes. Given the critical focus of the texts, the journal prompts, and the outside readings, Parks believed that the structure of the course represented a "decentering" of white, male, middle-class norms. While occasional discussion topics or foci would bring discomfort to some students, they became accustomed to adopting a critical stance toward mainstream community and school discourses. As he gained the respect of these students as "one of us," he also encouraged them to examine the limitation of their larger school status related to their white privilege. (This focus on challenging the white males' discourses of race and class led some of the Hmong students to feelings of resentment in interviews about the attention afforded on the white students' perceptions of race at the expense of the Hmong students' experiences with racism and class resentments.)

Parks also continually focused on the ways in which categories associated with race and class differences were cultural constructions serving to perpetuate social hierarchies (Bonilla-Silva, 2001). For example, during the course, the students prepared to attend an event at a local university that involved students from different, largely suburban, schools who were enrolled in the College in the Schools program. The students were to meet together to listen to a speaker discuss multicultural literature, and to then discuss the topic with students from other schools.

Parks anticipated that because the students would be interacting with students from different race and class backgrounds, that issues of race and class differences might arise, particularly in terms of how some of the largely white, suburban students perceived his students as coming from a diverse, urban, working-class school. He sensed that his students would encounter some stereotypical comments from some of the middle-class suburban students; he also believed that his students had ideas of who suburban and rural people were, and that these ideas could serve as a basis for a discussion of race and class.

Prior to going on the field trip, he asked the students to write about and then role-play their perceptions of a prototypical rural student and a prototypical suburban student. The students realized the stereotypes they employed in describing others is associated with how others may stereotype them. In describing the suburban students, students frequently referred to class markers, particularly money, as a feature that distinguished themselves from their suburban counterparts. They noted that physical markers such as dress, hair, as well as speech, served to differentiate them from suburban students.

This activity began to foster students' awareness of the culturally constructed nature of categories—how the categories they apply to others and themselves shape their perceptions of others. When students encountered people who challenged these categories, they could reject the person as inconsistent with their categories, or consider revising their categories in ways that account for the difference represented by the person.

Parks also challenged students' discourses of individualism through activities in which students examined institutional forces shaping social practices and public policies related to race and class difference. For example, students read Peggy McIntosh's (1997) essay on white male privilege and discussed examples of ways in which white males are afforded certain privileges through institutional practices in their community and in the school. Students also read excerpts from Jonathan Kozol's (1992), *Savage Inequalities*, describing the conditions of schools in East St. Louis related to lack of funding, as well as factors creating poverty in that city. And, students explored issues of class difference as portrayed on the PBS program, *People Like Us*, in terms of how institutional class markers function to define their own and others' identities. From these and from other activities, students began to recognize how identity construction is mediated by institutional discourses of race and class, a useful background for interpreting characters' identity construction in the novels they were reading in the course.

Given their socialization in the largely white, working-class culture of their school, many of these students resisted what they perceive as threats to their sense of white privilege in these discussions. At the same time, some of these students began to recognize the value of critically examining larger economic and institutional forces shaping their identities. Having to grapple with dialogic tensions in their lives led some students in this course to interrogate discourses of race and class shaping their perspectives, an awareness critical to their ultimately adopting a political critique of the conservative fast-track economy agenda (Linkon, 1999).

Responding to Literature

In responding to the literary texts read in the course, students were experiencing characters who themselves reframed their identities within shifting discourses and status quo systems. For example, one of the novels read in the course was the time-travel novel, *Kindred*, by Octavio Butler (1979). In this novel, the main character, Dana, is an urban, African-American female and professional writer living in Los Angeles in 1976. She is transported back to the world of slavery in antebellum Maryland in 1819 through a link to her great-grandfather and slave-owner, Rufus, who, in her new, 1819-reality, raped her. She understands her present self through understanding her past heritage as not only related to her white great-grandfather, who fathered her grandmother with another slave, but also as constructed in the contemporary urban world of Los Angeles.

In reading about Dana's time travel and in constructing her identity, the students experienced the ways in which her own perspectives on slavery and white privilege were located within the pre-Civil War South and contemporary American society. Because the novel highlights how she perceived her identity as constructed in different ways by the discourses operating in these two worlds, students recognized the ways in which identities were constituted by participation in historical and cultural worlds. They contrasted how Dana's relationships with white males were constituted by different roles, norms, tools, and beliefs operating in different systems—slavery versus contemporary Los Angeles. Examining how Dana's identity was constructed by conflicting discourses of slavery and contemporary civil rights helped the students further understand how identity is constituted by discourses. This led them to reflect on their own identity construction as shaped by culture and history as more than events distinct from their everyday lives, but as something that actually influenced their lives.

Another novel read in the course was Dorothy Allison's (1992) novel, *Bastard Out of Carolina,* a National Book Award finalist, which portrays a white, working-class South Carolinian family grappling with issues of economic oppression, job discrimination, and sexual abuse in the 1950s. The novel portrays a controlling, violent father, Daddy Glen—who was raised in a middle-class family but who has lost all of his money and is now destitute—and the female adolescent main character and narrator, Bone. After Bone's biological father dies, her mother, Anney, remarries Daddy Glen, who begins to sexually abuse her. Once the abuse is revealed, Anney sides with Glen against Bone, who then turns to her lesbian aunt for parenting and survives what was a brutal childhood.

In reading this novel, the students examined the ways in which discourses of class are used to marginalize and stigmatize working-class people through categories such as "white trash," "hardworking/lazy," and "respectful/shameful" (Baker, 2000). Bone's birth certificate falsely categorizes her as "illegitimate," something that her mother attempts to change during the entire novel against a corrupt legal system that positions working-class people as the "other," in ways that benefit those in power—an echo of the current Republican strategy. Allison (as quoted in Baker, 2000) describes her interest in "the politics of *they*, why human beings fear and stigmatize the different while secretly dreading that they might be one of the different themselves. . . .[A]ll the other categories by which we categorize and dismiss each other—need to be excavated from the inside" (p. 122, italics in original). She posits that the horror of class prejudice, racism, sexism, and homophobia is that they persuade people that their security "depends on the oppression of others, that for some to have good lives there must be others whose lives are truncated and brutal" (p. 126).

Having read novels only about poor people of color, the students in the course were surprised by the fact that they were reading about poor whites. One Hmong student noted, "It is different because the characters are white. It criticizes white people. It is something new about this book."

In responding to the novel, students examined the fact that the middle-class characters consistently marginalize the working-class characters in terms of institutional constraints—by putting up barriers to the courts, schooling, and employment. However, some of the white students were reluctant to frame the characters' practices in institutional terms related to the plight of working-class whites, preferring to perceive the characters through a discourse of individualism.

By responding to these and other novels in the course, students were interpreting characters' increasingly awareness of how systems shaped their identities—how slavery shaped Dana's past and present self, and how class structures shaped Glen and Bone. This led some of them to engaged in a similar shift in perspectives about how institutions shape their own identities and stances.

Students' Attitudes toward Affirmative Action

These different perceptions toward the relationships between institutions and individual practices were evident in the ways in which the students in the course responded to issues related to affirmative action. Many of the students in the course expressed opposition to affirmative action, both out of concern for future job-hiring practices and college admissions, expressions reflecting conservative political views expressed in the media, and in their own community in terms of a discourse of white privilege (Reisigl and Wodak, 2001).

In discussions of affirmation action, the students argued that because they did not participate in past instances of racism—as related, for example, to the portrayal of slavery in *Kindred*—they should not face reverse discrimination, which was evident for them, in affirmative-action programs. One student argued that accusations against the current white population as responsible for past misdeeds was misplaced because "we had nothing to do with what our ancestors did, but we are still the ones who have to face the consequences for it."

Noting that they needed to pay far more tuition to attend a competitive college than did students of color, they were critical of government tuition support programs and job-hiring policies. One student noted that "if you have a guy who goes in there, say a Native American person who is just as qualified as the person if not better, they will always be judged as better because of their color and because of their background than what a white person would be because they are used to the white person."

A number of students argued that affirmative action programs actually created a disincentive for students to "work hard" in school because they were given a "free ride." As one student noted, "Why do we have to keep giving the black kids help because it is not encouraging them to do something better . . . if you want somebody to be something better, you shouldn't give them money just for being good."

In challenging students' arguments related to affirmative action, Parks examined race and class inequities in terms of larger systems, as opposed to framing issues in terms of their own personal gains or losses. For example, one white student indicated that he was struggling with a journal prompt, "what race/gender, etc. would make your life easiest?" The student noted, "I have black people in my family. I don't want to say that whites are better." Parks responded that "it's not who you think is better, but in this system, this country, whose is easier?" He consistently responded to students by distinguishing between individual experiences of students and the perceived norms of societal behavior.

Parks also noted contradictions in students' positions regarding affirmative action related to assumptions about a history of exclusion operating in higher education. He created a hypothetical case of low-income families receiving more financial aid, a direct reference to the advantages afforded students in the course. He also supported those students who were resisting the shared, majority consensus emerging in the classroom, for example, that whites should not be held accountable for past historical events.

Rather than challenging students himself, he encouraged expression by other white students regarding the hegemonic control of the white system. As a result, some students began to shift their stances. One white student noted how she changed her view on affirmative action programs, which she initially resented, because she became increasingly aware of how race and culture serves to disadvantage some groups "because of their race and their culture and how they grew up and all of the things that they had to deal with that I wouldn't, being white." Another student noted: "I just thought just because you were a minority you could just get along in life a little easier when it comes to school and stuff like that. Get scholarships and all that other good stuff. And then when we got into it a lot of it kind of changed my whole aspect on it like how look at that now. The way earlier hurdles and that sort of thing and where you come from and your family situation. So that changed me a lot."

Another student noted that she became more aware of the institutional challenges facing students of color: "Now, at the end of class, my perspective of the whole issue has done a 180. Not like just one not two not three, but like, hundreds of things in class, different subjects and topics and even going to like the East Saint Louis thing about how certain people . . . I mean, you don't even realize how poor and how bad some people really have it."

By forging relationships with students and telling stories, Parks functioned as what Beverly Tatum (1997) described as a progressive "white ally" by emphasizing similarities between his experiences and those of his students. Through the use of effective metaphors and modeling approaches for self-interrogation of identity, he equipped students with the language and processes through which to articulate their alternative perspectives on race and class. As a result, some of the students began to perceive themselves as operating in a cultural and economic system perpetuating white privilege.

Changes in Individual Students' Perspectives

The degree to which students shifted their perspectives to adopt a more institutional perspective varied within the group. Many of the white males demonstrated little change.

Corey

Corey, a popular, white, athlete at Johnson identifies strongly with his "working-class" family background. Corey's father is a self-employed construction worker who bids out for construction work with his brother; his mother was not employed outside of the home. Corey will be the first in his family to attend college.

In class discussions, interviews, and journal entries, it's common to hear Corey voicing his family beliefs, using them to anchor his opinions. This reflects the strong socializing force of the family in shaping racial attitudes around the need for social conformity (Feagin, 2000)—in this case, family members who were uneasy about the increasing diversity of the school.

Much of Corey's identity revolves around his active participation in sports as a means of defining his status in school. His participation in sports was linked to discourses of self-discipline and competition in the school culture. As Corey noted: "I mean there's discipline in football so you learn that, but then I'd say hockey there's a lot more discipline . . . if you do something wrong you're gonna get punished for it. Even at school, he [the coach] finds out about everything I mean. And then baseball, baseball's like, a more relaxing sport, more fun, I mean still, you still gotta stay disciplined if you wanna play, you can't be going out, getting in trouble. . . ."

The emphasis on self-discipline reflects a larger discourse of individualism—that one's success in sports is a matter of one's individual ability to maintain self-control both in school and outside of school. Because Corey perceives everyone as having an equal chance at sports, he sees sports as "fair," depending on athletes' willingness to train and work hard—that their success is a function of their individual motivation.

Corey's discourse of individualism spills over to his strong belief in meritocracy—that anyone can succeed if they work hard enough and that everyone is given an equal chance to work, a discourse that shaped his perspective of affirmative action policies. He consistently argued that affirmation action policies discriminated against whites. He noted that Asian students "can come to the United States or be born here and get schooling for half or less than half of what white people go to school for." He perceived affirmative action as not only creating disadvantages in hiring, but also in college scholarship support: "White people get no help at all because they think every white person is rich. Minorities get enrichment programs to get help with their scholarships, when most white people don't get help with any money for college."

His belief in the value of meritocracy and hard work is evident in his response to the novel, *Bastard Out of Carolina*. He argues that Bone's future depends on her own self-initiative—that she herself is responsible for her own fate. As Corey noted: "I think she could if she stayed in school and went to college after, just like anybody else could. But, I don't know, the things that went on in her life might mess her up a little bit. She might need counseling or something, but I still think that she could get probably get through it. I just think that she has a chance like anybody else. *Anybody* [emphasis in the original] can, if you do the right stuff and work hard your whole life."

In discussing Daddy Glen's problems, Corey suggested that because Daddy Glen had not adhered to his family's expectations for him, he should begin living the way he was "brought up" in a middle-class family. "I thought that Glen sort of started off backward from his family. His family is rich, and he should have an easier life to start off with, but he kind of failed at everything and started going down the tubes and now he's got to rebuild his way back up. Like, you guys were saying, he didn't follow in his family's footsteps; he kind of funneled down. He's got to just build up and work harder now to get back up to where his family is . . . with expectations."

Corey's perspective on Daddy Glen reflected a lack of a discourse of class. He assumed that losing one's middle-class status resulted in Glen's decline, failing to recognize the ways in which the white middle-class people in the town actually discriminated against and stigmatized working-class people.

Corey is highly critical of instances in which affirmative action programs reward people for their skin color or ethnic background, undercutting his notion of "hard work." In a class discussion on affirmative action, Corey says that he has heard the following about his chances of becoming a police officer: "I want to be a police officer, but supposedly now a day it is not easy to be a cop if you are white. Now it is a lot easier to become a cop if you are a minority. If you are white and you are better than the person next to you and he is black, the white person might not get that job. Just because that person is a different color. It is also that way for college, white people get no help at all because they think every white person is rich. Minorities get enrichment programs to get help with their scholarships, when most white people don't get help with any money for college."

For Corey, both home and sports discourses are grounded in the belief in individually doing "right" as opposed to doing "wrong," and working hard. Confronting issues such as racial and socioeconomic oppression and affirmative action created tensions for white male athletes such as Corey, who are uncomfortable dealing with these tensions, because it requires a renegotiation of familiar, stabilizing discourses.

It could be argued that these students' immersion in a world of sports functions as a codified, defined defense against the complexities and contradictions of interrogating the system. In the first of the John Updike *Rabbit* series, *Rabbit Run*, the high school basketball star Rabbit Angstrom thinks approvingly about the clearly delineated lines on the basketball court and the smooth arc of the ball moving through the air, thoughts that contrast with the messiness of his deteriorating world after high school. As suggested by northeastern British adolescent males' football fan club activities (Nayak, 2003), sports functions as a nostalgic substitute for workplace bonding in what were, prior to the diminution of manufacturing jobs in the "New Economy," vibrant workplace contexts. These males' obsessive view of sports and the value of "winning" seems to serve as an avoidance mechanism to addressing complexities and contradictions associated with the declining status of working-class people.

Devin

However, not all of the male athletes in the class shared Corey's perspective. Devin is also a working-class, white, male athlete, whose father worked in the local post office and his mother is a daycare worker. Devin noted that his father "has been working in the post office for seventeen years. He has a twenty-three-year-old boss who thinks he knows it all. It's kind of tough on him because he works nights." He also notes that "I have to work for what I need and want. And so do my parents; we're a working family. I won't get a free ride, so to speak, to college; I'll have to work for it."

In contrast to Corey's discourse of individualism, Devin voiced perspectives reflecting an awareness of institutional aspects of white privilege. While he derived some of these perspectives from his participation in community and church organizations, he was also influenced by the course discussions and readings on white privilege, as well as Parks's perspectives as a working-class white adult whom he emulated.

In responding to *Love Medicine*, Devin posited that whites were responsible for Native Americans' dire conditions, in their co-creation of a reservation system and by imposing their beliefs onto Native Americans:

> We just kind of came over with all of our oppressionistic views and Catholicism and this is the way to be and this is the way you should be and oh yeah, this land is good for cultivating so I'll tell you what; we have guns and you have spears so we will kick you out of here and give you a crappy little plot of land up north. And, we'll let you sit there for a little while until we need more land, and then we'll take that from you. Then you can live in a more confined area and we'll take some more and then take some more. . . . It was their land in the first place. We had no right to cheat them out of their own land.

In rereading McIntosh's (1997) essay on white privilege a second time toward the end of the course, he noted that he was learning to recognize the institutional advantages associated with white privilege that blind people of the need for affirmative action. He noted that "There are people in this world that will give a job because of race and not of skill. We just don't see it because we have unearned advantages of being White. We don't see that because we are brought up this way—'a process of coming to see that some of the power which I originally saw as attendant on being a human being in the U.S. consisted in unearned advantage and conferred dominance. . . .'"

He continued, noting that many of his white peers "do not see 'whiteness' as a racial identity" because of the "way we were brought up and taught was all about the whites and how 'good' we are. But notice there isn't a whole lot on how poorly we treated others (people of minority). In a way we are dictators of other cultures. I say this because we enslaved a race for almost 200+ years because we were fat and lazy."

He perceived instances of racism in his everyday life: "Even today as I work at a gas station I see segregation. IDs will be checked on a black or Hmong customer but not on a white. During World War II we had Japanese prison camps for Japanese-Americans. So in reality, are we really all that great? I tend to think not. Our privilege system only seems to benefit us."

In response to his peers' valuing of individuals' "hard work" as opposed to affirmative action hiring programs, he argued that such programs were needed given the institutional racism shaping hiring practices: "They said if you work hard for it, you get what you deserve, and that's not necessarily true, because the racism in society is really strong when you try to get a job."

He was one of the several students in the course who changed his attitude toward affirmative action due to his exposure to the historical impact of institutional racism "given the history of what we put all of them through. About time we give something back to them."

In responding to the literary texts in the course, as well as Parks's perspectives, he experienced alternative discourses leading to his awareness of institutional aspects of racism. While he was not entirely consistent in his stance, and would occasionally voice more traditional discourses, in contrast to intransigent stances of the other white males in the course, he represented one of the students in the class who was willing to entertain new ways of thinking about issues of race and white privilege.

Conclusion

These two students varied in the degree to which they addressed issues of race and affirmative action. They differed in their willingness to engage with the dialogic tensions operating in Parks's course. Corey, a working-class white male, resisted these dialogic tensions as inconsistent with his stance of a discourse of individualism and "hard work" consistent with his identity as competitive male athlete. He voiced adopting a popular resentment toward the presumed advantage of people of color in job hiring. In contrast, Devin, also a working-class white male athlete, was more open to entertaining notions of institutional racism.

The results of this study point to the value of encouraging alternative, conflicting value stances in literature discussions as a means of challenging students' status quo discourses. Students were experiencing the voices of characters who challenge the status quo, as is the case in Butler's *Kindred* and Allison's *Bastard Out of Carolina*, in which the main characters adopt outsider, deviant perspectives on their worlds, and address dialogic tensions related to race and class differences. Constructing these characters' dialogic tensions transferred over to entertaining tensions in their own lives, tensions attributed to difference in race and class (Beach, Thein, and Parks, in press).

While the students had difficulty interrogating institutional discourses of race and class, some students such as Devin began to recognize that their worlds are mediated by discourses and by institutional forces. These changes in value stances are unlikely to occur from solitary interventions: reading multicultural literature alone, or discussions with diverse peers, or challenges from a teacher or peer. But a combination of all three may at least create possibilities that at least some of these working-class students, particularly white males, will resist the conservative discourses that attempt to divert their attention from the economic institutional forces shaping their lives.

References

Allison, D. 1992. *Bastard out of Carolina*. New York: Dutton.

Anaya, R. 1978. *Bless me, Ultima*. Berkeley, CA: Tonatiuh International.

Apple, M. 2003. *The state and the politics of knowledge*. New York: Routledge.

Appleman, D. 2000. *Critical encounters in high school English: Teaching literary theory to adolescents*. New York: Teachers College Press.

Aronowitz, S. 2003. *How class works: Power and social movement*. Cambridge: Harvard University Press.

Baker, M. P. 2000. The politics of "they": Dorothy Allison's *Bastard out of Carolina* as critique of gender, sexual and class Ideologies. In J. F. Folks (Ed.) *The world is our home: Society and culture in contemporary Southern writing* (pp. 117–41). Lexington: University Press of Kentucky.

Beach, R. 1997. Students' resistance to engagement with multicultural literature. In T. Rogers and A. O. Soter (Eds.) *Reading across cultures: Teaching literature in a diverse society* (pp. 69–94). New York: Teachers College Press.

Beach, R., Lundell, D., and Jung, H. 2002. Developmental college students' negotiation of social practices between peer, family, workplace, and university worlds. In J. Higbee and D. Lundell (Eds.) *Multiculturalism and developmental education*. Minneapolis: University of Minnesota, Center for Research in Developmental Education and Urban Literacy.

Beach, R., Parks, D., Thein, A. H., and Lensmire, T. 2003. High school students' responses to alternative value stances associated with the study of multicultural literature. Paper presented at the annual meeting of the American Educational Research Association, Chicago.

Beach, R., Thein, A. H., and Parks, D. in press. *High school students' competing social worlds: Negotiating identities and allegiances through responding to multicultural literature*. Mahwah, NJ: Lawrence Erlbaum.

Bettie, J. 2003. *Women without class: Girls, race, and identity*. Berkeley: University of California Press.

Blum, L. 2002. *"I'm not a racist, but . . .": The moral quandary of race*. Ithaca: Cornell University Press.

Bonilla-Silva, E. 2001. *White supremacy and racism in the post-civil rights era*. Boulder, CO: Lynne Rienner Publishers.

———. 2003. *Racism without racists: Color-blind racism and the persistence of racial inequality in the United States*. Lanham, MD: Rowman & Littlefield.

Brown T. N. et al. 2003. "There's no race on the playing field": Perceptions of racial discrimination among white and black athletes. *Journal of Sport & Social Issues, 27*(2), 162–83.

Burgess I., Edwards A., and Skinner J. 2003. Football culture in an Australian school setting: The construction of masculine identity. *Sport, Education and Society, 8*(2), 199–212.

Butler, O. 1979. *Kindred*. Garden City, NY: Doubleday.

Center for Individual Rights. 2004. Website. [Online] Available at http://www.cir-usa.org. Accessed May 25, 2004.

Century Foundation, The. 2004. Left behind: Unequal opportunity in higher education. New York: Century Foundation. [Online]. Available at http://www.tof.org/publications/education/leftbehindrc.pdf. Accessed June 5, 2004.

Cisneros, S. 1994. *The house on Mango Street.* New York: Knopf.

Dorris, M. 1987. *A yellow raft in blue water.* New York: Holt.

Eckert, P. 1989. *Jocks & burnouts: Social categories and identity in the high school.* New York: Teachers College Press.

Erdrich, L. 1989. *Love medicine.* New York: Bantam Books.

Feagin, J. R. 2000. *Racist America: Roots, current realities, & future reparations.* New York: Routledge.

Fine, M., and Weis, L. 1989. *Unknown city.* Boston: Beacon.

Frank, T. 2004. *"What's the matter with Kansas?" How conservatives won the heart of America.* New York: Metropolitan.

Fullinwider, R. K. 1998. Defending affirmative action from its defenders. *Intersections.* [Online] Available at http://www.crg.und.edu/publications/interssections98/defending.html. Accessed June 5, 2004.

Gee, J. P. 2002. Millennials and bobos, *Blue's Clues* and *Sesame Street*: A story for our times. In D. Alvermann (Ed.) *Adolescents and literacies in a digital world* (pp. 51–67). New York: Peter Lang.

Guinier, L, and Torres, G. 2003. *The miner's canary: Enlisting race, resisting power, transforming democracy.* Cambridge: Harvard University Press.

Harvey, D. 1989. *The condition of postmodernity: An enquiry into the origins of cultural change.* New York: Blackwell.

hooks, bell. 2000. *Where we stand: Class matters.* New York: Routledge.

Hurston, Z. N. 1986. *Their eyes were watching God.* London: Virago.

Kingston, M. H. 1989. *The woman warrior: Memoirs of a girlhood among ghosts.* New York: Vintage Books.

Kogawa, J. 1993. *Obasan.* New York: Anchor.

Kozol, J. 1992. *Savage inequalities: Children in America's schools.* New York: Perennial.

Lensmire, T. 2000. *Powerful writing, Responsible teaching.* New York: Teachers College Press.

Lewis, C. 2004. Resituating the self: The pedagogic possibilities of critical discourse analysis. Paper presented at the Critical Discourse Analysis Conference, Indiana University.

Lewis, C., Ketter, J., and Fabos, B. 2001. Reading race in a rural context. *Qualitative studies in education,* 14(3), 317–50.

Linkon, S. L. (Ed.). 1999. *Teaching working class.* Amherst: University of Massachusetts Press.

Maher, F., and Tetreault, M. K. 1997. Learning in the dark: How assumptions of Whiteness shape classroom knowledge. *Harvard Educational Review,* 67(2), 321–49.

McIntosh, P. 1997. White privilege and male privilege: A personal account of coming to see correspondences through work in women's studies. In R. Delgado and J. Stefancic (Eds.) *Critical white studies: Looking behind the mirror* (pp. 291–99). Philadelphia: Temple University Press.

Ohmann, R. 2003. *Politics of knowledge: The commercialization of the university, professions, & print culture.* Middletown, CT: Wesleyan University Press.

Nayak, A. 2003. "Boyz to men": Masculinities, schooling and labour transitions in de-industrial times. *Educational Review, 55*(2), 147–159.

Payne-Bourcy, L. and Chandler-Olcott, K. 2003. Spotlighting social class: An exploration of one adolescent's language and literacy practices. *Journal of Literacy Research, 35*(1), 551–90.

Phelan, P., Davidson, A., and Yu, H. 1998. *Adolescents' worlds: Negotiating family, peers, and school.* New York: Teachers College Press.

Pierce, J. 2003. "Racing for innocence": Whiteness, corporate culture, and the backlash against affirmative action. In A. Doane and E. Bonilla-Silva (Eds.) *White out: The continuing significance of racism* (pp. 199–214). New York: Routledge.

Reisigl, M., and Wodak, R. 2001. *Discourse and discrimination: Rhetorics of racism and antisemitism.* New York: Routledge.

Roediger, D. R. 2002. *Colored white: Transcending the racial past.* Berkeley: University of California Press.

Sadowski, M. 2003. Class and identity in a socioeconomically diverse high school: A discussion with Elaine Bessette, Joan Lowe, and Bill Quinn. In M. Sadowski (Ed.) *Adolescents at school: Perspectives on youth, identity, and education* (pp. 122–26). Cambridge: Harvard University Press.

Tatum, B. 1997. *"Why are all the black kids sitting together in the cafeteria?" And other conversations about race.* New York: Basic.

Updike, J. 1960. *Rabbit, run.* New York: Knopf.

Wiegman, R. 1999. Whiteness studies and the paradox of particularity. *Boundary, 2*(26), 115–50.

Yon, D. A. 2000. *Elusive culture: Schooling, race, and identity in global times.* Albany: State University of New York Press.

7

SOCIAL CLASS AND AFRICAN-AMERICAN PARENTAL INVOLVEMENT

Cheryl Fields-Smith

Parental involvement encompasses an array of home- and school-based activities that research frequently associates with student achievement (Epstein, 1995; Stein and Thorkildsen, 1999). In fact, a steady stream of research has led to federal, state, and local mandates that often require schools to include parental involvement in their programs. However, the discourse on parental involvement tends to favor the perspectives of white, middle-class parents (Gavin and Greenfield, 1998). Furthermore, school norms sometimes marginalize the school-based involvement of ethnic-minority and low-income parents (McGrath and Kuriloff, 1999).

In order to avoid the confounding effects of both race and class, researchers frequently examine the effects of social class among white parents. However, John Diamond and Kimberley Gomez (2004) observed, ". . . few studies have examined social class patterns within racial groups other than Whites." This is exemplified by William Jeynes's (2003) meta-analysis of forty-six studies of ethnic-minority parental involvement and achievement in which each article controlled for socioeconomic status or did not disaggregate findings by social class. Furthermore, the existing literature often suggests that teachers and administrators frequently perceive low-income, ethnic-minority parents as less actively involved in their children's education (Stein and Thorkildsen, 1999), or as not interested in their children's education (Smrekar and Cohen-Vogel, 2001; Trotman, 2001).

The purpose of this chapter is to examine the experiences of seven African-American families of elementary school-aged children representing four categories of social class (working class, working middle class, managerial middle class, and professional middle class). I will explore the complex and distinctive ways in which African-American families intersect with schools as I also consider the extent to which black parents emulate the parental involvement practices of white parents in order to support their children's education. Specifically, I will explore how the existing literature on social class and parental involvement helps to explain black parental involvement, as I also investigate where black and white parents of similar social class backgrounds diverge in their involvement with their children's education. Understanding social class differences in home-school interactions addresses issues of teacher misperceptions as well as informing teacher education programs. In addition, given the link between parental involvement and student achievement, investigations of parental involvement among African-American families may also provide insight regarding achievement disparity between white and black students.

As a starting point, I will incorporate Joyce Epstein's (1995) topology for parental involvement as a framework for my analysis. Epstein's topology of parental involvement activities and her home-school partnership model both serve as theoretical constructs in parental involvement literature. The topology classifies parental involvement into six broad categories: (1) parenting, which includes creating a home environment that supports children as students; (2) communicating, which refers to all forms of home to school and school to home communication; (3) volunteering at the school, which refers to school-based activities; (4) learning at home, which refers to family involvement with specific academics at home; (5) decision making, which refers to parents' participation in school planning, advisory councils, and other parent leadership roles; and (6) collaboration with the community, which refers to activities that identify and integrate community resources and services in ways that strengthen school programs, student learning outcomes, and families. Development of these varying types of parental involvement is believed to help schools develop a comprehensive parental involvement policy.

Epstein (1995) also developed a model of the ways in which home, school, and community should function as a partnership. Her model suggests that the types of involvement represent interactions between families, schools, and communities that should function as a partnership to influence students' success in school. In the model, home, school, and community each represent separate, but overlapping influences on student success. An underlying assumption of the model is that children will most likely succeed when they feel cared for and when they are encouraged to do well. The model posits that home, school, and community should all be responsible for the appropriate interactions and connections required to foster student success. Students are in the center of the spheres of influence because the partnerships themselves do not result in student success. Rather, partnerships support and encourage students to create their own success.

While Epstein acknowledges that home-school-community partnerships will vary from one to another, she assumes that each component of the partnership functions with a belief in shared responsibility between them. In other words, the model suggests that the adults in the home, school, and community form interdependent connections in relation to student success. Epstein's (1995) model guides parental involvement research and policy.

Middle-class parents tend to be more engaged within each of these forms of involvement than working-class parents. Several explanations have been offered for social class differences in parental involvement among white parents. For example, Lareau (2000) found that unlike their middle-class counterparts, white, working-class parents have a tendency to refrain from establishing working relationships with their children's teachers, which created a barrier to parents' knowledge of school events and classroom happenings. In addition, Thomas Gorman (1998) demonstrated that some parents' past negative experiences related to social class led to a devaluation of the role of education among white, working-class families. In fact, ". . . parents who experienced hidden injuries of class tended to harbor the most contempt for individuals with college degrees and/or upper-level, white-collar occupations" (p. 15).

In contrast, the research directed at African-American parental involvement at the elementary school level tends to focus on families of low social class. Studies have demonstrated that teachers can play a critical role in contributing toward increasing the involvement of low-income parents. For example, comparing teachers who were low and high encouragers of parental involvement, Karen Gavin and Daryl Greenfield (1998) demonstrated that parents' responses to teacher requests to be involved increased when teachers in both categories of parental involvement encouragement made requests for specific forms of involvement activity, which has been further supported by Kathryn Drummond and Deborah Stipek (2004). In addition, Kimberley Waggoner and Alison Griffith (1998) indicated that parents adopted some of the teachers' behaviors and language they observed while volunteering in their children's classrooms.

However, African-American parental involvement research has also identified differences between parent-teacher perspectives. For example, Waggoner and Griffith (1998) demonstrated that black parents and teachers are not always talking about the same thing when they speak of "parental involvement." They indicated that the African-American low-income parents included both home- and school-based activities in their definitions of parental involvement. Conversely, teachers defined parental involvement narrowly, only based on school-assigned activities. In fact, teacher comments included a remark of surprise when a black parent appeared to take the initiative assuming a role that was not assigned by the school. Similarly, James Bauman and Deborah Thomas (1997) documented the motivations and practices of a highly involved, low-income African-American single parent, who took the initiative to maintain communication with the teacher regarding her child's progress in school, which challenged the teacher's preconceived negative perceptions of black single-parents' involvement in their children's education. Claire Smrekar and Lora Cohen-Vogel (2001) revealed acute contrasts between school staff members' negative beliefs regarding parents' interests in their children's education and parents' desire to not only be heard, but also to be valued as a parent. In fact, parents repeatedly stated that they would become more involved, if asked. In comparison, teachers and administrators in the school characterized the parents as lazy and disinterested in their children's schooling. Studies that examine specific programs document successful strategies to involve parents in the educational process of their children (Edwards, 1995; Morris, 1999). In many cases, these studies highlight the crucial role of schools initiating the interaction between home and school.

Yet, such initiation may not be the norm in schools in which teachers may harbor doubts about the potential contributions of low-income parents. In such schools, the staff may not recognize the social capital of lower-social class parents or parents of color. Studies that employ social capital theory have shown that school personnel favor parental behavior that is deemed supportive of school policy and procedures, behaviors usually associated with middle-class, white parents (Gavin and Greenfield, 1998; Lareau and Horvat, 1999; McGrath and Kuriloff, 1999). Part of the social capital that parents bring to schools originates in their social networks. Within their social networks, families have different access to information about schools and about children. White middle-class parents are more likely than black working-class parents to have social networks that consist of school staff and other parents in the school (Marshall et al., 2001; McGrath and Kuriloff, 1999). Moreover, Steven Sheldon (2002) indicated that the size and location of a parents' social network predicted their involvement. Parents' interactions with adults in their children's school predicted involvement in school-based activities. Conversely, parents' interactions with adults outside of their children's school predicted home-based learning activities. In the absence of other outreach efforts from schools, homogeneous social networks, such as those found among working-class black families, were associated negatively with overall well-being and student progress in school (Marshall et al., 2001).

Although evidence of social network commonalities exists among black families, studies have also revealed considerable diversity among black parents of similar class backgrounds. Diane Scott-Jones (1987) compared the teaching styles of the low-income parents of high- and low-achieving children and found that mothers of high-achieving children tended to approach teaching their children at home naturally, incorporating it into the regular routines of the home. In contrast, mothers of low-achieving students approached learning at home more formally. Additional evidence of variance among low-income involvement was demonstrated by Scott-Jones's (1987) finding that high achievers' parents tended to stress the importance of good grades more often than parents of low-achieving children, who frequently stressed good behavior. Similarly, Smrekar and Cohen-Vogel (2001) found the low-income, ethnic-minority parents in their study were divided between viewing the value of education as their children's acquisition of particular knowledge of a subject area or the children's acquisition of social skills. Moreover, Robert Colbert's (1991) study of twenty-three African-American parents with primarily limited levels of education revealed that approximately half of the parents felt powerless in their interactions with their children's school and were characterized as nonassertive. The remaining half of the participants reported frustration, but also utilized strategies that characterized them as assertive and empowered in their ability to influence their children's educational experience. The author noted that 80 percent of the nonassertive parents reported an overall satisfaction with their children's progress in school, while 60 percent of the assertive parents expressed dissatisfaction, suggesting that parents' passive involvement may be associated with satisfaction in their children's performance at school. Alternatively, the low-income, ethnic-minority parents interviewed by Smrekar and Cohen-Vogel expressed deference toward their children's teachers. However, these parents did not report feelings of intimidation. Instead, like the parents in Colbert (1991), they articulated frustration with their interactions with school personnel.

The variations among African-American parents in these studies parallel those found in the literature on white parents. For example, Drummond and Stipek (2004) found that regardless of race/ethnicity, parents expressed a belief in the importance of involvement in their children's education, a finding that has been supported by previous research (Chavkin and Williams, 1993; Farkas et al., 1999; Stein and Thorkildsen, 1999). Racial/ ethnic congruence exists among some of the parental involvement literature related to social class. For example, some groups of working-class parents distinguished between parent and teacher responsibility in the educational process, suggesting an independent relationship, and they limited their roles to monitoring their children's homework (Lareau, 2000). Another similarity between African-American and white working-class families found in the literature is that "acceptable" forms of involvement are often learned through school norms (Lareau, 2000; McGrath and Kuriloff, 1999; Smrekar and Cohen-Vogel, 2001). Combined, such research attest to the existence of an institutionalized understanding of appropriate parental involvement actions. Usually these actions include attending school meetings, monitoring homework completion, and attending school programs.

In general, research on African-American parents of low socioeconomic status establishes that for the most part, they not only value education, but also desire to be involved in their children's education. Yet, the question remains as to what constitutes social class. M. Freeman (2004) posits that the use of measures such as income or free/reduced lunch eligibility may cause researchers to miss interpret the relationships and interactions that explain differences in social class. Similarly, Michael Zweig (2004) and Stanley Aronowitz (2003) suggest that social class should be understood as the degree of power or autonomy participants have as a result of their jobs. Degrees of power are observed in a person's ability to influence legislation and policy, to hire and fire workers, and to control their work environments. Zweig argues that defining social class in terms of power requires an examination of the relationships between social classes. In this chapter, I will employ power-based, rather than income-based definitions of social class in order to contribute toward a better understanding of the mediation of parental involvement among African-American families. As social classifications based on occupation are difficult in studies of parenting, where one parent often works at home during children's early years, I will follow Zweig's (2000) suggestion that unemployed spouses usually, "share the class position of their working mate" (p. 12). For this study, the social class of stay-at-home mothers was based on the social class of their husbands.

In sum, the literature not only informed the definitions of social class for this study, but also guided the research questions. School staffs tend to expect and favor the involvement practices of white, middle-class parents, which are often school-based. Working- and lower-class parents frequently face barriers to participation in such forms of involvement. However, working- and lower-class families often express a greater willingness and desire to be involved in their children's educational process than is perceived by teachers and administrators.

Most of the research on parental involvement has examined white families. In fact, ". . . few studies have examined social class patterns within racial groups other than whites" (Diamond and Gomez, 2004, p. 384). Therefore, we do not yet know the extent to which black parents carve out distinctive forms of parental involvement or whether they create distinctive ways of supporting their children's education. This study made the following inquiries: As their children attend schools in which black students continue to lag behind white peers, when do black parents create distinctive forms of parental involvement to support the specific challenges face by their children, and when do they adapt the forms of parental involvement of white parents, practices that schools most readily expect and recognize as supportive of children's achievement?

Methodology

This chapter utilizes data from a larger study (Fields-Smith, 2004) that investigated the parental involvement attitudes, beliefs, practices, and explanations of 19 African-American parents (14 mothers and 5 fathers) across levels of social class within the same southeastern school district. Each parent represented a different family. Originally, participants were selected through a community nomination process as described by Michelle Foster (1997). Three African-American parents representing three different schools were asked to nominate additional parents as potential participants. The final sample of parents ranged in age from 34 to 51 years. The average age of the group was 45 years old and their children ranged in grades from kindergarten to the fifth grade.

Interviews with seven parents from this original sample were used to examine differences in parental involvement among various levels of social class. Unlike previous studies on parental involvement, this study employs defines social class based on parents' occupational autonomy as described by Zweig (2004). Using this framework changed low-income, middle-income, and upper-income classifications to working class, working middle class, managerial middle class, and professional middle class. Working-class professions represented included a nursing aid and retail worker. Working middle-class families included essentially blue-collar workers who have acquired middle-class status through home ownership. Managerial middle-class occupations represented include business executives who have the authority to hire and fire employees; however, they lack the social and political influence afforded to the upper echelons of corporate America. Husbands who held managerial middle-class positions had greater flexibility in their work schedules than working-class families. In addition, managerial middle-class fathers had wives who stayed at home, worked part-time, or were retired. Occupations represented in the professional middle class include lawyers and a psychiatrist. None of the parents in this study represented families in poverty.

The seven parents selected from the original sample of 19 participants were chosen with the intention of providing a cross section of socioeconomic status levels found in the original study. In addition, the selected parents represent different types of school settings including a predominantly white magnet school (PWT), a predominantly black theme school (PBT), and two predominantly black traditional elementary schools (PBE1 and PBE2). Given the use of a community nomination process to identify participants, these seven parents represent highly involved families. In fact, all of the parents were members of the PTA executive board committee except for one. Four of the seven parents had previously, or were currently serving as, PTA president. Unfortunately, this study does not capture the experiences of parents who were less visible in their children's schools. Rather, the parents of this study represent the fairly typical parental leaders from this community. Table 1 provides a summary of background and demographic data for the seven parents represented in this chapter.

Table 1

Summary of Parent Background and Demographic Data

Parent and School Pseudonym	Age	Marital Status	Number of Children (Grades)	Social Class	Occupation	Native Community Type	Education
Betty (PBE1)	37	S	2 (5th, college)	Working	Retail Employee	Urban (Northeast)	Some College
Val (PBE1)	39	S	2 (1st, 4th)	Working	Nurse's Aide	Urban (North)	Some College
Vicki (PBT)	39	M	2 (5th, 7th)	Working-Middle	Admin. Asst.	(Military)	BA
Edward (PBE2)	50	M	3 (4th, 2 adult)	Professional-Middle	Lawyer	Urban (Southeast)	Advanced Degree
Robert (PBE2)	51	M	3 (K, 2nd, 4th)	Managerial-Middle	I. T. Manager	Suburban (Southeast)	Advanced Degree
Barbara (PWM)	46	M	2 (5th, 7th)	Managerial-Middle	Stay-At-Home Mom	Suburban (Midwest)	BA
Mary (PWM)	51	M	2 (2nd, 6th)	Professional-Middle	Retired Teacher	Urban (Northeast)	Advanced Degree

Research Setting

All of the parents who participated in this study had at least one child attending a public elementary school in Howard County Public Schools (pseudonym). Located in the southeastern region of the United States, the school district has experienced a 10% growth rate over the past ten years. Furthermore, census data revealed that the racial composition of the county has changed from majority white (71.3%) in 1980, to majority black (55.3%) in 2000. The percentages of Asian and Hispanic-Americans who attend schools in the county more than doubled in the same time period as well.

The increase in Howard County's population led to an increased enrollment of students in the county's public school system. The district's student enrollment increased from 90,837 in the year 2000, to 97,284 in 2003, according to reports presented on the State Department of Education Website. In 2003, 74,739 students of the total 97,284 identified themselves as African-American. Of these, 41,859 students attended elementary schools in the county, grades pre-K–sixth. In comparison, 10,372 Howard County school students identified themselves as white, and 6,097 of these attended elementary schools in the county.

Together, the seven parents represented four schools in the same southeastern district. These included two predominantly black, traditional elementary schools (PBE1 and PBE2), one predominantly black theme school (PBT), and one predominantly white magnet school (PWM). Table 2 provides a summary of the demographic and achievement data available for each school, as of 2003.

From table 2, it is evident that school PWM, the predominantly white magnet school, has the highest achievement levels and the lowest percentage of students eligible for free/reduced lunch of the four schools. School PBT, the predominantly black theme school, has the largest student population and the second best achievement levels and second lowest percentage eligible free/reduced lunch. Although the two predominantly black elementary schools have relatively similar-size student populations and achievement levels, the percentage of students eligible for free/reduced lunch was 75% at school PBE1 and 50% at school PBE2, respectively. In addition, schools PBT and PWM tend to require yearly lotteries to determine the placement of new students due to an access of applications from families attempting to have their children enrolled. Although the Howard County School District was majority black, the predominantly white magnet school (PWM) was centrally located in majority white neighborhoods. In contrast, the predominantly black schools (schools PBE1, PBE2, and PBT) were located in majority black neighborhoods. As described by Drummond and Stipek (2004), the location of school PWM most likely impedes the enrollment of African-American and other ethnic-minoritystudents. Barbara and Mary felt their

Table 2
Summary of School Demographic and Achievement Data for _____

Performance School	Total Enrolled	Black	White	Hispanic	Lunch	Student Reading Free/Reduced Standards
PBE1	798	660	30	32	600 (75%)	Not Met: 20% Met: 49% Exceeded: 32%
PBE2	758	735	3	5	445 (50%)	Not Met: 14% Met: 50% Exceeded: 36%
PBT	1,090	1,060	3	6	495 (45%)	Not Met: 5% Met: 37% Exceeded: 59%
PWM	414	125	236	2	40 (10%)	Not Met: 0 Met: 6% Exceeded: 94%

children would receive a better quality of education at school PWM than at their assigned neighborhood schools. They based their decisions to enroll their children in school PWM on the school's high test scores and reputation of excellence.

Research Design

This qualitative study utilized a modified version of Irving Seidman's (1998) multistage interview design. Data were collected from two interviews with each parent. This first stage of interviews was conducted early in the school year and focused on both background and current practices at home and at school. These initial interviews averaged one hour and fifteen minutes in length. The second stage of interviews queried parents' motivations to be involved in their children's education. These follow-up interviews occurred approximately six months after the first interviews and averaged forty-five minutes. Interviews were recorded and transcribed. Transcripts were reviewed by each participant for accuracy. Analysis of data consisted of a process of coding patterns and identifying themes (Creswell, 1998).

Findings

The results of this study will be presented in the four categories of social classes (working class, working middle class, managerial middle class, and professional middle class). Profiles of parents will be presented within each level of social class. Next, patterns and themes will be discussed within each of the four levels of social class. Finally, the report of findings will conclude with a discussion of patterns and themes identified across class levels.

Working Class

Describing the working class, Zweig (2000) writes, "On the job, most workers have little control over the pace and content of their work. . . . The job may be skilled or unskilled, white collar or blue collar" (p. 13) Accordingly, two parents in this study represent working class families. First, Betty, who works as a retail employee and who is the mother of two boys, one in the fifth grade and the other attending a local community college. Next, Val, who works as a nursing aide and who is also the mother of two boys, both in elementary school (first and fourth grades). Both Betty and Val were divorced and basically raising their children on their own. Neither Betty nor Val was a native of the southeastern region where they were currently raising their children. There were from the northeast and north-ern regions, respectfully. Both women's children attended school PBE1. As may be expected Betty and Val share similar parental involvement beliefs, practices, and motivations; however, they also reported several key differ-ences in their interactions between home and school.

BETTY: As a retail employee, Betty reported that she had little control over her work schedule to the extent that she frequently had to work twelve hours a day. However, she tended to have one day per week off, which she sometimes used to visit the school. Betty reported that she visited the school two to three times per month to volunteer, meet with the teachers, or make a surprise visit. Betty's volunteering was limited to single-event activities be-cause of the irregularity of her availability. Her volunteer activities include working with small groups of children, chaperoning field trips, providing baked goods, and helping teachers. Betty expressed the fact that her sched-ule keeps her from being a "PTA mom." She attends meetings when possi-ble because she believes PTA meetings tell her ". . . what's going on with education at the state and the quality of education" that her children re-ceived and she reported that so far, she was satisfied. Betty takes the initia-tive to demonstrate her desire to be involved in her son's education. She stated, "When I have the chance to be at the school, I'll call the teacher to try to make arrangements prior to the day to see if we can sit down and talk about where my son is in school so that the teacher and I can feel comfort-able. I'm letting the teacher know that I'm involved with my child and that I want to be involved."

This statement demonstrates Betty's awareness of, and desires to, comply with school expectations of parental involvement.

Betty's school visits served several additional purposes. First, she ex-plained, "I meet his teachers and establish a relationship with them." Betty's relationships with teachers primarily serve to keep informed of her children's progress in school. Second, she reported, "When I'm at the school I work with the teacher in class to make my son see Mom is there. I also get to meet his peers and it just does something." Betty also admit-ted that she conducted surprise visits to the school, ". . . just to let my son know I could appear at anytime."

Betty also conducted home-based activities including reading with her son at home, practicing math skills, reviewing spelling word lists, and checking his homework. In particular, Betty gave an account that demon-strated her knowledge of the importance of her son hearing himself as he read, and therefore, requiring him to read aloud.

When asked how she knew to use these types of learning strategies, Betty first reflected on experiences of her own mother reading with her at home. Then she commented, "I don't have a degree, but some of my friends are more educated than yourself, so that's the good thing about having friends and networking so that you can call them and ask them and they give you advice. So that's a good thing that has helped me." Some of these relationships had been established over time from high school, within her son's school, and from previous work experiences. For example, a friend, who was a school secretary, told her about a magnet middle school program that she will apply for when her son is old enough to attend. She also received strategies from suggestions made by teachers in the school reminiscent of the parent described in the Bauman and Thomas (1997) case study. Betty's social network also included neighbors who served as a "safety net" on occasions when she was not able to be home at night due to work.

Betty's motivations to be involved in her son's education extended beyond a general belief in the value of parental involvement. First, her own experiences served as the primary factor motivating her home- and school-based involvement activities. She confided that she did not finish high school because she was pregnant with her first child. Although she did return to school, Betty stated, ". . . once I started having children, then they became my main focus. So with my own children, I want them to fulfill their education. That's what drives me in the inside because I know what I sacrificed." Second, she admitted that teachers themselves inspired her to be involved. She expressed empathy for teachers through comments such as, "Teachers are very important people and a lot of times they don't get what they deserve." Reviewing her own experiences, Betty stated that she could not think of one negative experience with her teachers. Similarly, Gorman (1998) found that working-class parents with positive learning experiences in childhood were more likely to value education than working-class parents with negative experiences. Betty's belief in the importance of education and the need for education in society also motivated her involvement. She stated,

> It [education] is one of the keys of life that you've got to have if you want to be successful and be on the ball. You have to stimulate your brain and want to read and write. . . . Education is why we have doctors and lawyers and all of these different things. If you want to be one of them, you're going to have to go for the degree. If you just want to become part of the American workforce, you can do that too, but still you're going to have to read, write, add, and subtract. . . . So, no matter where you are in your life, no matter what level of workability you want to do, or education, you're still going to have to have basic fundamentals.

These comments demonstrate Betty's awareness of the possibilities related to education and indicate that she believes education to be a universal need regardless of one's social position.

Betty continues, "Not only do you want the basics, you want the best. You want to go up there and get your Master's. You want to get your BA. That's what I tell my son because like my mother sacrificed a lot for me and I end up sacrificing a lot for them. So I push my children like my mother pushed me because you always want better for your children, so you push them."

She has succeeded with one son who was already enrolled in college. However, while her comments may be inspiring and demonstrate an awareness of the possibilities of mobility with education, the remarks do not necessarily reflect an understanding of the limitations (e.g., social and economic) related to obtaining advanced degrees.

Overall, Betty's school- and home-based activities reflect her support of the educational process. She monitored her children's progress in school through school visits and through learning activities at home. The demands of her job led to sporadic school visits, but she still strived to maintain a connection with her son's teachers as part of monitoring his progress in school. Betty's heterogeneous social networks provided support and knowledge that enhanced her son's educational experience. However, very few of these contacts were within her son's school. Unlike the working-class parents described by Drummond and Stipek (2004), Betty expressed an overall satisfaction with her son's elementary school.

VAL: Val's two sons attended school PBE1 along with Betty's children; one was in the fourth grade and the other was in the first grade. Val also has a two-year-old daughter who attended a day care facility during the day.

Although Val's work as a nurse's aide provided limited financial resources and societal influence, her position fostered steady work hours, which made attending evening meetings more feasible than visiting the school during the day. Therefore, unlike Betty, Val was able to serve as an active member of the PTA. In fact, Val served as a chair of the Cultural Arts Committee of the PTA and reported that her goal was to have the group ". . . connect a little more with the teachers to make sure that it's [Cultural Arts programs] in conjunction with what we are doing." This comment reflected parental involvement with a broader, school-wide focus than Betty's. In fact, prompting was required to solicit Val's reflections on her parental involvement activities directed toward her own children.

Similar to Betty, the home- and school-based activities that Val engaged in for her children represented primarily monitoring, supporting, and reinforcing the educational process at the school. Val reported that she used the school agenda planner system at home and the school-wide, weekly notices to assist with the monitoring of her children's progress.

Agenda planners required teachers and parents to initial their children's homework assignments daily. This communication enable Val to review her children's homework and to make sure that it was placed in her children's backpacks for the next day. Moreover, Val served as one of the room parents for her son's class. This position kept her in contact with other parents, with classroom happenings, and with the teacher.

Unlike Betty, Val reported having numerous connections with other parents and teachers in the school that extended well beyond her neighborhood. Val became involved with the PTA executive board after she attended a general PTA meeting and heard the PTA president requesting more parents to become involved in PTA leadership roles. Since that meeting two years ago, Val and the current PTA president became friends. This is the second year that Val has served on the Cultural Arts Committee. As chair of the committee, most of Val's duties can be completed in the evening (e.g., making phone calls and attending meetings). She also reported that her PTA committee work fostered a working relationship with the school's principal. While this relationship did not extend beyond the school, Val was able to develop a rapport such that she felt comfortable bringing issues to the principal.

This also contributed to her broad parental involvement perspective. She confided, "I have seen teachers hollering just at the brink, to me, of a nervous breakdown. But luckily, a lot of the things that I've seen haven't been in my children's classrooms. But, I did voice what I had observed to some other teachers and I didn't mention any names to the principal, but you want to know what's going on in there [the school]. You want to make sure nobody's hollering at your kid, unjustly at least." Although Val was a highly involved parent, she felt her job kept her from serving as a "watchdog" on the behalf of the children during the school day. She explained, "I see grandparents and parents in the school all the time. I know they're not on the payroll, but they're helping as monitors and stuff. I'd like to be able to do that a little more too."

Val believed that it is every parent's responsibility to be involved in their children's education. She resented the seemingly complacent parents who do not show up even when the school scheduled important workshops or meetings on Saturdays. She lamented, "If I as a single parent can do it, then every parent should be able to do it." She further revealed, "Even though I can't be in the building on a regular basis, I can make phone calls for teachers, help coordinate field trips, and prepare items for a bulletin board." Val made a point to visit the school at least once or twice per week by dropping her children off to school in the morning. She used this time to informally maintain communication with staff members. Val ascribed to a "by any means necessary" approach to being involved in her children's education.

Similar to Betty, Val's at-home practices centered on reinforcing skills and concepts learned at school and monitoring homework and overall academic performance. Both parents valued the importance of getting to know their children's teachers and providing service to the classroom. However, Val's social network, primarily located with the school, enable her to have a broader perspective of parental involvement. Her PTA committee work fostered her ability to internalize and to work to implement part of the mission of the school. She was also able to influence school curriculum through the Cultural Arts Committee.

Discussion

As single, working-class mothers, Betty and Val faced work-related constraints on their parental involvement. The irregularity of Betty's work schedule challenged the consistency of her involvement and Val's daytime, inflexible schedule limited her ability to visit the school during the school day. However, for both mothers, the belief in the importance of education and contacts within their social networks influenced them to develop strategies to circumnavigate these barriers.

In fact, together, Betty and Val exhibit all six of the forms of involvement found on Epstein's (1995) topology of parental involvement activity. First, Betty and Val's parenting activities included close monitoring of their children's progress and providing routines that support learning. Second, communication occurred through informal visits, arranged meetings, and the school-initiated mediums of an agenda planner and weekly mailers. Next, both working-class parents engaged in volunteering at the school. Their volunteering activities tended to be single events such as chaperoning field trips, rather than ongoing tutoring. However, Val was able to serve as a room parent for her son's classroom. She found that she could conduct several activities on the teacher's behalf at home. In addition, the teacher had more than one room parent assigned, which made the job easier for Val because tasks could be shared.

Fourth, Betty and Val conducted learning activities at home. However, each of the mothers tended to support and reinforce learning at home similar to the working-class parents described in Waggoner and Griffith (1998) who incorporated teacher behaviors they observed while volunteering with interactions with their children at home.

Only Val displayed practices in the final two classifications of Epstein's (1995) typology, decision making, and collaboration with the community. Through her work as PTA Cultural Arts Committee chair, Val researched and coordinated artistic school performances from groups locally and outside of the district. This position gave her a deeper understanding of the school curriculum as she sought to make connections between the scheduled performances and curricula at various grade levels. Similarly, her PTA committee role enabled her to collaborate with various community resources to enhance learning for all of the children in the school. From observations of several PTA executive board meetings, I observed that the committee received direction from the school principal in identifying community resources. The principal also encouraged the committee to work with teachers at each grade level in order to connect the cultural performances and programs to the curriculum.

Epstein's (1995) topology in of itself might not capture fully the roles of parental involvement displayed by these parents. For example, the advocacy displayed by Val through her watchdog-like monitoring of teacher-child interaction as she visited the school may have been categorized as communication or volunteering. However, Val's sense of agency represented a stark contrast with typical everyday communicating or volunteering. In addition, Betty frequently initiated contacts with her children's teachers. Rather than wait for scheduled conferences, she called to arrange a meeting with the teacher when she had the time.

Concurrent with previous studies, the school played an important role in fostering these parents' involvement. Universal use of agenda planners and weekly school mailers provided Betty and Val with a medium through which they could not only communicate with teachers on a regular basis, but could also monitor their children's progress as well. In addition, the principal played an important role in guiding parents to connect programs to the curriculum. Moreover, teachers were open-minded toward flexibility in activities that parents engaged in to support the classroom.

Betty and Val differed from the working-class parents described by Drummond and Stipek (2004) in that they were not trying to make changes. In fact, Betty and Val appeared relatively content with their children's school and with their teachers, which was an attitude characterized by middle-class parents in Drummond and Stipek (2004). The working-class mothers also differ from the parents described in Colbert (1991), whose passive involvement reflected a general satisfaction with their children's progress in school. Although Betty and Val's children were performing fairly well in school (receiving A's, B's, and one or two C's), both parents maintained active involvement within the boundaries of their work situations and refrained from criticizing the school.

Working Middle-Class Parental Involvement

VICKI: As the daughter of a military family, Vicki grew up on both the East and West coasts. She also spent several years overseas. Her military childhood provided fully integrated schooling on military bases. Vicki recalled a sense of comfort in her mother being home when she arrived from school each day. At age thirty-nine, Vicki was the mother of two children, a fifth-grade girl and a seventh-grade son, and she strived to provide that same comfort for them as well.

After the birth of her first child, Vicki left her full-time administrative assistant position to become a part-time clerical worker at her church. She and her husband, a heating and air conditioning repairman, decided that it would be best for her to stay home with the children. In order to ease the loss of Vicki's full-time salary, her husband takes on additional jobs on the side. Her husband's long work hours made Vicki the primary parent who engaged in home- and school-based activities. She reported, "We were blessed that we could manage it, but it was a sacrifice." Twelve years later, Vicki's account demonstrates the advantages afforded them as a result of the sacrifice of her salary.

As a part-time employee, Vicki was afforded more time to be involved at her children's school. She invested her time by serving on several PTA committees, assuming PTA officer roles including president, volunteering in her children's classrooms, and supporting her children's extracurricular activities. While volunteering in school, Vicki engaged in a variety of activities. She worked with remedial children in small groups, assisted teachers with copying and correcting papers, and worked with other teachers in the school as well.

Like Val, Vicki approached parental involvement with a broad perspective and a strong sense of collective agency. Rather than taking an individualistic stance regarding the motivation and purpose of their involvement, Vicki and Val expressed beliefs and participating in ways that benefited children other than their own.

Vicki's children attended school PBT, a predominantly black theme school. Although the school is public, as a theme school administrators were able to be innovative with the learning process and instruction. The school also aimed to attract students beyond the typical neighborhood attendance boundaries. Vicki's children began attending school PBT prior to it becoming a theme school. Because the family resided within the attendance area for the school, the children were able to continue attending after it became a theme school. Vicki reports, "I was there before the theme school. You know, the theme school concept is around parental involvement. That's its strength." The theme school requires sixteen hours of parental involvement per year, per family. Prior to the school becoming a theme school, Vicki was ". . . a parent going on the field trips, coming in to the classroom as the teacher requested it and needed help and whatnot. Whereas with [school PBT], you know they have a whole list of things that they assign you to do. Involvement is expected. Teachers expect you to be there and they expect you to volunteer. If you didn't, then that would then jeopardize your child's place at [school PBT]." These comments suggest that when the school was a traditional elementary school, parental involvement was based on teacher needs. Converting the school into a theme school appeared to create additional opportunities for involvement. In fact, the theme school created a parent center where ". . . parents complete work orders that teachers have placed. So, for example, they might make copies or maybe make teaching tools. It really helps because not every parent is comfortable working side by side with teachers."

Vicki believes wholeheartedly that involvement in her children's educational process is part of the responsibility of raising children. She reflected, "As a parent you have to be there for them [children] and you have to nurture. You have to be there every step of the way in the development, both physical, mental, emotional development. It comes from being involved in what they do. You have to know who their friends are. You have to know where they are in school. You have to know who is teaching your child. What are the instilling? Because teachers have your children for a good part of the day, the majority of the day and this is a major influence on your child."

Contrary to parental involvement trends (Stein and Thorkildsen, 1999), Vicki believed that parents should get more involved as children get older. "In elementary school you feel like you just really have to be there. I mean, you're more inclined to help the little one, so to speak. Then as they get more independent, as they go one to middle school and higher, you feel like you don't need to be there, but actually, it's just the opposite. They need you just as much." Part of the reason why Vicki felt compelled to be involved even in the higher levels was due to her perception that she needed to maintain a relationship with her children's teachers to make sure that her children get the best education possible. She linked her being at the school to the proverbial squeaky wheel that gets the oil. She said, "Every once in awhile you have that exceptional teacher that goes beyond the call, with the majority of the students and making sure that each and every one of their students is on track and that's a good year, but they are rare." Another reason why Vicki became so active in her children's schooling is to foster relationships with teachers that would enable her to monitor her children's progress and to build a foundation on which to rely during times when they would have to advocate on her children's behalf.

Vicki spent so much time at her children's school that when asked about the forms of home-school communication she used she replied, "Well, generally I would be there. So, it would be more face-to-face. If I needed to call I would. But, generally, I'd see them pretty much daily and we'd talk. Also, I've been fortunate that my children's teachers felt that they could call me if they needed to contact me."

Similar to Val, Vicki described heterogeneous contacts in her social networks. She reported that she developed friendships with her children's teachers which, at times, extended outside of the school. In addition, she often became friends with the parents of her children's friends. She commented, "When your children become really good friends and you know, they're outside of the classroom, you have that socialization and socialization activities." Relationships also naturally developed due to her children's extracurricular activities such as soccer. Vicki served as team mom for her children's soccer teams and met a number of parents in her children's schools as well as in surrounding schools. Church attendance was another avenue for building relationships with parents and teachers. Vicki attended a church centrally located in her community. Members of the church had children, or taught in schools other than school PBT.

Vicki's report of home-based activities was reminiscent of Betty and Val's practices. "The big thing is giving them the amount of space and time to do homework and making sure that they had proper resources. It used to be that you would have to take them to the library for projects, but now because of the Internet . . . Well, we had to invest in a computer. It has because mandatory. Teachers tell them to type up their assignments." Like Betty and Val, Vicki's home-based learning activities represented their support and reinforcement of learning in school.

Overall, Vicki's home- and school-based practices represented all six of Epstein's (1995) topology of parental involvement. Like Val, decision making and collaborating with the community was mediated through participation on the PTA executive board. Unlike Val, Vicki discussed parental involvement issues beyond the school to the entire school district. At one time, she chaired the Legislative Committee of the PTA board and became more aware of political and legal issues facing schools at the state and district level. Her awareness of educational issues beyond school PBT was also fostered by the heterogeneous social network of friends and acquaintances.

Managerial Middle Class

ROBERT: The father of three girls, Robert is the manager of an information technology department of a major corporation. He works the graveyard shift, 11:00 pm–7:00 am. His wife is a nurse supervisor. Robert's three daughters attend a predominantly black traditional elementary school (school PBE2). At fifty-one years of age, Robert is one of the oldest parents interviewed. He experienced both segregated and desegregated schooling. In fact, he was among the first integrated classes in his mid-Atlantic school district.

Although Robert's parents did not graduate from high school, they stressed the value of education as he grew up. Robert describes his childhood community as "close-knit." He recounted, "If you acted up in school and your neighbors found out, they would tell on you."

Additionally, he described close relationships between his parents and his teachers, who also lived in the community. Robert's descriptions of his childhood community align with the documented histories of bonded communities and African-American teachers of excellence during segregated times (Foster, 1997; Walker, 1996) Robert also described his childhood community as, "lower middle class," meaning that his neighborhood was not in the projects, but they also were not in the plush suburb communities. This slight edge afforded him a college education and contributed to his self-efficacy with regards to his own children's rights to a good education.

Robert's positive childhood experiences led him to seek a close-knit community where his children could attend school, even though he had to go outside of his assigned school to find it. After his children attended three different schools, he used acquaintances and friends from work and church to find a predominantly black, traditional elementary school whose faculty and staff he described as ". . . deeply devoted to our children, sensational, and caring."

Robert and his wife were actively involved in their children's education. They both head a PTA committee for special needs children as one of their children was a special needs child. In this role, they worked closely with the principal to reduce the amount of time exceptional children spend receiving services outside of the classroom. Robert also served on the school council, which addresses school issues primarily at the district level. In addition, he reported that he and his wife participate by tutoring children weekly during and after school, volunteering on special event days, and by remaining available as needed throughout the school year. He and his wife divide parental involvement duties between them in order to maintain a daily presence at the school. Because Robert works at night, he visited the school most mornings. His wife tended to participate in school activities held in the afternoons, with the exception of tutoring days.

Given the inflection in his voice, tone of the interview, and amount of data collected as Robert described his beliefs regarding parental involvement, he was most passionate about the responsibilities parents have before children enter school and their responsibility to build relationships with their children's teachers. For example, he stated, "The first major role occurs before children even get to school. Parents have to teach their children that school is not playtime. School is not day care. School is for learning. You can't learn when your mouth is running." He further emphasized that parents' responsibilities included preparing their children for school. For Robert, preparing his children for school included making sure they get enough sleep each evening, ensuring that they maintain personal hygiene, fostering their independence, and instilling in them the importance of education. These beliefs mimicked the remarks of Val and Betty as well.

Robert also voiced a strong belief that parents should be visible in their children's schools. "It's only natural that a teacher responds to your child when she sees how you respond to your child. If you're up at the school, around your child, then that gives teachers a little faith. It's human nature. They see me, they know that's a child that they're going to make sure that they're going to achieve or they're going to make sure that they get the best out of them. And they're also going to keep me informed if my children are not giving their best."

Robert's comments demonstrate a belief in the advantages to be gained through parents' active visibility in their children's schools. His approach to parental involvement included a strong sense of agency similar to Val and Vicki. During the interviews, he often referred to the children he worked with as his own, illuminating his sense of shared responsibility and advocacy with children other than his own. Robert reported that he used school events to speak to parents of the students he worked with regarding the students' progress or behavior in school, both positively and negatively. His motivations to share with other parents mirrored the concept of the West African proverb, "It takes a village to raise a child." Again showing his ownership of agency for all children, he stated, "If we don't get the children to understand the boundaries of elementary school, then it's harder to get them to understand in middle school and it's futile in high school. It's the theory of growing a tree. They put a stick beside it to make sure it grows straight. If you don't put a stick beside it, the trunk will be all bent and you'll never get it straight again. It is the same with children."

Robert and Vicki's belief in shared responsibility for the betterment of schooling experiences for all children contrasts with the descriptions of white, middle-class parents who, at times band together in the interests of their own children only (McGrath and Kuriloff, 1999). Robert further evidenced a belief in his responsibility to other children in the school as part of his religious beliefs as well. "God put parents as stewards over the children." Robert acknowledged that he had advantages as an older parent. The parents of the children who he volunteers with at school tended to be younger than him; as a result they respected him.

Robert's maturity contributed to his social capital as well. He and his wife decided to wait before having children. This wait time enabled the couple to establish their careers, which provided each of them with the flexibility needed to volunteer in their children's schools regularly. Unlike

Betty and Val, Robert and his wife held professional positions with considerable seniority. In addition, as salaried employees, Robert and his wife were not faced with the consequence of sacrificed income as Betty and Val experienced when they volunteered at the school.

Similar to Vicki, Robert's sweeping social network including neighbors, teachers, professional colleagues, and politicians. While Betty and Val emphasized social networks as a "safety net" for child care and forgotten homework, Robert's description of social networks included accounts of advocacy and sharing strategies to improve the quality of educational experiences for his children as well as for other children. For example, Robert used his political connections to resolve an overcrowding issue on his children's school buses. The political acquaintance (whom he met at a community meeting) advised him to rally parents to sign a petition to seek resolution and also guided him as to where to send the petition. In another instance, Robert, along with other parental colleagues, worked together to petition the school board for flashing lights to be placed at the entrance of the school as a safety measure. Moreover, Robert relied on teacher contacts to develop an after school tutoring program.

Robert and his wife conducted learning activities at home just as Betty, Val, and Vicki did. Robert reported that his wife assumed the responsibility of overseeing homework primarily because he sleeps during the day since he works the night shift. However, unlike Betty, Val, and Vicki, Robert conveyed that they also expanded the school curriculum by teaching their children black history. The family visited museums, historical sites, and cultural events that help their children develop an understanding of who they were as African-Americans and also to develop an awareness of the world around them.

In general, Robert's report revealed participation in each of the six forms of parental involvement found in Epstein's (1995) topology. Through his social networks, PTA involvement, and school council work, he engaged in school decision making and collaborated with the community to employ resources to improve the educational experience. He volunteered and communicated with teachers on a regular basis, almost daily. Unlike the previous parents, Robert's self-reported home-based involvement included not only supporting and reinforcing school curriculum, but expanding it as well.

BARBARA: At forty-six years of age, Barbara was a married, stay-at-home mother of two children (in the fifth and sixth grades). Her husband was employed as a business executive. Barbara and her husband were raised in the Midwest. They met in college. Since that time, Barbara's husband has pursued an advanced degree. Barbara describes her childhood community as small, middle class, and very close-knit. She was the daughter of a Baptist minister. Her parents' high expectations for educational progress provided the motivation for her success in school; a tradition she has tried to pass on to her children.

Unlike the previous parents, Barbara was quite critical of her children's teachers. Barbara's children attend school PWM, a predominantly white magnet school that serves grades four to six. Negative experiences with teacher interactions and declining achievement scores led Barbara and her husband to seek alternatives to the traditional predominantly black elementary school her children initially attended. She described teachers in the previous school as "lazy, and not interested in going beyond what was expected." They chose school PWM because of its high test scores and for its reputation of excellence in the community. Transportation to the school was not an issue because Barbara was able to drive her children to the school herself.

As a parent, Barbara was compelled to be involved in the PTA, but not just as a member. She stated, "To be very honest, I choose involvement activities because I find it necessary in order to be in the loop. So, for example, I'm chairing a PTA committee this year, which enables me to attend PTA executive board meetings." She further clarified that being in the loop meant that she had opportunities to be involved in school decision making. Barbara shared an account of the first PTA meeting she attended. She and her husband left the meeting feeling as though all of the critical decisions had been decided and that the communication process was one-sided, from the school to parents only. In her view, PTA general meetings were for information only. From that moment on, they both agreed that they needed to seek greater access to input in decision making at the school. Through the yearly rotation of executive board or school council roles each year, Barbara and her husband have ". . . found a way to get in there to be in the know, to influence things at the level they want to." Barbara identified roles that enabled her to attend executive board meetings in order to be ". . . at the point of decision making, when I want to be." She avoided high-ranking positions such as PTA president or ". . . as high up in the hierarchy as to have a whole lot of work." Instead, she identified her purpose in assuming a role as finding ". . . a role that would grant me access." Even when granted access, Barbara's involvement in decision making is at her discretion. ". . . If I feel like I need to garnish support for a particular thing, then I'm in a position to go and do that. But if not, I at least know it's not that it's being brought to me at the level where 'this is it and this is how it is'."

As suggested by Vicki, Barbara wanted to get to know the teachers who were influencing her children's lives on a daily basis. The type of service she enjoyed most was her volunteer work with students rather than her PTA involvement. Barbara believed that volunteering at the school was part of a parent's duty in what she refers to as ". . . managing the parent-teacher relationship." She remarked, "We [parents] have to manage teachers. I find that I'm most effective as a parent in support of our children when I go and do things for the teachers. You have to go and volunteer to do things that are helpful to the teacher like copying. It is often a mundane task, copying for teachers hours at a time, but it is something that helps them [teachers]. I find that the way teachers work today, you really have to kind of get to know them in a way that allows you to have some inroad with them."

To Barbara, inroad with teachers provided access to a relationship such that later if there was a problem, teachers would be less likely to take the patented approach with your child. In this way, the time Barbara invested in doing "chores" for her children's teachers lead to the building of rapport and a reciprocal relationship throughout the year. Barbara points out that she performs "chores" for teachers whether she liked them or not because she was ultimately there for her children regardless of who the teacher may be.

Although school PWM required sixteen hours of volunteering from parents, Barbara contended that volunteering at the school requires a special effort on the part of parent volunteers beyond just showing up. In fact, she stated that she was distressed because she finds that she "works so hard to get what [she feels] is something that is just [her] right as a tax-paying citizen. . . . But, I often wonder, now what if I had to work? How would my children fare if I were not in the position to go and handle things?" Part of the barriers Barbara described included the cliquish environment of the school. It seemed that the same parents held particular positions. "Here I am, a willing, able-bodied person who's willing to invest in not only her child, but in the life of the school and then I've got to find things to do. I have had to ask, 'What can I do? What can I do?' The response was, Well maybe you could talk to a teacher about finding something.'"

Barbara attributed some of the difficulty she faced to the racial makeup of the school. She reported, "Part of the problem, well, you know, It's [school PWM] really not representative of the county at-large. It's truly a little private school within the county system. There's just enough African-Americans in there where I guess nobody can complain. There's diversity. They do have that, but it's very selective. . . . They kind of throw us a little bone, as it were. That's how I feel about it." Barbara's description support the findings of Daniel McGrath and Peter Kuriloff (1999) that school norms including the behaviors of white, middle-class parents contributed to the marginalization of ethnic minority and low-income parents. Barbara's middle-class status may have enabled her to overcome the barriers. Advantages afforded her due to social class included the fact that she was a stay-at-home mom, which provided the time to be persistent and consistent.

Barbara was also sensitive to issues of equity at the school. She protested, "They [school personnel] send home notices about different things and there's just an understanding that everybody has the ability to do whatever it is they're asking. It doesn't take into account that if you have any economic challenges, you know, you may. They assume no one has economic challenges. It's like, they pretty much state this is how you do it. You buy this." For example, school policies required children to have two recorders [flute-like musical instruments], one for home and one for school. Barbara further illustrated the effects of such policies when she remarked, "I can do this, but what if it weren't that way. There are parents that have challenges, so they may be the ones who leave, and of course they would be us [African Americans] because they other ones are, you know, it's no big deal." Barbara's comments suggest an underlying institutional assumption that all of the students have middle-class parents. For example, clubs choose specific types of, usually name brand, athletic shoes and T-shirts as a requirement for participation. Outside of these expressions of concern for financially challenged families, Barbara's comments suggested minimal collective agency, unlike Robert, Vicki, and Val.

Barbara reported that she supplements her children's schooling experience with learning activities at home. She further explained that she engaged in learning activities at home when she perceived that her children were not getting something she deemed important at school, or when she believed that the teacher was just teaching to the middle achievement level of the classroom and therefore, not challenging her child enough. At times, this meant that she needed to add to or reteach material covered in class. As an example, she believed that her son's teacher did not place enough emphasis on grammar in the classroom; therefore she and her husband reviewed grammar, punctuation, and writing skills at home.

Similar to the working class and middle working class, Barbara believed it was her responsibility to make sure that the home-school partnership exists. However, unlike the other parents, Barbara expressed an overall frustration in having to "work" for the quality education she believed her children deserved as children of taxpayers. Rather than express empathy as other parents did, Barbara displayed a sense of entitlement with regards to teachers' role in her children's educational process.

Barbara reported that she was very careful about developing relationships with parents that extended outside of the school and that developed into friendships. Unlike Vicki, Val, and Robert, Barbara's social networks from within the school were filtered in a way that the few parents she and her husband socialized with beyond schools appeared to have values similar to their own. These relationships had an influence on her children's education through the sharing of ideas. While she did not report relationships with her children's teachers that went beyond school walls, Barbara did state that she had friends and relatives who were teachers. Though Barbara's social network were slightly more limited than that of Vicki and Robert's, each of their networks reflected a departure from descriptions of African-American social networks found in the literature (McGrath and Kuriloff, 1999) that suggest that African-American parents do not employ social networks within the school.

Professional Middle Class

MARY: At the time of the study, Mary was serving as PTA president for school PWM, the same school that Barbara's children attended. At age fifty-one, Mary was a retired schoolteacher married to a higher-education administrator in a business department of a local college. Just like Robert, Mary and her husband had their children (second and fifth graders) later in life. At the birth of her first child, Mary was a stay-at-home mom; however, after a few years as a volunteer mom, she went back to teaching in the private Montessori school her children attended prior to going to school PWM. Mary's decision was prompted by her fascination with the Montessori concept. Mary and her husband decided to seek a public school provided they could attend school PWM, because of the excellent reputation of the school. The change from private to public school was contingent on Mary also becoming a stay-at-home mom again. Transferring from the Montessori school to school PWM was difficult. Mary reported having to walk up and down the hallways of the Howard County Board of Education building for two days before she found someone to answer her questions regarding the lottery process and the appropriate testing that would be required to transfer.

Dissimilar to Barbara's experience, Mary was able to head the Cultural Arts Committee within her first year in school PWM. She decided to take on the role ". . . to bring about cultural diversity in the school." She continued, "I worked with the Board a lot on decisions and how diversification could be made in a more positive light and not a struggle and a tug and pull." Unlike Val's cultural arts position, Mary's role influenced the diversification of the school staff and the student population, as well as programs and curricula. Similar to the middle-class parents described by Drummond and Stipek (2004), Mary was supportive of the school even while noting areas in need of improvement. However, Mary's positive stance toward improving the school differs from the frustration expressed by Barbara.

Very similar to the previous parents, Mary believed in a partnership between home and school. Like them, she also initiated the relationship between herself and her children's teachers. Describing her approach she stated, "I go and I introduce myself. I tell them who I am. I let them know

[who] my daughter is and if at any point in time you need to be in contact with me, please don't hesitate to do so. . . ."

Currently, she and her husband divide their time between school PWM and another school in the district because school PWM only serves grades four through six and their youngest was in the second grade. Distinctions exist in the parental involvement at each school. She observed, "At [predominantly Black regular school] you have a very small handful of parents who are actively or aggressively involved, whereas I find that at [school PWM] everybody is . . . I mean if it's, I think there's 146 kids in the sixth grade, I guarantee you, you're going to see twice that many at PTA meetings because the dads attend too." Like Robert and Barbara, Mary and her spouse take turns rotating positions of involvement at their children's schools such that during any given year, one of them served on the executive board.

Mary and her husband's social class, influence, and power were displayed in her frequency and flexibility of school-based involvement. For example, Mary stated she was ". . . like a fixture on the walls" when describing how often she and her husband visited the school. Moreover, when their daughter went on a weeklong field trip one to two hours from the school and neither Mary nor her husband were selected as chaperones Mary said, "That's okay that you didn't choose me because we'll be there every day. And I was. My husband got off work and we drove to [the destination of the field trip] every day so that I could see her and make sure she was okay." In addition, Mary and her husband made a personal choice not to have their children ride on the school bus. Instead, they each drop off and pick up their children. Their ability to do so reflected the proximity of their home to the school, and the ease in which Mary's husband could alter his schedule for drop-offs and pickups.

Similar to Barbara, Mary was selective in having relationships with other parents in the school that extended beyond the school. This year was the first time she allowed her daughter, age eleven, to sleep over a friend's house. Describing the mother of that child Mary stated, "Her mom is an extremely active mom, high-visibility. She's at the school every day. She's a Lunch Bunch Mom, so she does lunch daily. She's in the lunchroom and she's this and she's that. I know that her daughter has to move within certain boundaries so I felt that I could trust with her being three with the girl's mom, in their home, and the [her daughter] would come home in one piece." The mother's visibility in the school made Mary comfortable yet, describing the relationship with the parent Mary remarked, "I would say not friends, but our kids go to the same school. She's a mom. I'm a mom and we have the same interest as far as our children are concerned. But, friends outside of the school, no. No." Data was not collected related to the ethnicity of this parent.

Mary reported that she was motivated to be involved in her children's education due to several factors. First, she connects to her upbringing. "I do not know any other way to be because this is how my parents were with me. So, if I did anything less, then I would really feel like I would be doing them a disservice for me". Second, she has observed the ". . . excitement and the joy that comes from my children when we see each other at school." Third, she reported, "I make sure that I'm visible in both of their schools because I don't want there to be no mistakes mentally in the fact that I'm a highly proactive mom and highly involved." Finally, similar to Barbara, Mary sought access to decision making. She responded, "I'm able to have a strong voice in decisions. For example, when the issue of uniforms came up I was able to voice my opinion on colors and the inclusion of jeans." Other areas of input include budget issues and curriculum and instruction. Regarding her opportunity to have input, Mary stated, "My vote may not necessarily change it to what I see as being right, but at least, like I told them, you know how I feel and I'm going to be giving you my opinion as to how I would think things should be run or governed or done."

In all, Mary's practices in the home and school were similar to Barbara and Vicki; however, Mary had a more supportive attitude toward her children's school than Barbara. Even when Mary criticized her children's school she remained positive and offered a solution. Mary epitomizes the professional middle-class families discussed in Drummond and Stipek in that mobility from a private school to a prestigious, public magnet school was feasible, given the location of the school and the flexibility of being a stay-at-home mother.

EDWARD: Edward represented the professional middle class as a private practice lawyer. His wife occasionally helped run his office, but primarily was a stay-at-home mother. At age fifty-one, Edward was beginning a term of service as PTA president for school PBE2. Edward had three children, two were adult age and one was in the fourth grade. He was more involved now than he was when his older children were going through public schools. He attributed the difference to his own maturity level.

Prior to becoming PTA president, Edward had always been highly active with the PTA at school PBE2. He served on committees and volunteered in his daughter's classrooms. Reflecting on the five years he spent as a parent at school PBE2 he commented, "Parents that tend to be involved on some level, whether it's those who are involved heavily or those who you can call on to do things when you need them, they're usually parents who have had a college education or those who had some college and to my knowledge, they always have graduated from high school. So they know the value of education." He also commented on the fact that the most supportive parents tend to be homogeneous in age (forties and early fifties) as well, at school PBE2.

Edward remarked, "Educating a child is a never-ending process." He acknowledged the value of the home-school partnership, and he clearly believed that he played an important role in his children's education. He attributed his own educational process to his belief in interdependent relationships between home and school. He stated, "Because of my educated backgrounds, we're not going to sit back and allow other people [teachers] to do all the work."

As PTA president, Edward believed that advocacy was the primary function of the PTA. This differs from Barbara's view of the organization because she felt as a general member, the organization served to disseminate information. "Parents have to have some level of involvement. You don't have to be an active PTA member, but I think you need to be a member of the PTA. So at least your name will be on the roll. That way, if the PTA leadership asks how many members do you have you can say three hundred. Maybe all three hundred don't come to a meeting on a regular basis, but it would be great to know if you needed your three hundred members to come stand out in front of the building or meet you at the board office, they'll be there because advocacy is that main thing that PTA is about. It's not fundraising." Edward expressed a belief that once parents spend time volunteering in school they'll ". . . realize that they need to do something in terms of enhancing something at the school." He further stated that becoming a member of the PTA helps parents identify the process involved in meeting the need they have identified. He acknowledged disparities between the abundance of resources of the predominantly white schools in the northern part of the district and of the limited resources in the southern part, where school PBE2 was located. Of this situation he said, ". . . those northern end schools are predominantly white and supposedly have more resources than us, but most of those resources were brought into the building by parents. It is not that the system [is] giving more." Examples of areas that have been improved at school PBE2 included new books for teachers' classrooms, test-taking materials, a new playground, and equipment for the gym. Furthermore, Edward said, "What we have to fight against is that we have schools in neighborhoods that are perceived or actually not receiving resources."

Edward reported that he had used his leverage as a lawyer on behalf of the school to obtain resources for the school. For example, school PBE2 was originally built for a school population of 600, but due to increased new home construction the student population was approaching 1,000. Although the student population was growing, school resources such as the cafeteria were not being expanded. Edward reported, "The cafeteria, the freezer, and some other things were in real bad shape. You know, if you build a cafeteria for 600 and then you give them more kids, well you need more staff. You go in there during lunchtime. They're flopping around each other, burning, spilling. So the commitment that we got recently that some of these things would be addressed, is based on the fact that we have unsafe conditions. You know, when you start telling people you have unsafe conditions and then one of your PTA presidents is a lawyer, you don't have to say anything. No one wants a lawsuit!"

Edward's social networks included politicians, teachers in and outside of his daughter's school, church members, colleagues from volunteerism, community leaders, and neighbors. Before moving into this district, Edward served on the Board of Education. He maintained friendships from that experience. In addition, he was born and raised in a community very close to the district in which his daughter attended school. Therefore, he had a deeper understanding of the history of the community. He used his relationships with members of the community to advocate for legislative advocacy and politics. At the time of the second interview, Edward was running for political office.

Interestingly, Edward commented, "I often tell people, being a member of [the] PTA oftentimes pits your interest for your own child with the interest of all the children. [The] PTA is for all children. And sometimes you have to say, well I've got to make sure I take care of my own too because I'm spending so much time for the group." Edward strived for a balance between collective agency and advocating for his own child's education.

At home, Edward and his wife assisted with homework, and reinforced and supplemented his daughter's education. "You try to be a teacher at home and you realize how difficult it must be in a room with twenty-five of them. Trying to figure out how to teach a lesson from a different angle, trying to motivate. A lot of it at home is motivation, I think." Edward reported that he spent a lot of time monitoring his daughter's progress at school, trying to make sure that ". . . if she doesn't get it, it isn't because of behavior, not paying attention, sickness, or something else."

In order to monitor his daughter's progress in school, Edward emphasized that he worked to build relationships with her teachers. He stated, "She's in the fourth grade and I still walk her to her classroom everyday. She wants me to, but also I walk her to the door and ask the teacher how everything is going. For the most part she sees me one, twice, three times a week. And I ask, is everything alright? And I mean it sincerely because if there's something I can do as a parent, then I want to know about it and I'll try to do it."

In general, Edward's form of involvement demonstrated empathy for teachers and collective agency. He seemed to make parental involvement synonymous to raising a child. His perspective was expressed clearly as an advocacy organization. For him, PTA functions included disseminating information, fund-raising, volunteering, and taking political action, all for the purpose of advocating on behalf of the children in the school.

In sum, the various perspectives of parents in this study support and challenge previous research in parental involvement. Practices described by the African-American parents in this study demonstrate involvement in all six of the categories found in Epstein's (1995) topology. However, Epstein did not fully capture all of the nuances of African-American parental involvement found in this community such as advocacy and monitoring of teachers' actions. Furthermore, Epstein's home-school partnership model does not consider the sense of entitlement brought to school by more educated parents and by the subsequent willingness of these parents to be strong advocates for their children's well-being. This suggests that the more we learn about diverse families, the more we learn about family involvement in general.

The findings from this study also inform the intersection of race and class. Schools have been slow in acknowledging that working-class and middle-class parents might contribute in effective, albeit in different ways. Schools also seem to expect black and white families to become involved in similar ways. While the literature acknowledges that teachers do tend to expect less interest and involvement from poor parents of color, the experiences of the working- and middle-class families in this study suggest that expectations and compliance overall is remarkably similar for black and white parents.

The striking similarities between white and black parents' involvement and their explanations for why they are involved may be interpreted in several ways. One possible explanation is that similar forms of involvement may be effective for all children, regardless of background, suggesting that parental support is generic. On the other hand, the similarities in forms and explanations for involvement may be surprising as black students continue to lag behind their white peers in academic achievement. This selection of black parents engaged in forms of involvement very similar to those documented in the literature such as volunteering in classrooms, performing routine clerical tasks, supervising academic practice (primarily in the area of literacy), assuming leadership positions within established organizations, and in the case of middle-class parents, the assumption of more of a "watchdog" role to oversee their children's education. Middle-class parents were much more strategic in establishing networks and positioning themselves to have access to information; working-class parents sometimes had access to social networks through which they learned things in schools, but for these parents, this access was more accidental than strategically sought.

For the most part, the stories told by these parents represent compliance with conventional forms of involvement expected by schools. As parents invoke these forms of involvement, schools gain, but what losses occur if parents refrain from participating in practices more specifically responsive to the needs of their children? Possible losses include limited or no advocacy related to institutional racism. Barbara, whose children attended the predominantly white magnet school, described some of the injustices experienced at school, but did not indicate what she might be doing about it in her position of involvement. Another parent, Edward, insists that differences in resources at white and black schools are attributable to parents, not to "the system." Some of the parents talked of supporting curriculum enhancement around issues of diversity, but there was discussion about advocacy for specific educational needs of black children or achievement gaps that children like theirs were likely to experience. Parents also did not indicate a need for specific information about the ways in which their children might have to plan their futures in a different way from white children.

Finally, this study did not explore the perspectives of the specific schools represented regarding the ways in which school staff might draw on cultural or community strengths and the understandings of black parents to foster deeper partnerships in order to address achievement gaps. Further research is needed to examine the extent to which schools possess the characteristics of successful parental involvement programs as found in previous research.

As African-American parents invoke these forms of involvement rather than other possible forms, they will be more responsive to the needs of their children within and across social class. For example, regardless of social class, parents in this study took the initiative toward establishing and maintaining working relationships with their children's teachers. Working-class mothers purposely dropped their children off to school in the morning just like the professional middle-class parents with the purpose of providing frequent informal touchstones with the teacher throughout the year. In addition, parents subscribed to Epstein's (1995) overlapping spheres model of interdependence between home and school.

Epstein's (1995) six forms of parental involvement were well represented by the home- and school-based practices of the parents in this study. However, social class differences were observed in the motivations for learning activities at home. Unlike Drummon and Stipek (2004) the managerial and professional middle-class families in this study reported that they extended and surpassed learning at home, based on their observations of missing topics such as black history or parents' perceived shortcomings of a teacher's practice. This demonstrates that the degree of interdependence between home and school changed with the social class of the parents. Working-class parents reported engagement in learning activities at home that were supportive of learning at school. In comparison, professional and managerial middle-class parents indicated that they extended the school curriculum by having their children learn more about particular topics and at times middle-class parents also used learning activities at home to make up for a perceived weakness in teachers' practices. Furthermore, middle-class parents would be classified as more self-efficacious in that they voiced their intentions to be involved in school decision making. Unfortunately, in this study opportunities for decision making appeared to be mediated by the limited number of positions on the PTA executive board, which may explain the disparity between the large number of African-American parents who wanted to be involved in school decision making compared to the few parents who reported actual opportunities in Nancy Chavkin and David Williams (1993).

Examining social class in terms of occupational power not only demonstrated the extent to which parents could be in the classroom, but also indicated the quality and purpose of parents' social networks. Sheldon (1998) demonstrated that homogeneous social networks were associated with lower levels of achievement and that low-income parents tended to have more homogeneous social networks than middle-class parents. In this study, Val, the working-class mother who served as a PTA committee chair had more opportunity to forge relationships with teachers other than her own children's teachers. While achievement data were not collected as part of this study, data show that Val's perspective of parental involvement was broad compared to that of Betty's network, which was limited by the inflexibility of her work schedule.

Given the diverse experiences of parents in this study, the intersections of race and class merit much further consideration than has been available to date in the literature on parent involvement. This chapter represents one step in that direction.

References

Aronowitz, S. 2003. *How class works: Power and social movement.* CT: Yale University Press.

Baumann, J. and Thomas, D. 1997. "If you can pass Momma's tests, then she knows you're getting your education": A case study of support for literacy learning within an African American family. *Reading Teacher,* 51, 108–20.

Chavkin, N. and Williams, D. 1993. Minority parents and the elementary school: Attitudes and practices. In N. Chavkin (Ed.) *Families and schools in a pluralistic society* (pp. 73–83). Albany: State University of New York Press.

Colbert, R. 1991. Untapped resource: African American parental perceptions. *Elementary School Guidance & Counseling*, 26(2), 96–106.

Creswell, J. 1998. *Qualitative inquiry and research design: Choosing among five traditions.* Thousand Oaks, CA: SAGE Publications.

Diamond, J. and Gomez, K. 2004. African American parents' education orientations: The importance of social class and parents' perceptions of schools. *Education and Urban Society*, 36(4), 383–427.

Drummond, K. and Stipek, D. 2004. Low-income parents' beliefs about their role in children's academic learning. *Elementary School Journal*, 104(3), 197–213.

Edwards, P. 1995. Connecting African American parents and youth to the school's reading curriculum: Its meaning for school and community literacy. In B. Gadsden and D. Wagner (Eds.) *Literacy among African-American youth: Issues in learning, teaching, school.* Cresskill, NJ: Hampton Press.

Epstein, J. 1995. School/family/community partnerships: Caring for the children we share. *Phi Delta Kappan*, 76, 701–12.

Farkas, S., Johnson, J., Duffett, A., Aulicino, A., and McHigh, J. 1999. *Playing their parts: Parents and teachers talk about parental involvement in public schools.* New York: Public Agenda.

Fields-Smith, C. 2004. After "It Takes a Village": Attitudes, beliefs, practices, and motivations of African American parents in elementary school settings. Ph.D. diss. Emory University, Atlanta.

Foster, M. 1997. *Black teachers on teaching.* New York: New Press.

Freeman, M. 2004. Toward a rearticulation of a discourse on class within the practice of parental involvement. *Qualitative Inquiry*, (10)4, 566–81.

Gavin, K. and Greenfield, D. 1998. A comparison of levels of involvement for parents with at-risk African American kindergarten children in classrooms with high versus low teacher encouragement. *Journal of Black Psychology*, 24(4), 403–17.

Gorman, T. 1998. Social class and parental attitudes toward education. *Journal of Contemporary Ethnography*, 27. Retrieved April 23, 2001 from Academic Search Elite Database.

Jeynes, W. 2003. A meta-analysis: The effects of parental involvement on minority children's academic achievement. *Education & Urban Society*, 35(2), 202–19.

Lareau, A. 2000. *Home advantage.* New York: Rowan & Littlefield Publishers.

Lareau, A. and Horvat, E. M. 1999. Moments of social inclusion and exclusion: Race, class, and cultural capital in family-school relationships. *Sociology of Education*, 72, 37–54.

McGrath, D. and Kuriloff, P. 1999. "They're going to tear the doors off this place": Upper-middle-class parent school involvement and the educational opportunities of other people's children. *Educational Policy*, (13)5, 603–29.

Marshall, N., Noonan, A., McCarthney, K., Marx, F., and Keefe, N. 2001. It takes an urban village: Parenting networks of urban families. *Journal of Family Issues*, 22(2), 1–16 [On-line].

Morris, J. 1999. A pillar of strength: An African American school's communal bonds with families and community since Brown. *Urban Education*, 33, 584–605.

Scott-Jones, D. 1987. Mother-as-teacher in the families of high and low-achieving Black first-graders. *Journal of Negro Education,* 56(1), 21–34.

Seidman, I. 1998. *Interviewing as qualitative research: A guide for researchers in education and the social sciences.* New York: Teachers College Press.

Sheldon, S. 2002. Parents' social networks and beliefs as predictors of parent involvement. *Elementary School Journal,* 102(4), 301–16.

Siddle Walker, V. 1996. *Their highest potential: An African American school community in the segregated south.* Chapel Hill: University of North Carolina Press.

Smrekar, C. and Cohen-Vogel, L. 2001. The voices of parents: Rethinking the intersection of family and school. *Peabody Journal of Education,* 76(2), 75–100.

Stein, M. and Thorkildsen, R. 1999. *Parental involvement in education: Insight and application from the research.* Bloomington, IN: Phi Delta Kappa International.

Trotman, M. 2001. Involving the African American parent: Recommendations to increase the level of parent involvement within African American families. *Journal of Negro Education,* 70, 275–86.

Waggoner, K. and Griffith, A. 1998. Parental involvement in education. *Journal for a Just and Caring Education,* 4, 65–77.

Zweig, M. 2000. *The working class majority: America's best kept secret.* Ithaca: Cornell University Press

———. 2004. *What's class got to do with it?: American society in the twenty-first century.* Ithaca: Cornell University Press.

8

SOCIAL HETEROGLOSSIA

THE CONTENTIOUS PRACTICE OR POTENTIAL PLACE OF MIDDLE-CLASS PARENTS IN HOME–SCHOOL RELATIONS

Janice Kroeger

Within the last several decades researchers have documented the importance of parent involvement in academic achievement, measuring the effects of parents' activities with schools and children as one influence on school success (Booth and Dunn, 1996). Joyce L. Epstein has argued that the strategies teachers use with parents are key factors in increasing the active roles parents play in classrooms; parents, too, exert influence on school climate (1986, 1996). Recent discussions have accounted for active parent networks, uncovering the links within families' social groups. Steven B. Sheldon found that parents with more connections to other parents within communities engaged in heightened parent–school activity (2002). Although we realize the ways in which parents' beliefs and behaviors generate values about school and influence children's accomplishments (solidifying the link between involvement, expectations, and student skills and achievement), we also know that parenting strategies for success and thus cultural capital contrast with the variety of ethnic, social-class, and linguistic groups (Bright, 1994, 1996a; Diamond, Wang, and Gomez, 2004; Hidalgo et al., 1995; Okagaki and Frensch, 1998; Wentzel, 1998). What we know a great deal less about, however, is how schools with urban diversity support parent involvement when their family populations are intersecting, cross-racial, multilinguistic, and composed of a broad variety of social classes, such as those in many of today's schools. This chapter reveals tensions and possibilities within one diverse community.

National policies have urged "every school to promote partnerships that will increase parental involvement and participation in promoting the social, emotional, and academic growth of children"; many schools have used such policies as a springboard to important reform addressing disparities in achievement among children based on minority economic, racial, and language status (National Education Goals Panel, 2000). Such national foci suggest that the more parents are involved in schools, the better-off children will be; yet theorists have also uncovered the darker side of parent participation within the activity of the middle class, the aforementioned working individualistically to benefit their own with questionable consequences or counterresults for the children of others (Brantlinger and Majd-Jabbari, 1998; Lareau, 1989). Recent productive approaches to urban school reform suggest studies of school communities as "ecologies" with nested concerns of groups to be shared, acted upon, and improved, not by lone individuals but by powerful school and parent leaders marshalling resources (Giles, 1998).

This research focuses on the potential of the active middle class and the findings come from an ethnographic portrait in a diverse urban primary school. This chapter, which features an analysis of how home–school relations, are recast by, and in relation to, majority dominance, gives an account of a small group of people making sense of experiences in order to produce action and community. The findings reveal social checks and balances, highlighting the individualistic, collectivist, and seemingly interreliant manner in which middle-class parents operated vis-à-vis the school, children, and other parents, who came from the minority with respect to language, social class, and ethnicity. This chapter is a mirror on a portion of this school's ecology, implicating the critical nature of parent activity in schools.

Theoretical Frame: Social Heteroglossia

The nature of Highland School is best described by the term *heteroglossia*, a theoretical concept that describes a social and literary wholeness made of the particularistic elements of the languages of many groups in a culture (Bakhtin, 1935/1981). Bakhtin argued that "what languages have in common—the only thing they all have in common—is that they are each specific points of view on the world, forms for conceptualizing the world in words, specific world views, each characterized by its own projects, objects, meanings, and values" (pp. 291–92). Although Bakhtin used the terms *languages* and *utterances* in variation, his point was that utterances are always at least two-sided acts, belonging to both speakers and listeners and to those whose "voices are heard in the word"; therefore, the word discourse "lives, as it were, on the boundary between its own context and another, alien context" (p. 284). Overall, any spoken utterance has its own intention, *a social intention*, which is beyond the word, the speaker, and listener, as its own task or project (Morris, 1994; Morson and Emerson, 1990).

Much like the ways in which Bakhtin described shared utterances between speaker and listeners as existing on boundaries, the five neighborhoods of Highland and their constituents existed in an endless cycle of dialogic relations with one another. Without one faction of the community, the others could not exist; without describing low-income parents and their children, Highland could not be called an urban reformed school with the advantages conferred upon it by the middle- and high-income families from professionally situated lives. The double-sided nature of social relations at Highland seemed polemical, fraught with tensions, and ripe for possibility. As one parent stated: "Well, while we might like to think that we are all one population and one big happy family in the school, I really see there being racial and social divides and not a lot of crossing of that. Certainly there is no crossing of boundaries at the level of the families. One of the first things I noticed early on in William's [his son] schooling was that it was always the white families that were there. Minority parents weren't there. With the children I think there is a better connection across ethnic and racial divides" (Sol's father, October 29, 2000, pp. 5–6).

This parent reflects Mikhail M. Bakhtin's (1981) notion of heteroglossia, in which opposing forces collide and comprise as "close a locus as possible to moments in discourse when centripetal and centrifugal forces collide" (p. 123). In language, indeed in every utterance, social tensions are present: those that have the potential to unify social meanings and those that have the potential to disturb meanings. Thus, language as a living entity continuously re-creates culture and its possibilities. Bakhtin defined centripetal forces as social arrangements in language that unify a concept (or group) and centrifugal forces as outer-reaching, unpredictable, disorganized, and unwieldy forces breaking shared meaning and social purposes of language (or social organizations) apart. Bakhtin claimed that the discourse of the novel conveys the conflict between official and unofficial doctrines of culture. I use the concept of *heteroglossia* in this work to examine the ways in which informants in this study displayed the conflicting meanings of social groups within this particular time and place. The results of my interpretive analysis continually show the character of individual people and the characteristics of groups of people constructed relationally to each other. By rendering the social heteroglossia within Highland's parent and student community, I convey the existence of clashing social groups within the school's larger parent community.

Site Description and Interpretive Research Methods

Located in a large Midwestern city, Highland School[1] served students from kindergarten through the third grade. During the year of data collection, according to school records, the school population was classified as 38% impoverished, 34% ethnic and racial minority (consisting of African-American, Latino, and Hmong groups), and 66% European American. District leaders and school personnel developed desegregation strategies throughout the city to combat resource inequities (Confidential, Highland Principal, 1998). The school drew children and parents from five very different neighborhoods (see table 1).

Table 1
Highland School's Neighborhood Descriptions

Waterside International community	A multilingual and multiracial community. Residents live in a large public-assisted housing complex. Some of Highland's Latino and Hmong families live at Waterside. The area is home to low-income families of European and African-American ancestry as well as new immigrant status
Highland neighborhood	A neighborhood of mixed ethnic and racial groups from both white-collar and blue-collar occupations. Residents are both renters and homeowners and primarily speak English.
South Green Street area	A neighborhood zoned for residence and business, bordering both Highland and Waterside International. Residents are of mixed racial and linguistic groups and live in low-income, public assistance, and rental units. The area is home to African-American, Latino American, and European American groups, many earning a living in service industries, such as restaurants and retail.
Village Grove neighborhood	A residential neighborhood with rental properties, student housing, and single-family homes. Heads of households work in white-collar and blue-collar industry. The racial makeup is predominantly white with an ethnic and linguistic mix associated with university students.
Gravenswood neighborhood	A residential neighborhood populated by middle- to upper-middle-income families and professionals associated with a university, health fields, and civic occupations. The Gravenswood neighborhood contains Gravenswood Elementary School, Highland's paired school. Residents rent or own homes, and there is a heavy population of retirees, a small portion of students, and many families of mostly European American ancestry. There are very few Latino, African-American, or Hmong.

Each neighborhood had its own particular character, and economic, racial, and linguistic qualities often blurred at the edges. Reform strategies were used to accommodate neighborhood diversity at the school, including mixed-age grouping, in-class delivery of special services (including English as a Second Language [ESL], Talented and Gifted [TAG], and Special Education), smaller class size, and Developmentally Appropriate Practices, including active hands-on learning strategies and age appropriate curriculum (Bredekamp and Copple, 1997). Title I moneys were used for Reading Recovery Services and for empowerment groups for parents of racial and linguistic minority students who had a history of lower school achievement than their white counterparts (Confidential, Highland Principal, 1998).

The parent and school personnel informant pool for this study were derived from a first–second grade classroom with a veteran teacher, Marlene Spencer. Focal informants provided access to a full range of home–school–community events for the duration of the study, in which the researcher analyzed the content and process of home–school events for individuals and for groups of families and also studied the identity and social group memberships of a small number of parents.

In such an approach the distinctiveness of one person or group is downplayed, and "attention is redirected to the cultural forms that connect and construct various people in context" (Eisenhart, 1999). This multi-aged classroom was chosen because of the dimensions and range of differences in parents' race, social class, language, sexual orientation, ethnicity, marital status, and family structure. The perspective this researcher took was intentionally disruptive to the common use of *diversity*, usually defined as a minority-only concept; therefore, information was solicited from a range of parents from both majority and minority groups (Kroeger, 2001).

Among the families in the study classroom, 11 were of two-parent, middle or high income, professional European American background; 3 were of two-parent, working-class, European American, Hmong American, or Chinese American background; and 2 were two-parent or single-parent welfare recipients of Hmong American and African-American descent. The primary languages spoken by the parents were English, Hmong, and Mandarin. Focal parents included a first-generation Hmong father, a European American father who was a gay activist, and a European American mother who was one of several Parent Teacher Organization (PTO) leaders. For contrast with the focal parents, the researcher selected eight peripheral parents from the classroom who were queried about emerging issues related to community partnerships within the school.

Qualitative methodology was used, including observations made in the classroom, school, home, and community as well as short intensive interviews conducted before and after home–school events. Data sources included audio taped interviews with the focal teacher, school personnel, focal parents, peripheral parents, and a small set of children. A total of 81 observations, 59 interviews, and 79 memos were generated during the 2000–2001 school year. Analysis of data was ongoing, and the researcher attended to "the immediate and local meanings of actions" as defined by the "actors' points of view" (Erikson, 1986). Expanded field notes from observation (Emerson, Fretz, and Shaw, 1995) were coded for a priori and emergent themes in an ongoing fashion. Themes were triangulated among observations, artifacts, and interview transcripts[2] (Graue and Walsh, 1998). A uniform set of questions related to educational experience, social history, and student participation with Highland was posed to focal parents. A less intensive set of questions related to events and activities was posed to both focal and peripheral parents, based on themes arising within the community.

Member checks in the form of raw classroom field notes and written cases shared with the focal teacher and parents substantiated informants' meaning. For interviews and member checks with the parents of Hmong and Mandarin students, the researcher secured the translation and transcription services of speakers from each dialect or language (independent of those available in the school)[3] (Fielding and Fielding, 1986). Translations and transcriptions of Hmong and Mandarin data were then cross-checked for accuracy of meaning for a second time with another proficient speaker of each dialect or language.

Parent Involvement and Highland School

Three major categories of opportunity were available for parent involvement at Highland, including those structured by the first-grade teacher, Marlene Spencer, in the focal classroom, those relating to restructuring and school improvement created by school staff, and those created by the active Highland/Gravenswood Parent Teacher Organization. This analysis features the strong presence of the middle class in certain venues, particularly classroom volunteering and PTO activity (see table 2).

Parents from Spencer's classroom chose from among the many events produced at the school. Table 3 describes the families, their location in the community, and their participation and attendance at events during one year and illustrates the relationship among neighborhood location, event production, and parental attendance.

Table 2
Parent Involvement Opportunities at Highland School

Focal Classroom	Restructuring Plan	Highland–Gravenswood PTO
Ready-Set-Go conference	Title I adaptations	weekly community newsletter
fall Open House	parent handbooks in Hmong and Spanish	PTO monthly meetings
fall and spring parent–teacher conferences	parent call line in Hmong and Spanish	committees, dontations and funding
take-home folders	ongoing parenting groups for minority parents	Fundraisers
weekly newsletters		Sock hop
routine and novel	School Improvement Plan	fall and spring book fairs
volunteer opportunities	Market-Day celebrations	Gravenswood Carnival
report card discussions	assemblies for parents and children	miscellaneous sales
end-of-year classroom performance	mentoring program	PTO Academic Events
	ESL family potluck	Author's Tea
	International dinner	Star Math experiences
		After-school second-language classes

Table 3

Families in Spencer's Classroom Participate at Highland School Activities

Parents/Adults	Location in Community	RSG	Open House	Fall Parent Teacher Conference	Classroom Volunteer	Spring Parent Teacher Conference	End-of-Year Classroom Performance	Ongoing parenting meetings for AA, Hmong, and Latino	Boundary Issues meetings	Market Day Events	Mentoring Program	Balanced Literacy Review	ESL Family Potluck	International Dinner	PTO Monthly Meetings & Committees	Sock-Hop	Fall & Spring Book Fairs	Gravenswood Carnival	Author's Tea	Star Math Experiences	Afterschool Second Language Classes
								Events Offered at Highland School													
Sallie & Martin Arola	Gravenswood	◆	◆	◆	◆	◆	◆			◆							◆	◆	◆	◆	◆
Laurel Strauss & Joel Henderson		◆	◆	◆	◆	◆	◆		◆	◆	◆	◆		◆	◆		◆	◆	◆	◆	◆
Paige & Robert Cartier		◆	◆	◆		◆	◆		◆	◆					◆		◆	◆	◆		◆
Helen & James Jacobs		◆	◆	◆	◆	◆	◆										◆	◆	◆		◆
Michael Colton & Donald Lake		◆	◆	◆	◆	◆	◆			◆							◆		◆	◆	

(continued)

Events Offered at Highland School

Parents/Adults	Highland-Gravenswood				Village Grove		Highland	South Green Street & Waterside International	South Green Street	Waterside
Sandra Stewart & Paul Koester	◆									
Rachel Summers & David Cash	◆	◆	◆	◆		◆				
Betsy & Walter Cline		◆		◆	◆			◆		
Mae Chao & J. Smith		◆	◆	◆	◆	◆				◆
Eva Blasius & Howard Wilson (biological father)										
Stephanie & Mike Landers										
Angela & Anthony McNeal										
LaAsha Hurston										
Elisabeth & Nao Kao Moua								◆		◆
Mai Ling Cheng & Khang Shui										
Bao Ly Vue & Qhousa Vue										

Opportunities and Volunteerism
in Spencer's Classroom

Spencer provided routine opportunities for families who wanted to be involved in a variety of ways throughout the school year. These were designed to inform parents about classroom instruction and offered suggestions for supporting children at home (Epstein, 1996). Spencer's activities also gave parents a chance to discuss their knowledge of children or to contribute materials or skills to the classroom; however, several of Spencer's opportunities lay outside the realm of access of some parents, the forces of social class, ability, and linguistic clout influencing how and why parents participated (Delgato-Gaitan, 1991; Lareau 1989; Lareau and Horvat, 1999; Lareau and Shumar, 1996). In volunteering, parents participated in varying capacities, and all classroom volunteers came from upper middle-class professional families (see table 3). Although Spencer's class was diverse, volunteers were not. Spencer explained her strategies for recruiting parents. Realizing that not all parents would be able to assist, she framed volunteering as a request: "Before school begins, I always talk about the chance to volunteer. I try to have a schedule at that point with the times that I really need volunteers in the classroom. And I try to present it in such a way that they don't feel guilty if they can't do it, . . . but I want you to know that you are really welcome to participate in this way" (October 13, 2000, p. 14).

Spencer benefited from the parents' time, expertise, visits, and interest, but so did the entire class. Describing the parent volunteer cadre, she said: "I think we've had 9 [parent volunteers] on a regular basis, either weekly or biweekly. We also have a grandmother who volunteers" (October 13, 2000, p. 14).

Distributing Skill and an Emerging Ethos of Responsibility

Volunteers were integral to the smooth operation of the centers and to in-depth exploration of topics; and most importantly, they served as adult intermediaries, supporting children's experience and mastery of the curriculum. Seven parents and two community volunteers raised the adult-to-child ratio to about 5:1 during a typical literacy block, creating an active curriculum with many language opportunities.

Parent volunteers verbalized their desire to enjoy and to get to know the children, to support individual students and the teacher, and to support the classroom and school as a learning community. Volunteer experiences both perpetuated the power of middle-class parents and gave this active parent group insight into the perspectives and needs of students who were not their own offspring, thus sometimes altering their understanding of their own roles as members of a diverse urban school. Instructional time was not interrupted by pullout services; instead an in-class curriculum model with differentiated instruction was implemented (Confidential, Highland Principal, 1998).

Sallie, an European American mother who had worked as a lab technician but chose to stay at home with her young children, captured the essence of the parent volunteer community in the following way: "At Highland School I think many parents really care, and they are not only willing to do for their own kids, but they do for other kids. We realize that it is the right thing to do because not all kids have parents that can. It makes the community better for everyone. It becomes a caring group of people, and there are fewer kids to fall through the cracks" (May 17, 2001, p. 40).

Helen, another Gravenswood parent with an office managerial position, worked every other week in Spencer's room. She commented on the peer group: "A good thing about volunteering is that you get to know kids. I have loved it. It gives me insight, and certain things Margaret [daughter] talks about are clearer. I know almost all of the kids, and every other week either Margaret or Margaret's twin sister Gwendolyn has me in her room" (January 9, 2001, p. 1).

Helen expressed a sentiment common among parents. She had positive contact with other members in the children's group. She found it "interesting to see how different kids learn, work together, and help each other" (January 9, 2001, p. 1). She commented about the variety of learning occurring within Spencer's room and, like Sallie, could articulate how her involvement in the classroom mattered to students other than her daughter. She related an attempt to motivate a student to write: "I helped Chantilia to sound out words. She knew most of them. The group worked well together. [This was] the first time that I've worked with Chantilia in particular. She worked out words from the board. She had done five whole lines and then began to erase. I stopped her and commented that she'd done quite a lot of work to stop and quit. I said, 'Are you sure, Chantilia? You've done an awful lot of work. You have a good product'" (January 9, 2001, p. 1).

Volunteer parents worked in different ways, but they shared what appeared to be an emerging ethos of responsibility toward learners. Sallie volunteered at both Highland and Gravenswood schools (Highland's paired third- to fifth-grade school). She reflected upon her child's room, stating, "I benefit a lot when I am there. I help a lot of kids. And a lot of kids are getting special time and attention from me, not just my daughter" (May 17, 2001, p. 30).

The insight about Highland reflected the academic and social pressures with which teachers, children, administrators, and parents struggled. Sallie appreciated the heterogeneous grouping that supported her child's special learning needs as well as those of all children: ". . . Spencer mixes things up, and so my daughter, who has speech and language difficulty, didn't feel that she was at the low end. Students pick up on that, and it must've been Christmas before she even noticed that there were some other first graders who were reading better than she was. And at that point she was motivated to read at home with us. She forged ahead" (May 17, 2001, p. 14).

Sallie focused on classroom grouping experience, which together with reduced class size improved the odds that her daughter would continue to be motivated and master early reading. Consistent with parental involvement among middle-class parents (Lareau, 1989), Sallie monitored her daughter's progress; moreover, she noticed the reform strategies supporting all readers. She commented: "If everyone had known who is in the bottom group, that would have been very hard and affected reading for Anne . . . [Sallie's daughter]. She would have gotten into the perception that she is a poor reader. It would have been hard to encourage her to work on it. I give Marlene and Cathy [a special educator] credit for working with the kids in heterogeneous groups and designing it to really help them. I am amazed when I go in and see Marlene working with just one or two children on reading" (May 17, 2001, p. 14).

Sallie's concern extended the benefits of her involvement to children other than Anne. She drew attention to the importance of the Highland parent volunteers, especially altering the ratios of adults-to-children, which is advantageous for reading: "The new governor wants to increase class size from 15. I thought these kids just would not be where they are. In Marlene's room two kids who could not write their letters at the beginning of the year are now writing and sounding out entire words. That would not be possible if you have 24 kids! How many classrooms have the parent volunteers where you can have the ratio of 4 kids to one adult during a 2-hour language arts block? It doesn't always happen that way. If you have only one teacher, they [the students] are not going to be ready for the 3rd grade" (May 17, 2001, p. 15).

When she spoke of "the two children who could not write letters at the beginning of the year," Sallie referred to first-grade English language learners. This mother expanded her understanding of Anne's needs with recognition of the needs of other children. She continued, "And they've got to get that help at the lower grades. This is my very strong feeling from seeing kids make 2 years of progress in one."

Solomon is another child in Spencer's room; his father recognized the link between volunteers in this urban classroom and the current issues surrounding early school achievement. He described what he saw as a difference between his own upbringing and the needs of today's schools:

I went through public schools . . . in a wealthy district. . . . There was no ethnic mix till High School. There are many differences now. Then, parents' participation was only for field trips, and of course that was [for] mothers. . . . These days teachers really need the help in the classroom that parents give. . . . Parent helpers come in on a daily basis and help run math centers. A reason for appealing for the extra help is that there is such a wide range of abilities. I'm hesitating because this is sort of a negative comment about children from low socioeconomic backgrounds who have difficulty sitting still [and] staying on task, and an expert adult helps in certain situations. . . . Trying to attend to all of the kids is a tough job for a teacher. (October 2000, pp. 14–18)

Each of these parents recognized that the individualized instruction provided by teachers and supported by classroom volunteers mattered to everyone's school achievement. Although Solomon's father's comments were laced with critical evaluations of children from backgrounds of poverty, the perception of how volunteers support schools reflected an understanding common to Highland and to the literature (Epstein, 1996).

Spencer relied upon her volunteer cadre to assist small groups of children while she alternately worked with individual students and small instructional groups. In fact Solomon's father's comment reflected the classroom he saw. Parent involvement in Spencer's room was important, but it seemed especially so for those struggling in relation to peers— which, in this researcher's estimation, included children from both middle-income and impoverished backgrounds.

Participation in the classroom remained high but was hard won. Lengthy vacations and illnesses made volunteering impossible for some; other parents stepped in and filled empty slots (Memo, November 2000; Colton, April and May 2001). Although volunteering evoked strong compassion, charity, and altruism and could arguably be construed as a misguided obligation, volunteers' commitment and flexibility were qualities that circumvented the collapse of Spencer's learning community.

Cross-Family Associations and New Alliances

Parent volunteers learned about children outside their own neighborhoods. In certain instances, European American parents advocated for children who were not their own but for whom they had assumed a modicum of responsibility through their school connection. School-mentoring programs, individual motivations, and a focus on diversity, achievement, and community, all supported their efforts and intentions.

Village Grove and Gravenswood parent advocacy for children from the Waterside and South Green Street neighborhoods sometimes moved beyond classroom volunteering or school wide mentoring; however, when advocacy occurred, some parents' gestures were small, for example, making costumes for end-of-year productions or supporting and sustaining cross-neighborhood friendships or driving kids to and from school.

In contrast with smaller connections among parents of various neighborhoods, two unusually strong parent-to-parent networks operated on behalf of students and Highland's parent community. Each of these parent-to-parent networks was distinctive. Middle-class mothers moved out of their insular relations with other European Americans into Highland's communities of color. First, I will describe a series of connections arranged by a parent named Marietta on behalf of Spencer's student Weiyi; then I will describe an unusual cross-neighborhood alliance entitled PATHWAYS led by Laurel, a parent in Spencer's classroom. Both women were European American, middle class, and professional.

Supporting Weiyi

Marietta, a mother with an interracial marriage and bilingual and biracial children, was a source of uncommon support for Spencer. Marietta lived in the Village Grove neighborhood and supported second-grader Weiyi and his mother Mai Ling, relatively new arrivals living in the South Green Street area. Marietta, a medical language interpreter, commented: "Weiyi's dad and I used to stand outside and wait together and yack. And I would always talk to him because I knew he couldn't talk to anyone else at Highland. I think that is how Spencer got to know that it was possible for me to interpret for them" (Chang, February 5, 2001, p. 2).

Because Highland served few Mandarin families, no site-based interpreter was available for this group. Marietta helped Spencer arrange conferences and became an educational support person for Weiyi; likewise, she argued for her own children's maintenance of Chinese language and culture. She commented: "It is hard to raise bilingual children, especially in a place like Highland, where English is spoken a lot. They [my children] are never going to go out and meet that language [Mandarin] without our engineering it. And so, it makes them see that there are good reasons for them to be bilingual. We want them to be proud of being Chinese. We want to communicate to them in a big way so that they will feel that they can stand up to pressure to conform or assimilate" (February 5, 2001, p. 9).

Highland paid Marietta a small stipend for her services, but she vowed to translate regardless. Marietta was available throughout Weiyi's second-grade year, relaying messages from school to the parents' restaurant and back again to Spencer. Marietta updated Mai Ling on changes in Weiyi's academic needs, scheduled conferences for Spencer, and ensured that his parents knew of extended vacations or snow days. Chang helped Spencer discuss problems of concern to Weiyi's reading achievement and to interactions with other children.

Mai Ling attended every conference facilitated by Marietta. Mai Ling commented that before gaining Marietta's support, she and her husband were paralyzed in communications, stating, "Weiyi's father can listen, but if he did not understand, he could do nothing because there was no translator" (M. Cheng, trans. Yu, November 13, 2000, p. 4:11). Weiyi's parents came to no school events other than the conferences at which Spencer had requested their attendance; both worked long hours and managed a staff of twelve employees. Recognizing that better involvement, resulting from the translation support of Marietta, was more important than more frequent involvement, Spencer considered this relationship to be highly successful. Without the volunteer support, the relationship would have evolved differently; moreover, Weiyi's school success was altered in a positive and lasting way by a parent outside of his family.

Cross-Neighborhood Alliances in PATHWAYS

PATHWAYS was a cross-racial, multilingual parent–teacher group sponsored by Highland PTO funding and led by a parent in Spencer's room, Laurel, a psychologist with a private practice. Laurel's son Solomon was doing quite well; Laurel worked as a classroom volunteer and a school mentor, supporting a kindergartner in another room. Her role in PATHWAYS entailed shared leadership with a Latino mother. The group's purpose was to improve minority–majority relations. She stated: "PATHWAYS operates under the auspices of the PTO. We are a group of parents and some teachers. Last spring we met a couple of times. We don't have any Hmong parents in the group, but several African-American parents and a growing number of Hispanic parents, and a variety of others. Many are European American. We are trying to build bridges across all of the communities of the school" (June 25, 2001, p. 12).

PATHWAYS met, developed an agenda, and provided an outlet for the often tension-filled, cross-cutting concerns of education with race, language, economic status, sexual orientation, and student and family marginalization in the school.

The twelve to sixteen parents and two teachers attending PATHWAYS meetings were energized during conversations. Heated topics included the following: problematizing black children; minority overrepresentation in special education; language issues; cultural dissonance among teachers, students, and parents; problems of poverty; poor perceptions of low-income families and children; and equity regarding gender and sexual orientation.

PATHWAYS operated differently from other school-led organizations. The issues raised were those that parents felt school staff ignored,
and its members bridged the artificial divisions separating majority–
minority parents from different neighborhoods. Despite background
experience and professional or lay status, these parents of varying backgrounds operated as equals without a school-imposed agenda. PATH-
WAYS members had an opportunity to voice concerns and to listen to the
needs of people outside of their own, often insular, social groups. Participants of PATHWAYS raised cross-group awareness, discussed social
problems, and built alliances. The group, led by one middle-class parent
volunteer and her Latino collaborator, achieved social integration among
parents, something the school itself had achieved only in the classroom
but never fully among parents. PATHWAYS cut across the social divisions within the community, linking those European American parents
and teachers with an interest in issues of social justice and diversity with
parents of color.

Although PATHWAYS met every other month, they netted little attention from the wider Highland school administration. Spencer seemed
unaware of the group, and the PTO, its sponsoring organization, gave it
scant attention. Laurel expressed reservations about the continued existence of PATHWAYS: "It is hard to know what will happen with the
group next. I feel that many people care about these issues, but few are
willing to put the time and effort in or even know how to keep it going.
PATHWAYS is enormously draining. . . . The connections made across
groups were wonderful, but I worry that PATHWAYS is not going anywhere" (Strauss, June 25, 2001, p. 12).

Laurel questioned the events structuring the entire school community; these were typically disjointed entities (see table 2). As an active parent she questioned the long-term efficacy of maintaining separations
among the many groups of parents at Highland even if these separations
were inadvertent: "I think there is a definite place for groups to organize
within themselves and feel strong and powerful. There is a definite place
for individuals to form community when you are working with people
like yourself, but then I am not a separatist. I think an important next
step is to connect everybody and have a place where every group of the
school is coming together" (Strauss, June 25, 2001, p. 13).

For Laurel, mentoring and producing connections to the many parents in PATHWAYS grew out of her responsibility to her son as well
as to the children of others. Laurel noted that the work of PATHWAYS
would likely cease, especially if she reduced the amount of time she
dedicated to it. Nevertheless, she believed "simply to connect was
enormously important."

Volunteering and Contentions Boundary Reinscriptions

In the aforementioned sections, middle-class parents seemed receptive, even generative of an ethos of responsibility toward children and toward other social groups beyond their own. Their overarching concerns might lie on what Bakhtin would characterize as a discursive boundary. Although these parents' words were "populated with the intentions" of their own priorities (their own children), their words were simultaneously overpopulated with the primacy of the needs of others within this community.

Middle-class parents at Highland seemed positioned somewhere between their world of self-interest and individualism (Brantlinger, 2003), and yet their words and actions simultaneously maintained a foothold in the worlds of others. Middle-class European Americans (with emphasis upon independence) have been characterized in much research as intrinsically motivated toward actions that are self-enhancing (Hernandez and Iyengar, 2001), whereas other groups are often characterized as collectivist in action and intention, drawing motivation from activity that benefits the group (Hernandez and Iyengar, 2001; Trumbell et al., 2001; Valdes, 1996). At Highland, however, the self-enhancing activity of volunteering among many of the middle class generated action beyond a simple Judeo-Christian do-good mentality (Gans, 1978). The ethos captured here had the potential to increase understanding of the relations between those within the full community; moreover, many dealings mattered in the achievement of all children.

Drawing again upon Bakhtin to analyze the activity of Highland volunteers, I found that the discourse and activity of this middle-class group could not be split from the production of the culture within this school with its focus upon community. Although parent volunteers worked to support their own, they simultaneously identified a set of children and parents whom they perceived to be beneficiaries of their work. Parent volunteers were unified as part of the same whole to which children other than their own belonged; thus, all volunteers put the concerns they had as parents of their own child squarely next to the needs of the other. Each of these mothers discerned what she perceived to be the rewards of her labor, and each also neatly articulated community understandings in ways new and different from what the literature commonly portrays as those of the middle-class parent (Brantlinger, 2003; Graue and Smith, 1996; Lareau, 1989). Despite this evidence of volunteerism as a two-sided act, at times, division within the community prevailed. Some still wanted their own children to stay firmly on their own side of the fence.

Boundaries boldly reasserted themselves; the lines of demarcation put neither the middle class nor the lower economic class in a favorable light.

The wealthier European American mothers were wary of what they didn't know but expected from the poorer parts of the school's communities. One parent's discussion, depending upon interpretation, conveyed attitudes toward a child from a low-income family that were either less than flattering, reflective of differences in cultural value, or based on facts. The mother said, "I don't know her family, but I don't think that anyone would help her make a costume. We are going to make one for Chantilia, too, and they will each have one" (May 17, 2001, p. 35).

Furthering this line of contrasting evidence, Gravenswood mothers supported regular play dates between their children and those from the Waterside International or South Green Street neighborhoods, believing that play dates were beneficial for all children. Cross-neighborhood visits would not, however, be balanced. One mother commented: "There are kids that we have had over for play dates because they haven't had too many. It is a nice thing for them even though I know it won't be reciprocated because it is not a home that I feel comfortable sending [my child] to. And those are the kinds of kids that you say, 'Oh, [my child] has outgrown this, and we have these extra markers. Would you like these?' They are kids that might not have that at home."

Admitting her own bias, this mother did not allow her own child to visit the less affluent neighborhoods. Her summation—"*Those* children might not actually have had legitimate opportunities"—provided the impetus to support the children of others (on her own turf) but didn't allow her (or her child) an option to visit foreign territory. Limiting any opportunity to learn about a neighborhood, family, or lifestyle differing from her own, she also prevented the much-needed self-correction of negative perceptions. The Gravenswood mother's assessments of needs and risks in the South Green Street and Waterside neighborhoods remain open. While the children of Highland could experience cross-neighborhood alliances in the classroom, they were less likely to do so outside of school unless parents' desires concurred. The egalitarian social environment, which had been so carefully contrived in the desegregated, restructured school, was undone through parents' social selection for children.

Persistent Social Class Factors and the Caveats of Volunteerism

Parent networks, financial security, and education mattered in volunteerism. Parents secured after-school care or worked late to compensate for time in Spencer's room. Parents traded times, and their professional careers and part-time work schedules allowed them each some degree of flexibility. Predictably, all of Spencer's parent volunteers were European American. No parent of color, limited English proficiency, working class, or lower income worked with the focal classroom in this way. Bill's mother, Elizabeth, wanted to volunteer but could not get time off from her factory shift to work in the classroom (May 30, p. 8). Work obligations precluded Raphael's mother from this type of volunteering as well; his grandmother volunteered instead, traveling once a week from out of town. Chantilia's mother volunteered once but did not return. Jimmy's father participated in other ways with the assistance of Building Resource Instructional Support. Weiyi's parents worked long hours and believed it was important to "learn about Weiyi," not about the classroom or the school through involvement (M. Cheng, trans., Su, November 17, 2000). While volunteering produced and reinforced networks of association between Village Grove and Gravenswood, the classroom volunteer activity offered little room for bringing Highland, South Green Street, and Waterside families into the daily life of the classroom.

Levels of education may have excluded some from participating as Spencer requested. Parents from the South Green Street area or from the Waterside International Pavilion, many of whom were refugee and immigrant families or from countries with lower educational achievement, might not have experienced the volunteering event in a positive way. In fact, volunteering in this way would have called attention to what they lacked (Vue, March 28, 2001). Some first-generation refugees from Laos and Thailand typically had four to seven years of schooling as was the case with Jimmy's parents but not Bill's, his father and mother having both a high school education and some college. Many newcomers did not speak the language of the school.

Volunteering in Spencer's room followed a widely used model of participation recommended by school policy makers, but the experience presented many with challenges. Taking into account the nature of Spencer's classroom and an analysis of which parents did or did not participate, the researcher concluded that the experience of volunteering was as overwhelming and disengaging for some as it was rewarding and fruitful for others. A parent most at a loss in the role Spencer created was one with limited education of English language.

Middle-Class Parents and the Highland Parent–Teacher Organization

The Parent Teacher Organization, which structured ten of twenty-five opportunities, exerted a powerful force upon parent involvement at Highland School, contrasting with Spencer's classroom or the improvement and restructuring initiatives. PTO, largely uncontrolled by school staff, generated activities equal to either Spencer's efforts in the classroom and Highland's paid staff. The PTO board held meetings, raised money, elicited the support of other parents, and constructed academic and social opportunities for children and parents (see table 3).

Majority dominance prevailed in this venue. Active PTO board members were mostly white middle-class parents; the two parents in Spencer's classroom who were members of the board, Paige (treasurer) and Laurel (PATHWAYS committee member), were both Gravenswood mothers. Many others in Spencer's classroom attended PTO events; however, few parents came from Waterside or from South Green Street. Of all of the parents from Spencer's classroom attending or using the events provided by the PTO, most were from the wealthier neighborhoods. Of the four students in the focal classroom whose parents were of color, few attended PTO events.

The Persistent Social-Class Features and the Caveats of PTO Activity

School restructuring altered the quality and quantity of teacher–parent interactions; simultaneously, Danielle Dumas, the school principal, played an important role in challenging the active middle-class families on the PTO board. Majority class, race, and language shaped attendance at all PTO events, and certainly, board membership paralleled the dominant social-class standing at Highland.

Board members contemplated the absence of parents of color and featured their work as a way to make Highland School a successful community. Though members recognized unequal dynamics and professed a desire to integrate communities, they did not recognize their own place in constructing power relations. Paige, Catherine's mother, commented on her own experiences with the dynamics of power in the organization: "We have been trying to get more minority involvement on the board, but PTO is time-consuming. To be quite frank, there are a lot of really smart people on the board and smart parents in this district, and it can be quite intimidating. In my situation as treasurer, I've had people say, 'Well, how can this figure be this? Last month it was this.' I said, 'This is a volunteer job! Do not call me to the carpet in front of 20 people!' You have to say to yourself, 'There are people like this in all walks of life.' . . . It is intimidating for people at all levels" (Cartier, May 30, 2001, p. 15).

Paige's evolving role in the community was typical of the ways in which this network of parents inducted others into the traditional events and activities of the school. She explained how she began: "I went to functions, and I did these things; but I didn't really know or have any idea what they did or how they spent their money or how they got all this money. So I talked to a friend, asked her what it was like, what it entailed, and realized that is something I can do" (Cartier, May 30, 2001, p. 12).

As PTO treasurer during her daughter's years in Spencer's room, Paige balanced accounts, kept track of outstanding debts and fund-raising figures, located banking services with the most cost-efficient checking account, and invested Highland PTO funds. Her activity was another example of the ways in which Highland's middle class distributed some people's skills and maintained the cultural place of others.

The Principal's Role; Voicing the Rights of Others and Creating Tensions

Dumas raised concerns of parents whose presence was implicit in the words of the school's agenda to "alter the quality and quantity of parent interactions" (Confidential, Highland Principal, 1998). Dumas's perspective as a school leader aligned clearly with the perspective of ethnic and linguistic minority families. Dumas characterized the PTO support for the school as both a struggle and a benefit: "Overtly, I think the PTO has been extremely helpful with funding. They are extremely conscientious in terms of trying to help, but it is icing, not down to the cake. We have a lot of well meaning parents, who work very hard for the PTO and really reach out" (Dumas, June 11, 2001, p. 9).

Dumas saw the board come a short way during her four-year administration; nevertheless, she saw that the PTO had much work to do. As a school leader she played a role in shifting the PTO's worldview. She stated: "It is more than just paying for baby-sitting and transportation and making phone calls. It is facing your own racism; it is putting yourself in uncomfortable positions, . . . reaching out to African-American parents and inviting them to the PTO meeting at this school, but they know it is going to be all-white people from the Gravenswood neighborhood" (June 11, 2001, p. 10).

Dumas articulated an unlikely but more comfortable arrangement for many black parents, suggesting a strategy to attract African-American members of the community to the PTO board. She stated, "We'll bring our whole meeting to South Green Street Community Center, and you bring six of your African-American friends with you to make yourself feel comfortable. [That] would make the PTO feel uncomfortable." Dumas explained that the PTO board would have little understanding of how to involve black, Latino, or Hmong parents on the board because they had no understanding of exclusion: "None of them are overtly racist. That isn't the case with our PTO, but [it is a question of] how uncomfortable you are willing to make yourself to make someone else comfortable. It isn't about money. It is about having some sort of understanding of how you would feel if it were you were a minority parent" (June 11, 2001, p. 10).

Dumas saw progress in the way in which PTO handled issues of access to both places and information for some parents. She saw changes in delegation of responsibility among parents to facilitate communication with Latino American and Hmong American parents. She stated: "At first, it was the principal's responsibility to let them know that something needed to be done. Now every time they print something that it is going home in English, [they say] 'What can we do about that?' Every time we have a meeting, [they ask] 'How do we advertise to the parents that we will have a Building Resource Instructional Support person there to translate? That we will pay for cabs if there are transportation problems?' Or [they ask] whether people are willing to pick up other people" (June 11, 2001, p. 11).

Dumas saw the PTO shift its practices to create a slightly more accessible atmosphere for parents. Her descriptions of the state of the PTO contrasted with her memory of it in earlier years: "They are taking more ownership for the more superficial stuff, but you've got to start somewhere. They are looking around their group instead of looking at me for answers" (Dumas, June 11, 2001, p. 10).

Despite what Dumas saw as progress, her words convey criticism, an assessment that PTO's involvement within the larger structure of Highland School had an overarching position that failed to address the many problems, therefore maintaining the position of the powerful; the administration also benefited from PTO work. The same parents who were helpful and generous with time and resources, had as much or more to learn as a professional staff did. Dumas perceived her role as one of challenge to the PTO board. Her conversation implies an attempt to shift the thinking and behavior of the PTO, but the board controlled activities as well as important funds. She explained: "The budget PTO generates certainly isn't going to make our poverty-stricken parents at this school—who happen to be largely minority parents—more comfortable, especially when they look and see that the PTO has more money to use than their household income. That is the reality of what they are able to raise as an organization, and we need to appreciate and not condemn" (June 11, 2001, p. 12).

The PTO provided the schools with powerful financial backing through fundraising; however, looking closer at events created by PTO activity prompts further scrutiny.

Contentiousness of PTO Activity

Much of what the PTO did can be understood as beneficial, neutral, or counterproductive to the Waterside Community and South Green Street neighborhoods. Whether PTO board activity is regarded as helpful or hurtful to Highland as a whole depends on the ways in which events and experiences are analyzed. The Highland PTO structured opportunities that produced participation among groups; events themselves were more or less efficacious for particular children and families in specific ways. Below the surface, events reveal practices that perpetuated exclusionary behavior and that prevented many children and families from academic or social benefit because of culture-specific types of knowledge (Delgado-Gaitan, 1991).

The PTO voiced the desire to appeal to and support all families, yet their adaptations, such as providing transportation, securing interpretation skills, or supplying funds to purchase items that parents typically bought, weren't the only things that mattered. These modifications benefited some; however, the types of events offered and developed by the PTO during the year were comfortable, natural, and enjoyable only to some families in the school. This is implicit in Dumas's comments and manifested in the overall low turnout from the Waterside International and South Park Street areas.

Less than fully described but clearly implied by the principal's discussion is the culture-specific knowledge that parents needed in order to be part of the involved and visible community. It is no surprise that Waterside International Pavilion and South Green Street families infrequently attended many of the Highland activities. The sock hop, for example, was a pleasant experience for parents who enjoyed American pop music, dance, and customs; but it likely alienated many African-Americans, Mexican Americans, and certainly Hmong Americans, for whom their own music and dance represents identity.

Many events, such as the Authors' Tea and Book fairs contained pedagogically meaningful elements for children regardless of a parent's participation. In particular, these two events, with their focus on reading and writing, could be very helpful to children regardless of parents' attendance or language and educational backgrounds. In these instances, children experienced literacy and academic support through reading, writing, book purchases, and adult writing and story-telling interactions. PTO organizers took into account financial considerations, purchasing vouchers for children whose parents could not afford to buy them. This was to the credit of PTO event developers, but both literacy events had strong elements of linguistic and academic cultural capital embedded in their delivery. Persons who could not read English, for example, or write commentaries on children's work during the Author's Tea, would likely feel uncomfortable. An event designed to celebrate children's writing ironically exposed parents' lack of literacy in the presence of others.

By contrast, an activity like Star Math was academic in nature but more fully dependent upon a parent's skill and activity at home; therefore, it was inaccessible to many without the education, time, or desire. Star Math and after-school foreign language classes for children of necessity included elements of academic and economic cultural capital in order for them to be meaningful. Star Math required a parent to have at least a basic math education, English reading skills, and after-school time sufficient to facilitate the lessons.

After-school foreign-language classes were tuition based and included only Western languages. Organizers prioritized German, Spanish, and French, but members of the parent and child communities spoke Hmong, Spanish, and a handful of Asian languages (Japanese, Chinese, and Korean). Spencer's student Bill noticed that the languages in the entire parent (and child) community were not considered in the event planning, commenting, "Do they have Hmong? I speak Hmong really good" (classroom memo, winter 2001). Carnival, one of the few events in which parent communities merged, nevertheless relegated Mexican American and Hmong American parents to food donors and preparers, replicating class positions even within an event that many considered successful.

When close event analyses are juxtaposed against spoken desires, we see clearly that well-meaning individuals perpetuate hegemonic structures by capitalizing upon and valuing their own capacities. Looking deeply raises additional questions about the implicit purposes and social functions of large organizations like the PTO, which control experiences for children and families, simultaneously creating moments of possibility for some, yet largely reaffirming the positions of dominant classes of people.

During the study year the PTO Board approved $21,000 worth of line-item and one-time grant requests calculated from end-of-year grants and items reported in PTO minutes (September 2000 to May 2001). The organization purchased science materials, emotional literacy posters, Hmong cultural materials, maps, ESL items, and many other basic supplies throughout the school year. Of the total amount generated, most was devoted to the special needs of low-income and ESL students.

The treasurer commented on the tremendous fund-raising capacity of the PTO, which implicated a series of complex commitments, all of which supported communities of the school. An allocation of approximately $5,000 went to the Title I parent empowerment groups for families of color. Paige, one of the mothers, stated:

> We voted on grants. And the number one priority grant was for the minority parent empowerment groups. Most grants have to do with multicultural education materials. We granted money . . . for Hmong posters. Gravenswood School Plus is a program that the Gravenswood principal has at her school for kids in an after-school and homework group . . . and School Plus, a series of scholarships to support students in the PTO-sponsored foreign language classes who could not pay the

$50.00 to participate. It is for school improvement and community building and open-arms-for-all, a necessary after-school learning opportunity. (May 30, 2001, p. 16)

Much of the funding covered space and materials, and the treasurer's comments confirmed that funding provided for early literacy materials, not all print media or in English. Trade books supported bilingual learners, and importantly, all purchases supported early readers. She said, "We bought some Spanish trade books for Gravenswood, multilingual books on tape. This is the second year that they have granted SPARK bookbags, $1,300.00 for that."

The Highland–Gravenswood PTO responded partially to the larger learning community, by providing grants ultimately sought by staff. It was up to the teachers to use the moneys well and to establish an appropriate curriculum. In this instance, the PTO's capacity for funding was tremendous, and their time and allocation of materials indeed supported teachers on behalf of learners. Paige continued: "The majority of the 15 grants addressed the needs of all communities at Highland." Paige's comment partially contradicts the notion that the PTO wasn't stepping up to the challenge of the larger Highland school community. Seeing the PTO's goals in tandem with the larger vision of this integrated learning community, she stated, "I like to say that the PTO shares the same goals as the teacher and principals at Highland and Gravenswood do."

Like volunteerism, PTO work defies analysis solely as a funding mechanism or solely as a mechanism whereby groups of parents from Gravenswood, Village Grove, and Highland neighborhoods organized activities to benefit themselves and only their own European American middle-class children. Any close analysis of events, similar to parent volunteerism in classrooms, reveal practices that both perpetuate the status quo and alter opportunities for all children and families.

Implications and Conclusions Stemming from Social Heteroglossia and Parent Involvement

Home–school relations emerge and develop in a complex web of community networks that structured possibilities for particular people, revealing home–school relations as more complex than simple. This analysis of parent involvement shows the strong place of middle-class parents in an evolving ecology, thus fostering a realm of potential and contention for everyone. These findings, although supplemental to the existing and growing body of critical literature about middle-class parents (Brantlinger, 2003; Delgado-Gaitan, 1991; Graue, 1993; Lareau and Horvat, 1999; Valdes, 1996), do not endorse the abdication of responsibility by teachers and appropriation by parents, but instead focus more clearly upon parent leadership networks and upon the school staff's responsibility to analyze more carefully power relations within schools.

A simplistic analysis of this data would place middle-class parents fully in the seat of establishing and perpetuating hegemonic forms of schooling, and yet they do not fully do so. At times and in places, important cross-racial and social-class relations are established. These findings call attention to the oddly interdependent power plays between administrators, teachers, and various parents social groups, which recapitulated elements of positive and negative social practice.

A base of educational decision making was formed at Highland, and it had the power to move dominion more clearly underground or to solidly situate the activity of influential middle-class families within the realm of the powerful, affecting the lives of all of the parents and children in significant ways. These data show extensive interpretation of social and discursive data, fluidly constructing school participation, thus establishing a school climate of a particular type.

The critical role of dominants, illustrated in enactments of middle-class European American models of involvement, show a surface valuing of diversity and slight adjustments in delivery and form of school activities; yet these partial adaptations are not nearly enough to benefit its range of students. Highland appears at once to be a parent community in which people were in a much-needed process of grappling with the requirements of others and simultaneously supporting community within an ethos of responsibility. Aspects of what middle-class parents do also reestablishes their own place. Active European American parents from the Gravenswood, Highland, and Village Grove neighborhoods invested in what they saw as the school's needs through volunteerism and funding; yet they have also reasserted aspects of their cultural dominance through events and activities for families, which in many ways privileged their own. Home and school involvement at Highland as a heteroglossic endeavor simultaneously showed change and maintenance of the status quo with cultural domination gaining ground. Instances of deep "boundary spanning" among several middle-class parents (as in Marietta's translation support and the work of Laurel in PATH-WAYS) occurred (Lawson, 2003), showing clearly that the roles people play are not entirely dictated by social structure but by personal agency (Holland et al., 1998). These middle-class mothers, although individually driven, took action of collective merit.

Perhaps a combination of restructuring, teacher practices, and parent activities worked in concert to shift the conversation about the needs of learners, thus creating an emerging ethos of community. A restructured school environment with this determined cadre of parent volunteers changed the individualistic tenor of Anglo-American parents' activity. Findings suggest that the individualistic model of relational practice, in which Anglo-American parents work to benefit their own children, may have a potential to shift to one in which Anglo parents support communities of children as classroom volunteers provide instructional and social support to a fuller range of learning community members. Nonetheless, this ethos of responsibility downplayed any functional focus to question the larger forces at work in such an activity.

Rather than simply add to the literature of awareness about the power of the active middle class, I have highlighted the key features, which counteract and contest the notion that middle-class activity and discourse is solely individualistic and potentially counterproductive to the success of children from "other" families. The dominant activity of middle-class participation in school in this study, while arguably assimilational, may have potential that school and parent leaders can exploit for different types of community good. Furthermore, I have argued that normative types of parent involvement, situating an entire community, must be continuously challenged in order to meet the heteroglossic quality of families in many of today's schools.

The concept of heteroglossia allows interpretations of relatedness of groups within the school; in an attempt to be effective, people adjust and change their ways of thinking, living, being, and doing relative to the demands of the larger communities outside of the school. This chapter itself calls school leaders and teachers either to question more carefully and to stop the beneficial but recapitulative activity of the middle class, or to marshal their forces more powerfully to benefit schools in new and different ways.

Notes

This work originally appeared in *The Urban Review*, 31 (1–30). Copyright, Springer. With permission of Springer Science and Business Media.

1. All proper names in this account are pseudonyms.

2. The researcher transcribed all of the interviews that were generated from English speakers.

3. The researcher wishes to thank the Spencer Foundation and the Netzer-Wendt Scholarship Fund at the University of Wisconsin, Madison, which financed the years of data collection and analysis of supporting research work with Hmong and Mandarin informants.

References

Bakhtin, M. M. 1981. Discourse in the novel. In M. Holquist (Ed.) Trans. C. Emerson and M. Holquist. *The dialogic imagination*. Austin: University of Texas Press. (Original work published 1935)

Booth, A., and Dunn, J. F. (Eds.) 1996. *Family school links: How do they affect educational outcomes?* Mahwah, NJ: Lawrence Erlbaum.

Brantlinger, E. 2003. *Dividing classes: How the middle class negotiates and rationalizes school advantage.* New York: RoutledgeFalmer.

Brantlinger, E., and Majd-Jabbari, M. 1998. The conflicted pedagogical and curricular perspectives of middle-class mothers. *Journal of Curricular Studies,* 30(4), 431–60.

Bredekamp, S. and Copple, C. (Eds.) 1997. *Developmentally appropriate practice,* rev. ed. Washington, DC: National Association for the Education of Young Children.

Bright, J. 1994. Beliefs in action: Family contributions to African-American student success. *Equity and Choice,* 10(2), 5–13.

Bright, J. 1996a. Partners: An urban black community's perspective on the school and home working together. *New Schools, New Communities,* 12(3), 32–37.

Confidential, Highland Principal 1998. *Comprehensive school reform grant.* Midwestern Town Confidential.

Confidential, Highland Elementary School 2000–2001. *School improvement plan (SIP).* Midwestern Town Confidential.

Delgado-Gaitan, C. 1991. Involving parents in the schools: A process of empowerment. *American Journal of Education,* (November) 20–26.

Diamond, Wang, and Gomez 2004. *FINE Digest.* Available at www.fine network.org.

Eisenhart, M. 1999. Changing conceptions of culture and ethnographic methodology: Recen thematic shifts and their implications for research on teaching. In V. Richardson (Ed.) *The handbook of research on teaching,* 4th ed. Washington, DC: American Educational Research Association.

Emerson, R., Fretz, R., and Shaw, L. 1995. *Writing ethnographic fieldnotes.* Chicago: University of Chicago Press.

Epstein, J. L. 1986. Parents' reactions to teacher practices of parent involvement. *Elementary School Journal,* 86(3), 277–94.

———. 1996. Advances in family, community, and school partnerships. *New Schools, New Communities,* 12(3), 5–13.

Erickson, F. 1986. Qualitative methods in research on teaching. In M. C. Wittrock (Ed.) *Handbook of research on teaching,* 3rd ed. New York: Macmillan.

Fielding, N. G., and Fielding, J. L. 1986. *Linking data.* Vol. 4. Newbury Park, CA: Sage.

Gans, H. J. 1978. The positive functions of poverty. *American Journal of Sociology,* 78(3), 275–89.

Giles, H. C. 1998. *Parent engagement as a school reform strategy.* New York: ERIC Clearinghouse on Urban Education. EDO-UD-98-5.

Graue, M. E. 1993. Social networks and home–school relations. *Educational Policy,* 7(4), 466–90.

Graue, M. E., and Smith, S. Z. 1996. Parents and mathematics education reform: Voicing the authority of assessment. *Urban Education,* 30, 395–421.

Graue, M. E., and Walsh, D. J. (Eds.) 1998. *Studying children in context: Theories, methods and ethics.* Thousand Oaks, CA: Sage.

Hernandez, M., and Iyengar, S. S. 2001. What drives whom? A cultural perspective on human agency. *Social Cognition*, 19(3), 269–94.

Hidalgo, N. M., Siu, S., Bright, J. A., Swap, S. M., and Epstein, J. A. 1995. Research on families, schools, and communities: A multicultural perspective. In J. Banks and C. Banks (Eds.) *Handbook of research on multicultural education*. New York: Macmillan.

Holland, D., Lachicotte, W., Skinner, D., and Cain, C. 1998. *Identity and agency in cultural worlds*. Cambridge: Harvard University Press.

Kroeger, J. 2001. *Tracing the discourse of diversity in home and school relationships*. Seattle, Washington: 2001 Annual Meeting of the American Educational Research Association.

Lareau, A. 1989. *Home advantage: Social class and parental intervention in elementary education*. New York: Falmer Press.

Lareau, A., and Horvat, E. M. 1999. Moments of social inclusion and exclusion: Race, class and cultural capital in family school relationships. *Sociology of Education*, 72(1), 37–53.

Lareau, A., and Shumar, W. 1996. The problem of individualism in family–school policies. *Sociology of Education, Special Issue on Sociology and Educational Policy: Bringing Scholarship and Practice Together*, 24–39.

Lawson, M. A. 2003. School–Family Relations in Context. *Urban Education*, 38(1), 77–133

Morris, P. 1994. *The Bakhtin reader: Selected writings of Bakhtin, Medvedev, and Voloshinov*. New York: St. Martin's Press.

Morson, G. S. and Emerson, C. 1990. *Mikhail Bakhtin: Creation of a prosaics*. Stanford, CA: Stanford University Press.

National Education Goals Panel. 2000 March. *NEGP Monthly*, 2(15).

Okagaki, L., and Frensch, P. A. 1998. Parenting and children's school achievement: A multiethnic perspective. *American Educational Research Journal*, 35, 123–44.

Sheldon, S. B. 2002. Parents' social networks and beliefs as predictors of parent involvement. *Elementary School Journal*, 102(4), 301–16.

Trumbull, E., Rothstein-Fisch, C., Greenfield, P. M., and Quiroz, B. 2001. *Bridging cultures between home and school*. Mahwah, NJ: Erlbaum.

Valdes, G. 1996. *Con respeto: Bridging the distance between culturally diverse families and schools, an ethnographic portrait*. New York: Teachers College Press.

Wentzel, K. R. 1998. Parents' aspirations for children's educational attainments: Relations to parental beliefs and social address variables. *Merrill-Palmer Quarterly*, 44(1), 20–37.

PART 3

AFTER CLASS

These complex discussions of class and how class works with and against race and gender argue that we must keep working on the conceptualization of class. What is to come after class as we have historically understood it? Ellen Brantlinger's research has led her to conclude that schools do the work of social class in separating and preparing people for the stratification of the wider society. Her work leads her to argue that both the winners and losers in hierarchical forms of social relations are endemically linked to frustration, anger, and violence. She is also clear that it is the middle class that needs to change its behavior if we are reduce inequality.

Maike Philipsen takes this last argument a full step further. After class, we must be clear that the issue of poverty does not belong to the poor but rather to the non-poor. The non-poor derive disproportionate benefit from a stratified economic system. While Philipsen sees a role for educators in eradicating poverty she argues that direct economic changes are more likely to reduce income inequality. Nevertheless, she argues convincingly that academics themselves can play a more active role by naming who benefits including how we benefits ourselves.

One of the lessons of this volume is that class is contingent. Van Dempsey illustrates this by illuminating how the class in rural, Appalachia has a distinctive form. Youth are "pushed out" of home and region to take advantage of education while simultaneously "pulled back" by local culture and families. His work shows us that intersectionality involves more than race, class and gender. It also has a geography that will need to be accounted for, after class.

Finally, George W. Noblit returns us to the distinction drawn in the opening section, getting to class. The subjective and objective ways of getting to class were distinctly drawn. After all the work on class this and other volumes represent, Noblit argues that class is in danger of becoming déclassé unless it is reconstituted. He argues for instead of reducing all forms of stratification to a class base that it may be better to reconstitute class after race. This is to say that class may have to be thought of as maintaining difference as well as a strategy to reduce inequality. After class, we may have to think rather differently.

9

(Re)Turning to Marx to Understand the Unexpected Anger among "Winners" in Schooling

A Critical Social Psychology Perspective

Ellen Brantlinger

After conducting interviews with high- and low-income youths in Hillsdale, I concluded that the former were the clear winners in school and the latter losers. All school participation and outcome measures indicated this was the case (see table 1). In terms of reported grades, 24% of affluent adolescents received mostly A's, 67% mostly B's, and 9% C's or below. In contrast, no low-income student had mostly A's, 13% had B's, 38% had C's, and almost 50% had D's or F's. Low-income students felt that most of their teachers did not like or respect them, yet were effusive in praising teachers they felt cared about them and who supported their school careers. Affluent students took positive teacher attitudes and treatment for granted and, to some extent, saw teachers as social inferiors. Low-income students reported vastly higher rates of punished school infractions (80% compared to 30% of high-income youths) and more negative punishment (48% sent to the principal's office compared to 9% of high-income students, and 30% suspended from school compared to the case with high-income students where this did not occur). The most frequent penalty for affluent students was teacher reprimand—they were "talked to"; low-income students were "yelled at." I was familiar with poor children's difficult school circumstances from teaching and field experience supervision. In the latter role, I clocked in 7,000 hours of observations in Hillsdale classrooms. I was aware of the fact that subordinate status was not benign: "Failure becomes all the more aversive as society requires individuals to spend more time in formal education" (T. Thompson, 1999, p. 3).

I interviewed low-income adolescents first and was saddened by their unrelenting tales of failure, exclusion, and ostracism in schools. By the time I interviewed high-income students, I was predisposed to see them as villains who benefited from school at the expense of low-income youths' suffering. Sure enough, many affluent students came across as arrogant elitists—full of themselves and oblivious to, or dismissive of, difficulties experienced by low-income students. Their irritating cultural and moral deficit narratives about poor students and families matched those of middle-class mothers and teachers at higher income Hillsdale schools (Brantlinger, 2003a). I initially was so put off by these adolescents' assumptions of superiority and expectation for privilege that I ignored their hints at frustration about being unable to perform the ideal roles expected of students of their social class. I failed to notice high achievers' obsessive worries about not meeting parents' excessively high demands. I was not particularly empathetic to their concerns about the precariousness of their place in cliques and in prestigious activities. Nor did I think much about the hard data that showed that affluent adolescents were almost as negative about school as their low-income counterparts (see table 2). Instead, I saw high-income youths as winners who topped the school hierarchies and who monopolized cultural and social capital. A closer look revealed the undercurrent of dissatisfaction, even depression, which crackled the

Table 1
School Careers of High- and Low-Income Adolescents

Grade Level Status	Low-Income (N = 40)	High-Income (N = 34)
Above grade level	0	6 (18%)
On grade level	11 (28%)	28 (82%)
Retained one year	9 (23%)	0
Retained two years	6 (15%)	0
Class for mentally retarded	3 (8%)	0
Class for emotionally handicapped	1 (3%)	0
Class for learning disabled	10 (25%)	2*
Resource services	4*(10%)	2*
Previously in special education	4*(10%)	0
Referred but not placed	3*(8%)	0
Total special education	23 (57%)	2 (6%)

*Also included in first 3 categories (rows).

Table 2
High- and Low-Income Adolescents' Attitudes toward School

Attitude toward School	Low Income (N = 40)	High Income (N = 34)
Positive	15 (38%)	10 (30%)
Mixed	15 (38%)	18 (54%)
Negative	10 (25%)	6 (18%)

shining surface of apparent school success. In this chapter, I reinterpret the results of my studies of adolescents and parents from a critical social science perspective. First, I review the capitalistic nature of American society and schools and the damaging conditions for subordinates in the system. I also review liberal social psychology, contrasting it to a critical social psychology perspective.

The Capitalist Nature of American Society and Meritocratic Nature of Schools

Citizens dwell on defining America as a democracy, rarely noting the powerful influence of capitalism. Yet, capitalism does reign and schools mirror, or reproduce, its social order (Anyon, 1980, 1981; Bowles and Gintis, 1976). Indeed, capitalist control is intensifying as government regulations of public life erode and are superseded by the entrepreneurship of transglobal corporations. The key democratic ideals of liberty and equality have always been in conflict in the United States, with their balance fluctuating somewhat according to the president or political party in power. Equality portends a distributive justice in which resources and status are to be fairly similar for all citizens. In contrast, liberty and the pursuit of (individual) happiness set up a laissez-faire climate of competition for limited status and material resources. Competition and hierarchy are integral to free markets in and out of school. Weighing in on the side of liberty (liberalism or neoliberalism), capitalism validates people's right to carve out a good life for themselves, often to the detriment of others.

Lesser Schooling for Poor Children: The Travesty of Meritocracy

Americans tend to believe that people enter occupational and educational markets with equal chances to succeed. However, based on family income, gender, race/ethnicity, and language use, students bring different amounts of cultural and social capital to school. Pierre Bourdieu defines capital as the "capacity to exercise control over one's own future and that of others as a form of power" (Calhoun, LiPuma, and Postone, 1993, p. 4). Additionally, school quality varies according to the economic capital, or financial status, of clientele (Burton, 1999; Kozol, 1991). Hence, rather than being a leveler, education gives rise to, and perpetuates, inequalities. Given the ideal of equality, class-related distinctions call for an explanation, which usually is that children differ in merit. Although aware of inequities, Americans still like to believe that success in school and markets depends on such personal traits as intelligence, stamina, common sense, and a strong work ethic rather than social class and race privilege. Few patrons question the win/lose aspects of meritocratic schooling. Given that adults compete for lucrative jobs and career advancement, it seems natural and reasonable that children should compete for valued school circumstances and outcomes, hence that some should do better than others. Children are encouraged to develop skills that further their self-interests (Labaree, 1997). The fact that students do not have equal chances because playing fields are unequal is ignored as is the emotional impact of having subordinate status. Most lay and professional discourse centers on how to bring failing and at-risk students up to speed so that they will not be a drain on society. Over the past several decades student differentials have been named (note the proliferation of disability and at-risk categories) and institutionalized through legislation. Ethnographers describe how low-income students and students of color are placed in stigmatizing school arrangements, receive primarily negative feedback about schoolwork, and are subjected to discrimination by teachers and schoolmates (Casella, 2001; Fine, 1991; Grant and Sleeter, 1996; MacLeod, 1987; McLaren, 1986; Noguera, 2003; Oakes, 1985; Valenzuela, 2003; Weis, 1990; Wexler, 1992; Willis, 1977).

Americans continuously identify children's low educational outcomes as a problem. Touting the "self-made man" rationale, and alluding to room at the reified top for all, politicians and educators stress that if low-income students are to improve their life conditions, their academic achievement must improve as well. Indeed, No Child Left Behind is based on the premise that closing the educational achievement and attainment gap between classes will reduce economic and social disparities. The message is that it is up to poor children to replicate the achievement patterns of their higher-income counterparts if they are to become as one with the middle class. Prescribed remedies, however, inevitably solidify rather than reduce disparities. Solutions that call for increasing the ranks of the educated class as a way to end poverty do not take into account (1) that people with high school diplomas and even college degrees currently are unemployed or underemployed, (2) that there are not enough professional and other college attainment-based careers for all citizens, and (3) that working-class labor is needed. Tightening school standards and demanding higher test scores has negative repercussions, including social and emotional stress for both teachers and students and narrowing the schools' focus to measurable skills and knowledge (Brown, 1995; Reay, 1998).

Identity Formation and Distinquishing Relations under Capitalism

Identity is a psychological and a sociological concept; it involves the meaning making of the psyche and the role-defining language and context of social relations. Hence, explicating the dynamics of identity formation is a task for social psychologists. Identity combines the intimate or subjective world (who one feels one is) with an objective face (how one appears to others). Thus identity is never entirely under personal control. Dorothy Holland, William Lachicotte, Debra Skinner, and Carole Cain (1998) maintain: "Persons' capacities are implicated in reflexive mediation that objectifies, monitors, and evaluates their own behavior" (p. 19). They further argue, "socially constructed selves are subject to positioning by whatever powerful discourses they happen to encounter" (p. 27). The objective and subjective are intertwined to influence people's performances of self: "People tell others who they are, but even more important, they tell themselves and then try to act as though they are who they say they are" (p. 3).

In contrast to liberal social science theories that social life is neutral (sane) and pathology is due to problems in socialization or "bad seeds," individual problems can be logically understood as endemic to everyday interactional patterns in and among all classes under capitalism. George W. Noblit and William T. Pink (1995) claim that whereas the old sociology of education saw schooling as consensual and integrative, the new sociology sees opposition, resistance, and conflict in schools. Bourdieu (1984) argues that because social positions are relational and interdependent, the dominant class not only controls Others, but their power depends on Others' subordination. In meritocratic schooling, for example, for certain children to be deemed superior, Others must be designated inferior, dumb, and incompetent.

Scholars concur that bias and inferior schooling inflict damage on students and interfere with positive identity formation (see Hudak, 2001; Kihn, 2001). Arguing that "labeling is about politics, power, and representation," Glenn M. Hudak (2001) notes that it results in a "false" (imposed, rejected, inferior) self (identity) that is personally dislocating and fragmenting (p. 21). Children fight the stigma and pain of the label in order to feel "real and alive, not isolated and alienated" (p. 19). Researching "special needs" girls at an inclusive British high school, Shereen Benjamin (2002) shows the links between school micro-politics (power relations produced in interpersonal interaction) and students' identity work. The girls had difficulty constructing positive identities out of the dearth of constructive identity resources available to them at school. In spite of substantial evidence that labeling and separating are harmful, vulnerable students continue to be dubbed with stigmatizing names and segregated from mainstream schoolmates.

To explicate the grounding of distinguishing practices, Bourdieu develops the idea of habitus, or the "mutually constituting interaction of structures, dispositions, and actions whereby social structures and embodied (situated) knowledge of those structures produce enduring orientations to action which, in turn, are constitutive of social structures" (Calhoun, LiPuma, and Postone, 1993, p. 4). Although the deterministic character of class correspondence theory is criticized for being pessimistic in denying a role for human agency, Bourdieu does take beliefs and intentions, hence agency, into account. Agency is not free-floating, but constrained by socially received knowledge and social relations characteristic in one's habitus or field. Field accounts for "space of positions" and people's "position taking" (p. 5), and results from the interplay of habitus and access to cultural and economic capital. To translate Bourdieu's constructs into what happens in schools, clearly, status positions relate to students' sociocultural knowledge and dispositions, cultural capital (or lack thereof), and stratified school structure.

Other sociologists write about the connections between context and identity. Erving Goffman (1959) observes that "ordinary actors" manage and develop performances in relation to others in their social settings. For Goffman (1967), subjectivity and identity are embedded in the material features of contextually oriented scripts. Self-construction of identity is mediated by the material world (Holstein and Gubrium, 2000). Examining (con)textually mediated communication, action, and social relations, Dorothy Smith (1990) concludes that "people's lives are infused with the process of inscription of cultural text" (p. 209). According to Holland and her colleagues (1998), "cultural studies of the person is predicated upon a continuing cultural production that is a co-development of identities, discourses, embodiments, and imagined worlds" (p. vii). People's actions, then, are "related to social positions in social worlds that are structurally marked" (p. 7). Jane A. Van Galen (2004) refers to an absence of explicit mention of social class in educational scholarship. My studies reveal that although social class rarely is directly named, adolescents and adults do speak of poverty, wealth, and poor and rich people. More importantly, such student categories as smart and dumb, good and bad, and "those who care about learning" are coded words understood to be linked to student class affiliation. Like Van Galen, I conclude that social class has major cultural significance in the construction of identity and, in turn, influences social relations in school and in community life.

Agency, as identity, is situated within historically contingent, socially enacted, culturally constructed worlds (fields or frames of social life). Affluent people have the power to exercise agency in ways that enable them to reach their goals, whereas low-income people are compelled to comply with dominant class routines that rarely meet their needs or facilitate their agendas. The agency of low-income adults and adolescents is mostly suppressed, but surfaces in creative forms of resistance. Low-income students comply minimally with school routines or are passive aggressive in noncompliance (skipping school and classes, not participating in class, and not doing schoolwork). Others resist through confrontation or acting out. In *Learning to Labor*, Paul Willis (1977) illustrates how resistance worsens students' school circumstances and, ultimately, reduces their chances for an improved adult life. At some historical periods, working classes exercised more power and control over their lives. As labor unions are quashed and working-class economic and political clout declines, the collective and personal agency of working classes dissipates.

Even in the small town of Hillsdale, class-related distinctions in habitus mean that children and adults can be identified by class-bound personae and behaviors. While constellations of class-tied responses were evident in my interviews, consistent with Bourdieu's ideas about improvisation, each informant's narrative was to some extent idiosyncratic. Rather than being passive imitators of class-distinguishing ways of being, students and parents are agents who are innovative in performing class roles. Bourdieu argues that individual and group ingenuity contributes to the ongoing production and evolution of class characteristics. Yet, innovation is confined within class parameters. It also seems that innovation is inherently opportunistic. According to Gramsci's (1929–35/1971) idea of hegemony, because dominant groups intend to keep subordinates in relegated places and counterresistance from them, they are constantly energized to come up with new actions (improvisations) and original theories (ideologies) to sustain and legitimate domination. Resistance, by definition, is reactive, changing according to the domination patterns of elites.

Distortions in Perceptions and Interpretations of Others

Structuralist sociology defines a social world prescribed by norms, scripts, and socialized performances. Some scholars of this persuasion pay little attention to the innovative actions and personal feelings of actors. At the other end of the spectrum, with a decontextualized take on affect, psychologists see such emotions as anger as erupting from within. Emotions are seen to have an impact on the external world, but arise from internal sources. Perhaps social scientists perceive emotions this way because they often are men who hold unchallenged dominant positions. In the Victorian period, women's emotional symptoms (e.g., hysteria) were attributed to their fragile and unstable female physiology rather than a reaction to being subordinate. Similarly, the white world tends to see aggression as essential to blacks' genetic makeup, whereas blacks understand "rage" as a legitimate response to the continuing oppression of racism (Cose, 1993). In mainstream education circles, subordinate students' attitudes and behaviors are identified as problematic, but there is little recognition that teachers and high-status students act in disrespectful and uncivil ways. Following Maurice J. Elias (1989), I wrote about schools not being safe havens or even neutral venues for low-income youths (Brantlinger, 1991). Schools inflict symbolic violence (Block, 1997)—a potent source of anger and acting out. Rooted in frustration and depression, violence reveals the deeply emotional dimensions of classroom life (Boler and Zembylas, 2002). The institutional reaction, however, is to identify "misbehaviors"as personal pathology and to label the culprits "emotionally disturbed." Regardless of being disruptive, resistance has been touted as an inevitable and justified response to unfair treatment and hopeless situations (Ahier and Beck, 2003; Dyson, 1993; Fleischer, 2001; MacLeod, 1987).

Powerful people attribute their material and status advantages to their labors and talents. Correspondingly, they see Others' low status as due to their lesser aspirations and inferiority. Veiled by these distorted perceptions, social class privilege, in and out of school, goes mostly unnoticed. Dominant groups rarely speak about how students relegated to second-class status in class comprehensive schools or diminished education in class-segregated schools suffer (Brantlinger, 1993, 2003a, 2003b). They do not acknowledge obvious structural disparities in education or their own monopoly of high-status positions and white/class privilege. Professional educators, who should have been exposed to pluralistic society and diversity issues in teacher education or in-service courses, narrate stories that stress deficient genes or cultural heritage causes for class distinctions in school and society. The affluent believe that some people deliberately choose to be poor and prefer the lifestyles to which they are condemned by lack of funds (Bourdieu, 1984). That is, "Bourgeois observers see self-willed degradation in the slums" (Stallybrass and White, 1986, p. 135). In contrast to the invisibility of structural discrimination for affluent people, low-income parents and adolescents see and resent class-biased practices (Brantlinger, 1985a, 1985b, 1985c, 1993; Demerath, 2003). At the same time, illustrating the power of hegemonic discourse, to some extent low-income people share the dominant class perspective that their class is less smart, worthy, and respectable. Clearly, they internalize the distorted messages produced and circulated by dominant classes. Hence, they vacillate between blaming the system and blaming themselves. Self-blame results in their not protesting entitlements given to higher classes.

Commonsense Constructions
of Anger and Violence as Residing Solely
in Subordinate Youths

In spite of the general sense that poverty is self-induced, middle-class people appear to understand that denigration and subordination relate to anger and violence. Although empathy is not their strong suit, perhaps advantaged people can imagine how they would resent deprivation. Since the publication of my adolescent research in *The Politics of Social Class in Secondary Schools* (1993), a rash of shootings by white youths has occurred at suburban schools. The media has repeatedly drawn attention to the mystery of high suicide rates among students at elite universities and secondary schools. Studies of affluent and middle-class youths reveal their tendency to tease, bully, and reject each other and, especially, their lower-status counterparts (Burkett, 2001; Eder, 1997; Merton, 1994). Nevertheless, because success and wealth are associated with happiness, evidence of anger, cruelty, and violence in affluent, successful classes are counterintuitive. What cannot be explained by commonsense theories often gets ignored.

I was particularly puzzled by one of the findings of my adolescent interviews. Although both high- and low-income adolescents characterized low-income students as troublemakers, actual incidents of cross-class violence were perpetrated by high-income youths. High- and low-income informants described a frequent incidence in school hallways. High-income students would push a peer into a low-income student. When the low-income target reacted (usually verbally or with a threatening posture), the disruption brought teachers to the scene. The pusher proclaimed that the contact was accidental, the pushed peer would insist he was innocent, and both charged that the threatened retaliation on the part of the low-income student was not legitimate. Tense and upset by the incident—and by general feelings of vulnerability and powerlessness in the alienating school culture—the low-income youth would be belligerent toward all parties, hence was the one to be punished. Some affluent youths saw these occurrences as humorous pranks. Low-income adolescents were bitter about being singled out, slammed into, identified as perpetrators, and getting in trouble for defending themselves by "fighting back." When I discussed these incidents with college students, many recalled similar perceptions of who was violent and similar evidence of who was cruel in their secondary schools. They, too, did not understand why school winners would feel the urge to be mean to losers.

In my studies, high-income people conveyed that hostility and violence are endemic to the low-income Other. They conjectured that "angry" and "at-risk" youths imitated adult antisocial behaviors. Low-income adolescents and parents also tended to see negative attitudes, anger, and violence as unique to their class. Reflecting Willis's (1977) British working-class lads, they were animated in enumerating the ways in which they resisted domination. Except for passive aggression, however, what they detailed appeared to be fantasies of what they would like to do to get back at others' offenses. When asked to be specific about actual deeds, they admitted to not having engaged in cross-class aggression. Their anger inevitably was aimed at high-status Others; their fights were exclusively with their peers. Again, school-based cross-class attacks witnessed by adolescents were committed solely by affluent students. Regardless of consensus about who initiated the tussles, the reality did not interrupt stereotypes regarding the social class of troublemakers. Furthermore, the evidence of high-status youth infractions did not stick to their personal image—affluent adolescents were narrated as cooperative, peaceful, and moral.

Theories about the Origins of Violence

In a middle school study, D. Eder, C. C. Evans, and S. Parker (1995) observed a rigid ranking system acted out in official and unofficial spatial segregation. High-status youth involvement in cross-group shunning and teasing was ubiquitous. Students felt a high degree of insecurity about their social standing. The authors conjecture that by joining the ridicule of certain low-status students, high-income participants redirected their insecurities outward and deflected potential negative attention from themselves. Bystanders, who did not approve of peers' cruelty to vulnerable students, did not intervene to protect them. Eder and her colleagues found that that causes considerable stress. A low-income girl assigned to work in the lunchroom had such a strong fear of being mistreated that she went to great lengths to avoid high-status students. Scapegoats were special education students or students perceived as unattractive. Reputed to be the most popular and powerful males in the school, athletes were particularly prone to the use of degrading terms about homosexuality and weak (feminine) behavior.

Eder and her colleagues hypothesize that affluent youths' cruelty and aggression comes from a desire to physically differentiate themselves from those whom they feel embody negative characteristics. Worried about their own place in valued groups, they validate their status as insiders by casting Others as outsiders. Don Merton (1994) claims the heightening of family and community pressures result in middle school adolescents' need to establish themselves as better than others, which they do by bullying through negative epithets, put-downs, and physical aggression. Patrick M. Brantlinger (1990) describes the psychological phenomenon of dominant class groups projecting traits (stupidity, dirtiness, and violence) they do not want applied to themselves onto Others. David Harvey (2001) refers to the tendency to see evil in outsiders as a "geographic imaginary" that flourishes when there is little contact and hence little knowledge about Others. Dominant groups erect and preserve their own high status by creating rules by which outsiders' behaviors are constituted as deviant (Becker, 1963). Fitting in and belonging are important to adolescents, so they attempt to appear as nonexceptional members of school groups (Sacks, 1992). A. Michele Lease, Richard M. McFall, and Richard J. Viken (2003) argue that wanting to be ordinary correlates with perceptions of Others as different, which, in turn, leads to the exclusion and ostracism of outsiders perceived as inferior. In a global study of school violence, it was found that countries with the most stratified educational systems had the highest rates of school violence (Akiba et al., 2002).

The human tendency to create outsiders is conjectured to stem from deep psychological needs. The French linguist and psychoanalyst Julia Kristeva (1982) offers the concept of abjection to explain why apparently healthy individuals participate in forms of group-based fear, hatred, and oppression. People engage in intense self-creation work and defend their identity boundaries by constructing exclusionary social codes. They create a symbolic cultural order that assigns lesser identities to certain groups typically based on income-level, race/ethnic status, and religion. Individuals cast impure and offensive nonidentity elements to the borders of psychic as well as social structures. Within the daily operations of language and culture, humans express loathing and disdain toward Others, producing a regularity of rejection in the social order (see Smith and Danforth, 2000, pp. 138–39). George Lipsitz (1998) sees abjection in the possessive investment in whiteness. White [class] hegemony is maintained through the use of externalizing and decentering strategies that focus exclusively on Others (McLaren et al., 2001). Outward gaze serves to maintain privilege by externalizing difference, defining difference as inferiority, and resisting self-examination and critique. The practice of blaming the victim has long been condemned; however, the practice still pervades the social sciences and is reflected in the thinking of the lay public (Armstrong, 1993; Ryan, 1971; Valencia, 1997; Wright, 1993). Notions about deficits figure in classifications of anger as deviance and notions of causality pinpoint anger as residing in childhood or family pathology (see DSM IV). The image of personal and family dysfunction often is tacitly, if not explicitly, tied to minority race and lower class. Theories grounded in liberal social psychology (social science generally) assume that school and community life are neutral; hence dysfunction is not inherent to settings or mainstream students, schools, and families. These mainly psychoanalytic interpretations of identity formation and intergroup tensions address group processes, but tend to ignore the influence of the broader societal context.

The Puzzle of Violence among
Winners in the System

Due to the strength of commonsense constructions about who is hostile and why, people are surprised about violence committed by individuals from higher class backgrounds. After the first suburban school shooting by white students from middle- and upper-class families, the media and public expressed astonishment about the status of the perpetrators. However, after a few episodes at various suburban locations, people grew accustomed to the pattern of middle-class violence (Kimmel, 2003). Indeed, witnessing the televised spectacle of Washington, DC, shootings, media commentators as well as my acquaintances were surprised that the snipers were black. Recent events informed the public about middle-class, white perpetrators. Race and class stereotypes and commonsense notions that being at the bottom of the economic or social ladder causes anger are resilient. Concerned about increasing threats of violence from various quarters, Americans deal with school-based violence by investing in draconian security systems and toughening suspension and expulsion policies (Casella, 2001). In spite of suburban violence, the security measures and zero tolerance policies that are the most inflexible and punitive are imposed almost exclusively on schools in low-income areas (Devine, 1996).

The high suicide rate among students enrolled at Ivy League universities and elite high schools surface in press coverage as a paradox that cannot be explained by common theories about the origins and nature of anger and depression. It is assumed that prosperity, prestige, and success in competition make people happy. However, based on a study of business students at the University of California, Berkeley, Jennifer Chatman and Ariel Malka (2003) conclude: "In a capitalistic society, people generally believe that—all other things being equal—being rich is better. But that is not what we found" (p. 15). Just as I eventually came to realize that successful adolescents in my town were unhappy in school, these researchers found that wealthy people were not particularly content with their lives. So, although Americans have come to associate sniper incidents with white men and school violence with middle-class white boys, apparently these perpetrators continue to seem like unexplainable class and race aberrations—counterintuitive anomalies. The public cannot understand why middle-class persons (the winners in the system) are angry.

In this chapter, to explain the paradoxical discontent and aggression among the supposed winners in school and societal hierarchies, I turn to ideas about the ubiquity of human stress under capitalism. In particular, I draw from Philip Wexler's (1996) *Critical Social Psychology*. I had followed Wexler's (1992) advice to study the psychodynamic level of school relations for the perspectives of those involved. Yet, because I was fixated on low-income students' plight, I failed to notice problematic aspects of affluent youths' schooling. In this analysis, I revisit my interviews with 40 low-income and 34 high-income adolescents (1993) as well as with 36 low-income parents (Brantlinger, 1985a, 1985b, 1985c) and with 20 affluent mothers (Brantlinger, 2003a) and interpret the narratives by using a critical social psychology lens. I argue that frustration, anger, and violence toward others and self, are endemic to winners and losers in the hierarchical forms of schooling that exist under capitalism. First, I critique the flawed and biased theories put forth by liberal social psychologists.

Abnormality and Deviance according to Liberal Social Psychology

The liberal social psychology tradition attributes identity formation to a socialization model that is undergirded by the assumption that immediate family members and peers are key to identity formation. Ignoring capitalist context and social class relations, they define a separable core self that develops through identification with, attachment to, and imitation of, significant others. Given this framing of identity, the mainstream social psychology field sublimates and denies the presence and force of cultural domination (Wexler, 1996). At the same time, by aggregating individual deficiencies, scholars declare the existence of a set of undesirable traits in low-income children and families, which, in turn, are attributed to cultural patterns distinctive to their race or social class. Such individualistic theories about personal deviance and abnormality "shore up ruling class ideology by blocking from view social structural tendencies that are the identifiable source of personal conflict and suffering" (p. 14). Furthermore, the paradigm "normalizes and legitimates everyday cultural reifications" [of class-distinctive attributes] (pp. 79–80). Wexler criticizes the "fix-it shop of liberal society" that sees problematic identity as an idiosyncracy to be remedied on an individual basis by experts such as themselves (p. 89). He also derides liberals' inability to envision alternatives to market competition, noting that "the social can no longer be imagined as being anything different or other than the market itself" (p. xxiii). Hence, market relations become "a transhistorical, unalterable, constant fact of social life" (p. xxv). Liberal social psychologists see meritocratic schooling as neutral and normal. Dysfunctional school mechanisms are not considered; defects exist in students. Although social psychology purportedly pairs sociology and psychology, it dwells on individual (i.e., student and family) psychological aspects of human actions and not on macro-level, societal phenomena.

Moving from Liberal to Critical Social Psychological Views of Position and Affect

The conceptualization that framed my early reports of social class dynamics came from Bourdieu's (1977, 1984) clarification of habitus, cultural capital, and field as well as from social class reproduction theories of schooling. These concepts were useful in explaining the class-related character of adolescent and adult identity formation and the institutional processes that elevated and centered, or deflated and marginalized, students from each social class. In terms of theory, I mainly followed the sociological trend to focus on group processes. Bourdieu explains dominant groups' motivation to distinguish themselves from subordinates as well as their actions for doing so. He does not address people's personal reactions to within-class competition or emotions related to being in subordinate or dominant positions. Because an understanding of affect is necessary to account for the paradox of discontent and violence in higher classes, I turn to Wexler's application of Marxist concepts to link macro- and micro-levels of human experience and to explicate the nature and place of subjectivity in social life.

Wexler (1996) sees unsatisfactory identity and alienation as expected products of capitalist social relations. Claiming that "social class is a salient collectivity" and economic production a "salient institutional site of social relations" (p. xx), Wexler studies peoples' lived experience through "the sociopsychologic of capitalism" (p. 78). He examines the "relational interactional processes which make possible the production and reproduction of both the concrete individual and the structure of social relations" (p. 73). Karl Marx theorized that capitalist social formation arises from the relational processes of alienation, commodification (commodity fetishism), and exploitation of human labor power (see Bottomore, 1956). Wexler generalizes these aspects of capitalist production to a social psychology matrix for understanding human relations in schools. Because of their importance, brief definitions of these concepts are provided here.

Commodification or Commodity Fetishism

In modern capitalist societies this involves the construction of people's desires and felt needs around the material products of capitalism. Fetishism attaches to the products of labor; as commodities are produced [they affect] the social character of the labor that produces them (Marx, 1867, pp. 77–78). Due to commodity fetishism, humans' sense of agency reverses: products and things are understood as the source, rather than the effect, of human actions (Wexler, 1992, p. 85). Commodification also converts humans into commodities whose value in the market is based on their material resources and achievements (i.e., capital). Hence, self-value is attained by accumulating institutional products, e.g., test scores, grades, credentials, and professional status. People are constructed as deficient when they lack these exchange values. While personal status and power are elevated, personal control (agency) is diminished so that commodity accumulation is accompanied by a loss of imagination and capacity for self-directive planning (p. 86). In commodified cultures humans treat each other as objects so that, rather than being between people, social relationships are between products or outcomes of people's (students' school) labor. Material appearance is disconnected from concealed personal realities (Bottomore, 1973, p. 87). For example, in my study, high-income adolescents seemed intent on performing class-determined, commodified roles; however, they generally hid their insecurities about not fitting in or not succeeding academically from each other. In interviews, they first reeled off successes. As rapport and trust built, they confessed to considerable insecurity and emotional stress about their status.

Exploitation

This occurs when subordinate classes do not get the full value of their labor (surplus value goes to dominant classes), but also when social status is not equal and when relations are based on hierarchies. Some have more valued commodities (high test scores, good grades, participation and leadership in prestigious activities, and high-status labels and classroom placement) and others have less (low grades, exclusion, low-status placements, and negative labels). Recall that Bourdieu (1984) claims that social class distinctions are always interdependent: for some to have more desired commodities and higher status, Others must necessarily have less.

Accumulation of capital by dominant classes (exploitation) is obscured and routinized through ideology embedded in formal institutional structures (e.g., comparative evaluation, classification and placement, and legalized due process systems). The rationale for these systems are that some children are slower academically or have defects that need remediation. These rationale, or ideologies, naturalize and legitimate distinctions and disparities in school settings. Gramsci (1929–35/1971) and J. B. Thompson (1984, 1990) theorize that, as meaning in the service of power, ideology's role is to convince subordinates that status and material disparities are justified. High-income people in my studies believed that low-income students' lesser achievement and low-status placement resulted from their lesser intelligence or negative attitudes. In turn, these were attributed to genetics or to parents' inadequate child rearing practices. Echoes of these deficit narrative ideologies echoed in the responses of low-income participants. Wexler sees exploitation as central to structuring all social interaction. He contends that in exploitive situations the self becomes a battleground between social production (of what dominant groups reward) and individual ownership (agency, authentic identity, and agendas) (p. 87).

Alienation

According to Marx's definition, alienation occurs under capitalism when a person, group, institution, or society becomes (remains) alien to (1) results or products of their own activity (and the activity itself), (2) the natural environment, (3) other humans, and (4) human possibilities (Bottomore, 1973, p. 9). Self-alienation is not one among various forms of alienation, but is the essence and basic structure of alienation (p. 10). Bottomore claims that Marx felt that recognition of self-alienation would become an individuals or groups' incentive to call for a revolutionary change—for de-alienation. The cases of two high- and two low-income participants that I summarize illustrate that these three dimensions of capitalist relations affect participants of both classes, although in quite distinctive ways.

Wexler (1996) argues that Marx's general tendency laws (commodification, exploitation, and alienation) are "mediations which apply to all social relations in capitalism" (p. 78). In his own ethnographic work (Wexler, 1992) makes sense of "disabling tendencies in contemporary social life" (p. 8) by deconstructing "discourses which present themselves as explanatory in the everyday social interpretive practices of ordinary people" (p. xxi).

Referring to fundamental human drives for purposive labor and non-alienated activity, Wexler (1996) maintains that feelings of alienation under capitalism indicate "psychological resistance to socially patterned partialization and atrophy of human capacities" (pp. 82–83). Rather than attributing group formation and relations to value similarities, mutual attraction, and complementary needs (as liberal social psychologists theorize), Wexler claims collective grouping phenomena, forming cliques and rejecting and ostracizing Others, are due to individuals' efforts to overcome paralyzing fragmentation and powerlessness brought about by the alienating commodity fetishism and exploitation of capitalism. In my studies, both high- and low-income adolescents alluded to idealized others that were powerful, complete, and without personal flaws. As they referred to these ideal classmates, or entertainers, Others were described as inadequate objects. Wexler maintains that the assignment of these valences corresponds to students' socially patterned sense of personal lack and self-devaluation that predict interpersonal attraction and aversion. It is important to compare the dynamics of abjection and how identification with certain ideal others and securing a place in a powerful collective are "desired ways to turn alienation into intimacy with others as well as with self" (p. 84). Thus, identity formation represents a personalized mode of appropriation and accumulation (of commodities) (p. 90). Wexler argues that schizophrenia (fragmented experience, (con)fusion of the imaginary with the real, loss of boundary around ego or self, perception of self as object, and sense of fragility or isolation) are quintessential self-products of social relations in late capitalist commodity relations (p. 124). Commodity relations of fitting in and conforming to external standards happen among people of either class who have little control over their work (p. 125). These same dynamics are integral to alienation. Relatedly, both affluent and impoverished adolescents in my studies were upset about what happened to them in school and were worried about their post-school lives.

Questioning the Middle Class as the Model for Child-Rearing

Educated, middle-class parents are continuously held up as parenting models and are particularly praised for supporting their children's educational achievement. However, the intense, even exploitive, nature of their involvement is rarely addressed. Writing about college application, after noting that universities have become "a couple of clicks more selective," Jennifer Jacobson (2003) conjectures that families who are "very successful in their own lives aren't used to hearing 'no'" (p. A27). She cites an admission officer as saying, "parents today are used to being heavily involved in the daily lives of their children, and have long ferried them to and from ballet lessons, soccer practices, and many other 'enrichment opportunities,' and when it's time to select a college they can't turn it off" (p. A27). This official claimed that one mother came on "like a scud missile," reminding him more of "an agent than a parent, while her daughter was sitting next to her looking like 'can I please be anywhere but here?'" (p. A28). Another admission officer says that part of his job is to "remind parents that the process needs to be focused on the students' interests and not the parents' agenda" (p. A28). This evidence of parental pressure on gatekeepers may be the tip of the iceberg in terms of how some push their children to perform idealized middle class roles and unrealistically expect them to excel in a range of in- and out-of-school activities. Such students may have few choices because their lives are shaped by their parents' ambitions.

Commodification, Exploitation, and Alienation in Hillsdale

In a recent chapter I updated my portrayal of two adolescents, affluent Marissa and low-income Travis (Brantlinger, 2003b). I highlight these same two adolescents here, as well as a parent of each social class. Catherine, Marissa's mother, was interviewed for a study of affluent mothers (Brantlinger, 2003a). Rhonda, Travis's neighbor in "the Projects," was interviewed in a study of low-income parents (Brantlinger, 1985a, 1985b, 1985c). Marissa was the epitome of a successful student and Catherine of an involved parent. In terms of dissatisfaction with life circumstances, Marissa was fairly representative of affluent adolescents. Regarding excessive concern about social and achievement status, Catherine typified affluent mothers' worries about their children attaining a secure high-status place in a competitive world. Educational achievement and attainment not only were status markers for external evaluation, but were the grounding for positive identity for the educated professional class. Affluent mothers revealed their compulsion to produce smart, attractive, popular, and well-adjusted children. Travis was similar to other low-income youths in that he had emotionally disengaged from school by middle school and as a freshman in high school, he dropped out the day he turned sixteen. Rhonda's voice matched those voices of many low-income parents who expressed anger at the negative school circumstances that existed for their children and also for themselves in their earlier student days. They vacillated between critical insight and self-blaming as they reiterated the ideology of school as the site for social mobility.

Travis was a bright, athletic, and handsome teenager with a keen wit. Teachers liked him and did not give up on encouraging him to improve his schoolwork and to join athletic teams. In some ways they felt Travis had "class-exceptional" talents and could succeed in school, so were perplexed about why he did not make an effort and joined his less-competent peers' rejection of schooling. Travis did not identify with his teachers. Although Travis announced that "me and teachers didn't get along," when asked to describe a favorite teacher, Travis responded without hesitation:

> I loved Mr. E. [his fifth-grade teacher]; he was a real cool teacher. He helped me a bunch of times when I did not understand—he cared about me. Other teachers did not care. They'd just get mad and say, "You'll flunk if you don't do your work." They didn't care what happened to me. We'd argue a lot. I wouldn't understand something and they'd say, "Well I just showed you how to do it!" And I liked Mr. F. [middle school gym teacher and wrestling coach]. He was nice. All the kids liked him and he liked us. We had fun in his class. Most teachers was snobby;

some was all right. If you didn't understand, they didn't treat you like a piece of trash. Some teachers helped you if you had a problem. Most didn't. They helped some kids—their pets, but they didn't care about most of us, didn't care about me, if I flunked or anything.

When asked if some students had an easier time in school, Travis's immediate response was: "Yeah, preppies, rich kids. They got away with things. Teachers were hard on me and my friends." When asked about his relations in high school, Travis said: "I had some friends—we stuck together. The punks were smart alecks—we avoided them. They would start fights and things like that. The preps ran the school. They would smart off and call us grits [epithets for low-income people] and stuff like that. They didn't bother me. I just kept away from them. I didn't care." Travis stressed "not caring," but his animated and emotional tone belied the validity of this assertion. Before Travis dropped out of school, he had been suspended twice in the fall for "missing class and being late" and had not successfully completed any freshman courses. Travis felt that his mother "didn't want me to quit, but said 'if that's what you want to do, then do it.'" He explained, "She'd rather see me quit than [be] in trouble. Besides, she let my brothers drop out, so it wouldn't be fair [to] make me go. Anyway, she didn't finish herself, and my dad dropped out when he was real little." When asked why he dropped out, Travis reminisced: "The dean was giving me a bunch of trouble. She did that with all us boys. She'd hassle me about being late, missing school—I was having problems with everything. She'd call my mom and threaten her. When I quit going for a week after my dad died, she said she'd take me to court if I wasn't there every day. My mom said I did not have to go until we got things straightened out. So, she suspended me. She said I couldn't come back until I had a letter from the doctor or welfare. I never liked school anyway. It was all right at Hillview [elementary] some of the time, I guess. I did not like Downing [middle school] or high school. When I was 16, I stopped going. I just got tired of going."

Astute about class politics, Travis used the interview to express resentment about class disparities and to share his frustrations about the hopelessness of achieving the American social mobility dream. Along with other more self-confident low-income youths, Travis verbalized his anger at his second-class status in schools. Less insightful peers revealed their self-alienation by enumerating their inadequacies and feelings of inferiority. Commodified and exploited as losers, low-income youths were alienated from the student role, school personnel, and schooling.

Rhonda grew up in "the Projects" on "the Hill" (an impoverished area). When her second son was born, Rhonda moved to her own subsidized apartment in the same complex where she had been raised and where her mother continued to live. At the time Rhonda was interviewed, her sons were in the seventh and fifth grades and her daughter was in the second grade. Both sons had been retained a year in early elementary school. Todd, the fifth grader, had attended a self-contained class for students with mild mental handicaps for two years, although Rhonda was not clear about his label. Rhonda resented that no one listened to her during the case conference that resulted in Todd's special education placement; she admitted that she had not gone to subsequent conferences, "because it wouldn't make no difference anyhow." She recalled:

> I tried to tell them about how upset he was about his daddy so he could not stay still or pay attention. He wasn't like that when he was little. He used to mind better. When Todd was in second and third grades, he liked his teachers and he did okay then. Now, he didn't like Mrs. X, he said she was mean and didn't help him. I know some of them teachers wasn't fair. They have teachers' pets or something. They favor people that is more like in their type of society, their set-up. Like everybody has their own little group, little society, people you run around with, people you shouldn't talk about. Teachers favor ones more like themselves, or people who they feel is respectable, or whatever you want to call it.

In terms of evaluating the cause of Todd's problems, Rhonda alternated between blaming herself (and/or the boys' fathers), her sons, and school personnel. She recalled, "Todd had lots of trouble learning to read, he was backward about his learning, just did not catch on—and I know how that feels; I was a little like that myself." Rhonda complained: "I know some of them teachers wasn't fair, they only want to teach the smart ones—the ones who catch on fast—they don't bother with those ones having a hard time. It was like that back when I was in school; I know it's like that now." Although her other son Dean had been "held back in kindergarten," Rhonda said, "now he's making mostly B's and C's in middle school and don't mind school so much right now." Rhonda's valuing of education surfaced as she described her daughter's school performance: "Annette is real smart. She's making all A's. She likes school. She loves her teacher and now she is even saying that she wants to be a teacher when she gets big. You should hear her read. She brings all these hard books home from school and instead of playing outside or watching t.v., she just sits there reading out loud. She reads better than Todd. She helps him when he lets her. I bet she even reads better than Dean. She's my smart one."

When asked about her own educational attainment and whether she expected her children to graduate from high school, Rhonda elaborated:

I never went back after eighth grade. I was failing lots of classes and I just got fed up with school. You know, in a sense, you're degraded by people smarter than you. So, I really, actually know how Dean and Todd feel because I've experienced the same thing. And teachers like certain kinds of kids—they're talkative, which I wasn't. I was real shy and stayed back. I felt really sort of degraded myself. Got discouraged. I think my boys feel the same way. I hope they finish school, I really hope they do, but I don't know, maybe they won't if things keep on going the same way. Annette, now, she'll finish, I know she will. She loves school. She's a smart one.

When asked about other people's attitudes toward her neighborhood schools, Rhonda explained, "See, this part of town up here is run-down and stuff and a lot of people don't like Hillview and Downing. They don't like the Hill Schools 'cause they're by the projects and stuff." In terms of discrimination, Rhonda said: "Well, you can see the difference between them people that come by the money—they're treated different and that's not right. I think kids should be treated equal, but they're not. They're differencing them. They done that way back even when I was in school."

When asked if she would prefer her children to go to the schools in affluent neighborhoods that she categorized as "real good schools—hotshot schools for rich kids," Rhonda pondered the question, then said: "I don't think they'd feel that easy over there. Well, I just think it's more well-to-do kids there, and whenever a child is poor—when the others got more things, better clothes, and stuff like that, then they're going to make fun to a certain extent. Around here it's more people who are down to our level."

Crossing over to the affluent eastside of Hillsdale, Marissa was admired by peers for "having it all." Marissa got straight A's in advanced tracks, was a cheerleader, and in the competitive swing choir. In her interview, after glibly detailing accomplishments as they might be listed on a résumé for college admission, Marissa confessed to feeling insecure on a number of fronts. Reassurance that sterling grades meant she was intelligent met with prompt denial. Marissa reiterated that her good grades were the result of her own hard work as well as parental tutoring and intervening with teachers on her behalf. She insisted that she did not "catch on easily" or "really understand most subjects." Claiming to be "tone-deaf with two left feet," Marissa surmised she made swing choir only because the director knew that she could afford the expensive costumes and her mother would be helpful. After describing hanging out at the mall and the lake with friends, Marissa launched into a vehement attack on her peers—they were two-faced, dishonest, and disloyal. She complained that her parents favored her brother. She charged that her parents "only cared" about the impression she made on others—her popularity and achievements. When alternative explanations were offered, Marissa insisted that they did not really care about her. She cynically admitted to being a teacher's pet, but went on to attribute preferential treatment to her brother's sterling reputation and her mother's school involvement. All was not well in Marissa's seemingly ideal world. Her airhead image allowed her to mask her insecurities and anger. Marissa frantically detailed problems in her life, conveying she had no one to trust to confide her feelings to on a regular basis. Pittu Laungani (1999) claims that individualism creates conditions that do not permit an easy sharing of one's problems and worries with others (p. 95). According to Abraham Maslow (1970) and Eric Erikson (1968), achieving a fulfilling identity is difficult and stressful in an individualistic culture and in extreme cases leads to an identity crisis. Marissa was a prime example of conflicted and angry feelings about herself and her world.

Marissa's mother, Catherine, grew up on the East Coast and moved to Hillsdale when her husband became a college professor. She preferred her own "classic, rigorous" private church-affiliated education to her children's public schools, although they had attended the "best schools in town." She and her husband selected their first home because it was in the Kinder School zone. Kinder was an exclusive high-income elementary school with no children on free or reduced lunch. They declined sending their son to the gifted and talented program he qualified for because "we felt our own school, Kinder, was a better school, really, and so we did not think it was worth it to bus him to the other side of town." They later moved to a posh suburb because they could afford a large home in the catchment zone of a new, more homogeneously high-income middle school. Catherine's version was: "We heard from teachers that it had better quality programs and was more academic." Catherine claimed that her children had "natural talent and were motivated to excel." Both were in advanced placement sections in middle school and in high school honors classes, although Catherine admitted that Marissa had not always done well on these tests; so she was "grateful that principals were responsive to our requests" [for Marissa to be in these classes].

Catherine was proud that her children were active in extracurricular activities. Marissa was "more social than Christopher," who was "more of a scholar (like his dad), interested in science." Catherine was pleased that Marissa was clothes conscious, in a prestigious clique, and engaged in high-status activities. In contrast, after proudly describing Christopher's athletic prowess in tennis and track, she quickly returned to discussing his academic strengths: "Chris is interested in the subject matter he is studying and motivated to learn far beyond what he is given to learn. He . . . will speak up for himself when he does not understand or feels something like a grade is unfair. I often have to intervene with teachers for Marissa. He cooperates with teachers and has a good attitude about learning and is energetic and conscientious about his work. Christopher has always . . . looked forward to going to school."

One complaint Catherine had about public education was that her children occasionally had been in untracked classes, where they "weren't pushed because teachers had to teach to the common denominator and water down the curriculum." Catherine recalled: "At times, with my daughter, she was bothered by the school environment. In high school, in a few classes, they both were with kids sometimes where many students do not emphasize education and our kids had to deal with that, whereas in my time, I studied in schools where all kids came from families that stressed education and learning. They have had to associate with a wider group of people in public schools than we did in private schools. I think in some school environments here they stress mediocrity."

When specifically asked about whether she would support local social class desegregation, without hesitation Catherine replied: "I prefer them to attend schools in this area [affluent suburbs] because this is where the better students are." She explained: "Ideally, a public school should have a mixture of socio-economic groups. The problem is when a lot of low-income kids whose parents don't have much education come into contact with high-income kids then there is not much stimulation for good, um, they don't stimulate each other and they aren't going to have good programs. I know I am equating low-income with lack of interest in education, but I think that is the way it is. My son says that grits [epithet for low-income people] are not interested in school—that's what he says and he is tolerant of everybody."

When asked about the contact her children had with low-income children, Catherine conjectured: "I don't know how much contact they have with lower-economic children. I doubt if they have any in most of their classes." Then she quickly changed the subject.

> What I have heard is that it is never the parents of students who need help and have problems that come to meetings with teachers and it is always parents of kids who are doing well in school or are from high socioeconomic groups because they value education and, . . . maybe do not feel intimidated. There are differences in abilities, whether that is that low-income kids don't have abilities or whether it is lack of encouragement of learning by the home, I don't know, but I think low-income parents don't think learning is important. They have to . . . think about jobs and making money. I admit, high-income

kids do have more educational options, but they are more interested in those options too. Really, on a practical level, now, you would not want your children to go to those schools [points to four low-income schools on the list of local schools]. . . . I would want my kids to go to a mixed school but one with an emphasis on, and value for, education with a good faculty. My kids should be with kids who are motivated and interested in learning.

Catherine had a master's degree in education and taught high school for two years before she married and moved to Hillsdale. She had chosen to stay home when her children were young, intending to go back to work when they finished elementary school but "got so involved with volunteer work that I just never tried to find a job." Much of this work had been at her children's schools, in the library, and as room mother. Although parental participation even for middle-class parents typically drops at the secondary level, Catherine continued to be active in the high school Parent Teacher Organization and in fund-raising to support for their extra-curricular activities.

As might be noted in these interview summaries and quotations, Catherine and Rhonda continuously referred to themselves and their children as members of a social class. Similar to all affluent mothers' narratives, Catherine revealed assumptions about her class's intellectual and moral superiority. She implied that because her children were academically advanced, they needed and were entitled to privileged conditions and class-segregated school circumstances. In contrast, Rhonda wavered between resentment about the social class biases that she knew were quite profound and making comments that indicated that she had internalized class-related messages about intellectual and competency inadequacies. Low-income people's responses revealed a resignation to class distinctions in schooling. Because school disparities match the lesser conditions of all aspects of low-income life, they may seem natural and normal. The inequities that shock and dismay middle-class people who are concerned about educational equality, may be taken for granted by those in subordinate positions. At least to a certain extent, poor parents and adolescents seemed to buy into the dominant class ideology that schools are fair meritocracies and that all students can do well if they are smart, have the right attitude, and exert an effort. In spite of having considerable insight into the nature and extent of social class bias, they still attribute lesser status to their own, class-related inferior personal attributes rather than to structural factors that limit access to quality education. To confirm the main point of this chapter, substantial evidence of commodified, exploitive, and alienating circumstances riddled the narratives (see table 3).

Table 3
Impact of Capitalist Schooling on Adolescents and Parents

Participant	Commodification	Exploitation	Alienation
Low-income adoles- cents	socialized by schooling to accept inferiorized identity and low-status	possibility for acceptable status and self-image are sacrificed so affluent students can be superior	school facilitates positive outcomes for affluent students; low-income students have no constructive place in school
Low-income parents	learned through her own schooling to accept low school status and negative outcomes for offspring	surplus labor position (chronic unemployment and low wages) benefit capitalists; the children must suffer second-rate status so others can excel	little or no power to influence the schooling of offspring; negative school experiences and outcomes result in not seeing school as beneficial
Affluent adoles- cents	pressured to be perfect in academics, appearance, activities, and popularity	must conform to class expectations, little room for her feelings and agendas	little sense of solidarity with her parents, siblings, or peers; out-of-touch with own feelings
Affluent mothers	learned through schooling that they were superior products who must retain that status	excessively high expectations to raise perfect children; personal needs sacrificed to facilitating children's status	by insisting on perfect school performance from offspring she loses the intimacy she might otherwise have with them

Who Wins in School Hierarchies?

When examining the ubiquity of hierarchical schooling, it is easy to conclude that high-income students are winners and low-income students
losers. Certainly that has been the message of most of my own scholarly
work and that of critical theorists generally. It is undeniable that low-
income people have a much harder time and suffer most from life under

capitalism. Clearly, school inflicts the most damage on students who are relegated to second-rate classes and who are bombarded with evidence that they are losers. Wexler (1996) maintains: "Even now, but in the neutralized language of science [used by educational professionals, politicians, and the general public] rather than one of morality and personality, the bourgeois self ideal is used as a standard by which to inferiorize any working-class subjectivity that resists its hegemony. The working class, despite resistance, was subjectively colonized in schools and families. The powerlessness dimension of commodity effects had historically had the greatest impact on this class" (pp. 128–29).

As I reread the transcripts of interviews with affluent adolescents, I began to realize that there were no true winners in the complex and troubled dynamics of social class relations under capitalism in or out of school. The convergence of evidence that winners in capitalist educational meritocracies are not particularly happy, provided the incentive to seek out theories that might explain this ironic paradox. And, as noted in my review of Wexler's critical social psychological perspective, I found Marx's ideas about capitalist exploitation to have sound explanatory value.

Low-income students clearly suffer from humiliating classroom arrangements, negative evaluation of their work, and exclusion from prestigious activities. Yet, low-income students and parents understand these negative circumstances from their position/perspective as subordinates. Many of the low-income adolescents who were interviewed had the comfort of knowing that their parents empathized with their school problems because of their own degrading experiences. Low-income adolescents and parents could externalize blame for conditions and name common enemies (snobby teachers, stuck-up preps, and useless homework). They felt within-class solidarity based on a shared sense of injustice. In addition, they were able to invert the moral hierarchy by espousing alternative values (it was important not to be snobby or think you were better than others) and by validating their own interests (race cars and heavy metal music) and personal styles. They conveyed that they exercised certain choices that accounted for their low status in school (attributing low grades to not caring about school and not trying). Just as with Willis's (1977) British working-class lads, some Hillsdale youths claimed that they purposefully did not fit into the mainstream and intentionally failed their courses. However, based on the emotional intensity of these claims, this resistance bravado appeared to be a feigned position and defensive fiction.

In contrast to low-income youths who could take school or leave it because they knew their social class had been disenfranchised from the benefits of school and society, school was an essential testing ground for affluent adolescents. They were to follow in their parents' footsteps and to compete with their peers to attain a respectable level of middle-class status. They felt pressured to pursue professional careers, whether or not they found them interesting or believed they could reach their parents' goals. They aspired to being the brightest, most athletic, and most talented in the arts—just doing their best was not good enough. Some who had not made it into the advanced course arrangements or did not get top grades were dejected about being second rate. Those who excelled were worried about maintaining their high status through each stage of their education and life careers. Some, who would be considered exceptionally high achievers by any standard, said they felt like imposters, attributing success to intensive personal effort and family intervention rather than to "natural talent." A star athlete (described by others as a "popular jock") was upset that his best friend had received the most valuable player award, which he felt he deserved. A junior, who played piano well enough to accompany classmates' vocal performances, compared herself unfavorably to someone who had preceded her in this role and who had been admitted to a prestigious music school—she was convinced that she would not be admitted. If affluent students were not successful academically or were excluded from peer social life, they could not excuse themselves on the grounds of social class discrimination. They were personally accountable. Combined with arrogance about their worth and entitlements, signs of anger and/or depression about family life and social relations in their neighborhood and school arose in affluent youths' narratives. Some seemed guarded in expressing their feelings. Others openly confessed to considerable anxiety about meeting parents' (and their own) demands. Like their troubled low-income counterparts, they used the interview opportunity to express intense feelings. Affluent adolescents were to enact a commodified superior performance. Even when they succeeded, some felt exploited and alienated.

The irony of the social reproduction milieu under capitalism is that there are distinctions even within the dominant class that prevent their solidarity and create friction within the collective of privileged students. Competitive ranking dynamics do not sort zombies or mannequins but real people with feelings and desires. Being at the top echelon does not guarantee a happy, problem free life. The turmoil and angst of having to be the best affect the psyche of students who should be content with their winning status. The theme that she was to perform an idealized middle-class role and could not be valued for herself dominated Marissa's narratives. As a commodity, albeit a valued one, Marissa was exploited and alienated by the competitive/capitalist climate of school and home. At twenty-five years of age, Marissa returned to her parents' home because her marriage was troubled and because she had quit a fairly lucrative job after being passed over for a promotion. Catherine confided that Marissa "did not try hard enough to work things out," but also confided that her son Chris had started and dropped out of two master's degree programs and had "a temporary job."

The smart and talented Travis had mostly disengaged from schooling by the eighth grade. Learning that high school was not designed in his social class interests, Travis skipped as often as he could and had no regrets about quitting. He experienced the chronic unemployment and underemployment as had his parents and brothers. Hillsdale working-class jobs had disappeared when factories relocated to Mexico and when part-time service jobs relied on a ready pool of university students. About ten years after I interviewed Travis, I read of his suicide in the local newspaper obituary. He left three children to fend for themselves in a difficult low-income world. Other interviewed adolescents were not as bitter as Marissa and Travis; however, none glowed with contentment about their life in schools and in the community. Few parents of either class were totally at ease and satisfied with the present and future lives of their offspring.

A close look at the complex reality of the processes and products of schools under capitalism reveals that nobody actually wins in terms of having their intimate personal needs satisfied. Regarding the foundations and functions of capitalist relations and meritocratic schooling, it is important think about the nature of human needs. Maslow (1970) presents a continuum of essential human needs. The first two are biological (sustenance and safety); the next three regard emotions and social life (need to belong and feel loved, feel esteemed and respected, and reach potential—self-actualization). Positive identity is linked to a sense of personal wholeness embedded in feelings of solidarity with valued others. Drawing from Erving Goffman (1959, 1967), Roy F. Baumeister (1996) claims the desire to think well of oneself is a fundamental and pervasive motivation of human psychological functioning. A cause of frustration and anger, then, is having one's hoped for identity thwarted or satisfying personal relations threatened. Consistent with Baumeister's and Maslow's claims about human needs, based on a meta-analysis of anthropological studies, David E. Brown (1991) found that societal hierarchy that corresponds to uneven distributions of social status and material resources was a human universal. Brown also found that support for a social reciprocity morality based on recognition of commonalities across social borders was simultaneously present.

Possibility of School and Societal Reorganization

Some might argue that the social and emotional climate in schools might be improved without touching the societal context. In my years of field experience supervision, I observed caring and committed teachers. I also witnessed whenever they conformed to the meritocratic standards of schooling: grading, ranking, and sorting students. Yet, focusing on the way in which school organization affects teachers and students, Valerie E. Lee (1995) observes that in Catholic schools, teachers and students use the word community to describe their schools, whereas personal and communal dimensions had largely disappeared in public school life. She attributes problems to bureaucratization and to efficient delivery of services, not to the inherent anticommunal dynamics of capitalist relations. Lee claims that two measures of communal organization are shared values and shared activities among school community members. I would question whether these might ever be realized in schools under capitalism. Perhaps some vestiges of communal life remain in homogeneous private schools or in rural schools less influenced by the rampant commodity fetishism of capitalism with its exploitive and alienating impact on humans.

In contrast to Lee's separation of school from its societal context, Michael W. Apple (1995) insists that institutions and events of everyday life be understood not in isolation from the relations of domination and from exploitation of the larger society, but in a way that stresses interconnections, especially for the institutions, policies, and practices of formal education. According to Apple, social class is an analytic construct, but also a set of relations that exist outside our minds. For Apple, as for Wexler, capitalism "exists as a massive structuring force" (p. 180). Certainly, the divisive strains of capitalism are strong in Hillsdale and in its schools. What should be stressed as a concern for all Americans is that school and societal inequalities (Perrucci and Wysong, 2003) threaten the very democracy we hold so dear (Rorty, 1998; Young, 2000).

An unfortunate aspect of the American capitalist system and its meritocratic schooling is that they depend on social hierarchy and on uneven resource distributions of resources rather than on equality. If Bourdieu, Samuel Bowles, Herbert Gintis, and other critical theorists are right, schools in capitalist societies are bound to remain individualistic, competitive hierarchies that privilege children from dominant families and marginalize subordinate children. These divisive relations are bolstered and mystified by social mobility and economic advancement ideologies that have little to do with reality. Generations ago, George Counts (1932) worried that stratifying interactions would be hard to change. It is clear that transformative school reform is difficult precisely because schools are controlled by the middle classes who think they benefit from stratification and exclusion (Brantlinger, 2003a). My studies indicate that it is time for these powerful people to look at the kind of schooling they have created and think harder about the kind of schools they want for their own and for other people's children. Losers in the system are likely to be too demoralized to imagine a more just world. Moreover, they lack the power to engage in the collective action needed for monumental change. To alter capitalism in society and meritocracy in schools, there would have to be a profound change in Americans' thinking. The only hopeful aspect of the widening income gap and economic downturn of our troubled country is that citizens' consciousness may be raised enough to consider alternatives that are more consistent with the distributive justice and equality dimensions of democracy.

References

Ahier, J., and Beck, J. 2003. Education and the politics of envy. *British Journal of Educational Studies*, 51, 320–343.

Akiba, M., LeTendre, G. K., Baker, D. P., and Goesling, B. 2002. Student victimization: National and school system effects on school violence in 37 nations. *American Educational Research Journal*, 39, 829–53.

Anyon, J. 1980. Social class and the hidden curriculum of work. *Journal of Education, 162*, 67–92.

———. 1981. Elementary schooling and the distinction of social class. *Interchange*, 12(2/3), 118–32.

Apple, M. W. 1995. Part III introduction: Power, politics, and knowledge in education. In W. T. Pink and G. W. Noblit (Eds.) *Continuity and contradiction: The futures of the sociology of education* (pp. 177–84). Cresskill, NJ: Hampton.

Armstrong, L. 1993. *And they call it help: The psychiatric policing of America's children*. Reading, MA: Addison-Wesley.

Baumeister, R. F. 1996. Self-regulation and ego threat: Motivated cognition, self-deception, and destructive goal setting. In P. M. Gollwitzer and J. A. Bargh (Eds.) *The psychology of action: Linking cognition and motivation to behavior* (pp. 27–47). New York: Guilford.

Becker, H. 1963[1973]. *Outsiders*. New York: Free Press.

Benjamin, S. 2002. *The micropolitics of inclusive education: An ethnography*. Buckingham: Open University Press.

Block, A. A. 1997. *I'm only bleeding: Education as the practice of violence against children*. New York: Peter Lang.

Boler, M., and Zembylas, M. 2002. Discomforting truths: The emotional terrain of understanding difference. In P. P. Trifonas (Ed.) *Pedagogies of difference: Rethinking education for social change* (pp. 110–36). New York and London: RoutledgeFalmer.

Bottomore, T. B. 1956. *Karl Marx: Selected writings in sociology and social philosophy*. New York: McGraw Hill.

———. (Ed.) 1973. *Karl Marx*. Englewood Cliffs, NJ: Prentice-Hall.

Bourdieu, P. 1977. *Outline of a theory of practice*. Cambridge: Cambridge University Press.

———. 1984. *Distinction: A social critique of the judgment of taste*. Cambridge: Harvard University Press.

Bowles, S., and Gintis, H. 1976. *Schooling in capitalist America.* New York: Basic.

Brantlinger, E. A. 1985a. What low-income parents want from schools: A different view of aspirations. *Interchange,* 16, 14–28.

———. 1985b. Low-income parents' perceptions of favoritism in the schools. *Urban Education,* 20, 82–102.

———. 1985c. Low-income parents' opinions about the social class composition of schools. *American Journal of Education,* 93(3), 389–408.

———. 1991. Social class distinctions in adolescents' reports of problems and punishment in school. *Behavior Disorders,* 17, 36–46.

———. 1993. *The politics of social class in secondary school: Views of affluent and impoverished youth.* New York: Teachers College Press.

———. 2003a. *Dividing classes: How the middle class negotiates and rationalizes school advantage.* New York: RoutledgeFalmer.

———. 2003b. Who wins and who loses? Social class and student identities. In M. Sadowski (Ed.) *Adolescents at school: Perspectives on youth, identity, and education* (pp. 107–21). Cambridge: Harvard University Press.

Brantlinger, P. M. 1990. *Crusoe's footprints: Cultural studies in Britain and America.* New York and London: Routledge.

Brown, D. E. 1991. *Human universals.* Philadelphia: Temple University Press.

Brown, D. K. 1995. *Degrees of control: A sociology of educational expansion and occupational credentialism.* New York: Teachers College Press.

Burkett, E. 2001. *Another planet: A year in the life of a suburban high school.* New York: HarperCollins.

Burton, R. L. 1999. A study of disparities among school facilities in North Carolina: Effects of race and economic status. *Educational Policy,* 13, 280–95.

Calhoun, C., LiPuma, E., and Postone, M. 1993. *Bourdieu: Critical perspectives.* Chicago: University of Chicago Press.

Casella, R. 2001. *"Being down": Challenging violence in urban schools.* New York: Teachers College Press.

Chatman, J., and Malka, A. 2003, July 18. Sometimes, money can buy happiness. *Chronicle of Higher Education,* 49(45), A15.

Cose, E. 1993. *The rage of a privileged class: Why are middle-class blacks angry? Why should America care?* New York: HarperPerennial.

Counts, G. 1932. *Dare the school build a new social order?* (reprint). Carbondale: Southern Illinois University Press, 1978.

Demerath, P. 2003. Negotiating individualist and collectivist futures: Emerging subjectivities and social forms in Papua New Guinean High Schools. *Anthropology and Education Quarterly,* 34, 136–57.

Devine, J. 1996. *Maximum security: The culture of violence in inner-city schools.* Chicago: University of Chicago Press.

Diagnostic and Statistical Manual of Mental Disorders, 4th ed. 1994. Washington, DC: American Psychiatric Association.

Dyson, M. E. 1993. *Reflecting black: African-American cultural criticism.* Minneapolis: University of Minnesota Press.

Eder, D., 1997. Sexual aggression within the school culture. In B. Bank and P. Hall (Eds.) *Gender, equity and schooling: Policy and practice* (pp. 93–112). New York: Garland.

Eder, D., with C. C. Evans and S. Parker 1995. *School talk: Gender and adolescent culture.* New Brunswick, NJ: Rutgers University Press.

Elias, M. J. 1989. Schools as a source of stress to children: An analysis of causal and ameliorative influences. *Journal of School Psychology, 27,* 393–407.

Erikson, E. 1968. *Identity: Youth and crisis.* New York: Norton.

Fine, M. 1991. *Framing dropouts: Notes on the politics of an urban public high school.* Albany: State University of New York Press.

Finders, M. J. 1997. *Just girls: Hidden literacies and life in junior high.* New York: Teachers College Press.

Fleischer, L. E. 2001. Special education students as counter-hegemonic theorizers. In G. M. Hudak and P. Kihn (Eds.) *Labeling: Pedagogy and politics* (pp. 115–24). New York: RoutledgeFalmer.

Goffman, E. 1959. *The presentation of self in everyday life.* New York: Doubleday.

———. 1967. *Interaction ritual: Essays on face-to-face behavior.* Garden City, NY: Doubleday.

Gramsci, A. 1929–35/1971. *Selections from the prison notebooks.* Eds. Q. Hoare and G. N. Smith. New York: International Publishers.

Grant, C. A., and Sleeter, C. E. 1996. *After the school bell rings.* London: Falmer.

Harvey, D. 2001, November. *Geographical knowledges/political power.* Lecture at the Institute for Advanced Study. Indiana University-Bloomington.

Holland, D., Lachicotte, W. Jr., Skinner, D., and Cain, C. 1998. *Identity and agency in cultural worlds.* Cambridge: Harvard University Press.

Holstein, J. A., and Gubrium, J. F. 2000. *The self we live by: Narrative identity in a postmodern world.* Oxford: Oxford University Press.

Hudak, G. M., 2001. On what is labeled 'playing': Locating the 'true' in education. In G. M. Hudak and P. Kihn (Eds.) *Labeling: Pedagogy and politics* (pp. 9–26). New York: RoutledgeFalmer.

Jacobson, J. 2003, July 18. Help not wanted. *Chronicle of Higher Education,* 49(45), A27–A28.

Kihn, P. 2001. Labeling the young: Hope and contemporary childhood. In G. M. Hudak and P. Kihn (Eds.) *Labeling: Pedagogy and politics* (pp. 55–71). New York: RoutledgeFalmer

Kimmel, M. S. 2003. "I am not insane; I am angry": Adolescent masculinity, homophobia, and violence. In M. Sadowski (Ed.) *Adolescents at school: Perspectives on youth, identity, and education* (pp. 69–78). Cambridge: Harvard University Press.

Kozol, J. 1991. *Savage inequalities: Children in America's schools.* New York: HarperPerennial.

Kristeva, J. 1982. *Powers of horror: An essay in abjection.* New York: Columbia.

Labaree, D. F. 1997. *How to succeed in school without really learning: The credentials race in American education.* New Haven: Yale University Press.

Laungani, P. 1999. Cultural influences on identity and behavior: India and Britain. In Y. T. Lee, C. R. McCauley, and J. G. Draguns (Eds.) *Personality and person perception across cultures* (pp. 191–212). Manwah, NJ: Lawrence Erlbaum.

Lease, A. M., McFall, R. M., and Viken, R. J. 2003. Distance from peers in the group's perceived organizational structure: Relation to individual characteristics. *Journal of Early Adolescence*, 23(2), 194–217.

Lee, V. E. 1995. Two views of high school organization: Bureaucracies and communities. In W. T. Pink and G. W. Noblit (Eds.) *Continuity and contradiction: The futures of the sociology of education* (pp. 67–100). Cresskill, NJ: Hampton.

Lipsitz, G. 1998. *The possessive investment in whiteness.* Philadelphia: Temple University Press.

MacLeod, J. 1987. *Ain't no making it: Leveled aspirations in low-income neighborhoods.* Boulder, CO: Westview Press.

Marx, K. 1867. *Das Kapital: Kritik der politischen oekonomie*, Vol. 1. Hamburg: Otto Meissner.

Maslow, A. 1970. *Motivation and personality.* New York: Harper.

McLaren, P. 1986. *Schooling as a ritual performance: Towards a political economy of educational symbols and gestures.* London: Routledge & Kegan Paul.

McLaren, P., Carrillo-Rowe, A. M., Clark, R. L., and Craft, P. A. 2001. Labeling whiteness: Decentering strategies of white racial domination. In G. M. Hudak and P. Kihn (Eds.) *Labeling: Pedagogy and politics* (pp. 203–24). New York: RoutledgeFalmer.

Merton, D. 1994. The cultural context of aggression: The transition to junior high school. *Anthropology & Education Quarterly*, 25(1), 29–43.

Noblit, G. W., and Pink, W. T. 1995. Mapping the alternative paths of the sociology of education. In W. T. Pink and G. W. Noblit (Eds.) *Continuity and contradiction: The futures of the sociology of education* (pp. 1–32). Cresskill, NJ: Hampton.

Noguera, P. A. 2003. "Joaquin's dilemma": Understanding the link between racial identity and school-related behaviors. In M. Sadowski (Ed.) *Adolescents at school: Perspectives on youth, identity, and education* (pp. 19–30). Cambridge: Harvard University Press.

Oakes, J. 1985. *Keeping track: How schools structure inequality.* New Haven: Yale University Press.

Perrucci, R., and Wysong, E. 2003. *The new class society: Goodbye American dream?* Lanham, MD: Rowman & Littlefield.

Reay, D. 1998. Setting the agenda: The growing impact of market forces on pupil grouping in British secondary schooling. *Journal of Curriculum Studies*, 30(5), 545–58.

Rorty, R. 1998. *Achieving our country: Leftist thought in twentieth-century America.* Cambridge: Harvard University Press.

Ryan, W. 1971. *Blaming the victim.* New York: Random House.

Sacks, H. 1992. *Lectures on conversation*, Vol. 2. Oxford: Blackwell.

Smith, D. 1990. *Texts, facts, and femininity: Exploring the relations of ruling.* London: Routledge.

Smith, T. J., and Danforth, S. 2000. Ethics, politics, and the unintended cruelties of teaching. In J. L. Paul and T. J. Smith (Eds.) *Stories out of school; Memories and reflections on care and cruelty in the classroom* (pp. 129–52). Stamford, CT: Ablex.

Stallybrass, P., and White, A. 1986. *The politics and poetics of transgression.* Ithaca: Cornell University Press.

Thompson, J. B. 1984. *Studies in the theory of ideology.* Berkeley: University of California Press.

———. 1990. *Ideology and modern culture: Critical social theory in the era of mass communication.* Stanford, CA: Stanford University Press.

Thompson, T. 1999. *Underachieving to protect self-worth: Theory, research and interventions.* Aldershot, England: Ashgate.

Valencia, R. R. (Ed.) 1997. *The evolution of deficit thinking: Educational thought and practice.* London and Washington, DC: Falmer.

Valenzuela, A. 2003. "Desde entonces, soy Chicana": A Mexican immigrant resist substractive schooling. In M. Sadowski (Ed.) *Adolescents at school: Perspectives on youth, identity, and education* (pp. 50–54). Cambridge: Harvard University Press.

Van Galen, J. A. 2004. Seeing classes: Toward a broadened research agenda for critical qualitative researchers. *International Journal of Qualitative Studies in Education*, 17, 663–84.

Weis, L. 1990. *Working class without work: High school students in deindustrializing America.* New York: Routledge, Chapman & Hall.

Wexler, P. 1996. *Critical social psychology.* New York: Peter Lang.

———. 1992. *Becoming somebody: Toward a social psychology of school.* New York: Falmer.

Willis, P. (1977). *Learning to labor: How working class kids get working class jobs.* New York: Columbia University Press.

Wright, S. E. 1993. Blaming the victim, blaming society, or blaming the discipline: Fixing responsibility for poverty and homelessness. *Sociology Quarterly*, 34(1), 1–16.

Young, I. M. 2000. *Inclusion and democracy.* Oxford, United Kingdom: Oxford University Press.

10

THE PROBLEM OF POVERTY

SHIFTING ATTENTION TO THE NON-POOR

Maike Ingrid Philipsen

What Is Poverty?

Poverty may be the most basic and fundamental form of stratification that exists in many societies. Of all the forms of stratification: race, ethnicity, gender, disability, age, sexual orientation, religion, political affiliation, and even physical attractiveness, class seems different. Class, and particularly poverty, is more at the "bottom of it all" than the others. Social class determines in a fundamental way a person's being, existence, and options—or lack thereof. To live at the extremes of social class is to live in poverty.

The central topic of this chapter is the issue of poverty. More precisely, I will explore the question of what poverty means in relation to schooling and in what we place our hope as we think about the educational institutions at all levels, including higher education. I will speak to the role of the non-poor in perpetuating poverty and the changes in perspective it may take in order to do what, despite its feasibility, has not been done: to eradicate poverty once and for all. It is meant to spur reflections about the issue of poverty and to encourage those participating in debates about its origins and effects to investigate the roles of the non-poor in perpetuating a social order that continues to be marred by poverty.

Poverty can be defined in many ways. Federal definitions express poverty in terms of income per family unit. According to the Department of Health and Human Services, for instance, a family unit of four whose income does not exceed $18,850 annually can be defined as poor (Department of Health and Human Services, 2004).

Despite such definitions, I still have difficulty imagining what it means to live in poverty, although I have been poor for the duration of a few years as a graduate student, married to another graduate student, with one child, living on $13, 000 per year. That *was* poor but it was *not* poverty. There were parents in the background who paid for medical expenses and could be counted on in case of emergency; they provided a safety net. One characteristic of poverty, however, is the *absence* of a "safety net," and, instead, the real possibility that one unfortunate event such as an accident or medical emergency produces economically catastrophic consequences.

In addition, we "poor" graduate students were healthy in body and spirit. We did not suffer from the effects of growing up poor: years of malnutrition, physical or mental neglect, and abuse. Most importantly, though, there was the prospect of getting out of poverty. Graduate school does not last forever (though it may at times seem that way). In short, we were allowed to view our state of affairs as temporary, as an investment, perhaps even as a challenge: how far can you stretch that dollar? How creative can you be trying to make ends meet? We were poor, in short, but never experienced poverty.

According to the U.S. Census Bureau's statistics, poverty has been rising to 11.7 percent in 2001 from 11.3 percent the year before. This figure translates into 32.9 million people who, in 2001, lived below the poverty threshold, a figure 1.3 million higher than in the year 2000 (U.S. Census Bureau, 2001, p.1). These statistics were published in the *Richmond Times Dispatch*, alongside an article entitled, "Espresso Tax Stirs Debate in Seattle." The latter mentioned Starbucks coffee shops where coffee costs about $11 per pound (*Richmond Times Dispatch*, 2002, A2). Poverty and wealth exist side by side, figuratively, in this local newspaper and literally, in our society and in other societies. This coexistence deserves attention. It is imperative, I argue in this chapter, for those of us who belong to the so-called haves, to look at what poverty means, "looking" not to satisfy curiosity but as a necessary step in the eradication of poverty. What, then, does it mean to be poor?

A workshop organized by the United Methodist Church Southeastern Jurisdictional Multi Cultural Convocation generated a report presented at a Poverty Coalition conference in March 2003, defining poverty as,

> . . . being just barely able to get by.
> . . . the inability to live at a reasonably comfortable level due to economic circumstances.
> . . . living below what $7.00 per hour can provide in the U.S. No basic sanitary provisions, not enough to exist on.
> . . . hunger, substandard housing; health issues; job/jobless and the dehumanization of the human being. (p. 104)

One of Jonathan Kozol's important contributions more than a decade ago consisted in his vivid descriptions of the ramifications of poverty and, specifically, of poor schools, in his classic publication *Savage Inequalities* (1991). More recently in *Amazing Grace*, Kozol once again uses testimony, especially the voices and experiences of children, to describe in shocking detail what poverty means (1995). Examples of life in poverty abound in *Amazing Grace*, stories about drugs, prostitution, children falling to their death in elevator shafts, pain, and neglect. The city put a waste incinerator into Mott Haven which is, after all, a residential neighborhood, clearly an example of environmental classism.

Numerous other social critics have attempted to capture and communicate the experience of poverty, especially for children (Kotlowitz, 1992). In *Nickel and Dimed*, the journalist Barbara Ehrenreich tries on the life of the working poor (Ehrenreich, 2001). For several months, she struggles to get by on wages earned in one, at times two, low-paying jobs. She works at a WalMart, for a maid service, and as a waitress. Granted, she is not truly poor. She is a successful journalist in real life and knows that she will return to that life once her stunt as a poor person is over. Ironically, she also knows that at some point she will be able to collect the royalties generated by her best-seller about the life of the poor.

Despite these obvious limitations, Ehrenreich's work conveys many lessons. It teaches those of us who never had to think of such things, about the gritty details of having very little money and no prospects of change. Ehrenreich finds herself forced, for example, to live in motels because she is lacking the security deposit required to rent an apartment. Those who cannot afford a car do not shop at Sam's Club or Costco; they shop at the corner convenience store, at the Seven Eleven. Those without storage space or a freezer are unable to buy large quantities of food, which is cheaper than buying one meal at a time. Those who do not even own a stove—and motel rooms typically do not provide such access—have to eat out, and even fast food eventually gets to be more expensive than preparing meals. Ehrenreich describes the health problems caused by strenuous repetitive work done by people who are on their feet all day, standing, carrying heavy trays, bending, scrubbing, reaching, and lifting. These workers typically cannot afford high-quality shoes, healthclub memberships, or regular chiropractic adjustments. Often, they cannot afford health insurance and proper medical care. So-called wellness is not for the poor. Wellness is based on two conditions: money and flexibility, both of which Barbara Ehrenreich, the journalist, has, neither of which Barbara Ehrenreich, the maid, has.

Kozol writes about children. I have two young children and know what it is like to get that phone call from school: "Your child is running a temperature of 102. Please come and pick him up." My typical response is: "I'll be right there," knowing I can find a colleague to teach my class, cancel office hours or a meeting, and do my writing at night. It is unimaginable that I would have to worry not only about where to quickly get some Children's Tylenol but whether or not I will lose my job because of missed work. When my kids get sick, we worry about sore throats and coughs. When poor people's children get sick their caretakers may face an existential crisis.

Poverty, in other words, is its own world, with its own dynamics and laws and realities not captured by statistics. Poverty is dehumanizing. It undermines the essence of being because it prevents people from taking care of basic needs. It violates what the Brazilian educator Paolo Freire calls a "universal human ethic," an ethic unafraid to oppose exploitation of labor, an ethic that does not show obedience only to the law of profit, an ethic not restricted to the forces of the market (Freire, 1998). He calls on us "[to] condemn the fabrication of illusions, in which the unprepared become hopelessly trapped and the weak and the defenseless are destroyed" (p. 23). Poverty is the brutal manifestation of an unethical system, not only degrading and dehumanizing but also impeding the development of the mind. While solving the problems of poverty will inevitably involve education, schooling is now mired in the problems of poverty.

Disparity of Educational Resources

As we have all come to understand, the system of school funding in the United States rewards the wealthy and middle class with well-funded schools while depriving schools with a high concentration of low-income students. Rather than helping to equalize economic conditions, schools themselves differ greatly in terms of the quality, safety, and aesthetics of buildings, the variety and quality of programs, the equipment they are able to make available, access to technology, science labs, libraries, extracurricular programs, gyms, pools, and playing fields, and, of course, the ability to attract and retain quality teachers.

Disparities of resources available to schools are largely the consequence of a funding system that relies heavily on local property taxes. As a result, wealthy communities are able to pay a smaller share of their income to fund public schools for their children and nevertheless spend relatively large amounts on their children's schools. Poor communities may tax themselves at a higher rate but end up with less money to be spent on schooling. While inherently unequal, the system continues to exist because the American public at large refuses to examine how the non-poor perpetuate poverty and the myriad ways in which middle- and upper-class students benefit from the existence of the poverty of schools attended by others.

Rather than blaming teachers for the underachievement of poor students, we also need to do much more studying by looking at the extraordinary efforts that many middle-class parents put into gaining advantages for their children's education. The standards of recent school reform movements are not going to remain a static target for everyone to attain because it is not in the best interest of middle-class parents to have others catch up to their children (Van Galen, 2004). What needs to be envisioned, instead, is a system of schooling in which wealthier students do not have students in poor schools as a benchmark against which to gauge their own achievement. One of the insidious characteristics of a stratified system, in other words, consists in its appeal to those who find themselves better off than many others and who are benefiting from the existence of the underprivileged. White middle-class parents may embrace ideologies of equality and justice, and may well teach their young children to "share," this "ethic of sharing" is neither far-reaching nor does it translate into a sharing of privilege (Brantlinger, 2003; and this volume). "Sharing of privilege" would, after all, constitute a contradiction in terms, almost a violation of a person's "habitus," to use the terminology of Pierre Bourdieu.

Bourdieu saw "habitus" as the basis for a person's daily actions, and to be understood as a system of long-lasting dispositions, created and changed through a mix of objective social structure and personal experiences. Players (in other words: individuals in a given society) learn certain dispositions, often subconsciously, according to their position in the "field," the social sphere, the "game of life" (1984). Examples include such seemingly insignificant things as body techniques, ways of walking, eating, talking, body posture, and sense of social distance. They also include, however, habits of classification, making sense of, constructing, and evaluating the social world. Habitus can be interpreted, in other words, as a set of instruments individuals possess and use, often subconsciously, as "trump cards" in "the game," thus determining success or failure in achieving a desired position on "the field" (Mahar, Harker, and Wilkes, 1990, pp. 10–12). Meritocractic ideas, or the notion that "one gets what one deserves," are attempts of making sense of an existing social world, of explaining what is and why. These ideas have been deeply instilled as part of the habitus of both the poor and the non-poor. Among the poor, Bourdieu speaks of an ingrained "sense of limits" (1984, p. 471), mirroring the sense of entitlement shared by those who are better-off. This sense-making that assumes that individuals attain what they deserve may be at the core of our collective reluctance to address, and ultimately to resolve disparities in resources available to poor children and to their more privileged peers.

As far as school funding is concerned, there have been efforts to equalize it; poor school districts have taken the matter to the courts many times and often achieved legal victory. Those victories, however, hardly ever led to effective reform. Things stayed the same, often because those who gain from the existing system did everything in their power to sabotage the court decisions. It seems taboo to seriously consider a redistribution of resources for it would run counter to both the notion of meritocracy and the related idea that freedom means the ability to reap all of the benefits of one's own labor, no matter how obscene those benefits might be.

I encounter such attitudes in my college classes: every so often I propose to institute an income cap based on the argument that no person can possibly need more than half a million dollars per year to live comfortably. In fact, I argue, more money is likely to cause harm, to be spent unwisely. Consequently, income exceeding half a million dollars per year ought to be taxed at a rate of 100 percent and redistributed among those of lower income. The students' reactions are always strong, and mostly negative. They view the proposal as an entirely "un-American" idea, a significant limitation of personal freedom. They wonder how anyone can be expected to stay motivated if deprived of the opportunity to reap the full benefits of labor or success. Such a cap, they argue, would certainly lead to fraudulent behavior; people would simply hide their profits to avoid paying taxes. While the students are appalled by vivid accounts of how a wealthy nation like the United States allows for poverty to exist, they are equally outraged at the tax proposal. One of the reasons for their strong negative feelings, I think, is a deeply rooted belief that the wealth of some is unrelated to the poverty of others and that, despite all rhetoric, it must be the poor's own fault if they find themselves in an economically deprived situation.

Shifting Perspective: Focusing on the Non-Poor

The purpose of initiating conversations in the classroom like the one just described is similar to Ehrenreich's attempt to focus the attention on us, on the non-poor, and on the myriad ways in which we keep a system alive that continues to breed poverty. This particular idea is in sync with a proposal made by the president of the Poverty Coalition in North Carolina, Dr. Gordon Chamberlin. He proposed at a meeting of the South Atlantic Philosophy of Education Society in 2002 that the organization's members interview four colleagues in academia about whether and if so, how, the issue of poverty is addressed in their teaching. Chamberlin's theory was that while poverty and the poor are hardly understudied, academics do not address how academia benefits from the existence of poverty. His proposal was intended to refocus the camera on those of us who are *not* poor, a major shift in the history of how American society has dealt with poverty for centuries.

The question arises how, exactly, the non-poor benefit from poverty. In thinking about the routines of daily life, examples abound. Salaried professionals benefit from the fact that child care workers' wages are low—it makes child care affordable for them. As consumers, we benefit from low prices charged at large chain stores that keep employees' pay and benefits to a minimum. We benefit from underpaid cleaning and maintenance workers who take care of our office buildings and our homes—often as part-time workers, often without job security or benefits, often being paid "under the table." We benefit from the cleaning crew who sweeps and wipes and polishes for minimum wage once we have left our offices, or the cafeteria workers who serve meals they may be unable to afford themselves. One could add the adjunct professors who teach classes instead of full-time faculty because the market permits the academy to build, exploit, and maintain its own reserve army. More precisely, an excess of Ph.D.'s in most academic disciplines supplies the academic job market with large numbers of people who are highly specialized and thus prepared only for a relatively small number of jobs. Unless they find alternative positions elsewhere, the colleges and universities are able to string them along with uncertain and temporary offers, without benefits or reliable long-term prospects. This trend remains largely unchallenged by full-time faculty who benefit from the minimum wage labor of those who lack alternatives and who thus do not argue with unattractive assignments such as teaching large classes, undergraduate entry-level classes, survey classes, or those that are offered at undesirable times or in undesirable classrooms and locations.

In regard to schooling, several scholars have made the argument that the "have's" benefit from perpetuating a system that produces "have-not's." Bruce Biddle addresses the "resource management used by the rich and powerful" to ensure their advantages. He refers to analysts who, similar to this author, argue that in order to understand a major cause of poverty one ought to look at the conduct of those who are not impoverished. In education, affluent parents will use their resources and influence in order to assure that the system works in their children's favor. They are "playing the system" in myriad ways, including the support of policies such as tracking which, under the cloak of merit, tend to benefit their children, lobbying legislators that support their interests, manipulating school personnel, and working to keep an unequal school funding system in place (2001, pp. 21–22). Others have studied and shown how not just extremely wealthy but middle-class parents make use of an existing system in order to benefit their children. Middle-class parents are more prone than lower-class parents to intervene on behalf of their children. They tend to influence decisions regarding their children's placement in advanced courses and make use of their own college experience to navigate the system and to obtain information about what courses are beneficial for their children's future. Making use of one's "clout" or social capital, however, means bolstering structures that allow some to enjoy advantages at the expense of others (Brantlinger, 2003; Roundfield Lucas, 1999).

The next question that arises is how can it be that generally goodhearted people consciously or inadvertently keep alive and rationalize a system so blatantly unfair if it works to their advantage? This is a difficult question. Ellen Brantlinger seems convinced that the educated middle class, who takes advantage of relative privilege, is only believed to be liberal, progressive, and generally generous. She writes that "[o]n a theoretical level this class is populist and democratic, but on subconscious and unspoken levels we eschew both equitable distributions of resources and substantial inclusion of others into our exclusive communities" (2003, p. 192; see also Brantlinger, this volume). Generally, good-hearted people may be good examples of contradictions between "values-spoken," or that what is professed, and "values-lived," meaning actions and behavior (Philipsen, 1999), although they are probably acting in the best interests of their children.

One could also use Bourdieu's ideas once again in order to attempt an answer to this question of the seeming indifference among otherwise good-hearted people. Considering the power of habitus as, among other things, a way to make sense of the world, it becomes clear that much of what people do is based on a system of deeply ingrained assumptions that do not need to be revisited unless something significant happens, such as the confrontation of a "disorienting dilemma" (Mezirow, 2000, p. 22). It is thus not surprising that "perfectly good-hearted" people can go through the world, playing the game, benefiting from it at the expense of others, and still feel good about themselves. In a way, we don't know what we are doing.

What, however, would bring about change? If it takes the agency of the non-poor to solve the issue of poverty who—since they benefit from the system have no reason initiate change—and if people only change once they have encountered "disorienting dilemmas," then what will bring about the necessary dilemmas to spark that change?

Instead of asking these kinds of questions, American history provides ample examples of how poverty has been addressed solely through efforts to change the poor. The historian Michael Katz delineates this history (1995). He points to deeply ingrained thinking and habitual policy making that concentrate solely on the poor when seeking to address the problem of poverty. Katz makes it clear that in order to understand contemporary poverty we need to look at the past. He shows how nineteenth-century reformers attributed poverty to drinking, laziness, and what is generally considered "bad behavior." Subsequently, they designed public policy to improve the character of poor people rather than structural factors such as the exploitation of cheap labor at the core of industrialization and the subsequently growing gap between the rich and the poor. Katz writes: ". . . reformers emphasized individual regeneration through evangelical religion, temperance legislation, punitive conditions for relief, family breakup, and institutionalization. Of course, as a reform strategy, improving poor people did not end with the nineteenth or early-twentieth centuries, as almost any contemporary discussion of 'welfare reform' reveals. Indeed, in the 1990s, discussion of inner-city poverty invoke an 'underclass,' defined primarily by bad behavior, not by poverty, and deemed to be more in need of improvement than cash" (pp. 3–4).

Katz claims, furthermore, that education has been given a "starring role" in the effort to improve poor people. Public schools have been expected to solve social problems, assigning them an impossibly great load and setting them up for failure. He concludes that "as the history of education shows, improving poor people not only misdiagnosed the issues; it also time and again has deflected attention from their structural origins and from difficult and uncomfortable responses they require" (1995, pp. 3–4). It is worth considering to what extent current educational policies continue to reflect this legacy and to what extent we have now moved beyond it and are content with simply creating and operating schools for poor children.

One "difficult and uncomfortable response" to poverty, to use Katz's words, consists in a call to us, the non-poor, to take poverty personally and to realize our role in its existence. It is a call to stop focusing on the poor alone when we talk about poverty. What, exactly, does that mean, and how does this idea translate into practice other than charity giving on the part of the non-poor who may say something like "What can I do? I don't even *know* any poor people!" For one, I am advocating the conceptual development of the twin ideas of (a) redistributing resources; and (b) reevaluating the value of work, on the basis of which it might become possible to act, for instance, in revamping the welfare system. Harrell Rogers Jr. (1996) argues that Americans might take cues from Western European and Scandinavian countries, especially from innovative programs in Sweden, Germany, and France (p. 128). Although international comparisons tend to be tricky, it ought to be mentioned that while the major industrial nations of Western Europe have not eradicated poverty, their poverty rates are significantly lower than the U.S. rate (p. 108).

The dominant focus on the poor when addressing poverty in policy or academic discourse, however, is not merely habit but also beneficial to the non-poor. Martin Packer argued that the traditional classification of "middle class" and "lower class" no longer adequately describes the job structure in the United States (2001). Rather, the emerging class structure consists of an "inner" ring of permanent skilled workers and an "outer" ring of temporary, semi-skilled, disposable workers without benefits, vacations, or sick leave. The two-tiered job structure is not confined to the manufacturing industry; it is growing in academia, for instance, where tenured, salaried faculty constitute an inner core while the outer core consists of temporary, untenured, and underpaid adjunct professors hired by the course and moving from job to job. At any rate, the argument continues, the new economy demands a flexible workforce willing to work varying hours at a high pace, rendering the economy competitive and productive, always prepared to be laid off and rehired. Schools, Packer claims, are expected to produce the "human bricks with which the global economy is being built" (pp. 278–79).

For those who find themselves in the "inner ring" of the economy, there is little reason to focus on *us*, the well-to-do, and how we might be able to address poverty. Those who feel secure within the system are able to ignore those who are not. Others worry primarily about their own lot given that recent shifts in the economy and layoffs in managerial ranks have rendered even members of the middle class feeling vulnerable, sharing a "fear of falling" (Ehrenreich, 1989). The Chamberlin proposal, however, suggests a change in perspective. It resembles the recent shift in the literature on race relations where some have begun to argue that the focus of discussion needed to be on "white privilege," and on "whiteness" in general instead of viewing racism as a "black issue." In order to address racism it seemed no longer sufficient to solely focus on past and present issues shaping the lives of African-Americans. Addressing racism meant more than studying the history of racial segregation and discrimination or becoming knowledgeable of disturbing statistics illustrating such things as the achievement gap or minority poverty, incarceration, dropout, and single parents, which illustrate continuing inequalities. It is not sufficient for well-intentioned whites to participate in discussions about "oppositional cultures" and programs designed to level the playing field such as affirmative action, head start, remedial education, the Afrocentric curriculum, multicultural education, culturally relevant teaching, bilingual education and resegregation movements. It was time, some began to say, that we stop focusing on blacks and on other minorities and instead look at whiteness, at those who benefit, possibly without conscious acknowledgment, from a system and from practices that continue to be discriminatory in myriad ways.

Christine Sleeter (1997) talks about a dualism embedded in white consciousness: on the one hand the belief that we are good and caring people while, on the other hand, an unwillingness on the part of whites to jeopardize our relative comfort and privileges by questioning the existing social system which, after all, does not afford equal opportunities to all. Alice McIntyre, in her research of racial identities among white teachers, concluded that participants in her study found it difficult to generate enough rage at contemporary white racism to decenter the privileged racial positions they currently hold. It seemed that, for them, racism was a thing of the past and had over time been replaced by the American Dream and by the belief in the power of the individual. McIntyre calls for a myriad of things in order to address these misconceptions, and they all involve the agency of whites, for example, whites becoming more self-reflective about understandings of race, racism, and constructions of what it means to be white in this country (McInryre, 1997, pp. 135–139, 14). Specifically in regard to white teachers, one of her proposals is to address our own complicity around issues of educational racism and to be held accountable for exlusionary practices in schools (p. 148).

It is not clear how much of an effect on racial discrimination this shift in the debate about race has had so far (focusing on whiteness may not have led to significant improvements for those who are non-white). Be that as it may, a similar shift might well be productive in debates about poverty. Race can only cease to matter if whites take it personally, understand the implications of their privilege, and translate that understanding into action such as, in the case of teachers, questioning tracking and testing practices that have been shown to work out better for whites than for non-whites. Along the same lines, class will only cease to matter greatly, and poverty will only disappear, if those who benefit from class stratification and poverty of others begin to take poverty personally. This could take the form of political advocacy, for instance for a living wage, or for other forms of participation in what Brantlinger (2003) sees as currently emerging movements. She argues that rapid technological developments and political globalization have led to a "revolutionary period" during which growing and extreme social class polarization cause many individuals to react in ways that are both idealistic and activist. She names as one example recent protests against the World Trade Organization in Seattle and cites other authors who have called for people to generate "positive fantasies and mental images depicting future events" (Oettingen, 1996) and to capture the national imagination with a large moral mission (Schudson, 1998). In short, she sees a distinct possibility for transformative movements that would disrupt the existing social order (Brantlinger, 2003, pp. 198–99).

In What Ways Can Schools Address Poverty?

Concerning education, it is an appealing notion that schools are able to make a significant difference and improve students' lives. Educational scholars have repeatedly argued that teaching has a "moral dimension" (Goodlad, 1990; Noddings, 2002; Strike and Soltis, 1998), a dimension not confined to shaping student character or to the teacher's ability to make informed ethical decisions in the classroom. Rather, the moral dimension of teaching, and of schooling at-large, includes the mission to make substantial contributions to building a social system based on social justice, one, I might add, in which no one would be subjected to poverty. Gloria Ladson-Billings argued more than a decade ago that good schools and effective teaching indeed matter in that they can make a difference in students' lives and learning (Ladson Billings, 1994).

Thoughtful work has been done since by educators who searched for ways to make schools more responsive to the children of the poor without blaming the children or their families. Michael S. Knapp and Associates, for example, published *Teaching for Meaning in High-Poverty Classrooms* in 1995. Knapp argues that teachers and administrators in high-poverty schools are faced with manifold factors that complicate school life. They need to deal with a high mobility rate among children who not only have many diverse needs but who are also not very savvy at "doing school," playing the game, and knowing how to function effectively within the institution. In addition, poor schools have relatively few resources and second-rate facilities. Teaching and learning, in other words, are challenges. Knapp argues, however, that dwelling on the conditions of poor children's homes and communities—which has been a widespread response to the problem—is one-sided and ultimately not productive. Such focus ignores the relationship between teachers and learners. If one were to look at this relationship, he writes, questions other than the "deficiencies" of the students become important, questions such as, what does each party know about the life of the other? One is reminded here of Freire's work, a scholar who has repeatedly inspired educational communities around the world with his insistence on the importance of viewing teaching as a two-way street, where both the student and the teacher learn in the process (1998).

Viewing teaching as a mutual process, Knapp and his colleagues delineate what, exactly, it takes to construct productive teacher-student relationships in high-poverty classrooms. They focus on matters over which teachers exert most control in the daily operation of the classroom: establishing order and responding to cultural diversity. The authors challenge conventions undergirding most of the teaching in high-poverty classrooms, namely, the focus on children's deficiencies, sought to be remedied through the teaching of discrete skills. The curriculum is typically based on fixed sequences, from basic to advanced skills, accompanied by a teaching style that is fast paced and tightly controlled to "keep the students on task." Students are segregated by ability; they are tracked and their achievement is measured through standardized tests.

An alternative to this type of teaching is captured in the literature on "teaching for understanding," a philosophy of teaching that informs

Knapp's work. Proponents view knowledge as connected rather than discrete and attempt to relate classrooms to the students' world and experiences. The ultimate goal is for students to be able to *make meaning* of their instructional experiences. Making meaning connotes being able to make sense of school experiences, viewing things as parts of a whole rather than as disconnects, and, finally, connecting new learning experiences to already existing knowledge (Knapp, 1995, pp. 1–10).

In summary, a great deal of hope continues to be invested in schools and in the idea that schools can be instrumental in bringing about social change rather than succumbing to structural confines. This notion of hope, of course, has a long history. In fact, it is rooted in the very mission of the public education system.

Ever since the public schools came into existence, their advocates argued that one of the schools' central missions was to help eradicate social class stratification and poverty. "Education, then, beyond all other devises of human origin, is the great equalizer of the conditions of men,— the balance wheel of the social machinery," as Horace Mann phrased it in 1849. He argued that education would ". . . give each man the independence and the means by which he can resist the selfishness of other men. It does better than to disarm the poor of their hostility toward the rich: it prevents being poor. . . . The spread of education, by enlarging the cultivated class or caste, will open a wider area over which the social feelings will expand; and, if this education would be universal and complete, it would do more than all things else to obliterate factitious distinctions in society" (p. 60).

At least in the minds of some, the common schools were supposed to ameliorate, if not eradicate, the influence social class had in shaping an individual's life. Schools were promoted as being essential for the provision of equal opportunities, for "leveling the playing field" and realizing the dream that everyone has a chance to succeed in America, irrespective of class background. Such notions of schools as equalizers are not entirely confined to the American context but can be found in other countries as well. There are indications, however, that while educators in particular wish to embrace the notion that schools can truly affect students' positions in society and ultimately lead to a more just social order, the reality may be sobering.

Limitations of Educational Reform
for Addressing Poverty

Comparing changes in educational opportunities in thirteen countries (including the United States, Germany, England and Wales, Italy, Switzerland, the Netherlands, Sweden, Japan, Taiwan, Poland, Hungary,

Czechoslovakia, and Arabs living in Israel), Hans-Peter Blossfeld and Yossi Shavitt argue that inequality of educational opportunity remained rather stable over time in most of the countries under study, despite significant expansions of the educational systems in all of them (Blossfeld and Shavitt, 1993). While the average level of educational attainment rose, and primary and even some lower secondary education became nearly universal, the higher levels of education did not expand at the same pace, creating a "bottleneck" effect, unable to absorb the increasing numbers of graduates from the lower school systems. Effective equalization occurred only in two countries, Sweden and the Netherlands, both of which made attempts to equalize socioeconomic conditions. According to the authors, economic reform precedes educational equalization, rendering educational reforms ineffective in changing educational stratification and reducing educational inequalities between socioeconomic strata. Simply stated, social class is a powerful factor in shaping educational opportunities, and it seems as if social class diminishes in influence through economic, not educational reforms.

The preceding analysis illustrates a dilemma: schools do provide opportunities in people's lives, and yet they do not, or only within limits. To what extent they *can* provide opportunities depends to a large extent on the labor market. Recent statistics reveal that higher levels of education cannot necessarily solve the problems generated by economic shifts to part-time and temporary employment. To illustrate the point, the U.S. Department of Labor projects that the occupations characterized by the largest job growth between 2002 and 2012 are occupations that—with few exceptions—neither require advanced degrees nor promise substantial earnings. While registered nurses and postsecondary teachers are leading in terms of projected job growth, the next greatest growth will be in retail salespersons, customer service representatives, combined food preparation and serving workers (including fast food), cashiers, janitors and cleaners, general and operations managers, waiters and waitresses, nursing aides, orderlies, attendants, truck drivers, receptionists, and security guards (U.S. Department of Labor, Bureau of Labor Statistics, 2004). As far as numbers are concerned, in other words, the vast majority of jobs are created in low-income service occupations. This data needs to be combined with another trend, however, namely, that ". . . since the late 1970s, average premiums paid by the labor market to those with higher levels of education have increased" (Horrigan, 2004, p. 16). While the *number* of high-paying jobs is not increasing, in other words (quite the opposite, low-paying jobs show the greatest increase) monetary rewards for those who have been able to obtain advanced educational degrees and landed one of the relatively few high-paying jobs, have been increasing. ". . . [I]t is the growing distance, on average, between those with more education, compared with those with less, that speaks to a general preference on the part of employers to hire those with skills associated with higher levels of education" (p. 16). In other words, while higher education used to be a sufficient but not necessary condition for economic advancement, the trend has been reversed: advanced degrees are now necessary preconditions for economic success, yet they do not guarantee it (Diamond and Wergin, 2001, p. 4).

Conclusion

Poverty is a dehumanizing condition without a defensible place in a nation as wealthy as the United States. Yet it continues to exist and even increase. I have made the argument that perhaps it is time to shift the locus of analysis as to why poverty exists and how it can be eradicated from the poor to those of us who are not poor, as captured by the Chamberlin proposal. This proposal does not suggest that the nation can rely on schools and on other educational institutions to fix the ills produced by the economy and reflected in the labor market. Neither does it suggest what statistics question anyway, namely, that schools can be expected to enable everyone to escape poverty and low-paying jobs through education. Such is the myth, which is defied by current economic trends and by experiences in other nations. So what *can* be done? Chamberlin appeals to academics, in particular, not to solve the ominous problem of poverty but to take the first step and to focus our analysis on the non-poor, on ourselves as academics, in other words. *That,* if nothing else, is what academics ought to be able to do: shape ways of thinking and talking about a certain matter, and provide reasons for changing a nation's discourse. I would like to speculate what that could mean for academics' teaching and research practice. What, in other words, do we need to do? The following represent suggestions for initial steps:

- Academics should begin to look at "our own shop" and discuss how we benefit from adjunct faculty exploitation through wage compression, the same dynamic that produces the working poor.
- Academics should examine their curricula and research agendas to find out whether and if so, how, we address the issue of poverty. Perhaps we do, and if so, we ought to deal with another set of questions, namely, could critical academics find stature in their fields if the problems of poverty were solved? What would we then write about? As K. Lynch and C. O'Neill argued, oppressed groups have long been the subjects of research conducted by educational sociologists (and by scholars in other fields, one might add). As such, they have been ". . . generally excluded from the dialogue about themselves" (Lynch and O'Neill, 1994, p. 308).

- Teach students in various disciplines not merely *about* poverty and the poor but shift the focus and analyze structural origins of poverty, economic dynamics that *produce and perpetuate* poverty.
- Include in our teaching, discussions about responsibilities of the non-poor for existing structures and practices that perpetuate poverty, "wealthy privilege," and the myriad ways in which the non-poor take advantage of and, in turn, rationalize poverty.
- Do something this one chapter cannot do alone: pool the creative energies of academics and propose realistic, practical, doable ways to eradicate poverty once and for all. It takes the non-poor to do that. It takes us.

References

Biddle, B. 2001. *Social class, poverty, and education: Policy and practice.* New York and London: Routledge/Falmer.

Blossfeld, H. P., and Shavitt, Y. 1993. *Persistent inequality.* Boulder: Westview Press.

Bourdieu, P. 1984. *Distinction: A social critique of the judgement of taste.* Cambridge: Harvard University Press.

Brantlinger, E. 2003. *Dividing classes.* London and New York: Routledge, 2003.

Department of Health and Human Services. February 11, 2004. FR Doc. 04-3329 Filed 2-12-04; 8:45 am. Accessed on July 20, 2004 at http://aspe.hhs.gov/poverty/04fedreg.htm.

Diamond, R. and Wergin, J. 2001. The changing world of faculty work. *National Teaching & Learning Forum,* 11(1), 3–7.

Ehrenreich, B. 1989. *Fear of falling: The inner life of the middle class.* New York: Pantheon Books.

———. 2001. *Nickel and dimed: On (not) getting by in America.* New York: Metropolitan Books.

Freire, P. 1998. *Pedagogy of freedom: Ethics, democracy, and civic courage.* Lanham, MD: Rowman & Littlefield.

Goodlad, J. 1990. *The moral dimensions of teaching.* San Francisco: Jossey-Bass.

Horrigan, M. 2004, February. Employment projections to 2012: Concepts and context. *Monthly Labor Review,* 3–22.

Katz, M. 1995. *Improving poor people: The welfare state, the "underclass," and urban schools as history.* Princeton: Princeton University Press.

Knapp, M. S. and Associates. 1995. *Teaching for meaning in high-poverty classrooms.* New York: Teachers College Press.

Kotlowitz, A. 1992. *There are no children here: The story of two boys growing up in the other America.* New York: Anchor Books.

Kozol. J. 1991. *Savage inequalities.* New York: HarperPerennial.

———. 1995. *Amazing grace: The lives of children and the conscience of a nation.* New York: HarperPerennial.

Ladson-Billings, G. 1994. *The dreamkeepers: Successful teachers of African American children.* San Francisco: Jossey-Bass.

Lynch, K. and O'Neill, C. 1994. The colonisation of social class in education. *British Journal of Sociology of Education,* 15(3), 307–24.

Mann, H. 1848. *Twelfth annual report to the Board of Education of Massachusetts, 1849.* Boston: Dutton and Wentworth.

Mahar, C., Harker, R., and Wilkes, C. 1990. *An introduction to the work of Pierre Bourdieu: The practice of theory.* New York: St. Martin's.

McIntyre, A. 1997. *Making meaning of whiteness: Exploring racial identity with white teachers.* Albany: State University of New York Press.

Mezirow, J. 2000. Learning to think like an adult: Core concepts of transformation theory. In J. Mezirow (Ed.) *Learning as transformation: Critical perspectives on a theory in progress* (pp. 3–33). San Francisco: Jossey-Bass.

Noddings, N. 2002. *Educating moral people: A caring alternative to character education.* New York: Teachers College Press.

Oettingen, G. 1996. Positive fantasy and motivation. In P. Gollwitzer and J. Bargh (Eds.) *The psychology of action: Linking cognition and motivation to behavior* (pp. 236–59). New York: Guilford Press.

Packer, M. 2001. *Changing classes: School reform and the new economy.* Cambridge: Cambridge University Press.

Philipsen, M. 1999. *Values-spoken and values-lived: Race and the cultural consequences of a school closing.* Cresskill, NJ: Hampton Press.

Poverty Coalition. 2003. *Program on understanding poverty: A multi-discipline approach.* Second report. Greensboro, NC: Poverty Coalition.

Richmond Times Dispatch, Wednesday, September 25, 2002, A2.

Rogers. H. Jr. 1996. *Poor women, poor children: American poverty in the 1990s,* 3rd ed. Armonk: M. E. Sharpe.

Roundfield Lucas, S. 1999. *Tracking inequality: Stratification and mobility in American high schools.* New York: Teachers College Press.

Schudson, M. 1998. *The good citizen: A history of American civic life.* Cambridge: Harvard University Press.

Sleeter, C. 1997. Foreword. In A. McIntyre, *Making meaning of whiteness: Exploring racial identity with white teachers* (pp. ix–xii). Albany: State University of New York Press.

Strike, K. and Soltis, J. 1998. *The ethics of teaching,* 3rd ed. New York: Teachers College Press.

Tozer, S., Violas, P., and Senese, G. 2002. *School and society: Historical and contemporary perspectives.* Boston: McGraw-Hill.

U.S. Census Bureau. *Poverty: 2001 Highlights.* Retrieved September 4, 2003, from http://www.census.gov/hhes/poverty/povert01/pov01hi.html.

U.S. Department of Labor, Bureau of Labor Statistics. 2004, February. *Employment projections, Table 4: Occupations with the largest job growth, 2002–12.* Retrieved September 8, 2004, from http://stats.bls.gov/emp/emptab4.htm.

Van Galen, J. 2004. School reform and class work. *Journal of Educational Change,* 5, 111–39.

11

INTERSECTIONS ON THE BACK ROAD

CLASS, CULTURE, AND EDUCATION IN RURAL AND APPALACHIAN PLACES

Van Dempsey

Introduction

This chapter, as it focuses on rural and Appalachian contexts, is about white within white intersectionality, and about how power and privilege are enacted within whiteness. It is also about the juxtaposition of complexities of culture within rurality and Appalachia and the monolithic treatment of that context from outside observers and critics. This analysis comes out of an intersection of race, class, and place to, as Kimberlé W. Crenshaw recommends, ". . . account for multiple grounds of identity when considering how the social world is constructed" (n.d., p. 2). It is also, according to Crenshaw's work on intersectionality, ". . . a project that presumes that categories have meaning and consequences" but with the caveat that the ". . . most pressing problem . . . is not the existence of the categories, but rather the particular values attached to them, and the way those values foster and create social hierarchies" (p. 13). Finally, Crenshaw's thesis legitimates the position that critical acts of resistance for the marginalized in these hierarchies include "defending a politics of social location" rather than vacating and destroying it (p. 14).

To understand identity is to understand the point where categories intersect, and this chapter is an effort to shed light on those points for poor and working-class people in rural and Appalachian places. Of particular importance for understanding rural and Appalachian social hierarchies is the way in which the hierarchies create tensions for young people, as they are "pushed out" of the context by education, ambition, and economic pressures to leave the local world around them, and are simultaneously "pulled back" by parents, families, and local communities that treat the exodus as a betrayal to the local culture and familial ties and obligations. Rural and Appalachian children and young adults in particular, as will be seen later in this chapter, are positioned low in social hierarchies, and the "pulling" and "pushing" are as much acts of resistance as they are the inculcation of low ambition as it sometimes seems to be portrayed by cultural observers and critics. Given the changing economic dynamics of rural places, this pulling back and pressure to stay can be difficult for young people. For example, the old extractive economic base of Appalachia around coal, other mineral resources, and timber is increasingly disappearing, and not being replaced in all places where it disappears. Where it is being replaced, it tends to be by tourism, low-wage labor, and service economies (e.g., Walmart). As is often the case, education is held up as the solution to economic woes. But this tends to be a double-edged sword as public schools have been one of a host of public institutions which, in the control of privileged white citizens, fail to serve well children in poverty and the working class. Also, for children and young people who do realize access to the promises of higher-quality education, the road to economic opportunity tends to lead out and away. Finally, social class hierarchies themselves are convoluted by the layering of whiteness within rural and Appalachian places. The complicating factor is not always—or even usually—race or gender (alone) but the limitations and stratification within whiteness around constructions such as "poor white trash," "rednecks," and "hillbillies."

A complicating factor for doing this work where white intersects white is that much of the history and narrative of the shades of whiteness within rurality and Appalachia includes marginalization of others by marginalized poor and working-class whites. Even limited power and privilege gives power over some group somewhere. In the context of intersectionality, whites in rural and Appalachia places can be run down and simultaneously run down others in the intersections by their own vehicles of marginalization. This is a critical, though not totalizing, aspect of whiteness outside of urban and suburban America.

This chapter will consider the ways in which identity can be misunderstood and misrepresented in a social context that is typically treated simplistically and monolithically by observers (both inside and outside the social context). Many of the representations of rurality and Appalachia are simplified due to a lack of understanding and recognition of the contexts' social and cultural complexities, and also as part of marginalization: representation is easier to manipulate in simple culturally constrained terms such as the ones sometimes applied to rurality and Appalachia. This "mistaken identity politics" will be examined in light of broader cultural assumptions and in media and pop culture treatments of rural and Appalachian people. To turn a phrase, all politics may be local, but all politics of identity are not. Important parts of the construction of identity around class in rural and Appalachian settings involve infiltrations from outside the local area. These infiltrations include mythologies about rural and Appalachian America, images of chronic poverty and dispossession, the failure and corruption of public institutions (in particular schools), and the long-standing control of local Appalachian economies by external forces that sent profits elsewhere. These factors suggest that in representations, critiques, research on, and analysis of, rurality and Appalachia, there is a "real" and the "surreal," and it is not always obvious which is which and where the two meet.

This chapter will be structured around several ways of looking at the relationships of class, culture, and education in Appalachia and in rural America. First, a picture of rurality and Appalachia will be presented from statistical data and analysis of the impact of poverty and economic challenges in these two worlds. This will be followed by a summary of research and writing that frames some of the impact of class history and economic restructuring, and how these have altered the lives of rural and Appalachian children. Finally, cultural assumptions about rurality and Appalachia will be presented in the context of broader assumptions and portrayals of "whiteness" as a marginalizing effort imposed on poor and working-class whites in the context of rurality and Appalachia.

The Economics of Class in Rurality and Appalachia

In an examination of poverty in the United States in 2002, the Save the Children Foundation, focused specifically on rural poverty in the United States, and identified central Appalachia as one of six areas of concentrated poverty in the country. The report identified five key themes as the basis for chronic poverty in rural America, including Appalachia (Save the Children, 2002):

- Education that is often substandard;
- Limited opportunities for child and youth development;
- Inadequate health care;
- Limitations in transportation and limited access to other physical infrastructure;
- The difficulty in attaining and maintaining family self sufficiency.

These key themes undergird the more general themes highlighted in the introduction to this chapter, including problems of access to public institutions for citizens in poverty and the working class. Even where they are available at all, geography, local politics, and generally lower levels of public funding create situations where support taken for granted in some areas may not be assumed resources for people in rural places. These resources, more readily available and accessible in other places, may not close the gap left by parents', families', and communities' inability to provide them.

Similar data can be found from other sources. Research from the Annie E. Casey Foundation exhibits how class and economic issues play out in West Virginia as a landscape of both rurality and Appalachia. The 2001 statistics on West Virginia include the following (AECF, 2002):

- The median incomes of families with children in West Virginia were at $37,500 compared with a median income in the United States of $51,100, putting the state 36% below the national average.
- Twenty-one percent of West Virginia youths are "disconnected," defined by the foundation as 18–24-year-olds not enrolled in school, not working, and holding no degree beyond high school. Nationally, 15% of youths are "disconnected," according to this definition.
- Nationally, 8% of teens age 16–19 are neither working nor in school, compared to 14% of West Virginia teens. West Virginia is fiftieth among the states on this measure.
- Of all the children in West Virginia, 33% live in families in which no parent has full-time year-round employment. The average for the United States is 25%, putting the state 32% above the national average, and ranking it forty-eighth among all states in this category.
- In West Virginia, 22% of all children live in poverty, compared to 16% for the United States, putting the state 37% higher than the country and ranking it forty-sixth among all states in this category.

There are obvious obstacles to success for Appalachian young people, and these economic conditions complicate the work of the schools. Some of these barriers to success and access are cited by Katherine Cason 2001. Compared to wealthier peers, she argues, poor children in rural areas

- Are more likely to experience emotional and behavioral problems and are at higher risk for mental health problems including depression;
- Are two to four times more likely to be admitted into psychiatric outpatient care.

- Are retained at grade level more frequently;
- Are more likely to be born to parents who are not married;
- Are more likely to be victim of violent crimes;
- Are more likely to transition from childhood poverty to adult poverty;
- Score lower on state tests and are more likely to be drop outs. (p. 30)

Cason concludes by citing additional concerns for children in poverty, including data that shows that children in extreme poverty are more likely to experience physical health problems, cognitive-related barriers to learning, and experience lower levels of school achievement in early grades. Finally, Cason argues that family income is a greater predictor of these problems than race or family structure.

Dehaan and Deal (2001) cite similar research, with parallel conclusions, comparing rural adolescents to their urban counterparts. Among the problems and barriers faced by adolescents, Dehaan and Deal (p. 44) include the following stressors and barriers:

- Higher concentrations of adolescent poverty;
- Higher concentrations of single parent homes;
- Higher incidences of gangs;
- Higher incidences of crime among adolescents;
- Fewer school curriculum choices;
- Fewer structured out of school activities;
- Fewer employment opportunities;
- Greater frequency of social isolation.

Looking at families living at the intersections of rurality and poverty, the authors amplify the differences between rural and urban contexts for rural mothers: Poor rural women remain in poverty longer than poor urban women. Contributing to these deeper experiences of poverty are cultural and structural factors: work outside the home is not always valued in rural communities and families; rural women are often less educated; and rural families are larger and therefore more stressed. Meanwhile, women have access to fewer childcare options in rural settings (DeHaan and Deal, 2001, p. 47).

While educational researchers have long attended to the many consequences of urban poverty for children, educators may be less aware of the fact that rural children face many of the same barriers and problems. More poor children live in rural areas than in cities. Rural children are likely to remain in poverty for longer periods of time, and rural children attain lower levels of education. Rural children experience greater levels of hunger, have more health-related issues, and are more likely to experience substance abuse than urban children. Rural children are more likely to be involved in criminal activity. Finally, rural children are more likely to be depressed and experience chronic loneliness (Deehan and Deal, 2001, p. 53).

This general pattern of sociocultural realities is extended in research by Erik Stewart and his colleagues (2001) on parenting and its connection to outcomes for adolescents in rural places. Their work on the relationships between parenting practices and educational outcomes suggest that rural families are hesitant to ask for help in social networks because "individualism" carries the day as a preeminent value. Rural adolescents are less likely than their counterparts in other social settings to access or attempt to access supports that may alleviate life stresses. This is a particularly strong pattern where loneliness is an issue, as loneliness is connected to depression. Parents in rural places exert greater pressure on their children to attend to the needs and goals of the parents, and rural children are more likely to concede to the pressure as teenagers when they are simultaneously feeling a need to be independent (p. 132). As rural teens begin to feel the pressure of this psychological stress, they are simultaneously experiencing the constraints of the limited rural economy. Thus, rural teens act in opposition to their own sense of occupational aspiration, and instead limit their options to local realities (p. 143). Hence, the research concludes, the problems are not so much academic failure as aspirational displacement. In the end the researchers argue, parents are unable to serve as adequate support mechanisms, in part because of their own depression, mental health issues, and lack of economic opportunity in their own lives.

The problems cited by Stewart and his colleagues are compounded during periods of general economic decline. The economy in Appalachian areas is chronically depressed, and there do not appear to be easy remedies. As Robert Moore (2001) argues, the very incentives employed to spur economic growth in other areas, instead deplete fiscal resources in rural areas. When rural areas offer incentives for economic development such as lower taxes, tax breaks, and subsidized infrastructure investments, the resources that public institutions need to alleviate the effects of economic hardships are diminished. The sparse population in rural areas further complicates the potential for economic vitality given the contexts of geography and demography; public resources—where they exist—are more likely to be regional rather than local.

Economic growth is confounded by all of these factors: a historically and culturally based tendency for individuals to "go it alone" rather than access public services where they exist; the absence of local institutions that offer support for children and families; lack of resources; and, the spiral of failed access to, and failed delivery from, public institutions. Together, the economic picture is bleak, and high rates of poverty can be inescapable. If rural areas fail to offer incentives for economic development the likelihood of economic development there is diminished. Yet offering the public fiscal resources for development reduces public services available to address needs. Rural adolescents facing these barriers are unable to access a productive economy. They are in many cases undereducated, and face familial and local pressure to stay. Their parents and extended families press the importance of ties to the local culture, ties to place, and ties to "the land." Those very connections virtually ensure in most rural and Appalachian settings that it will be difficult to connect to any significant economic opportunity that will allow them to support themselves. Equally important, it is difficult, if not fallacious, to make the claim that dedicating oneself to becoming educated will pay off in quality of life when most young people would have to leave the area to put their education to use in the work force. It would appear that there is no way out, literally and figuratively. Parents, families, and the sense of connection to place become a source of connection and betrayal. Stay and you show your ownership of local values, local culture, and "where you come from." Leave to take advantage of opportunities that exist elsewhere, and betray your sense of place and familial and culturally based identity. For the 21 percent of 18–24-year-olds in regions of Appalachia who are "disconnected" from high schools, jobs, and further education (AECF, 2004), class is experienced in destructive ways at the intersections of economic deprivation and cultural resistance.

Class, Education, and Intrusion into the Local Area

Economic data such as this is hard to square with broader cultural assumptions about meritocracy. The work of providing public education and other public services to young people in Appalachia is profoundly complicated as they attend schools and attempt to access services at the intersections with economic realities of a region devoid of economic opportunity. As has been said earlier, the assumption that access exists is erroneous, and the promise of opportunity where access exists may not be legitimate given economic realities. As John Gaventa, Barbara Ellen Smith, and Alex Willingham (1990) have noted, the general lack of economic development and activity in Appalachia creates a "blame the victim" reaction where critics such as those in political power and those who control economic and social institutions blame lack of economic progress on schools—and indirectly students—for not being educated "enough" to generate prosperity. Appalachian children are treated, in essence, as a bad "raw product."

Yet research deflects this blame on two grounds. (1) Education difficulties are tied to a history of segregated and underfunded schools; hence there is no schooling structure for high performance relative to actual economic opportunity and vitality. (2) Poor rural communities are not a draw for high-paying jobs even if educational levels were higher. Recent research on economic development suggest that rural areas are more attractive for underpaid, low-salary jobs and less so for more lucrative employment, in part because underfunded education systems in rural areas cannot compete with suburban urban resource bases for education (Gaventa, Smith, and Willingham, 1990, p. 283). Under current funding structures for schools, some Appalachian children may be able to turn education into a ladder, but rural schools do not provide systemic or institutionally strategic avenues of mobility. In spite of the profound affect of class on education, and in spite of the large numbers of poor children in rural areas, rural America (particularly Appalachia), has become invisible in the discourse on social class. Recent scholarship on the intersections of social class with other identity frames such as gender and race have focused primarily on urban settings. In fact, little information exists in the current literature that looks at rurality as a compelling and signature location of narratives and research relative to class; work on class and schooling in rural areas is even rarer.

An exception is Cynthia Duncan (1999) whose work cuts across multiple rural contexts, including specific portraits and examinations of class in Appalachia. Duncan discusses three components of class in rural areas: (1) class as part of the broader social structure of rural contexts; (2) the way in which caricatures and monolithic identities of Appalachian poverty affect rural places and influence identity formation within them; and (3) how class is played out against a backdrop of locally corrupt politics in public institutions, particularly schools. Duncan uses these elements to expose the struggles that people experience in attempting to (or failing to) access the social, cultural institutional resources needed to negotiate the world outside of the immediately local area. Young people grappling with identity in these contexts have limited access to resources that might help them to build alternative narratives of their lives. Furthermore, the outright abuse of power and privilege in their communities often denies them access to whatever limited resources might otherwise be available (Duncan, 1999).

Duncan's (1999) work spotlights the importance of understanding Appalachian poverty and working-class struggles as important social and historical narratives in themselves; they are also important because of the connections to similar themes for the poor and working class in urban contexts. She suggests that "Studying rural communities offers advantages for making the connection between the face-to-face relations and common experiences people have and larger social processes involving structures of class and power (p. 192). Duncan makes a strong claim that the process of critiquing and understanding class relations must be done within the perspective of *place* in rural settings. This is particularly true in Appalachia where geographic inaccessibility and confinement, and the prominence of natural resources and land, are such crucial elements in defining identity through place. The combination of rigid class structure and corrupt institutional politics such as those in school systems are central in the stories of these places and in the way in which the historical and social class narratives play over time (p. 197).

Duncan centralizes schooling as the main source of hope for communities to turn their fate toward more opportunity. She believes that of all possible access points, public schools still stand as the most likely window of opportunity in Appalachia (1999, p. 208). It is important to note that she makes this claim in the process of revealing the stories of the poor and working-class citizens in rural Mississippi, in the mountains of West Virginia, and in a rural small town in New England. Her claims are based on hope for the first two locations (what could be), and based on evidence (what has happened) from her assessment of the progressive community values of the third. This claim is also made in the context of her own analysis of the corrupting and limiting institutional culture of schools that helped to create the marginalization of the poor and of the working class in the first place. While their track record is clearly inconsistent, Duncan believes that public schools can be a critical access point for economic opportunity and accessibility. But the record and the strategic opportunity must be understood in a broader examination and understanding of rural social and historical analysis, and understanding of the cultural contexts in which schools and the local economy are situated.

While Duncan's analysis brings her to the door of the school, Ruth Panelli (2002) employs a more wide-ranging and contested framework of what it means to be poor and working class in rural areas, especially what it means to be a poor or working-class rural child. She cites four contexts in which youth identities are constructed, each of which, she argues, must be understood in rurality: space (local and beyond), culture, politics, and economy (p. 120). This set of frames adds ". . . details, complexity and diversity of young people's rural lives" to the discourse on how young people construct identities in rural places (p. 120). Panelli's four areas of contextual analysis pull the construction of "rural" into the intersection with class, education, and other elements in the construction of identity for rural youths. Her strategies (p. 117) for contextual analysis all serve to constrain and enable how identities are constructed. The first, "cultural context," includes the family and local community, their belief systems, the social capital used for wider interpretations and negotiations of identity, and how they all ". . . serve to "shape the practices and values in a young person's immediate rural experiences. . . ." The second, "political—economic," includes the material and work conditions, the wider economic processes that young people experience, and access to institutional resources—including schools—that position young people for work and education. The third, "sociopolitical," includes structures and social/power relations, roles of ethnicity, gender, class, and how they intersect with class. The fourth, "spatial," includes issues such as the freedom of movement (or lack of it) within a social context, the panoptic effect of adults in close proximity in a rural fishbowl. Critical to this transparency is making explicit the ways in which local politics and social identities are constructed in rural places, and understanding how the places themselves are social-cultural constructions. In the context of rural places where poverty and the working poor are pervasive, class is a critical component of the construction (p. 114).

Offering yet another layer to our consideration, Roger A. Lohman (2002) gives four frameworks in his analysis of the intersections of poverty and culture in rurality. His work focuses on explanatory models that link poverty in critical ways to the broader understanding of culture within the region. These perspectives include the following:

1. Poverty as lack of economic development ("Bureaucratic Realism");
2. Poverty as beliefs, attitudes, and regional folkways as factors for understanding poverty (subsistence and high levels of poverty are "normal"); resignation, fatalism, family patterns, health, and child rearing ("Appalachian Culturalism");
3. Poverty as a necessary condition of labor markets in capitalism; outside profit requires regional and local exploitation ("Predatory Capitalism");
4. Appalachia as a colony; absentee ownership; political control and corruption; and maximum internal profit with minimum internal benefit ("Domestic Colonialism"). (pp. 240–44)

Lohman layers into this a complicating element of the importance of "localism," which exacerbates problems by creating and reinforcing indifference to the values, beliefs and norms of the "outside world" (2002, p. 242). Of these four lenses, Lohman argues that two—Appalachian Culturalism and Domestic Colonialism—are unique to understanding poverty in Appalachia compared to other contexts within the United States (p. 240). There are also two elements of Lohman's critique that he believes help to provide greater insight into understanding how we, as a broader society, view Appalachian poverty. Through the lens of Bureaucratic Realism, we tend to view poverty in the region as a result of "bad choices," as the rational result of bad decision making by those in poverty. As the author sarcastically makes the point held by some: "Unemployed? Then move where the jobs are!" (p. 244). Through the lens of Appalachian Culturalism, we tend to view the culture of the region and its poverty as a romanticized, "developmental experience, moral challenge." As Lohman observes, Appalachians are viewed as "poor, but happy" (p. 244).

Stephen L. Fisher (1993), in his analysis of the intersection of class, culture, and region, argues that class in and of itself is inadequate to understanding culture in Appalachia, particularly in the contexts of a long history of dissent and resistance by poor and working-class citizens to oppressive and marginalizing forces. He makes the case that issues such as "tradition," "shared values," and "shared cultural memory" are better lenses for understanding marginalization in Appalachia than class or economic access or income (p. 317). He believes that understanding "class" as a basis for resistance needs to be connected to class as a construction that comes out of family, community, place, and religion, but that is clearly connected to issues of income and economic access. In other words, "class" is as much a cultural phenomenon as it is an economic one.

Fisher's work serves to add complexity to our understanding of class in Appalachia by exposing it as a complex social construction that goes beyond conditions created by economic factors typically associated with "wealth" or "poverty." Understanding the way in which class is constructed in Appalachia requires that we look into the local, community-based social networks and structures, histories of political resistance, local traditions in the ways family relationships are built, and the role of churches and how religious beliefs are tied to social values. Much of what may typically assumed to be "class solidarity" is actually the complex intersections of all of these constructions played out as economic resistance and as political dissent tied to labor unions and economic struggle. He cautions that critics and observers of Appalachia and its poor and working class must be able to understand the borders between the need to promote new progressive or resistance politics from traditional institutions such as schools, and the history of racism, sexism, and homophobia that many believe have been markers in Appalachia culture and history (1993, p. 327). In what he frames as the "neopopulist debate" in the region, Fisher argues that we need to understand that "What is needed is a critical discourse and practice rooted in an awareness of popular traditions and resistance, but not blind to the wider contours of power within national and international capital" (p. 327). Class in other words, is not only an Appalachian construct in itself; it is only one element of the broader construction of Appalachia as lived and perceived, with the task being to sort how class conflict in Appalachia is part of the broader cultural and political structures and narratives that people live out. This includes understanding how the local intersects with the dominant broader culture, and how it provides a resource in the struggle against the marginalizing effects of the dominant culture (p. 328). This position is supported by the work of Alan Banks, Dwight Billings, and Karen Tice (1993) in their research on political resistance activities in Appalachia and how it reflects Appalachian culture more broadly. They highlight the importance of not re-presenting Appalachian culture as a fixed metanarrative or "the way it really is" instead struggling with ways in which to inscribe people such that their "subjecthood" is not diffused (p. 296).

In an examination of how class issues play out over time and between generations, Anna Kraack and Jane Kenway (2002) provide insight into the complexity of social class, and the deconstruction of class within class, in their research on intergenerational change in rural communities during economic transition. Their focus is on the breakdown of working-class order within class over time, creating an identity of "bad boys" as the values and expectations of social behavior change with a new economy transitioning away from traditional working-class structures. As economically driven needs shift from those associated with manual labor and "blue-collar" work to a softer economy driven by activities such as tourism and service work, economic activity becomes restructured to redefine what is considered "acceptable" and "unacceptable" behavior by teenagers and young adults. In the communities that are the basis of their research, the local economy has been through these transitions, settling into a new, service-oriented structure, creating a new "economic base of place" (p. 147). Their analysis describes how young boys were stripped of historical resources available locally for identity construction and left with destructive tensions based in hangover expectations and values from a different socioeconomic context (pp. 145–46).

The authors nest these tensions in differences between the generations over temporal, spatial, individual and community identities, and the socioeconomic forces helping to define them. An old economic and social order is in conflict with the new order, and the younger generation is caught in shifting structures and redefined expectations. As this transition settled out in the local communities, the values and expectations about work ethics and social relationships of the older, working-class generation did not change to meet the new socioeconomic conditions, but their expectations for the younger generation's values did change, creating intergenerational tensions. For example, the older generation pressures the younger to hold on to what they see as blue-collar work ethics (i.e., manual labor, working to the clock, routinized schedules, and "up and out" early in the day), but there is no longer blue-collar work to do, framed in those expectations. The older generation subsequently makes value judgments about the younger generation around these assumptions about work ethics. Feelings of worthlessness among young adults are created as there is no appropriate work in what has historically been identified as a "working man's town" (Kraack and Kenway, 2002, p. 150). Bad behavior associated with laziness and idleness (note the "Kids Count" on "Discounted Youth" statistic cited earlier) results as fear of failure prevails among the younger generation. In response, the younger generation sees leaving the community for broader opportunities as an escape, but simultaneously feel pressure to stay and not be a traitor to the local culture and community. The identification with "bad behavior" plays out in many forms. For example, for the older generation, visits to local pubs after work and "blue-collar drinking" were seen as part of the culture and as a process of letting off steam after a hard day's work. In the new economy, such behavior is unwanted by the older generation and by those invested in different economic opportunities because it clashes with the image the community wants to present to tourists who come to the area to spend money. The tourist economy holds no place for loud drinking and rowdy behavior in public places (p. 152). Drinking that was once expected as part of the class structure is now suppressed—by the older generation and from those benefiting from the new economic realities— as threatening to economic vitality. In response, young people try to move their "letting off steam" to places the local citizens don't go, but that puts them into contact with the tourists who are looking for an "idyllic" rural retreat.

In short, the realities of the new economy do not allow for a context where the old working-class values can be exhibited. There is no "work" to do in the old sense, and no acceptable "leisure" to enjoy as a result. While there is no context for learning the lessons of "hard work," there is still the expectation that that form of industriousness will be valued. The younger generation had no contextual basis for "learning the value of hard work" in the sense that their fathers had, but they are expected to practice it nonetheless (Kraack and Kenway, 2002, p. 153). Less "respectable" soft labor replaced the hard physical labor of the past. The lingering elements of social and class culture left to the younger generation impose meanings from a context that doesn't exist anymore, but the behaviors and values that the older generation wants to sustain are still demanded. The shifting economy has inscribed new class meanings in the context of rurality and into the local landscape, at the younger generation's expense. As Kraack and Kenway conclude, "The changing economic base, the altered demography and the tensions between the traditional and the different groups of new residents [e.g., retirees and those connected to new industries like tourism] have profoundly destabilised the social and cultural character of the township. Difference and instability have replaced sameness and stability" (p. 151).

David Whisnant takes a more philosophical approach to critiquing the transitions that have come with the introduction (or intrusion, depending on the perspective) of "modern" standards into mountain society in Appalachia. His primary concern is with the hegemonic nature of the broader cultural pressures affecting local culture. He takes the position that the economic problems of Appalachia are not technical-rational problems to be solved with commensurate "solutions," but are instead based on cultural assumptions of those imposing technical solutions from the outside. The economic problems of Appalachia require examinations that are as complex as the social structures and cultural contexts in which the problems are embedded (1995, pp. 192–93). In his perspective, class in Appalachia plays out as a cultural drama, not as a technical, social structural process. Any attempt to understand and change in any way, the lives of communities and groups of people in the region will necessitate an understanding of the culture of the region, the values and assumptions embedded in the social and class history and present-day situation of the region, and the ability to negotiate the social constructions that are part of that history and present.

Moving from broader analyses of schooling in rural America to a more focused consideration of literacy development, Laura Payne-Bourcy and Kelly Chandler-Olcott, studying working-class, rural adolescents, highlight class as cultural as well as economic. The authors argue that because class issues have been lost in social and political efforts to hide class in the United States, educators do not consider class as a confounding factor in schooling (2003, p. 553). As did Duncan (1999), Panelli (2002), Lohman, (2002), and Fisher (1983) their analysis assumes that social class structures in rural areas are multifaceted, not monolithic (Payne-Bourcy and Chandler-Olcott, 2003, p. 560). Payne-Bourcy and Chandler-Olcott identify numerous ways in which class limits working-class, rural adolescent in their academic worlds:

- Working-class, rural children do not believe that they are capable of "making knowledge";
- Working-class, rural children tend to experience more emotional and psychological separation from parents;
- Working-class, rural children do not believe that their parents can "fight for them" in the systems and institutions that are supposed to serve their interests;

- Working-class, rural children avoid authority structures and agents and define themselves in opposition to them. (pp. 553–54)

This literature that considers the intersections of class, whiteness, education, and rurality is consistent in drawing attention to the complexity of class in rural settings. This research also is consistent in spotlighting the contested role of schooling and education in this context. Brian McGrath (2001) reflects these themes in his analysis of children's experiences in rural settings, using school as one of three contexts for critique (work and housing being the other two). He argues from a theoretical framework that examines the duality of agency and structure in rural children's lives, looking at how young people respond to and reproduce change in terms situated in available resources as "actors in context" (p. 485). His inquiry emerges from the question of what children have at their disposal as social actors within social structures, and how that plays out for them as children who "mediate, negotiate and interpret their lives" (p. 485). McGrath claims that rural children have two kinds of resources available to them—allocative and authoritative—with critical attention to the authoritative. Allocative resources are those used to build material access and command and control over the object world. Authoritative resources are those that we use to organize opportunity and possibility in life as we construct and negotiate identity. How we exercise authoritative resources is a matter of the level of capability and capacity (and education is a central enabler or limitation to that) (p. 486). McGrath argues that a critical issue in identity construction is how the interplay of agency and structure plays out in rural contexts vis-à-vis class and education. How these authoritative resources are shaped through social relationships and practices influence children's capacity for agency: how do children act and what choices do/can they make (p. 486)?

Education exists as an authoritative resource because it (1) institutionalizes opportunity and limitation, (2) provides an arena for control, (3) regulates children's behavior, and (4) limits the sense of options in a limited economy (McGrath, 2001, p. 492). McGrath counts education as an authoritative resource, as he examines why rural students opt out of school as a potential resource and source of opportunity. He cites four reasons: (1) "negative teacher pupil relationships," (2) "bullying" within the social group, (3) "lack of intellectual and social support in schooling," and (4) students who see the qualifications required in school as irrelevant to their futures (p. 490). In essence, in a context of economic restructuring, schooling often fails to be one of the resources at rural youths' disposal, and provides limited capacity for enabling of possibility and choice.

Shades of White

Karen Anijar (2001), in an examination of education in rural America asserts that ". . . discourse only happens in the spaces where you can be heard" (p. 241). As rural and Appalachian youths negotiate the construction of their identities in the social, class, race, and geographic spaces to which they have access, there are multiple critical questions that must heard. What do rural and Appalachia youths hear in the discourses around them, in the ones that the broader culture offers to or imposes on them, and what do we hear from youths in their negotiations? One clear element of that discourse is the "white noise" that provides background and foreground to the discourses. Anijar contends that these students are aware (at least in its impacts) of the intersections of race, sex, politics, and localism with class in the representations in available discourses, particularly as they relate to schooling. And, they are aware of how these other elements tend to obscure class within their broader experiences as poor, working-class, rural, and/or Appalachian culture bearers (p. 251). In particular for rural children, class is "bound up" in place; children see how race can hide the noise of class that would otherwise be heard more clearly (p. 253). The students Anijar studied exhibited an awareness of how their own culture and language were not represented in an explicit way in the curriculum used in schools, and how language valued in schools tended to marginalize their local language use.

This emerging tacit silencing of discourse on class is evident in an autobiographical sketch of Roxanne A. Dunbar's (1997) own experience as a poor white child who transitioned into the middle class. Dunbar describes the struggles and tensions of being from a poor white community and all the stereotypes and prejudices (ignorance, lack of education, and caricatures of familial and social networks) about people from poverty that can entail, and moving on as an adult to membership in the middle class as an educated professional and by marriage. She writes from the standpoint of a person who has "betrayed" her poor white background by taking on the "values" of more privileged classes (i.e., getting beyond one's raising), and with the experiential knowledge of a white person who sees white privilege from her background. As she reflects on her life experiences that have become, in reflection, both enabling and wrought with stress, she asserts, "Poor rural whites (the original white trash) have lived by dreams, at least the ones I come from did and, in a perverse way, still do, albeit reacting to 'broken dreams'" (pp. 74–75). Moving on, by her own analysis, from much of the baggage that our culture attaches to poor whites, she still struggles with where she is going and where she left to go to. She identifies herself as a "class traitor," betraying class through her personal experiences and schooling success and leaving behind the contexts and conditions of poverty and working-class life that were her early and primary experiences. She is caught in the imbalance of being pushed out, pulled back, and wanting to claim elements of both (p. 85).

Dunbar's thesis brings us to a critical component of understanding how class and race in rural and Appalachian communities and contexts is connected to broader marginalization in ways connected to race, ethnicity, and gender. The invisibility of white poverty as a critical social problem is masked, according to Dunbar, by giving limited access to economic opportunity to poor whites in roles in service (literally) to the more privileged white classes. As a social critic, she offers the following analysis of poor and working-class whites in these contexts:

> We dregs of colonialism, those who did not and do not "make it," being the majority in some places (like most of the United States) are potentially dangerous to the ruling class: WE ARE THE PROOF OF THE LIE OF THE AMERICAN DREAM. However, self-blame, a sprinkling of white-skin privilege with license to violence against minorities, scapegoating, and serving as cops and in the military (give them a gun and point to the enemy) conspire to neutralize or redirect our anger. But above all it's that dream and the ideology, the "sacred" origin myth—the religion of "Americanism"—which keeps us doped and harmless, that and alcohol and drugs and cheap consumer items, especially sex and violence. But without the dream/ideology none of the other tricks would work. (1997, pp. 76–77)

Poor whites are held down; those who make it are poor whites who achieved or took advantage of the opportunities presented to them, and those who don't, constitute the trash. The problem is not in the mythology of success and opportunity; it is in the failures of the losers. Dunbar's point draws the critical line where the real, surreal, and unreal meet in understanding class and race—at least as whiteness—in rural American and Appalachia in particular. Horace Newcomb (1995) draws this distinction in region, geography, history, and myth, at least in Appalachia. His critique of representations of poor Appalachians calls into question the representation of Appalachian culture by researchers, cultural observers, and others external to the context, suggesting that many of our images of the region's poor whites are more a landscape of the mind than one of real life in a geographic region. Much of what we as a broader culture "believe" Appalachia to be is more a monolithic representation driven by the surreal images of fictional constructs than by the complex narratives of the region (p. 317).

Many common slurs and slams are used to compartmentalize caricatures and stereotypes of poor and working-class whites with rural and Appalachian identities, including "redneck," briar hopper," clodhopper," "white trash," and "hillbilly." Many social critics, writers, and researchers focus on the use of "white trash" as a way in which poor whiteness is framed in rural communities and in Appalachia. According to Analee Newitz and Matt Wray (1997), "white trash" is racialized (whiteness), classed (waste, detritus, and throwaway), and hybridized (race and class), while "white" is marked out with the "underclass" as a social class (p. 4). White trash as a construction helps to unpack issues of race, exposes the degree to which class in rural and Appalachia contexts is complex as typically framed, and illuminates our ability to understand social relationships around class and social power (p. 4). The label helps us to examine class identity and how we construct it with race and region, the material conditions of poverty, and the divisions in racial and nonracial communities (p. 8). White trash as a social and class construction helps to localize and specify constructions of whiteness, in particular, social and class distinctions among whites as a group (p. 9).

White trash as a construction allows for an "outlet" for explaining how race or ethnicity really can be the basis for class conditions, by creating a class of whites who do not belong to the privileged or on-their-way to privileged classes. White trash as a class group becomes a buffer. This is particularly critical in an area where there are few people of color on whom to blame economic or political segregation, or where large numbers of whites in poverty need to be explained as something other than a failure of capitalism.

Pem Davidson Buck (2001) makes similar arguments as to the potential benefit to come from an analysis of how we use white trash as a label and framing element of class. Buck argues that understanding how we construct white trash as a category helps to unpack the economic impact on the current middle class that has been caused by economic restructuring and globalization. This impact on the middle class, Buck claims, is parallel to what has been experienced by poor and working class rural and Appalachian whites for decades. "Whiteness no longer provides protection from the consequences of policies that make larger and larger portions of the United States into a Third World labor force. Nor does middle-class status provide complete protection. The results are similar to those of the 1920s and 1930s in the United States . . . when the middle class began losing privileges as a result of intense competition among national elites. As usual, when faced with widespread anger at their policies, the elite has been encouraging nativist, exclusionary reactions to facilitate divide and rule (p. 222).

Buck couches this critique in what she sees as ". . . the pervasiveness of the propaganda that blames people at the bottom of the drainage system for the loss of security being felt by people slightly higher, a security they once felt was theirs by virtue of white privilege and male privilege

(2001, p. 222). The economic exploitation of poor and working-class whites threatens the "illusion of whiteness" that is necessary for exploitation of racially identified ethnic groups. If there are larger numbers of poor whites, race can't be leveraged as easily for blame for a host of social ills. As more working-class and middle-class whites face economic deterioration, it becomes harder for elites to use race and "poor" as a mechanism for exploitation (p. 223). The necessary backlash calls for the creation of images that allow for the marginalization of people on some grounds other than race, so a new group of whites is created to justify the exclusionary tactics. Whites have to "other" whites; whites have to fade into other shades of whiteness to protect whites with privilege. White trash becomes the point of departure for reclassification of the white underclass (pp. 222–23).

Newitz's analysis of white trash constructions is consistent with the claim that the identification serves to exploit poor and working-class rural and Appalachian whites for the purposes of exploitation. According to Newitz, "white trash" as an identification, emerged as a way to differentiate segments of the white population from segments that wished to maintain the ability to exercise power. White trash makes whites in the group visible because of their being poor in ways that set them off from the rest of the whites. Newitz argues that this is done by making poor whites seem "monstrously poor" and appear in the popular culture as images that "terrorize the middle class." Class difference among whites is presented as differences in "civility" and "being civilized" (or not) (1997, p. 134). Newitz extends this critique to address the ways in which poor whites in rural areas and in Appalachia are presented as images in film and in the media, where white trash is positioned in ways that allow middle-class and privileged whites to resolve their racial problems without having to do it through racial and ethnic terms (p. 139). (One can marginalize a group as the source of the problem without taking on the identity of a "racist.") Typically in these images and narratives, whites (other than white trash) have to turn on white trash because they are forced to; in essence, the white trash was "asking for it" and those in the middle class have to defend themselves (p. 144). Middle-class whites are actually the victims in the mythology of white trash; white trash has divided the race, and the other classes are just trying to survive the threats.

This image is played out time and time again in movies where unsuspecting whites find themselves embattled by caricatures of white trash, such as *Deliverance*, *Wrong Turn*, and *Texas Chain Saw Massacre*. Newitz (1997) captures the process of representation this way:

> Ultimately, whites in poverty make a perfect target for displaced white racist aggression, for one can denigrate them but avoid feeling like or even

being called "racist." Furthermore, the idea that poverty is "primitive" shores up many of the most cherished beliefs of a capitalist—and imperialist—culture. First, it confirms the idea that those who are mature, and hence deserving, always achieve upper or middle-class status. And secondly, it undergirds a myth of economic "progress," in which the developed First World is naturally superior to the undeveloped Third World; or, likewise, upper- or middle-class people in the First World should "lead" their urban and rural poor. As savage Others, poor whites in the U.S. and abroad become unruly children who need discipline, strict boundaries, and (coercive) guidance from the upper classes. And as the savagely humiliated, the upper classes are absolved of guilt—either by directly engaging in class combat, or by consuming images of white self-punishment at the movies, on TV and radio, and in social criticism. (p. 152)

Anthony Harkins (2004) focuses specifically on the image of the "hillbilly" and the way it is portrayed in the media and popular culture. Harkins discusses the recent attempt by a major television network to create and air a realty show that would put on a public stage in Beverly Hills a "hillbilly" family from West Virginia. This life imitating entertainment imitating life (the original being the 1960s television show, *The Beverly Hillbillies*) was an effort by the network to put a poor, white, Appalachian family in the context of wealth and privilege in the same vein as the fictional Clampett family. After significant backlash from citizens, some media outlets including news and entertainment, and political leaders at the state and national level, the show was scrapped before being aired. While some critics panned the attempted show as socially demeaning and exploitative, some media observers explicated their own inability to see the complexity of the rural and Appalachian poor and working class. One media critic, cited in Harkins' analysis, argued that the show would never air or work because the network would never air a "real" Appalachian family. According to Harkins, the backhanded commentary gave this assessment:

> Yet confirming regional critics' worst fears . . . reporters have also used the chance to question the show's motive to trot out demeaning stereotypes largely formed by earlier media depictions of the hillbilly as both monster and dirt-poor fool. For example . . . the show [according to one critic] could not possibly be realistic for the network would not dare show the mountaineer family as it really would be—rabidly Pentecostal, anti-Semitic, violently homophobic, and interested only in sex and drugs. More in keeping with earlier comedic depictions, a story in *E! Online News* called on would-be applicants to "brush your tooth" and warned that "livestock" would not be counted as a member of the multigenerational family. The article also questioned the efficacy of CBS's hotline to field calls from applicants because there is "no word on how many members of the *Deliverance* set have phones. (p. 225)

Both ways—well-meaning critics or media-driven caricatures—Appalachia's poor and working class lose. The hillbilly image, Harkins concludes, is a way for mainstream American culture to position rural and Appalachian counterparts to afford power and privilege to itself (2004, p. 226).

Conclusion

Understanding class in Appalachia and in other rural places requires traveling through a complex intersection of race, gender, and class *and place*. To make the point most succinctly, rural places matter. To understand class in rural places is to understand the role of political and social geography as a complicating factor in people's lives, in terms of how social and political spheres are created and work in places with geographically isolated populations, low tax bases, and rurally based social networks. Also, economic development, and therefore economic opportunity, is a much different process in rural places than that found in suburban and urban places. This is particularly true in Appalachia, where topography plays a dominant role in access to places, moving from place to place, and defining the spatial limits within which people live their lives. These factors, coupled with the difficulty of economic development beyond extractive industries such as coal, gas, and timber highlight the chronic issues of poverty, economic disadvantage, the difficulty of creating public resources to offer institutional and public agency support, and high quality, well-funded public schools. (It should not be ignored that low-wage labor and cheap, low-tax natural resources do serve the interest of corporate, suburban, and urban America.) This alone would represent a daunting challenge for breaking down class barriers on a systemic scale; add in the complicating factors of historical (and sometimes current) institutional corruption and destructive, local micro-politics, and public and service institutions can fail to be or appear to be sources of help at all.

Finally, Appalachia offers more visibly and explicitly a class-based narrative about the broader culture in general, relative to issues of class in the United States. Appalachia powerfully illustrates the intersections of economics and identity politics as elements of class in this country. Constructions around "white trash," "rednecks," "hillbillies," and others that create "white within white" social structures, marginalize rural and Appalachian whites and give energy to agendas that "blame the victim" and make class issues tied to poverty a part of life in these places, in some cases something "they really want or they would do something about it." This is not to suggest that all economic limitations in these places are unchangeable or not in some ways due to social and political conditions that have been created from within. As a poignant example, the dream and promise of education for young people is juxtaposed with a strong culturally based pressure to tie oneself to place. The "pushing and pulling" of young people in rural and Appalachian places, in particular for those in poverty and working-class contexts, is the critical illustration of the complexity of class in rural and Appalachian America.

Schools, schooling, and education—like any other element of life in rurality and in Appalachia—are as much constructs as tools for cultural construction. Schools in particular in rural and Appalachian places are critical institutions that can create possibilities or opportunities as well as barriers and obstacles. In many ways schools are actually counterweights in that they represent on the local level much of the gateway out of rurality that so much local culture works against. (The more educated one becomes, the more likely they are to leave to be seen as traitors to the local culture.) The centralizing claim about schooling as enunciated by Duncan only works if schools can get beyond the historically corrupting tendencies of local control. Duncan's claim about schools does not take into consideration the problem that the identities that have become so closely tied to poverty and lack of economic opportunity in Appalachia are in a significant way *externally* imposed. Duncan's treatment of schools actually contradicts many of her important claims about the complexity of rural and Appalachian culture in general. Schools are a complex element of complex cultures, and are institutional subjects as well as objects of change. Finally, Duncan's claims do not appear to incorporate in a critical way the phenomenon that many students in Appalachia experience—in particular, teenagers and high school graduates—of being "pulled back" by community and family expectations that to leave is to dishonor local values and place. Given these last two points, many of Appalachia's children are held back by internal value structures and expectations, and are "pushed back" by external assumptions, caricatures, and media and popular culture pressures.

"Whiteout" travel conditions in snow are a well-known weather phenomenon to people who live in Appalachia, particularly in the higher landscapes of central Appalachia. In a whiteout, snow is so intense and the wind turbulent enough that the background becomes uniform and distinctions cannot be seen in the road. It essence, it appears that there is no background or foreground—no dimensionality—to the road. The situation creates hazards and dangers for travelers because they lose perspective and depth about what is around them, and cannot see the complexities of the terrain around them. All of the potential resources and securities laid out before the travelers are lost in the one-dimensional picture left out front; the hazards and potential risks made all the more threatening by the inability to negotiate the complexity of the path.

Whiteouts are further complicated by a looming silence that typically accompanies this weather conditions, the usual noise and commotion of negotiated traffic silenced by the seemingly quaint effect of snowfall and apparently less traffic.

This element of life in the mountains of Appalachia provides an apt metaphor for understanding the complexities of "whiteness" in the culture of the region and in the way in which the region is viewed and interpreted by those outside it. Whiteness in Appalachia and in rural places in general, is not a "one shade fits all" identity construction. It cannot be used as an all-encompassing, totalizing construct to understand culture in rural and Appalachian places, and it must be confounded by issues of class. Rather, it is one of white-within-white, with varying shades and layers both constructed within the negotiations of identity in place and imposed and coerced through the mythology and impositions of broader cultural negotiations. There is an important paradox in this intersection. On the one hand, the negotiation of whiteness and class in Appalachia and in rural America is limited by the tendency to treat it as monolithic and/or invisible. From this perspective, distinctions in whiteness and how it is negotiated are treated as not so different from whiteness and class writ large, so it therefore requires suggests no particular analysis, critique, or even research in its own right. "White is white," and the focus on understanding the intersection of class with other elements of identity is put on other places in suburban and in urban America. On the other hand, when whiteness in a rural place such as Appalachia is highlighted, it is too often done so to marginalize, fantasize, and mythologize, many times to justify exploitation and marginalization from the privileged and elite layers and shades of whiteness. In essence—and literally no pun intended—the caricatures and distortions created separate the dulled and faded shades of white from the bright whites. Many issues behind the negotiated identities of rural and Appalachian places provide a backdrop to this imagery. In West Virginia, for example, citizens struggle with the no-win choices of housing the nation's federal prisons and opening the landscape for toxic landfills to provide jobs, and scrapping off mountaintops to provide energy in the era of escalating oil and natural gas prices. The broader society literally "throws away" its human and material castoffs into the country's backyard and hauling off its valuables, all the while painting a picture that attempts to justify that it was the right place to do it because it is a place that has "done it to itself" historically. Valuable resources—human and material—leave and are taken because they need to or are needed and taken elsewhere, creating and leaving behind the dust and debris to make the place dirty for our cultural conveniences, and creating the contexts used to color in the shades of white that underlie the marginalization that suits the broader society. Finally, many times those who claim those places as home and who are tied to place, exacerbate the problems by becoming implicated in the process or by taking advantage of what they may see as the last measure of opportunity that does not require self-selected expatriation.

Appalachia and rural America, like other cultural contexts, deserves a "richer" perspective on the complexities of the intersections of race and class, and how identity around class is constructed in those contexts. It can neither be totalized as the textureless veneer of an intersection of "white" and "class" that masks the negotiated meaning of "place," nor can it be left to the simplistic twist of white-on-white marginalization when drawing out mythologized distinctions that privileges one imaginary shade over another. We have to understand the dangers and pitfalls of both, and recognize the noise and contestation of the intersection of whiteness and class in the backyards of America's urban and suburban places.

References

Anijar, K. 2001. Reframing rural education. In R. M. Moore III (Ed.) *The hidden America: Social problems in rural America for the twenty first century* (pp. 234–58). London: Associated University Presses.

Annie E. Casey Foundation (AECF). 2004. *Kids count data book: Moving youth from risk to opportunity. State Profiles of Child Well-Being* (ISSN1060-9814). Baltimore.

Banks, A., Billings, D. and Tice, K. 1993. Appalachian studies, resistance, and postmodernism. In Stephen L. Fisher (Ed.) *Fighting back in Appalachia: Traditions of resistance and change* (pp. 283–301). Philadelphia: Temple University Press.

Buck, P. D. 2001. *Worked to the bone.* New York: Monthly Review Press.

Cason, K. 2001. Poverty in rural America. In R. M. Moore III (Ed.) *The hidden America: Social problems in rural America for the twenty first century* (pp. 27–41). London: Associated University Presses.

Crenshaw, K. W. (n.d.). *Intersectionality, identity politics, and violence against women of color.* University of Washington Curriculum Transformation Project. Retrieved September 30, 2004, from http://www.hsph.harvard.edu/grhf/WoC/feminisms/crenshaw.html.

DeHaan, L. and Deal, J. 2001. Effects of economic hardship on rural children and adolescents. In R. M. Moore III (Ed.) *The hidden America: Social problems in rural America for the twenty first century* (pp. 42–56). London: Associated University Presses.

Dunbar, R. A. 1997. Bloody footprints: Reflections on growing up poor white. In M. Wray and A. Newitz (Eds.) *White trash: Race and class in America* (pp. 73–86). New York: Routledge Press.

Duncan, C. 1999. *Worlds apart: Why poverty persists in rural America.* New Haven: Yale University Press.

Fisher, S. L. 1993. New populist theory and the study of dissent in Appalachia. In
S. L. Fisher (Ed.) *Fighting back in Appalachia: Traditions of resistance and
change* (pp. 317–36). Philadelphia: Temple University Press.

Gaventa, J., Smith, B. E., and Willingham, A. 1990. Toward a new Debate: Development, democracy, and dignity. In J. Gaventa, B. E. Smith, and A. Willingham (Eds.) *Communities in economic crisis* (pp. 279–91). Philadelphia:
Temple University Press.

Harkins, A. 2004. *Hillbilly: A cultural history of an American icon*. New York:
Oxford University Press.

Kraack, A. and Kenway, J. 2002. Place, time and stigmatized youthful identities:
Bad boys in paradise. *Journal of Rural Studies*, 18, 145–55.

Lohman, R. A. 2002. Four perspectives on Appalachian culture and poverty. In
P. J. Obermiller and M. E. Maloney (Eds.) *Appalachia: social context past
and present*, 4th ed. (pp. 239–416). Dubuque, IA: Kendall/Hunt Publishing
Co.

McGrath, B. 2001. A problem of resources: Defining rural youth encounters in
education, work and housing. *Journal of Rural Studies*, 17, 481–95.

Moore, R. M. III. 2001. Introduction. In R. M. Moore III (Ed.) *The hidden America: Social problems in rural America for the twenty first century* (pp.
13–21). London: Associated University Presses.

Newcomb, H. 1995. Appalachia on television: Region as symbol in American
popular culture. In W. K. McNeil (Ed.) *Appalachian images in folk and popular culture* (pp. 315–29). Knoxville: University of Tennessee Press.

Newitz, A. 1997. White savagery and humiliation, or a new racial consciousness
in the media. In M. Wray and A. Newitz (Eds.) *White trash: Race and class
in America* (pp. 131–54). New York: Routledge Press.

Newitz, A. and Wray, M. 1997. Introduction. In M. Wray and A. Newitz (Eds.)
White trash: Race and class in America (pp. 1–12). New York: Routledge
Press.

Panelli, R. 2002. Young rural lives: Strategies beyond diversity. *Journal of Rural
Studies*, 18, 113–22.

Payne-Bourcy, L. and Chandler-Olcott, K. 2003. Spotting social class: An exploration of one adolescent's language and literacy practices. *Journal of Literacy
Research*, 35(1), 551–90.

Save the Children. 2002, June. *America's forgotten children: Child poverty in
rural America. A report to the nation* (ISBN 1-888-393-14-9). Westport, CT.

Stewart, E. R., Gavazzi, S. M., McKenry, P. C., and Sheidegger, T. H. 2001. Parenting practices of rural families and their relationship to adolescent educational and emotional outcomes. In R. M. Moore III (Ed.) *The hidden
America: Social problems in rural America for the twenty first century* (pp.
131–50). London: Associated University Presses.

Whisnant, D. 1995. Cultural values and regional development. In R. J. Higgs,
A. N. Manning, and J. W. Miller (Eds.) *Appalachia inside out: Culture and
criticism*. Vol. 2. (pp. 192–94). Knoxville: University of Tennessee Press.

12

CLASS—DÉCLASSÉ

George W. Noblit

This book is devoted to a rethinking of social class in education. The other authors offer perspectives on how social class is useful, and in what ways, for understanding how education works to produce a stratified population both within schools and in the wider society. As coeditor of this volume, I have read and reread these pieces many times and find them all compelling if in rather different ways. Yet when the authors of the chapters in this volume began this discussion several years ago, we were compelled by how the new understandings of race and gender made social class (of the trilogy: race, class, and gender) seem, well, déclassé. Neither academics nor those they studied were using it as an analytic category. In part, this is because the concept of social class had been captured twice: once by Karl Marx and once by status attainment studies (Aronowitz, 2003). It remained central in neo-Marxist critical theories if only to be challenged by feminist and critical race theories. Social class also remained embedded in the abstracted empiricism of status attainment studies (Karabel and Halsey, 1977). Creating a conception of class that might reengage both social science and public discourse meant that we, as authors, had to do so in the context of these competing conceptions of class. Nevertheless, we realized that we had to also imagine beyond these existing formulations of class if we were to address the failure of class:

> . . . class is a largely absent category in American public, private or scholarly discourse. Its elision is due in part to the lingering legacy of the Red Menace, Marx and the Evil Empire, but also to shared beliefs that (almost) everyone is "middle class" and only a residual category of nonpersons qualify as the "underclass." Class in the American context is seen primarily as the product and consequence of individual enterprise

313

rather than that of a complexly configured historical, social and political economic location. The lack of class analysis also is attributed to American "exceptionalism" as defined by the absence of a strong labour movement or socialist party. . . . (Ferguson and Golding, 1997, p. xvi)

Class analysis also has had its problems in England as well. As Margaret Somers (1997, pp. 73–74) writes:

Was there a class struggle in the industrial revolution? The questions remain unresolved. . . . Indeed "why the peculiarities of the English?" has been an intellectual complaint since the birth of the theory of class. Paradoxically, however, the yardstick used to measure the English working class and find it "peculiar" was constructed by classical sociological conceptions of class formation for which *English working people served as the putative historical model.* Surely something is amiss when the original historical actors whose lives were appropriated for a theoretical schema of class formation are subsequently judged deviant by that same theory.

Regardless of the interpretive and theoretical problems with class, many theorists, including ourselves, realize that social class affected our lives. At one point, theorists collectively reasserted the race, class, and gender trilogy with the clumsy phrase: the nonsynchronist parallelist position (McCarthey and Apple, 1988). This assertion was to signal the move away from the sense that class was the ultimate category, that all difference was reducible, in some senses, to an economically structured stratification. In this phrase we wished to signal that class continued to work both analytically and in the lives of people, but also to signal the lesson from critical race and feminist studies, that race and gender could not be reduced to social class analytically. Each contributed something unique and all worked together to mark and construct status and relative power in the United States. Ultimately, however, this reassertion of the trilogy was unsatisfactory because it did not reinvigorate the conception of social class. Something was terribly wrong with how we thought about social class and many began working on rethinking the concept (i.e., Aronowitz, 2003; Hall, 1997. Mahony and Zmroczek, 1997. Walkerdine, 1990; Wright, 1987). Patrick Joyce (1997, p. xi) in his forward to the Hall volume argued that the collections of essays ". . . resuscitates a concept that was almost dead." While this is surely hyperbole, it does demonstrate that there is much to be done. Perhaps more dramatically, Stanley Aronowitz (2003, p. 1) describes the response to his recent work:

When I tell friends that I have written a book on class, especially class in the United States, the news is received with either incredulity or cheerleading. The "posts"—liberals and postmodernists—question whether the concept is still useful and often suggest I use another term. If they acknowledge the salience of class at all in these times, most relegate it to a narrative—one of the stories Americans tell about history—or a figure of vernacular speech. The other response is gratitude that someone is (finally) going to blast the myth of American classlessness and its contemporary displacement, stratification. Stratification designates distinction without conflict. Those who replace class with strata deny that society is propelled by social struggles; for the stratification theorists, people are arranged along a social grid by occupation or income. The category is merely descriptive of status and differential opportunities for jobs and goods. Enthusiasts are frequently outraged that any intelligent social thinker can fail to observe the obvious signs of class difference, especially the ample evidence that at the political level the U.S. democratic system retains considerable deference to money and its bearers in the determination of social and economic policy. Plainly there is no longer agreement that the concept of class tells us anything about how social structure or history is constituted.

This paragraph names many of contending schools of thought at play in the reconceptualization of class, but in doing so understates the actual complexity of current thinking about social class. For example, the "posts" are not *a* school but rather a set of contending schools—postmodernism and poststructuralism being but two of them. They may both question the usefulness of class analysis but the latter's insistence that power permeates society and the former's focus on social life as narrative makes their perspectives more incommensurate than Aronowitz acknowledges. On the other hand, those who wish to reassert the salience of class in the United States are similarly varied. Some are essentially trying to reassert Marxist or neo-Marxist perspectives as the correct analysis while others are vexed by the the fin de siècle redistribution of wealth that began with President Ronald Reagan's presidency and continues through today. The latter assert that in the context of global capitalism the United States is now only a two-class society. Marxist thought, then, would be only a starting place rather than the end of the deliberation. Finally, the stratification theorists have been challenged by recent work conceptualizing class not as distinct economic categegories but as a continuum in which boundaries between high and lower status positions are increasingly blurred. Furthermore, some of this recent research also has undercut the notion that the United States is a meritocracy that was central to early status attainment researchers (Hallinan, 2000). All this is to say that while there is agreement that class needs to be rethought, there are a host of perspectives on how that might be redone.

We should also learn from Aronowitz (2003) that what seems to be called for is not the reassertion of existing perspectives but the reconsideration of these perspectives. He writes (pp. 1–2): "Unfortunately this book may give little comfort to those who defend the received wisdom about class and class struggles. . . . For them people like me are apostates. To this state of being I plead guilty. I remain loyal to the questions posed by the founders of historical materialism and to their reliance on history to provide solutions to vexing problems of power. But it cannot be true that the answers are immutable." I want to embrace the spirit that Aronowitz signals here, even if I want to go further with it. Aronowitz's (2003, p. 52) approach allows him to shift the focus from class struggle to class formation and thus to embrace social movements: "Genuine social movements are struggles over class formation when they pose new questions concerning the conduct of institutional and everyday life and entail new arrangements." Genuine social movements, for Aronowitz, reconfigure the "power situation (p. 53)" in terms of ". . . who constructs the rules of inclusion and exclusion in institutional and social life; who tells the story of past and present, what Antonio Gramsci calls common sense; and who has the power to define the future" (p. 53). I find much of this of interest even as I note that embracing social movements has long been championed by poststructuralists (see Wexler, 1987) and the focus on the narration of life is quintessentially postmodern. That is to say, Aronowitz seems to offer a synthesis of prevailing critical perspectives.

To my way of thinking, we need a host of approaches to break the conceptual logjam about social class: syntheses, reassertions, critiques, in-depth studies, and thought experiments. In this chapter, my focus is on one way in which we might break the conceptual logjam. I will do so by doing the unthinkable—reversing the "isn't it all just class anyway" logic of liberal thought. I will argue that we should consider the implications of "reducing" class to race and do so not as a statement of empirical reality, but rather as a *strategy* to reveal the hegemonic forces that have distanced the concept and experience of class from political traction.

This project is, of course, full of pitfalls that must be acknowledged. First, it is focused on the theoretical idea of social class. It is an exercise in the sociology of knowledge—examining social class as a reified reality. John Hall (1997), in *Reworking Class,* argues that "the end of class as a historical subject" is a failure of ideas. He concludes that the materialist dialectical model of capitalism development is being replaced with the view that the "many social struggles over material and ideal, social and cultural interests that do not always look like the surface manifestations of a dialectical class struggle" (p. 7). He also argues that the "the deconstruction of class as a theoretical object" (p. 7) emerges as part of the recent economic and political transformations within and between nations and "the postmodern crisis of knowledge" (p. 15), which has resulted in "contingently historical and discursive analyses of classes" (p. 15). Hall argues that the discrediting of social theory of class itself is actually a failure "to theorize in nonstructuralist ways" (p. 15). That Hall wishes to return to Weberian analyses and toward the institutional school of thought is of less interest to me, although in what follows I will, in part, call upon such traditions. Ultimately, the project requires a *reimagining* in which returning to classic theory or to existing schools of thought will only be of partial use.

Second, if "class is déclassé" in social theory, then the project here is marked by filling a void. This void must be carefully circumscribed if we are to try to explore ways of filling it. In the next section, I will begin this project by taking on the reality of class. My argument is that class is déclassé because for too long, social theorists had insisted that it is objectively real. The failure of working people to behave in ways in which class theory requires, forces us to admit that materiality is insufficient for class to be constructed as objectively real. We may wish to temper our theorizing in this vein in an effort to create the possibilities for strategic action. Moreover, part of this is also to ask how we can help everyday people understand how social reality gets constructed and to whose benefit. This is not only to be able to effectively strategize for action but also to reconceprtualize power itself.

Third, the persistent existence of inequality in the United States is full of evidence that there are important differences that must be dealt with. As Maike Philipsen in this volume argues, we have more and more people living in poverty. Her project of working with the non-poor to realize that we create and benefit from the poor resonates with me. Yet saying this and actually getting those who benefit from a state of affairs to change seems to be a daunting project in itself. It may well require a coalition from which what we call "the social classes" can emerge, and this as a strategy will require more imagination than empiricism. This will be the basis on the strategy I embrace here. By "reducing" class to race we may be able to achieve such a coalition around what Lani Guinier and Gerald Torres (2002, p. 10) term *political race*. Their project is to create coalitions that reach across differences while maintaining differences at least in some respects.

Finally, class as déclassé does not mean that we will not return to class. In fact, I will argue that the way to get to class at this point in history is by reducing it from its earlier historical dominance as a category ("isn't it all class anyway?) to one of the explanations of oppression, and a complex, all too subjective one at that. This means that I will, in the end of the chapter, return to class as one vector in intersectionality (Crenshaw, 1991). I have chosen "political race" as my strategy because it will reveal that race is not the sum total of one's identity nor the only category used to subjugate. From race we have learned that what must be changed is whiteness, from gender we have learned that what must be changed is patriarchy, and from class I will argue that we learn that what must be changed is hierarchy. In the end, class analysis and action should not be primarily targeted toward revealing the problems of the lower classes or the ways in which the middle classes try to shore up their imperiled advantage (Brantlinger, 2003; Erhenriech, 1989). Rather, the project is to reveal how hierarchy is created and how we learn from this process while creating a new definition of power—"power with" (Guinier and Torres, 2002, p. 141). We must return to class by doing more than name it—we must also name that which must be changed.

Class as Material Reality

John Meyer's Critique

I grew up working class, and was an active participant in all of the "social problems" that we have historically associated with lower-class existence: crime, single-parent families, gangs, and so on. I still live with these in many ways. They are and were real for me, and they were real to our neighborhood, the schools, and the police force. Yet I want to argue that social theory has given class a weight it cannot bear. By making it a central trope in social theory we have pulled it out of existence and into our intellectual projects. It is time to return class to everyday life—to unmask its seeming reality and materiality. Class must be understood as a product of human life and interpretation. In what follows, I will use two critiques of the reality of class, one by John Meyer and one by Pierre Bourdieu, to help define the void that must be filled if class is déclassé. Defining this void then will outline what is needed in way of strategic action—in effect, leading to reimagining what struggles may have traction in our current era.

Meyer (1994), in reviewing a set of chapters on social stratification, started his commentary by noting that those who study stratification tend to do so from "a realist vein" (p. 730). This, in turn, led him to argue that, regardless of theoretical approach, stratification studies "nearly all share a vision of society as a system made up of interdependent parts"— "a view rooted in a realist vision of modern society as a functioning system" (p. 730). While those more rooted in a Marxist perspective may wish to deny this, it is clear that Marxism has its own version of functionalism stressing the role of elites and economic forces. Meyer argues:

"The story is a standard sociological one, told with varying emphases on conflict and consensus; it is also very similar to the stories modern societies tell about themselves" (p. 730). His point is that stratification theories are as much products of modern societies as independent explanations—cultural products. Meyer is arguing that we have mistaken for an explanation what is actually a central myth of modernity. That is, our understanding of class is not outside of cultural assumptions but rather an expression of it. Our theories are constitutive of our society. Thus the claims of the reality or materiality of class do not unpack the assumptions and hierarchies of modern societies but rather are part of producing class as we know it. He in turn offers an alternative to realistic portrayals of stratification, arguing that modern societies themselves are cultural accomplishments and stratification is "highly constructed—as the product of meaning and interpretation in modern schemes and scripts" (p. 731). Moreover, the status accorded to groups "arise from cultural ideologies (which in the modern world commonly take the form of functional theories) as much as from "real" interactive dominance and dependence" (p. 731). That is, stratification is ideological hegemony—and real in this sense primarily.

Meyer argues that because stratification theorists underplay culture they misunderstand the place of the theories and analyses they generate. He writes: "Stratification theorists may understate the importance of the cultures of modern systems *because stratification theories (though not necessarily only narrowly academic ones) are the central cultural elements involved.* Recognizing the cultural character of stratification would weaken the realist vision of society as a real system. It would also undercut some of the scientific claims of stratification theorists: If stratification is cultural theory, the theorists (as classic phenomenological critics have had it) are studying themselves. (1994, pp. 731–32; emphases in the original)

For Meyer, stratification theories are central elements of modern cultures. He notes the irony of seeing stratification theories of premodern societies as cultural constructions while we fail to do so for our own societies. He offers two cultural "principles" (1994, p. 733) built into modern cultures that enable the extant understanding of class and stratification. First is the principle that societies are systems and thus only functional considerations can justify inequality. The theories offer critiques that are of the essential form that specific inequalities are not functional, either by opposing achievement with ascription or with "legitimate achievement against power" (p. 733). Second is the principle of "moral individualism" (p. 733). In this, individuals are regarded as equal and justice is determined by the relative equality of individuals. In the analyses of stratification, individual income equality, trumps analyses, if done, of groups.

For Meyer, these principles are contained in the cultures of modern societies. The first principle of society as a system is implicated in the theory of progress that in many ways defined modernity. This theory of progress also has an ideology of rationalism within it: ". . . rationalistic and progressive ideas have played a role in supporting a great deal of modern social differentiation. Activities can be pulled out of social life and bundled into rationalized elements or roles; their inequalities are thus justified" (1994, p. 734). Thus, occupations are constructed by the ideology of rationalism as is our understanding of their relative status. . . . Yet instead of accepting a functionalist view that modern societies require specific forms of stratification, Meyer argues that a better explanation is to see ". . . the cultural (functional) theories of modernity as widespread and as generating a good deal of stratificational isomorphism" (p. 734). Indeed, education becomes central to modern stratification not because it provides needed skills (as is argued by stratification theory) but because ". . . the myths of rational progress have made educational institutions culturally central" (p. 734).

The principle of individualism in stratification theory also has had important effects. It has led to stratification theorists largely ignoring how the status as citizen is a key dimension of social differentiation. That is, nationally and internationally individuals are not equal in access to nation-state resources that come with being a recognized member of the nation-state. The ideology of individualism also justifies the expansion of education under the guise of developing human capital. The contradiction is that "Not only is education the crucial certifier of inequality, but mass education is a most important constructor of equality as well" (p. 735). With the myth of individualism, we miss the dilemmas built into our educational systems.

Finally, ideologies of individual equality have also led to the development of professions and organizations designed to protect the vulnerable, including the young and aged. Education as an institution thus embodies modern myths in central ways.

Conjointly, the ideologies of rational progress and individualism, in Meyer's analysis, also generate considerable role differentiation in modern societies, which in turn sustains functional myths that work is defined by social tasks rather than by status, and that roles are distinct from persons within them. The significance of class differences, therefore, is downplayed in public discourse and in scholarly analyses because they do not give real people purchase on their lives. This is true even as "differentiation permits increasingly equal individuals in a system of increasingly unequal and ordered activities" (p. 736). The functionalist separation of role and person allows us to limit analyses of differences in income, for example, to comparisons of individual pay for the work they perform, while ignoring the fact that those who run organizations also have access to wealth and power well beyond their official "income."

Meyer's argument, then, is that stratification, as we understand it in theory and in life, is based on the culture of modernity and on its ideological bases rather than having an independent, real or material, basis. That is, people have real differences in what is possible in their lives but class theories fail to capture them in ways that theorists or everyday people find useful to either unpack or change the life situations of the poor. Worse, social theorists and analysts are key cultural workers in the maintenance of the culture of modernity and of its presumptions of rationalism, progress, and individualism. Work in stratification theory—even that which critiques stratification—results in the conception that stratification is a fact of life and that some differentiation is justifiable and others not so. In the end, academic protestations about inequalities end up justifying social differentiation.

Some may wish to argue that this decertification of realism is debilitating—that class analysis is not possible because we cannot escape our cultural assumptions. Yet Meyer's analysis shows that this is an overstatement. The actual debilitating argument is to the assertion that class has an objective existence beyond that constructed by humans. Moreover, it is clear that Meyer is arguing that a constructed notion of class is, to paraphrase W. I. Thomas (Merton, 1957, p. 421), "real" in its consequences. Myths and ideologies work in the social world precisely because they are interpretive schemes that make sense of everyday life. Such a cultural understanding of class and stratification should free us to strategize about how it could be otherwise. Meyer only ventures into this in a minor way. The question that remains is how that delegitimation may be accomplished.

Pierre Bourdieu's Critique

Pierre Bourdieu offers a second critique of realism in class analyses. Like Meyer, Bourdieu (1987–88) embeds his argument in the intersection of the "primary social experience" (p. 1) and in the "problem of knowledge" (p. 1). Bourdieu rejects a "false opposition" between objectivism and subjectivism: "In reality, agents are both classified and classifiers, but they classify according to (or depending on) their position within the classifications" (p. 2). In this, there is both a partial subjective moment and an objectivist moment taken from a "determinate position in an objective social space" (p. 2).

Bourdieu also makes it clear that addressing the question of whether classes exist as reality is in many ways a politicized scene. He argues that whatever answer is given ". . . is based on political choices" (1987–88, p. 2). Those asserting the existence of classes will tend to take a realist

stance, while those denying the existence of classes tend to indicate that
there are no categorical differences, but rather continua upon which social
scientist inscribe their versions of reality—"theoretical artifacts" (p. 3). Yet
Bourdieu argues that both share a "substantialist philosophy" (p. 3)

> . . . which recognizes no other reality than that which is given directly
> given to the intuition of ordinary experience. In fact, it is possible to
> deny the existence of classes as homogeneous sets of economically and
> socially differentiated individuals objectively constituted into groups,
> and to assert at the same time the existence of a space of differences
> based on a principle of economic and social differentiation. In order to
> do so, one needs only to take up the relational or structural mode of
> thinking characteristic modern mathematics and physics, which identi-
> fies the real not with substances but with relationships.

With this, Bourdieu displaces the real from phenomena to the relations among phenomena. These he equates with a structure that is not
discernible by "sense-experience" (1987–88, p. 3). Structure itself is a
space, a "*social space*" (p. 3, italics in original) that can be understood ".
. . by discovering the powers or *forms of capital*" (p. 4, italics in original)
that are used to appropriate scarce goods. He then returns to his classic
distinctions of forms of capital:

> In a social universe like French society, and no doubt in the American
> society of today, these fundamental social powers are . . . firstly *economic*
> capital, in its various kinds; secondly *cultural* or better, informational cap-
> ital, again in its different kinds; and thirdly two forms of capital resources
> that are very strongly correlated, *social* capital, which consists of re-
> sources based on connections and group membership, and *symbolic* cap-
> ital, which is the form the different types of capital take once they are
> perceived and recognized as legitimate. Thus agents are distributed in the
> overall social space, in the first dimension according to the global *volume*
> of capital they possess, in the second dimension according to the *compo-
> sition* of their capital, that is, according to the relative weight in the over-
> all capital of their various forms of capital, especially economic and
> cultural, and in the third dimension according to the evolution in time of
> the volume and composition of their capital, that is, according to their *tra-
> jectory* in social space. (p. 4, italics in original)

In this way, people are positioned relative to others not in one dimension, the verticality of class, but on multiple dimensions. Here Bourdieu then notes that the danger is that people will then interpret this
analysis in a substantialist manner—changing analytic constructs into
"real, objectively constituted groups" (1987–88, p. 4). He concludes:
"Ironically, the more accurate the theoretical construction of theoretical

classes, the greater the chance that they will be seen as real groups" (p. 4). Here he joins Meyer in arguing that theory has within it "the means of regrouping individuals into classes in such ways that agents in the same class are as similar as possible . . . and in such a way that the classes are distinct as possible from one another" (p. 5). This in turn obscures the social space from view, making realism apparently accurate.

Thus the idea of a class comes to have a life of its own. People affected by the classification, according to Bourdieu, are affected both "intrinsically" (as being about themselves) and "relationally" (in relation to other classes) so as to create a "homogenizing effect" (1987–88, p. 6). That is, the categorization itself sets in motion the creation of a group with some semblance of similarity.

This account of how classes are socially constituted shares elements of Meyer's argument. Theory and social analysis are not irrelevant to social life but constitutive of it. Knowledge names elements of social life. This is in turn taught to the elite and to the "educated" who attend college. They use these categories to constitute their own lives and through the media the tentative analytic constructs of intellectuals come to be the terms we all use to describe ourselves—to constitute and situate ourselves and the meaning of our lives. As intellectuals we cannot escape complicity in this. Bourdieu even argues that the Marxist tradition "confuses the things of logic with the logic of things" (1987–88, p. 7)—the theorized classes are equated with a mobilized group with a self-consciousness. This, of course, is how both the American and British working class becomes "problems" for class analysis. Bourdieu then concludes his discussion of the objectivist moment: "Social classes, or more precisely, the class which is tacitly referred to when we speak of social classes, namely, 'the working class exists sufficiently to make us question or at least deny its existence, even in the most secure academic spheres, only inasmuch as all sorts of historical agents, starting with social scientists such as Marx, have succeeded in transforming what could have remained an 'analytical construct' into a 'folk category,' that is, into one of those impeccably real social fictions produced and reproduced by the magic of social belief" (p. 9).

It is important to note that Bourdieu does not center politics in the objectivist moment. Rather, he focuses on how theory can create reality, sufficient that we mistake our categories for real life and thus the categorical imperative makes such things as social class appear to be objectively constituted. There is a politics involved in this, of course, but Bourdieu places this politics firmly in the subjectivist moment. His argument has implications for how intellectuals behave as well. He argues that it makes little sense for theorists to try to adjudicate which beliefs, analytic constructs, and/or folk theories are more real since this "theoreticist epistemcentrism leads one to forget that the *criteria* used in the construction of the objective space and of the well-founded classifications it makes possible are also instruments—I should say weapons—and stakes in the classsification struggle which determines the making and unmaking of the classifications currently in use" (1987–88, pp. 9–10, italics in original).

Here he points to how the objectivist claim about class is founded on the subjectivist moment, meaning that the former is at best loose fitting and at worse distant from the social space being categorized because it is a social constitution of modern society—not of empirical reality. His argument is that which had to be set aside to create an objective account of social position must be reinterred in the space it was exiled from. Ideologies, for instance, are not problems but better understood as one set of the strategies of representation at play in the social space of stratification.

This leads him to reject the objectivist/subjectivist distinction, or as he puts it:

> One can and must transcend the opposition between the vision which we can indifferently label realist, objectivist, or structuralist on the one hand, and the constructivist, subjectivist, spontaneist vision on the other. Any theory of the social universe must include the representation that agents have of the social world and, more precisely, the contribution they make to the construction of the vision of that world, and consequently, to the very construction of that world. It must take into account the symbolic work of fabrication of groups, of group-making. It is through this endless work of representation (in every sense of the term) that social agents try to impose their vision of the world or the vision of their own position in that world, and to define their social reality. Such a theory must take as an incontrovertible truth that the truth of the social world is the stake of a struggle. And, by the same token, it must recognize that, depending on their position in social space, that is, in the distributions of the various species of capital, the agents involved in this struggle are very unequally armed in the fight to impose their truth, and have very different, and even opposed aims. (1987–88, pp. 10–11)

Bourdieu's politics then is played out the "plurality of visions" such that ". . . the space of objective differences (with regard to economic and cultural capital) finds an expression in a *symbolic space* of visible distinctions, of distinctive signs which are so many symbols of distinction" (p. 11, italics in original). In this politics, there is considerable room for manuevering and manipulation of relations of group membership. The struggle then is one of symbolism aimed at "the definition of boundaries between groups," which in turn imposes a vision of divisions that enable the constitution of "properly political collective struggles" (1987–88, p. 13): "In these struggles whose ultimate aim, in modern societies, is the power to nominate held by the state, i.e., the monopoly over legitimate symbolic violence, agents—who in this case are almost always specialists, such as politicians—struggle to impose representations (e.g. demonstrations) which create the very things represented, which make them exist publicly, officially. Their goal is to turn their own vision of the social world, and the principles of division upon which it is based, into the official vision, into *nomos*, the official principle of vision and division."

Bourdieu is pointing to how ideas that seemingly "work" for analytic and discursive purposes can become reified over time and lose both their historical and spatial particularity (Abu-Lughod, 1991; Noblit, 1999). With reification, these ideas and practices take on a life of their own. People begin to organize their lives with them moving literally from "is" in a specific time and space, to "ought" in a wider set of spaces. As I have argued elsewhere (Noblit, 1999), this move is often then coupled to power and legitimation, creating a fortification around what was once simply a seemingly good idea about the particular into the "right" way to think and act. Legitimation becomes fortified when it is embedded in a set of practices all seen as the right way to believe act and ultimately when the power at play in everyday interaction to enforce an "ought" is coupled with the state, law, and ultimately law enforcement. For Bourdieu, the stakes are the imposition of legitimated rules about the construction of reality. Thus power over symbols becomes the power to objectify in public and formal ways.

Bourdieu concludes by arguing that the dominated have imposed the categories of preception that foster the acceptance of a given order of things as the dominant strive to impose a vision of the world that makes their privilege justified. Yet the dominated have a "practical knowledge of the social world" that can be "a truly creative power" enabling a reconceptualization, a new naming, which allows for groups conscious of their position to emerge where mere collectives once had been.

The Irreality of Class

Meyer and Bourdieu have somewhat different arguments. Meyer's critique is that stratification theorists are decidedly structuralist, and in this they miss the role of culture in promoting widely shared belief systems. Even opposition to stratification reproduces the structuralist view. Bourdieu shares this view but rejects the distinction that Meyer makes, arguing the point that there are objectivist *and* subjectivist moments in understanding social class. Meyer is willing, moreover, to embrace a strategy of decertification of myths that seems fully consistent with Bourdieu's argument, but Bourdieu is less willing to jump to this decertification—possible because his dualistic portrait of the objective and subjective moments lends less certainty to the outcome of intention. He would argue that decertification seemingly requires an objectivist moment that Meyer seems to otherwise decry.

While Bourdieu and Meyer construct their arguments somewhat differently, they are agreed on a key point that will serve as the basis for my arguments to follow. The point is that social analysts play the role of creating a symbolic system, a theory and analysis, which plays back into the social world as an account that others use as part of the struggle to name social reality. Our theories play as strategies and given the alignment of knowledge and power, serve the interests of domination. This is true whether we focus on analyses purportedly to emancipate the subaltern, or whether we advance a more functionalist analysis. The latter enables a strategy that justifies existing distinctions under the guise of a universal system analogy. The former reifies class distinctions through its analysis and unwittingly teaches the dominant the "arts of resistance" (Scott, 1990) that can then be countered via representational strategies that Bourdieu might see as symbolic violence toward the "lower" classes.

This, of course, creates a conundrum for social analysts and activists alike. Naming comes back upon us, and can be used by those with more power over symbols and representation to strategically create realities. Perhaps an analogy to the field of cultural studies might help us circumscribe the void left by the irreality of class. A central theme of cultural studies is that naming comes back to us and is one reason why cultural studies is reluctant to name itself definitively. By embracing the fuzziness and the indeterminacy that results from this, cultural studies can open representation itself for interrogation. Such rhetorical devices as accepting multiple interpretations as all real (both/and instead of either/or) highlight the issue of symbolic representation itself as it undercuts efforts to use social analyses to undergird definitive distinctions like those used in the study of stratification. In this then cultural studies provides a vision of how to "do class" without reproducing class distinctions. If class is dé-classé, it is because we have asked it to carry too much. It had to be both real and transcendent in the same moment. It seems then that to save the idea of social class from itself we need to supplant it with an approach like that of cultural studies. Importantly, however, our new conceptualization must enable strategic action even as it disclaims definitiveness.

Intersectionality

It is telling that when it was clear that race and gender were not reducible to class and thus class could no longer be the base upon which social distinction was built, the response of intellectuals was to first move to détente. The argument was that class, race, and gender were parallel in how they worked to stratify society. Raymond Morrow and Carlos Torres (1998) and others argued for a nonsynchronistic, parallelist position. For them, this argument was not just about the salience of class but also a defense against a postmodernism that they saw as undercutting the project of critique itself. I have no wish to argue the specifics of whether class, race, and gender operate in parallel or their relative synchrony. In large part, this is because I take this project to be rooted in claims of realism and objectivism. Rather, I want to note that when we start from another vantage point than class, different conceptualizations are possible. That is, when one is not defending the basis of social class it appears that other alternatives are possible. Emerging from critical legal studies and critical race studies, a different conceptualization is termed *intersectionality*. Intersectionality recognizes that analytically, separate categories actually exist together and in tension in everyday life. As African-American women have argued to white feminists, it is not possible to separate one's gender and one's race. To this, I could add one's class, sexual orientation, physical and mental ablism, and so on. Yet let me stay closer to the project at hand, social class, even though all are ultimately salient to intersectionality.

Intersectionality is a term used by Kimberle Crenshaw (1991) to describe how race and gender act together. She drew heavily on feminist theory and antiracism theory in arguing that the law and court actions in antidiscrimination cases forced black women to chose race *or* gender as the basis of their claim to having been discriminated against. Intersectionality is Crenshaw's way of highlighting the fact that race and gender (in her argument) are not parallel in their effects and are not simply additive in their effects. That is to say, together they constitute something more than the analytic distinctions capture separately.

Crenshaw (1994) is also careful not to argue for a new definitive theory. In fact, she is careful to eschew a totalizing theory. Rather she simply argues that the emphasis ". . . on the intersections of race and gender only highlights the need to account for multiple grounds of identity when considering how the social world is constructed" (p. 94). Here Crenshaw reclaims class not as an objective social position but as a form of identity.

This conceptualization of class as identity makes intersectionality possible. It has also led to a theory of identity as not a fixed stae of self but rather as cultural performance. For example, in *Girls Without Class*, Julie Bettie (2003) describes the experiences of young women in high school. She sees them as navigating class, race, and ethnicity and gender in multiple ways. She saw that class categories are ". . . infused with and intersect with gender and racial/ethnic meanings" (p. 7). In her work, class is understood as an identity performance that could not be separated from gender and race:

> Because middle- or working-class performances were experienced differently across race/ethnicity, and further, because those performances were read differently by others, dependent on the race/ethnicity of the

performer, and because it is impossible to uncouple these meanings, I used the hyphenated "race-class performances of femininity" as a way to indicate that class performances have race and gender specific meanings. But I could just as well speak of "gender-class performances of race" or "race-gender performances of class." That race, class, gender and sexual meanings and identities intersect is not simply an abstract theoretical insight. (pp. 55–56)

Intersectionality posits that multiple bases of distinction work together. It is more difficult to reify this conceptualization inasmuch as it is a performance of identity rather than an objective and definitive position. This offers a way to approach distinctions such as class in a way that makes it more difficult to be appropriated for stratification.

In fact, by highlighting intersectionality, Bettie offers an explanation for the quotes I began with declaring class to be déclassé. She explains:

Class is largely missing as a category of identity offered by popular culture and political discourse in the early-twenty-first century United States. Class is not a central category of thought, making it difficult to have a cultural or political class identity. Class is often conceptually displaced onto or read through other categories of difference like gender and race is such a way that class is rendered invisible. While it is not a more fundamental axis of identity or mechanism of social organization, it is perhaps more often obscure. Given the U.S. ideology of upward mobility, class is either not a present category of thought at all or is present but understood only as a difference of money and therefore as temporary. Consequently, categories like race and gender, which *appear* to be essentially there, fixed, and natural, readily take the place of class in causal reasoning, rather than being understood as mediated by or inextricably intertwined with class and one another. Thus, commonsense discourses on race and gender can work to preclude class visibility. (p. 195, italics in original)

Here we see an important aspect of intersectionality. Without a commitment to examine intersectionality critically, these young women could not see how class had been made invisible to them. This situation is filled with ironies, first, that the physical markers of identity that enable forms of oppression also enable identities with which to live with and to address forms of oppression. Second, these same physical markers upon which racism and sexism are built come to have such salience as identity material that class is hidden from view. Part of the project of this chapter, then, allow class to be recognizable. Without this, Bettie shows that young women she worked with had a "discursive absence" (2003, p. 194). She argues that the "*essentialized* conceptualizations" (p. 196, italics in original) of gender and race work against recognizing class differences.

Because they are taken to be "natural and inevitable" (p. 196), class was outside the discourse of difference: ". . . class meaning was routinely articulated through other categories of difference (race, gender, sexuality) and in other terms (family values, individualism, self-esteem" (p. 196). The taken for grantedness of race and gender organized the discourse of difference even as it helped mask the reproduction of class difference.

Yet Bettie (2003) wants to be clear that class was being actively played out:

> Working class performers, across race/ethnicity, had their dignity wounded through exposure to middle-class performers who routinely, and often unknowingly, inflicted class and race-based injuries in their practices of exclusion. Differing race-class performances of femininity took hold as girls defined themselves relationally in opposition to multiple others and as working-class girls adopted alternative badges of dignity that worked, at times, as a kind of resistance to symbolically heal class and race injuries. In short, girls began constructing future class positions for themselves without the awareness that they were engaged in doing so, and future class positions were constructed for them as their limited economic and cultural resources ensured that the vast majority of working-class girls would both opt out and be tracked out of a middle-class trajectory. (p. 190)

Her argument then is that class operates in social disclosure but is obscured by the conceptions of race, gender, and sexuality as categorical givens. As importantly, though, Bettie argues that class is "not simply reproduced but constantly re-created and co-created with processes of racialization and gender and sexual formation" (p. 194).

In this, she takes intersectionality to a new place. It is not that just that they act together in ways that have more salience than each alone. They are co-constitutive in a particular way. Race, gender, and sexuality constitute class as invisible. Class is not "there" in ways that race, gender, and sexuality are in the discourses available in everyday life. This seems to invite an "unveiling" of social class in our public discourses. Bettie strategizes: "It is important to locate instances of class cultural awareness, to make visible the everyday politics of resentment, and to go beyond this to provide a discourse which offers to transform that into a politicized class identity, alongside other political positionings" (2003, p. 201). She is after a discursive equality to the politics of difference: class should take its deserved position alongside race, gender, sexuality, (dis)ability, and so forth. Assuredly this is the ultimate goal. Yet unfortunately I believe that this task has the forces of history and culture against it. From Karl Marx on, the direct assault has been repelled repeatedly, and I will argue, it has been part and parcel of creating the essentialized views we have of race and gender especially. In the pages that follow, I will discuss how, in trying to make class more "real," our efforts have instead fed the "reality" of other forms of difference. Thus, I suggest, in our ongoing efforts to name "class," we undercut our efforts to demonstrate that these categories are socially constructed and legitimated in relations of power and knowledge. In what follows, we will need to reconstitute class in relation to other identities, enabling its character to be recognizable in its relation to other identities at the intersection.

I want to propose that intersectionality allows us a way to think about relations between identities and oppression. We can, for example, focus both on conceptions of race and gender as well as conduct a concerted assault on how class is understood. In the past, the reduction of difference to class was usually argued as a way to unite people in a common struggle. This has not come to be for many reasons, including the self-interests of credentialed middle-class scholars. Yet, class was unable to be used as a rallying point for shared concerns of oppressed groups because it was interpreted as an assertion of whiteness and patriarchy. To non-whites and women, rallying as a social class meant submitting once again. What is needed is an assault on many fronts: race, gender, sexuality, (dis)ability, and so on. Rather than reducing difference, we need to acknowledge difference and strategize how we can use categories of difference as a counter story (Ladson-Billings and Tate, 1995) to that of individualism and functionalist meritocracy that Meyer has identified as the key myths of stratification in the West. This task is beyond the scope of this chapter or even this book. Rather, I will simply point to one such approach from the perspective of race. I hope others will develop approaches from other *standpoints* as Patricia Hill Collins (1991) would term them. In the end, however, I will return to argue that the multiple standpoint approach may enable the discourse to be opened up but there will need to be a new discourse of class to help fill the void. Class needs to serve race and gender rather than to seek to reduce them. In this I want to advance Bettie's interest in moving to a place where class can be named, but want to emphasize that this naming be in the context of specifying the relation of class to other forms of difference.

Race into Class

I must admit that there are times when I wish to argue that class may be usefully understood as what whites do to each other and this is then visited on other categories of difference as a cultural model of how to stratify. Thus, we get class differences within races and genders and so on, yet beyond what whites do to each other whites and men also race and gender others as well. The heterosexual, white male then visits his distinctions on sexuality and on (dis)ability. While I acknowledge that this understates the roles of subalterns in creating difference, it helps remind me that it is my race, gender, and sexuality, and the power that has been pulled to these, which act together to stratify the social world. It reminds me that when I make arguments like I wish to do here, that it is also an act born of this power.

While I try to pursue equity broadly I am most intrigued by race. Race offers one way to leverage intersectionality, and it involves asserting race not as a category of difference but as a source of relation. Clearly, gender is another way to leverage intersectionality and, may offer real advantages in some coalition building. I will limit my discussion here to how gender may be a lever within education so as to advance a different conception of class. The larger point is that class needs to be understood in its relation to other forms of difference and thus starting from any of other forms would seem to push toward a more complex view of class and of a lived intersectionality of identity and experience.

The project I take on here is to use race to get to other forms of distinction, other irrealities that have been made real by distinctions drawn to conserve the power of the dominant. I think of the idea as starting with race to get into class—but ultimately understand a fuller complex of the relations of difference and dominance. That is, we remake class by understanding how it is constructed coterminously with race. The goal is not to reduce class to race but to enable class to be possible. In this, embracing race as a first move enables us to constitute class and gender (and ability as well as other forms of domination) in their own rights and in the context of each and all. Class need not be left to be déclassé.

Given my analysis of the problems of asserting the reality of class, it is also essential that race not be treated as real as well. It must be seen as a particular historical and social construction and thus is malleable. The goal has to get beyond the conceptualization used to begin—that is, it must be transformative in intent and outcome. An explicit embracing of intersectionality is thus necessary, but this must move beyond the multiplicity of identity and identity politics to engage domination and democracy more fully. For me, these conditions are best satisfied by critical race theory (Crenshaw et al., 1995) with its intent to reconceptualize race and politics. Here, the move in critical legal studies to consider the implications of changing the basis of law from property rights (which enscribes domination) to civil rights (which inscribes human possibility). The move to narrativity in critical race theory is also to embrace imagination over reality since reality inscribes race as a problem not as a possibility. Third, and most importantly, there has been a theoretically based project articulated that can be a basis for getting to class. Guinier and Torres (2002) have argued for a project around race to alter hierarchy generally. In doing so, they also engage class and gender (though not ablism, sexuality, and other forms of subjugation as directly). They do not directly, however, address how their project can help us reinvigorate class. I will argue this as but an extension to their work, one that is implicit if not fully explicit in their argument.

Guinier and Torres (2002) term their effort *political race* (p. 10), a project to "topple the hierarchy itself" (p. 9): "It is a fundamentally creative political project that begins from the ground up, starting with race and all its complexity, and then builds cross-racial relationships through race and with race to issues of class and gender in order to make democracy real" (p. 10). They are clear about why they see race as a better place to begin such a project than class. They argue that class in our society has become so individuated that it has been impossible to build a sense of "linked fate" (p. 101) that has been possible around race. They respond to critics who argue that emphasizing race undermines coalitions with the white working class by pointing out that de-emphasizing race means that no coalition will be possible across races because this is understood as a reinscription of whiteness. De-emphasizing race also undercuts the racial pride that that is the basis of community and solidarity. Thus, they argue that one must build from race not from class because "There is simply no American vocabulary for class as linked fate or as a basis for critique of systemic failure" (p. 103). This is because the "narrative of the American Dream" (p. 103) that individual hard work will lead to social mobility is also linked to a narrative that if whites fail in the mobility game then racialized others are to blame. "Because class in not named in this society, to collapse race into class would be to make *both* invisible, disabling a social movement from forming around either variable" (p. 103, italics in original). Furthermore, "a political race analysis can help identify class barriers" leading to "conscious coalition-building while acknowledging existing racial divisions" (p. 102). They document the viability of this strategy in cases of union organizing that explicitly addressed race. One result for working-class whites was a repositioning of themselves about race so that they could see themselves as part of the civil rights movement.

Moreover, they are clear that political race must go beyond itself, embracing intersectionality: "political race must assert its linkages to class, gender, and sexuality or else risk fragmentation" (Guinier and Torres, 2002, p. 298). That is to say, political race is argued to be the starting point but is not the only subjugation that must be interrogated. This then is the beginning of a transformative moment. Political race does not reduce other forms of difference to race but is a way to develop linkages to other forms of difference.

Transformation, of course, is not defined by linkages per say. Rather, transformation indicates that something becomes something it was not. For Guinier and Torres (2002), the political race project is to transform both power and democracy: ". . . we seek to use political race to create a dialogue about interactive forms of representation and more inclusive practices of democracy. Political representation becomes less about relinquishing power or seizing power or surrendering power. Instead, it becomes more about facilitating a dynamic engagement that begins to tell new stories about democracy. These stories involve organizing at the grassroots level, sharing power, and engaging the people themselves in actions that dissipate fear and build confidence" (p. 221).

For Guinier and Torres, the nature of power is to be transformed from the "zero-sum conception" (2002, p. 138) into "power–with" (p. 141). Fueled by both Foucauldian and feminist conceptions, the political race project rejects the view that because power operates everywhere that struggle is a hollow exercise. Following some feminist thinkers, they argue that power is constituted through relationships and cannot be done away with. Yet power, since it is socially constituted, can be transformed: ". . . what we can imagine is the transformation of the relationships and interactions among human beings. To imagine that such a transformation would eliminate the circulation of power is fantasy; rather, this reorientation seeks to capture power's generative capacity" (pp. 139–40).

Power-with then is that form of power generated "through collective action and struggle and through the creation of an alternative set of narratives" (Guinier and Torres, 2002, p. 141). Moreover, such participation not only leads to direct results, but allows a form of dignity even in the face of that dignity being potentially denied. Guinier and Torres go on to argue that power-with contains elements of power-over, and that indeed the two forms of power will likely exist side by side in any struggle and change in relation to one another. Yet they offer the analogy that if power-over is a pyramid, then power-with is an egg with two centers of gravity. This embodies the notion of shared and changing power relations. They conclude that power-with can be understood as having elements of "(1) working together over time in groups rather than as individuals in isolation; (2) seeing problems in context rather than as small units independent of the whole; (3) approaching problem-solving in ways that spark joint participation from diverse perspectives; and (4) defining problems locally, by the immediate stakeholders and then networking to similar efforts going on elsewhere" (p. 146).

Power-with, however, is not the only transformation sought in the political race project. The nature of democracy itself is to be changed. The transformation sought is from the current system where elites conduct deliberations about policy and supposedly are held accountable through elections. The chimera here is that this process is supposedly one of representation, when it is the justification of an elite. Guinier and Torres argue that this process violates the true sense of democracy whereby people are brought into "public decisionmaking as participants, not as spectators" (2002, p. 171).

They review experiences within the Latino community and see Hispanic/Latino identity as having a promising role in "destabilizing the black-white binary" (Guinier and Torres, 2002, p. 252). They also take two lessons from the Latino experience. First, when coupled with the promise to increase democracy in general, political race is more easily legitimated. Second, using political race only makes sense when coupled to efforts to undercut the dominant zero-sum definition of power.

Transforming power also involves directly resisting one of many mechanisms of securing a hierarchy based on race: the racial bribe. The bribe promises advancement on the color hierarchy (becoming whiter) in exchange for dropping a racial group's oppositional agenda. This is done by whites offering incentives that encourage the affected group to disassociate themselves from those seen as "of color," and by securing high status for individual members of the affected group within existing hierarchies. All this makes "whiteness" appear less monolithic, making the definition appear less problematic. Thus the strategy of political race requires that naming and destabiliizing be coupled with refusing to accept the racial bribe. ". . . political race requires that we exercise constant vigilance in renegotiating the black-white binary. The internal dynamics of race within each national group are complex. And like any historical moment, the contingencies admit many possible futures" (Guinier and Torres, 2002, p. 249).

These futures must be imagined in ways that whitestream (Denis, 1997; Grande, 2000; Urrieta, 2004) worldviews cannot. Here the turn is to narratives, to aspiration, and to magic realism as ways to conceive the possibilities for the future. Narratives are to speak of the experiences of those whose experiences have not counted in the social construction of power. These narratives are to "disrupt racialized hierarchies by changing the background stories we tell each other about race, wealth and power" (Guinier and Torres, 2002, p. 293).

Narratives allow new perspectives to be expressed and invite interpretation by others (Benjamin, 1968). Aspiration is argued to go beyond the descriptive and to be "both explanatory and motivational" (Guinier and Torres, 2002, p. 18). It accepts a view of power, drawn from Michel Foucault, that emphasizes the circularity and distribution of power throughout human life; and our agency that is "generative of new forms of creativity" (p. 18). The possibilities also have to be imagined. Magic realism is employed in the political race project as part of conceiving new possibilities: "By liberating the imagination, magical realists give voice to the possibilities of futures that are not held hostage to either the military

juntas in power or the juntas' neoliberal defenders" (p. 23). Magic realism also engages the reader-witness-participant in the interpretation of a
dislocation, a defamiliarization, a discrepancy:

> . . . magic realists . . . narrate the fantasies, myths and quotidian life in
> the same frame. The reader sees the previously familiar things in a com-
> pletely new context. The change in context is critical, for it provides the
> foundation for radically different meanings. Though the new reality may
> astonish and disorient readers, the characters in the story react to it with
> curiosity and faith rather than with confusion, uncertainty, fear, or disbe-
> lief. This discrepancy between the reader's and the character's reaction is
> key. The reader enters a reality that is fantastic yet remains empirically
> grounded through the actions and reactions of the characters. (p. 23)

It is this distance between the grounding and the fantastic that can
generate possibilities not imaginable either within the dominant whitestream view nor the resistance and opposition to it. Political race is
expressly committed to "clarity about the possibilities" (Guinier and Torres, 2002, p. 300) and to renewal through practice, accepting that people
choose "by their actions" (p. 300).

Political race as a project is transformative in another way. In the end,
reconceptualizing power, disrupting hierarchy, narrating counterstories,
and imagining new possibilities come full circle for race itself to be reimagined as well: "While political race is a form of black race-consciousness, we
do not reduce it to its biological expressions nor to its expression as "anti-
whiteness" (Guinier and Torres, 2002, p. 99). Race can be reconstructed
without biological essentialism, allowing the positive aspects of racial identity to be asserted into building coalitions. It also means leaving something
behind. As they write:

> Political race, in other words, involves several dramatic dislocations
> in conventional wisdom. The first will occur when white progressives
> recognize a more complex notion of racial consciousness that exists out-
> side of, yet is connected to, conventional class analysis. They will come
> to understand that energy for social change is often created when blacks
> and other racial minorities are encouraged to organize as a group with-
> out merely retreating into an exclusionary racial consciousness. The sec-
> ond disruption involves moving away from the anti-discrimination
> model that has dominated the discourse of civil rights. This discourse, in
> fact, sometimes inhibits the development of a broader coalition to chal-
> lenge the status quo. Such a change might require black leadership and
> the leadership of other marginalized communities of color to articulate
> the consciousness of racialized identity in broader terms than the current
> remedial strategies of the civil rights paradigm. (p. 25)

Political race then is a project of building coalitions "that puts the democratic process in direct opposition to the dominant ideology of individualism, as reflected in the consumerism of the market, in order to articulate the needs of those whom the market neglects" (Guinier and Torres, 2002, p. 101).

The political race project rejects our current definition of racism. They argue that the current definition is too tied up with "fighting irrational prejudice" (Guinier and Torres, 2002, p. 292) and individual bigotry. Guinier and Torres are "less interested in measuring blame and more concerned with developing a political framework that spurs us to respond and act" (p. 292). Their "definition then of racism relies on whether people *naturalize* racialized hierarchies" (p. 292, italics in original). The political race project is to "disrupt racialized hierarchies by changing the background stories we tell one another about race, wealth and power" (p. 293).

The coalitions are fashioned in rather context specific ways, but they invariably are to bring whites, both working class and the elites, to a view of linked fate with racialized peoples. Power is more likely to bring added energy and innovation across-the-board and benefit all racialized groups even if it is explicitly about reducing hierarchy. Thus, some white elites may find coalitions in their own interest. Many projects that they cite as achieving the coalitions moving toward power-with, have broad leadership that includes some white leaders as well. These projects also share a realization by whites that "they, too, were, in fact, functionally black" (Guinier and Torres, 2002, p. 290) in the existing hierarchy.

In these, I would argue we see how political race allows us to return to social class not as a category but as an engaged opposition. Racialized difference remains as the coalition inscribes the linked fate of the members. Class can be a coalition of difference engaged over time. This of course has some resemblance to Aronowitz's (2003) argument that we should think about class as a social movement. Yet I read Aronowitz to be speaking about more sweeping movements than Guinier and Torres use as their cases. He argues for forming alliances in a global context and accepts the fact that "struggle on a class basis—which invariably entails playing the zero sum game," is necessary for gains to be made (Aronowitz, 2003, p. 170). Guinier and Torres see coalitions as formed not across race but between races, with less necessity for sweeping movements given their rather different conception of power than Aronowitz. Sweeping movements are more demanded when preserving the zero sum definition of power. Power-with does not seek to simply replace who is in power, but more significantly to replace how power itself is deployed.

Class, from a political race perspective, is not as much determined by economics as it has the potential to be economically realized as coalitions work on their linked fates to address inequities and hierarchies. Class does not become a superseding category but rather the *sign* of a particular type of coalition—a coalition to use racial difference constructively to address their linked fate while changing the definition of power itself.

In my claim that political race allows us to construct class differently, I must also be tempered by what are acknowledged limitations of the political race project (Guinier and Torres, 2002). First, most current progressive organizing efforts are premised on the suppression of difference in efforts to create an alliance to deal with race-neutrally defined issues. Thus, racial hierarchies become institutionalized within these efforts. The challenge of political race projects then is to create a new mode of organizing itself, one that is not premised on erasing differences, but rather premised on enlisting differences. Second, political race is not directed toward conventional electoral coalitions. Rather, it more about activating the grassroots: "the losers of society stand to gain the most, and risk the least, from mobilizing for change, and they already have the tools for analysis at their disposal" (p. 296). Third, power is currently mobilized in a zero-sum manner, and thus political race functions in this context even as it works to change the definition of power. This means that coalitions must help each party to the coalition resist internal hierarchies, and that projects will likely be "in-between" (p. 297) existing deployments of power-over. As a result, they are likely to change with time and conditons and will have to be continually renegotiated. Thus, arguing that we can create a new conception of class, one that is not déclassé, is to argue that class is unstable and must be constantly renegotiated as well, that class-as-coalition of difference actively works against racial hierarchies in the coalition as much as in the wider society. In this way, class works to maintain race differences, to construct conceptions of linked fate, and to work against internal hierarchies within the coalition and within the parties to the coalition as well.

Education, Political Race, and Class

The political race project as developed by Guinier and Torres is based on examples that portend that a new notion of social class could be seen in such coalitions. Yet they were not as concerned, as I am here, with reconstituting class itself. They also have not tried to argue for a role for education in the project. My argument has been that over the last forty years or so, we have developed new understandings of race and gender that are not reducible to class. This challenge has meant that the claim that class is an objective condition that explains inequality and injustice must be rethought. This rethinking has taken many modes: from outright rejection of class as category of worth to retheorizing class (as contending groups, as social movements, etc.) to staunch reassertions of the value of class analysis. My argument here has been that if the lessons of race and gender analysis are taken seriously, then class cannot be what it once was. If gender and race are social constructions, historically situated and changing across time and space, then class is not "real" as well—it is a social construction that must be now be accomplished in ways we have not theorized.

My argument is that we may gain the most from going to class through race. In doing so, race is preserved as a source of identity, conceptualization, and mobilization rather than reduced or superseded in moving to class. Thus, class is a coalition of racialized groups that will continue to maintain their separate identities as they work in concert on fates they share. Class then does not sweep across society but is the accomplishment of localized coalitions in action. The coalitions are to resist internal hierarchies, to maintain productive elements of racial difference, and to foster a different definition of power. To the extent that class-as-coalition of racialized groups is achieved, then it both reaches into race and projects itself into localized and specific injustices. Class-as-coalition then is likely to have somewhat different forms in different contexts, depending on what the racialized groups agree is strategic. Therefore, we understand class not as an objective condition, but as a strategy that is likely to be reformed as contexts change. In this as well, we should admit that as strategy, class could then disappear from any single scene if it no longer has a purpose. Guinier and Torres seem to think that the experience of successful strategic action will strengthen and develop the coalition. As a sociologist, this optimism seems well placed to me, with the caveat that if inequity is successfully remedied or if the strategizing fails repeatedly, then class-as-coalition of racialized groups may disappear. I will not address this issue any further here, but this would seem to present the possibilities of futures that critical race theory may find useful to address.

What remains then is to consider how political race and class-as-coalitions of racialized groups may be sponsored. While this needs to take place across institutional and community venues, I want to focus on how schools can help with the project of reconceptualizing power, disrupting hierarchy, narrating counterstories, and imagining new possibilities. I do this with a set of misgivings for I fully understand that schools inscribe differences as deficits so that inequalities are both created and reproduced. Moreover, schools embody and reproduce the myths of rationalism and individualism that Meyer critiques. This is to say that the project of political race and class-as-coalition of racialized groups meets institutionalized ideology and power in schools—it meets the definition of power that is its nemesis. Moreover, schools are also being increasingly pulled into the neoliberal agenda of the right through accountability policy and privatization and as a backlash against the intransigence of the bureaucracy (Apple and Oliver, 1998). Yet I would also argue, with Foucault, that there is more than just institutionalized power in schools. There are fissures that may be exploited for this project. One of them is the gendered nature of schools. Within schools, "caring" relations (Noddings, 1984) between teachers and students mediate other forms of power. This mediation can itself be a source of leverage.

Some educators see caring as unproblematic, an ideal form of relation. It is much more complex for me. Caring relations in many ways can be seen as the basis of human development but they too exist in contexts that complicate and even contradict this form of relation (Rolon-Dow, 2005; Valenzuela, 1999). I agree with Emily Abel and Margaret Nelson (1990) that caring is also used to subjugate women. That is, the role of women is constructed so that women "naturally" care, and then men arrange occupation statuses so that caring work is devalued. Teaching is a prime example of this. Teaching became women's work for many reasons. In early American proprietary schools, only men were allowed to handle the fiduciary affairs of the schools. Men were seen as capable of handling money while women were regarded as "naturally" able to oversee the development of children. The feminization of teaching was coupled with the belief that oversight by men was needed to correct for the tendencies of women to coddle children. The feminization of teaching is such that males today who choose to be teachers must also address teaching as a gendered occupation. Indeed, many males choose teaching precisely because it allows them to develop caring relationships and to center these in their work lives. This is not without trade-offs of course. Men who believe that caring is the necessary relation at the base of teaching see their own claims to maleness questioned. Thus, some male teachers find it necessary to assume a hypermasculinity to bolster their claim to being males.

Not all women teachers embrace caring as the necessary relation of teaching. Yet even in this we see the gendered nature of the teaching profession. These women are often regarded as not as "feminine" as others and, in the everyday life of schools, are asked to assume more "male" roles in disciplining students and in managing the wider school community. Yet my argument is that regardless of the gender of the teacher, in American schools, caring is a relationship that we can use in the reconstruction of class. As I have written elsewhere (Noblit, 1993), race is overlayed here as well. African-American women teachers may be regarded by white teachers as authoritarian (and less caring), when in fact African-American women teachers situate caring as moral *authority*. Moreover, caring is also a power relation: one is cared for by the one caring. Caring as a form of mediation of institutionalized power is important here as well. In some regards, caring relations make the "symbolic violence" of education less evident (Bourdieu, 1977). One gains a relationship and possibly access to the whitestream social world as one's home culture is devalued and ultimately subtracted from oneself (Valenzuela, 1999). Caring, then, exists in fields of power and in fields of relationship. This makes caring one way to use schools to advance the political race and class-as-coalition of the racialized groups project. Caring touches on so much of schooling that it is a powerful lever.

I will not reargue the nature of caring or how it is gendered in our society here. This has been done well elsewhere (Abel and Nelson, 1990; Eaker-Rich and Van Galen, 1996; Gilligan, 1982; Noddings, 1984; Prillaman, Eaker and Kendricks, 1994; Rolon-Dow, 2005). What I wish to focus on is how we might use the fact that women are the primary socialization agents in schools, and that, as a gendered occupation, women and men teachers develop relations with students that both make schooling possible (without outright rebellion) and that competes with institutional controls as well. This dualism for me has the potential of being strategically productive—gender formations can be used to undercut racial formations. As the African-American teaching force was largely decimated by school desegregation and by its aftermath, this is also a strategy that argues a role for whites at this point in history. To be sure, I would want African-American teachers to in many ways lead the way— but to develop the political race project via schools, we must face the reality that whites will need to be effectively deployed.

Following Guinier and Torres, the strategy should focus on developing coalitions around linked fates. Today schoolteachers experience as much subjugation as students. High stakes testing is the bedrock of much of this. Accountability policy (Noblit, Malloy, and Malloy, 2001) decenters relationships in schools, denying women teachers their gender (as constructed currently) and denying men and women teachers their morality (Noblit, 1993). These forms of denial then can be the basis of establishing the political race project through schools.

It is also important to recognize that women have a highly developed pedagogy for the oppressor—one that has been fashioned over history in direct relation to their male oppressors (Noddings, 1989). Nel Noddings has argued that this pedagogy involves moderation, mediation, and sharing. That is, the acknowledged power of the oppressor means that women intercede with men to reduce the brutality of oppression especially toward children. Mothers all too often take the beating that was initially directed at the offspring. Women also work to broker an agreement, to effect a reconciliation between the oppressor and oppressed. Finally, women work through relationships in this pedagogy to renarrate the "transcripts" (Scott, 1990) of oppression. Here, they educate the oppressor in the limits of the oppressor's perspective, as well as educating the oppressor on how the exercise of power undercuts its own claims to legitimacy. Through sharing their perspectives, women position themselves between adult males and vulnerable children. Men have much to learn from this pedagogy.

Caring relations then can be leveraged for their potential in two ways. First is to reclaim the moral responsibility of teachers for the welfare of their students. Ironically, at least to me, this may mean that teachers would find it helpful to rearticulate child development. In part, this could be done in a conventional mode by aligning with specific reform efforts that problematize simplistic notions of child development and the role of schools. The work of James Comer (1993) is potentially of use here and enables a coalition across race as well. Here the goal is for teachers to offer counterstories to that contained in the media. The presumption of the failure of schools to teach could follow the lines of argument offered by David Berliner and Bruce Biddle (1997) that schools have failed but not in the teaching of content knowledge. They have failed to counteract poverty and inequity. Teachers are well situated to tell this story in a wide number of venues, especially those that address parents and public more directly. Following critical race theory, the counterstory is to challenge that told by the dominant media. Moreover, the story should emphasize that accountability has not led to a narrowing of the gap between whites and blacks. Politicians point to isolated cases, but this is the limit of the evidence. Accountability policy can be countered, at this point in history, by narrating it as both anti-child and racist. In this, white teachers and families of colors share a linked fate that can be built upon.

Teachers also need to sponsor counterstories told by parents and students. Here the goal is to design curricula that invites students and their families to narrate their experiences and struggles. Such narrative work values the lives of those stigmatized by our myths, ideologies, and education practices. These narratives may take the form of describing the learnings that come from our lives. Such stories counter the centrality of education in learning and rearticulates what schools as credentialing agents can and cannot offer students and families. The result may be Meyer's decertification of legitimacy but our experience is that much more complex understandings emerge (Noblit and Dempsey, 1996). These require people to engage more deeply in how the world is socially constructed.

Yet these counterstories are insufficient in part because teachers currently consider parents as a key problem (Van Galen, 1987). This blaming of parents, whatever its veracity in specific cases, undercuts the possibilities of new coalitions. This blaming also permits teachers to discount their own moral responsibility for educating children. Reclaiming this will be necessary if counterstories are to lead to reimagine schooling as a vehicle for the political race project. For schools to facilitate the political race project, teachers need to rearticulate the stories told about parents in ways that fashion a coalition with parents to address inequities in the community and nation. This would require teachers to accept the fact that they are responsible for the learning of the children even if parents are not helpful. It also requires that parents be understood not solely in terms of their instrumentality to the school. The role of parents then is reimagined not as primarily facilitating children's learning but in articulating to the wider world the linked fates of families of different racialized groups. This is difficult to be sure, but we have seen this in practice.

George Noblit and Michael Jennings (2001) have shown how parents can be mobilized around shared fates without requiring racial differences to be suppressed. In this case, the school's multiracial staff and two minority communities, one African-American and one Chinese, were able to directly intercede in large city school board politics to benefit students from both communities. Parents who found it hard to help their children with school-defined learning coalesced around a political project for the school and for their children. Educators sponsored the coalition by recognizing race differences as important and to be maintained. They also became part of the coalition with the parent groups to affect the fate of the entire school—in this case thwarting the disbursement of school populations to other schools as a new school was built on the old site. The result was not a lessening of race, but an engagement of race as what the school stood for. Parents ended up understanding that the teachers cared for both races of children and were willing to act to preserve not only the school but also the racialized communities the school served. The school also found that a focus on the needs of the children also enabled it to address accountability policy directly. The school articulated for the community that high stakes testing was being used to gain more control over education by the state legislature. Thus, the coalition made it possible for the school to articulate testing preparation as a political strategy rather than as a way to hold the school accountable as the political rhetoric had maintained. Accountability was driving a wedge where the school used its opposition to engage with parents about the real needs of their children. The educators for their part demonstrated they cared for all groups of students by focusing on a wider definition of responding to the needs of children. Parents then saw the school as key to their survival as separate racialized groups and as accepting the responsibility to counter the policies that were geared to define their children as problems. Incidentally, the test scores were rising rapidly as a result of this new coalition, revealing the effects of the coalition that had been formed. More important for our concern in this chapter is that they provide an example of how schools might embody a political race project and accomplish class-as-coalition of racialized groups. Class in this sense is but a strategic accomplishment—one that was based on the belief that the educators at the school cared about the children of both races and about both racialized communities. The communities were not brought together to diminish race but to act to maintain the productive elements of race differences in addressing their shared fates. The coalition also did not lead to hierarchy among the groups and with the school. All were brought together as parties to the coalition.

Conclusion

Social class has unfortunately become a concept that is overweight. Clearly, class had some traction at the time of its initial articulation. Yet instead of being treated as constructed category that had strategic uses, it became caught up in the science project that came to characterize social science (Pink and Noblit, 1995). The science project tried to mimic the natural sciences in its emphasis on objective reality and deterministic models. Yet this has had only a partial success. Human life is complex and reactive. The critical tradition in sociology and education found itself fighting a functionalist tradition that created a metaphor for social life that was in many ways beyond human experience. As a result, from the late Marx on, the critical tradition contested functionalism on the grounds of the science project. In this, class lost its origins in historical specificity. After the Frankfort school of critical theory shifted the grounds away from science and toward culture and politics, it became possible to recognize that the experiences of racialized and gendered peoples not only limited the reach of the concept of class. It made the claims of class as an objective reality déclassé. Fighting to maintain the critical tradition meant that many scholars were hard-pressed to accept this lesson. Class, for them, was the concept upon which critique and change was based. Yet these same scholars recognized the fact that gender and race were socially constructed concepts and as a result have tried to rethink class. However, the critical tradition's insistence that objective reality needs to exist for critique to have grounds has meant that women and people of colors other than white have found that they had to move away from class analysis in order to analyze the experience of people like themselves. Other scholars articulated postmodernist and poststructuralist perspectives to step away from objectivism and determinism while maintaining a critical perspective. Class has become déclassé in social analysis (Wexler, 1987) because it has had to take too much weight.

Recent reworkings of the concept of class have proved ineffective largely because of the insistence on the primacy of the concept. My argument here has been that for class to be reconstituted, it must reaccomplished through other forms of difference. My own project is to do this via race and secondarily via gender, but following Crenshaw (1991), a host of strategies may be possible in particular contexts, embracing the intersectionality of identity. Race and gender have primacy at the moment because they are believed to be central aspects of one's identity, whereas class has proven to be problematic on these grounds. Yet the wider point is that intersectionality offers us not a way to reduce difference to one or another concept but to elaborate it to a constellation. By considering critical race theory and its implications here, I have attempted one way to reconstruct class as a strategy. Thus, I have argued that it is possible for class to serve as a vehicle to maintain productive aspects of race differences and in suppressing internal hierarchies within the coalition while focusing on the "linked fates" of the different races.

In another move, I have argued that the gendered nature of schooling may serve as a lever for us to construct political race projects and to constitute the strategic class-as-coalition. There are other ways to argue from intersectionality as I indicated earlier. I believe that the role of theorizing thus is not to determine the best truth but rather to strategize possibilities that people may employ in everyday life to address inequities. As Guinier and Torres (2002) argue, however, theorizing is a limited part of the project. In practice we can learn what is possible in specific contexts, and recognize possibilities that theorizing has not considered. After all, the point is not to analyze the world but change it, even if change does not forever accomplish our goals.

References

Abel, E. and Nelson, M. (Eds.) 1990. *Circles of care: Work and identity in women's lives.* Albany: State University of New York Press.

Apple, M. and Oliver, A. 1998. Becoming right: Education and the formation of conservative movements. In C. Torres and T. Mitchell (Eds.) *Sociology of education: Emerging perspectives* (pp. 91–120). Albany: State University of New York Press.

Abu-Lughod, L. 1991. Writing against culture. In R. Fox (Ed.) *Recapturing anthropology* (pp. 120–142). Sante Fe, NM: School of American Research Press.

Aronowitz, S. 2003. *How class works: power and social movement.* New Haven: Yale University Press.

Benjamin, W. 1968. *Illuminations.* New York: Schocken Books.

Berliner, D. and Biddle, B. 1997. *The manufactured crisis.* White Plains, NY: Longman.

Bettie, J. 2003. *Women without class: Girls, race, and identity.* Berkeley: University of California Press.

Bourdieu, P. 1977. *Outline of a theory of practice.* Cambridge: Cambridge University Press.

———. 1987–88. What makes a social class? On the theoretical and practical existence of groups. *Berkeley Journal of Sociology,* 32–33, 1–17.

Brantlinger, E. 2003. *Dividing classes: How the middle class negotiates and rationalizes school advantage*. New York: Routledge/Falmer.

Collins, P. H. 1991. *Black feminist thought: Knowledge, consciousness, and the politics of empowerment*. New York: Routledge.

Comer, J. (1993). *School power*. New York: Free Press.

Crenshaw, K. 1991. Demarginalizing the intersection of race and sex: A black feminist critique of antidiscrimination doctrine, feminist theory, and antiracist politics. In K. Barlett and R. Kennedy (Eds.) *Feminist legal theory: Readings in law and gender* (pp. 57–80). Boulder, CO: Westview.

———. 1995. "Mapping the margins: Intersectionality, identity politics, and violence against women of color. In K. Crenshaw, N. Gotanda, G. Peller, and K. Thomas (Eds.) *Critical race theory: The key writings that formed the movement*. New York: New Press.

Crenshaw, K., Gotanda, N., Peller, G., and Thomas, K. (Eds.) (1995) *Critical race theory: The key writings that formed the movement*. New York: New Press.

Denis, C. 1997. *We are not you: First nations and Canadian modernity*. Ontario: Broadview Press.

Eaker-Rich, D. and Van Galen, J. (Eds.) 1996. *Caring in an unjust world: Negotiating borders and barriers in schools*. Albany: State University of New York Press.

Erhenriech, B. 1989. *Fear of falling: The inner life of the middle class*. New York: Pantheon Books.

Ferguson, M. and Golding, P. 1997. Cultural studies and changing times: An introduction. In M. Ferguson and P. Golding (Eds.) *Cultural studies in question* (pp. xiii–xxvii). Thousand Oaks, CA: Sage Publications.

Gilligan, C. 1982. *In a different voice*. Cambridge: Harvard University Press.

Grande, S. 2000. American Indian geographies of identity and power: At the crossroads of indigena and mestizaje. *Harvard Educational Review*, 70(4), 467–98.

Guinier, L. and Torres, G. 2002. *The miner's canary*. Cambridge: Harvard University Press.

Hall, J. (Ed.) 1997. *Reworking class*. Ithaca: Cornell University Press.

Hallinan, M. 2000. On the linkages between sociology of race and ethnicity and sociology of education. In M. Hallinan (Ed.) *Handbook of the Sociology of Education* (pp. 1–14). New York: Kluwer Academic/Plenum Publishers.

Joyce, Patrick, 1997. Foreword. In J. Hall (Ed.) *Reworking class* (pp. xi–xiii). Ithaca: Cornell University Press.

Karabel, J. and Halsey, A. (Eds.) (1977). *Power and ideology in education*. New York: Oxford University Press.

Ladson-Billings, G. and Tate, W. 1995. Toward a critical race theory of education. *Teachers College Record*, 97(1), 47–68.

Mahony, P. and Zmroczek, C. (Eds.) (1997) *Class matters: "Working class" women's perspectives on social class*. Bristol, PA: Taylor and Francis.

McCarthy, C. and Apple, M. 1988. Race, class, and gender in American educational research: Toward a nonsynchronous parallelist position. In L. Weis (Ed.) *Class, race and gender in American education* (pp. 9–39). Albany: State University of New York Press.

Merton, R. 1957. *Social theory and social structure*. Glencoe, IL: Free Press.

Meyer, J. 1994. The evolution of modern stratification systems. In D. Grusky (Ed.) *Social stratification: Class, race, and gender in sociological perspective* (pp. 730–38). Boulder, CO: Westview Press.

Morrow, R. and Torres, C. 1998. Education and the reproduction of class, gender and race: Responding to the postmodern challenge. In C. Torres and T. Mitchell (Eds.) *Sociology of education: Emerging perspectives* (pp. 19–46). Albany: State University of New York Press.

Nodding, N. 1984. *Caring*. Berkeley: University of California Press.

———. 1989. *Women and evil*. Berkeley: University of California Press.

Noblit, G. 1993. Power and caring. *American Educational Research Journal*, 30(1), 23–38.

———. 1999. *Particularities: Collected essays on ethnography and education*. New York: Peter Lang.

Noblit, G. and Dempsey, V. 1996. *The social construction of virtue: The moral life of schools*. Albany: State University of New York Press.

Noblit, G. and Jennings, M. 2001. Gregory Elementary School. In G. Noblit, C. Malloy, and W. Malloy (Eds.) *The kids got smarter: Case studies of successful comer schools* (pp. 35–50). Cresskill, NJ: Hampton Press.

Noblit, G., Malloy, C., and Malloy, W. (Eds.) 2001. *The kids got smarter: Case studies of successful comer schools*. Cresskill, NJ: Hampton Press.

Pink, W. and Noblit, G. (Eds.) 1995. *Continuities and contradictions: The future of the sociology of education*. Cresskill, NJ: Hampton Press.

Prillaman, R. Eaker, D. and Kendrick, D. (Eds.) 1994. *The tapestry of caring: Education as nurturance*. Norwood, NJ: Ablex Publishing Corporation.

Scott, J. 1990. *Domination and the arts of resistance*. New Haven: Yale University Press.

Rolon-Dow, R. (2005). Critical Care: A color(full) analysis of care narratives in the schooling experiences of Puerto Rican girls. *American Educational Research Journal*, 42(1), 77–111.

Somers, M. 1997. Deconstructing and reconstructing class formation theory: Narrativity, relational analysis and social theory, In J. Hall (Ed.) *Reworking Class* (pp. 41–72). Ithaca: Cornell University Press.

Torres, C. and Mitchell, T. (Eds.) 1998. *Sociology of education: Emerging perspectives*. Albany: State University of New York Press.

Urrieta. L. 2004. Dis-connections in "American" citizenship and the post/neo-colonial: People of Mexican descent and whitestream pedagogy and curriculum. *Theory and Research in Social Education*, 32(4), 433–58.

Valenzuela, A. 1999. *Subtractive Schooling: U.S.-Mexican Youth and the Politics of Caring*. Albany: State University of New York Press.

Van Galen, Jane A. 1987. Maintaining control: The structure of parent involvement. In G. Noblit and W. Pink (Eds.) *Schooling in social context: Qualitative studies* (pp. 78–90). Norwood, NJ: Ablex Publishing Corporation.

Walkerdine, V. 1990. *Schoolgirl fictions*. London: Verso.

Wexler, P. (1987). *Social analysis of education: After the new sociology*. New York: Routledge.

Wright, Erik Olin 1987. The Debate on Classes. In J. Hall (Ed.) *Reworking Class* (pp. 41–72). Ithaca: Cornell University Press.

CONTRIBUTORS

MICHAEL W. APPLE is John Bascom Professor of Curriculum and Instruction and Educational Policy Studies at the University of Wisconsin, Madison. He has written extensively on the relationship between education and power and has worked with researchers, governments, unions, and dissident groups throughout the world to democratize educational research, policy, and practice. Among his books are *The State and the Politics of Knowledge*, the twenty-fifth anniversary third edition of his classic *Ideology and Curriculum*, *The Subaltern Speak*, and the expanded second edition of *Educating the "Right" Way: Markets, Standards, God, and Inequality*.

RICHARD BEACH is Professor of English Education at the University of Minnesota. He is the author of *A Teacher's Introduction to Reader Response Theories*, and coauthor of *Inquiry-based English Instruction: Engaging Students in Life and Literature*, *Teaching Literature to Adolescents*, and *Teaching Media Literacy through the Web*. He is a former President of the National Conference on Research in Language and Literacy and former Chair of the NCTE Research Foundation.

ELLEN BRANTLINGER retired from the Department of Curriculum and Instruction at Indiana University. She has written four books: *Politics of Social Class in Secondary Schools*, *Fighting for Darla*, *Sterilization of People with Mental Disabilities*, and *Dividing Classes: How the Middle Class Negotiates and Rationalizes School Advantage*, and edited a multiauthor volume entitled, *Who Benefits from Special Education?: Remediating (Fixing) Other People's Children*. As a critical theorist, she has always been interested in understanding and overcoming oppressive power differentials among individuals and groups. She has become a strong advocate for qualitative inquiry and has published articles on that research design. Although she has researched and written on such diverse

347

topics as sexuality, sexuality education, social class, ethnicity, gender, disabilities, teacher education, and testing, the connecting thread consistently has been understanding oppression and enabling human rights and social inclusion. She is perhaps best known for her article, "Using Ideology: Cases of Nonrecognition of the Politics of Research and Practice in Special Education," published in the *Review of Educational Research*. She directed the Undergraduate Special Education Teacher Education Programs at Indiana University and then the Graduate Program in Curriculum Studies.

VAN DEMPSEY is Dean of the School of Education at Fairmont State University in West Virginia. Prior to this, he served as director of the Benedum Collaborative and the Benedum Center for Educational Renewal at West Virginia University, a school-university partnership built on the philosophy of the simultaneous renewal of educator preparation and K–12 schools. His primary teaching responsibilities include teacher leadership and the socio-cultural context of schooling. His primary areas of research and publication include school-university partnership work, education policy, and school renewal.

CHERYL FIELDS-SMITH is Assistant Professor of Early Childhood Education at the University of Georgia, Athens. Her research interests include family-school-community partnerships, the development of cultural sensitivity among teacher educators, and home schooling among African-American families.

MARGARET A. (GRETA) GIBSON is Professor of Education and Anthropology at the University of California, Santa Cruz. She has focused her research on the school performance of immigrant and minority youths with particular attention to home-school-community relationships and to how school context and peer relations influence student participation and achievement in high school settings. Her research looks at factors that promote and impede success in high school for Mexican-descent migrant youths. In addition to her ongoing work in several multiethnic high schools in California, she has conducted field research in the U.S. Virgin Islands, northern India, and Papua New Guinea. Her major publications include *School Connections: U.S. Mexican Youth, Peers, and School Achievement* (edited with P. Gándara and J. Koyama), *Minority Status and Schooling* (edited with J. Ogbu), and *Accommodation without Assimilation: Sikh Immigrants in an American High School*.

BETH HATT is Assistant Professor of Educational Administration and Foundations at Illinois State University, where she teaches research methods and social foundations of education. Her research interests focus upon issues of race, class, and gender equity within educational contexts. She is coeditor (with George Noblit) of *The Future of Educational Studies*. Her current research explores smartness as a cultural practice in schools.

DEBORAH HICKS is an educational scholar who studies the language, lives, and literacies of youths coming of age in poverty. Her latest project draws from a long-term ethnographic study of young girls growing up in working poor America. Her work is interdisciplinary in nature, drawing from the fields of education, gender studies, cultural studies, anthropology, psychology, and linguistics. She is currently a Visiting Professor in Women's Studies at Duke University and Professor of Education at the University of Cincinnati.

BILL J. JOHNSTON is Professor and Chair in the Department of Educational Leadership and Foundations at the University of Texas, El Paso. His research interests include the examination of educational policy primarily as the outcome of a coincidence of interests between the state and global corporations for their mutual benefit; examination of schools as sites to mediate the effects of corporate policy relative to social justice and equity; and finally the examination of strategies of instructional leadership for powerful teaching and learning to counter the effects of accountability centered pedagogy.

STEPHANIE JONES is Assistant Professor of Literacy at Teachers College, Columbia University where she teaches courses on literacy, culture, and language. Her commitment to social justice through critical literacy practices informs her pedagogy in graduate courses, working with teachers in classrooms, and working with elementary-aged children in New York City and across the Cincinnati metropolitan area. Her research, writing, and advocacy centers on the intersections of social class, literacy, identity, and family-school relations. She is the author of *Girls, Social Class, and Literacy: What Teachers Can do to Make a Difference.*

JANICE KROEGER is Assistant Professor of Early Childhood Education, Teaching, Leadership and Curriculum Studies at Kent State University. Her research and teaching interests are focused on issues of power and identity in home, school, and community partnerships, early years teacher development, early childhood policies and practices, and qualitative research methodologies. She has researched in, and written scholarly work about, social action, agency, and culture and cultural and identity change in diverse communities. She has focused on the intersections of social justice work, activism, school formation and the formation of schooled subjects (students). Her published works have appeared in such journals as the *Journal of Educational Change* and *The Urban Review*, she has contributed to or coauthored works in *English Education, The American Educational Review Journal, Early Childhood Research and Practice*, and *Contemporary Issues in Early Childhood*.

TIMOTHY J. LENSMIRE is Associate Professor of curriculum and instruction at the University of Minnesota, where he teaches courses on literacy, race, and critical pedagogy. His past research and writing focused on the possibilities and problems of progressive and radical approaches to education, especially in the teaching and learning of writing. His current work draws on cultural and critical white studies to investigate how white people become white. His books include *When Children Write: Critical Re-Visions of the Writing Workshop* and *Powerful Writing/ Responsible Teaching*.

GEORGE W. NOBLIT is Joseph R. Neikirk Professor of Sociology of Education and Chair of Culture, Curriculum, and Change Department in the School of Education at the University of North Carolina, Chapel Hill. He specializes in the sociology of knowledge, school reform, critical race studies, anthropology of education, and qualitative research methods. He has three ongoing funded research strands: school reform, race and education, and arts and education. His studies of school reform, especially "Comer" schools (funded by the Rockefeller Foundation and OERI) have resulted in three books: *The Kids Got Smarter: Case Studies of Successful Comer Schools, Cultural Matters*, and *Bringing Systemic Reform to Life*. Continuing a career of research on school desegregation and race equity in education, he is currently conducting an oral history study with James Leloudis titled, "Roads Not Taken in School Desegregation," funded by the Spencer Foundation. He is also completing nine years of research by writing a book about the A+ Schools Program, an arts-based school reform program, with funding from the Kenan Institute for the Arts and from the Ford Foundation. He also coedits *The Urban Review*.

DARYL PARKS is Assistant Professor of English Education with the Urban Teacher Program at Metropolitan State University, St. Paul, Minnesota. He has received numerous awards for teaching English to urban high school students and for service within urban communities. In addition to teaching methods courses to preservice urban teachers, he serves as a consultant to school districts on cultural influences in education. His primary interests are in the relationships between identity constructions (race, class, and gender), literacies, and critical pedagogies.

MAIKE INGRID PHILIPSEN is Associate Professor in the Social Foundations of Education at Virginia Commonwealth University. Her research interests center on issues of social justice and equality in education, specifically the roles of race, gender, and social class in shaping schools and institutions of higher learning. She studies questions relating to equal opportunities at both the K–12 and college/university levels, employing primarily a sociological perspective and qualitative methodologies. One of her publications analyzed the cultural consequences of an African-American school closing for the sake of desegregation. She is the lead faculty member at the university's Pff (Preparing Future Faculty) program.

AMANDA HAERTLING THEIN is Assistant Professor of English Education at the University of Pittsburgh, where she teaches courses on teaching literature and media, and theory and practice in teaching multicultural literature. Her research focuses on sociocultural dimensions of student responses to literature, particularly in terms of gender and social class. She is studying the ways in which working-class girls' responses to literature are negotiated through competing social worlds and cultural models.

LUIS URRIETA JR. is Assistant Professor of Cultural Studies of Education at the University of Texas at Austin. His general research interests center on issues of identity and agency, activism, altruism, new social movements, and social practice theory. He is specifically interested in Chicana/o and Indígena identity, and in activism as a social practice in educational spaces both in the United States and internationally. Methodologically, his work is grounded in anthropology and in qualitative research methods. His work specifically makes claims for native anthropology and native educational research as a political practice and method.

JANE A. VAN GALEN is Professor of Education at the University of Washington, Bothell. She has published articles on class and education in the *Journal of Educational Change* and *QSE*. She is coeditor of *Caring in an Unjust World: Negotiating Borders and Barriers in Schools*.

Name Index

Subject Index